# THE REBEL'S CLINIC

# THE
# REBEL'S CLINIC

———

## THE REVOLUTIONARY LIVES OF
## FRANTZ FANON.

———

## ADAM SHATZ

FARRAR, STRAUS AND GIROUX
NEW YORK

Farrar, Straus and Giroux
120 Broadway, New York 10271

Parts of this book previously appeared, in slightly different form,
in the *London Review of Books*.

Library of Congress Cataloging-in-Publication Data
Names: Shatz, Adam, author.
Title: The rebel's clinic : the revolutionary lives of Frantz Fanon / Adam Shatz.
Other titles: Revolutionary lives of Frantz Fanon
Description: First edition. | New York : Farrar, Straus and Giroux, 2024. | Includes
    bibliographical references and index.
Identifiers: LCCN 2023030996 | ISBN 9780374176426
Subjects: LCSH: Fanon, Frantz, 1925–1961. | Intellectuals—Algeria—Biography. |
    Revolutionaries—Algeria—Biography.
Classification: LCC CT2628.F35 S53 2024 | DDC 965/.04092 [B]—dc23/eng/20230927
LC record available at https://lccn.loc.gov/2023030996

Designed by Patrice Sheridan

Our books may be purchased in bulk for promotional, educational, or business use. Please
contact your local bookseller or the Macmillan Corporate and Premium Sales Department at
1-800-221-7945, extension 5442, or by email at MacmillanSpecialMarkets@macmillan.com.

www.fsgbooks.com
Follow us on social media at @fsgbooks

3   5   7   9   10   8   6   4   2

*This book is dedicated to the memory of three friends who,*

*in different ways and in different fields,*

*carried on the work of Frantz Fanon:*

MARIE-JEANNE MANUELLAN,
French social worker, activist, and secretary to Fanon
(1927–2019)

OKWUI ENWEZOR,
Nigerian American curator and critic
(1963–2019)

AMINA MEKAHLI,
Algerian poet and novelist
(1967–2022)

# CONTENTS

---

## PART IV: THE AFRICAN

## PART V: THE PROPHET

# THE REBEL'S CLINIC

# PROLOGUE

---

IN NOVEMBER 1960, a traveler of ambiguous origin, brown-skinned but not African, arrived in Mali. Issued in Tunis two years earlier, his passport identified him as a doctor born in 1925 in Tunisia, height: 165 cm, color of hair: black, color of eyes: black. The pages were covered with stamps from Nigeria, Ghana, Liberia, Guinea, Italy. The name on the passport, a gift from the government of Libya, was Ibrahim Omar Fanon, a nom de guerre. The psychiatrist Frantz Fanon was not from Tunisia but from Martinique. He had not come to Mali to do medical work: he was part of a commando unit.

It had been a long journey by car from the Liberian capital of Monrovia: more than twelve hundred miles through tropical forest, savanna, and desert, and the eight-man team still had far to go. From the journal he kept, it's clear that Fanon was mesmerized by the landscape. "This part of the Sahara is not monotonous," he writes. "Even the sky up there is constantly changing. Some days ago, we saw a sunset that turned the robe of the sky a bright violet. Today it is a very hard red the eye encounters." His entries move freely between rousing expressions of hope and somber reminders of the obstacles facing African liberation struggles. "A continent is on the move and Europe is languorously asleep," he writes. "Fifteen years ago it was Asia that was stirring. Today 650 million Chinese, calm possessors of an immense secret, are building a world entirely on their own. The giving birth to a world." And now an "Africa to come" could well emerge from the convulsions of anti-colonial revolution. Yet "the specter of the West," he warns, is "everywhere present and active." His friend Félix-Roland Moumié, a revolutionary from Cameroon, had just been poisoned by the French secret service, and Fanon himself had narrowly escaped an attempt on his life on a visit to Rome. Meanwhile, a new superpower, the United States, had "plunged in everywhere, dollars in the vanguard, with [Louis] Armstrong as herald and Black American diplomats, scholarships, the emissaries of the Voice of America."

Yet in the long run, Fanon believed, the African continent would have to reckon with threats more crippling than colonialism. On the one hand, Africa's independence had come too late: rebuilding and giving a sense of direction to societies traumatized by colonial rule—societies that had long been forced to take orders from others and to see themselves through the eyes of their masters—would not be easy. On the other hand, independence had come too early, empowering the continent's narcissistic "national middle classes" who "suddenly develop great appetites." He writes: "The deeper I enter into the cultures and political circles the surer I am that the great danger for Africa is the absence of ideology."

Fanon recorded these impressions in a blue Ghana School Teachers Book No. 3 that he had picked up in Accra. It is now stored at the Institut Mémoires de l'édition contemporaine, a research library housed in a former monastery in Normandy that sheltered partisan fighters during the Second World War. To take it in one's hands sixty years later and leaf through the pages is to inspect the thoughts of a dying man: Fanon did not yet know he had leukemia, or that his life would end in 1961 in a hospital in Maryland, in the heart of the American empire he despised. On the road in West Africa, he was open, thoughtful, and intrigued by the continent from which his ancestors had been carried on slave ships to the French colony of Martinique.

In Mali he imagined himself home, among his Black brothers, yet he remained a stranger. He had come as an undercover agent of a neighboring country in what he called "White Africa": Algeria, then in the seventh year of its liberation struggle against French rule. The aim of his reconnaissance mission was to make contact with the desert tribes and open a southern front on Algeria's border with Mali so that arms and ammunitions could be moved from the Malian capital of Bamako through the Sahara to the rebels of the Front de libération nationale (FLN).

The head of Fanon's commando unit was a major in the FLN's military wing, the Armée de libération nationale (ALN). He was a "funny chap" who went by the name of Chawki: "small, lean, with the implacable eyes of an old maquis* fighter." Fanon was impressed by the "intelligence and clarity of his ideas" and his knowledge of the Sahara, a "world in which Chawki moves with the boldness and the perspicacity of a great strategist." Chawki, he tells us, spent two years studying in France but returned to Algeria to work his father's land. When the war of liberation launched by the FLN began on November 1, 1954, he "took down his hunting rifle from its hook and joined the brothers."

Not long after, Fanon, too, had joined "the brothers." From 1955 until his expulsion from Algeria two years later, he had given sanctuary to rebels at the psychiatric hospital he directed in Blida-Joinville, just outside Algiers. He had provided them with medical care and taken every possible risk short of joining the maquisards in the mountains—his first impulse when the revolution broke out. No one believed more fervently in the rebels than the man from Martinique. He had gone on to join the FLN in exile in Tunis, identifying himself as an Algerian and preaching the cause of Algerian independence throughout Africa. Every word that he wrote paid tribute to the Algerian struggle. But he could never really become an Algerian; he did not even speak Arabic or Berber (Amazigh), the languages of Algeria's indigenous peoples. In his work as a psychiatrist, he often had to depend on interpreters. Algeria remained permanently out of reach for him, an elusive object of love, as it was for so many other foreign-

---

* The word "maquis" comes from the French term (originally of Corsican origin) for an underground resistance movement. It literally means "the bush" and was used to evoke the dense, hilly terrain in which French resistance fighters hid during the Second World War. The Algerian nationalist movement lifted the term from the lexicon of the World War II resistance, from which it drew inspiration. When young Algerians left their cities and villages to join ALN units in the mountains of the Aurès, they were said to *prendre le maquis*, "take to the maquis."

ers who had been seduced by it—not least the European settlers who began arriving in the 1830s. He would be, at most, an adopted brother, dreaming of a fraternity that would transcend tribe, race, and nation: the kind of arrangement that France promised him as a young man and that had led him to join the war against the Axis powers.

France betrayed its promise, but even as he turned violently against the colonial motherland, Fanon remained faithful to the ideals of the French Revolution, hoping that they might be achieved elsewhere, in the independent nations of what was then known as the Third World. He was a "Black Jacobin," as the Trinidadian Marxist C. L. R. James described Toussaint Louverture in his classic history of the Haitian Revolution. Nearly six decades after the loss of Algeria, France still hasn't forgiven Fanon's "treason": a recent proposal to name a street after him in Bordeaux was struck down. Never mind that Fanon had bled for France as a young man, then fought for Algeria's independence in defense of classical republican principles, or that his writing continues to speak to the predicament of many young French citizens of Black and Arab descent who have been made to feel like strangers in their own country.

In 1908, Georg Simmel, a German Jewish sociologist, published an essay called "The Stranger." The stranger, he writes, "is not a wanderer, who may come today and leave tomorrow. He comes today—and stays." This was Fanon's experience throughout his life: as a soldier in the French army, as a West Indian medical student in Lyon, as a Black Frenchman, and as a non-Muslim in the Algerian resistance to France. Simmel suggests that even as the stranger arouses suspicion, he benefits from a peculiar epistemological privilege since "he is offered revelations, confessions otherwise carefully hidden from any more organically embedded persons." Listening to such confessions was Fanon's trade as a psychiatrist, and it was in doing so that he decided to throw himself into the independence struggle, even to become Algerian, as if a commitment to his patients' care and recovery required an even more radical kind of solidarity, a marriage to the people he had come to love.

The twentieth century was, of course, full of foreign-born revolutionaries, radical strangers drawn to distant lands upon which they projected their hopes and fantasies. Yet Fanon was unusual, and much more than a sympathetic fellow traveler. He would eventually become the FLN's roving ambassador in Africa—his complexion a decided asset for a North African movement seeking support from its sub-Saharan cousins—and acquire a reputation as the FLN's "chief theoretician."

This he was not. It would have been highly surprising if such an intensely nationalistic movement had chosen a foreigner as its theoretician. Fanon's task was mostly limited to communicating aims and decisions that others had formulated. But he interpreted Algeria's liberation struggle in a manner that helped transform it into a global symbol of resistance to domination. And he did so in the language of the profession he practiced, and at the same time radically reimagined: psychiatry. Before he was a revolutionary, Fanon was a psychiatrist, and his thinking about society took shape within spaces of confinement: hospitals, asylums, clinics, and the prison house of race, which—as a Black man—he experienced throughout his life.

Fanon was not a modest man. He struck some of his contemporaries as vain, arrogant, even hotheaded. Yet to his patients he could hardly have been humbler.

What he saw in their faces, and in their physical and psychological distress, were people who had been deprived of freedom and forcibly alienated from themselves, from their ability to come to grips with reality and act upon it independently. Some of them were mentally ill (in French, *aliénés*); others were immigrant workers or colonized Algerians who suffered from hunger, poor housing, racism, and violence; still others suffered from performing the dirty work of colonial repression. (Fanon treated French soldiers who had tortured Algerian suspects, and wrote with remarkable lucidity and compassion about their traumas.) What they shared was an invisible, lacerating anguish inscribed in the psyche, immobilizing both body and soul. This anguish, for Fanon, was a kind of dissident knowledge: a counternarrative to the triumphal story that the West told about itself.

In a 1945 essay on Richard Wright's memoir *Black Boy*, Ralph Ellison observed that racial oppression begins "in the shadow of infancy where environment and consciousness are so darkly intertwined as to require the skills of a psychoanalyst to define their point of juncture." Fanon was a psychiatrist, not a psychoanalyst, but he read deeply in the literature of psychoanalysis. His first book, *Peau noire, masques blancs* (*Black Skin, White Masks*), published in 1952, when he was twenty-seven, was an attempt to reveal the shadow that racial oppression cast across the lives of Black people. In his later writings on Algeria and the Third World, he powerfully evoked the dream life of societies disfigured by racism and colonial subjugation.

"History," in the words of the Marxist literary critic Fredric Jameson, "is what hurts, it is what refuses desire and sets inexorable limits to individual as well as collective praxis." Fanon had a rare gift for expressing the hurts that history had caused in the lives of Black and colonized peoples, because he felt those hurts with almost unbearable intensity himself. Few writers have captured so vividly the lived experience of racism and colonial domination, the fury it creates in the minds of the oppressed—or the sense of alienation and powerlessness that it engenders. To be a Black person in a white majority society, he writes in one of his bleakest passages, was to feel trapped in "a zone of nonbeing, an extraordinarily sterile and arid region, an incline stripped bare of every essential from which a new departure can emerge."

Yet Fanon himself had a fervent belief in new departures. In his writing, as well as in his work as a doctor and a revolutionary, he remained defiantly hopeful that the colonized victims of the West—the "wretched of the earth," he called them—could inaugurate a new era in which they would be free not only of foreign rule but also of forced assimilation to the values and languages of their oppressors. But first they had to be willing to fight for their freedom. He meant this literally. Fanon believed in the regenerative potential of violence. Armed struggle was not simply a response to the violence of colonialism; it was, in his view, a kind of medicine, rekindling a sense of power and self-mastery. By striking back against their oppressors, the colonized overcame the passivity and self-hatred induced by colonial confinement, cast off the masks of obedience they had been forced to wear, and were reborn, psychologically, as free men and women. But, as he knew, masks are easier to put on than to cast off. Like any struggle to exorcise history's ghosts and wipe the slate clean, Fanon's was often a confrontation with impossibility, with the limits to his visionary desires.

Much of the power of his writing resides in the tension, which he never quite resolved, between his work as a doctor and his obligations as a militant, between his commitment to healing and his belief in violence.

Fanon made his case for violence in his final work, *Les Damnés de la terre* (*The Wretched of the Earth*), published just before his death in December 1961. The aura that still surrounds him today owes much to this book, the culmination of his thinking about anti-colonial revolution and one of the great manifestos of the modern age. In his preface, Jean-Paul Sartre wrote that "the Third World discovers itself and speaks to itself through this voice." An exaggeration, to be sure, and an inadvertently patronizing one: Fanon's voice was one among many in the colonized world, which had no shortage of writers and spokespeople. Yet the electrifying impact of Fanon's book on the imagination of writers, intellectuals, and insurgents in the Third World can hardly be overestimated. A few years after Fanon's death, Orlando Patterson—a radical young Jamaican writer who would later become a distinguished sociologist of slavery—described *The Wretched of the Earth* as "the heart and soul of a movement, written, as it could only have been written, by one who fully participated in it."

*The Wretched of the Earth* was required reading for revolutionaries in the national liberation movements of the 1960s and '70s. It was translated widely and cited worshipfully by the Black Panthers, the Black Consciousness movement in South Africa, Latin American guerrillas, the Palestine Liberation Organization, and the Islamic revolutionaries of Iran. From the perspective of his readers in national liberation movements, Fanon understood not only the strategic necessity of violence but also its *psychological* necessity. And he understood this because he was both a psychiatrist and a colonized Black man.

Some readers in the West have expressed horror at Fanon's defense of violence, accusing him of being an apologist for terrorism—and there is much to contest. Yet Fanon's writings on the subject are easily misunderstood or caricatured. As he repeatedly pointed out, colonial regimes, such as French-ruled Algeria, were themselves founded upon violence: the conquest of the indigenous populations; the theft of their land; the denigration of their cultures, languages, and religions. The violence of the colonized was a *counter*-violence, embraced after other, more peaceful forms of opposition had proved impotent. However gruesome it sometimes was, it could never match the violence of colonial armies, with their bombs, torture centers, and "relocation" camps.

Readers with an intimate experience of oppression and cruelty have often responded sympathetically to Fanon's insistence on the psychological value of violence for the colonized. In a 1969 essay, the philosopher Jean Améry, a veteran of the Belgian anti-fascist resistance and a Holocaust survivor, wrote that Fanon described a world that he knew very well from his time in Auschwitz. What Fanon understood, Améry argued, was that the violence of the oppressed is "an affirmation of dignity," opening onto a "historical and human future." That Fanon, who never belonged anywhere in his lifetime, has been claimed by so many as a revolutionary brother—indeed, as a universal prophet of liberation—is an achievement he might have savored.


THE WORLD IN WHICH we live is not Fanon's, yet he has become even more of an intellectual and cultural icon in recent years. In a postcolonial world, nostalgia for the ostensible clarities of the national liberation era is, to be sure, one of the reasons for this. Fanon wrote some of the most memorable catchphrases of the liberation struggle, and, what's more, he lived the life of a revolutionary. He spoke to racial injustice, the exploitation of the poor world by the rich world, the denial of human dignity, the persistence of white nationalism. And his insistence that liberation is a psychological as well as a political project echoes contemporary calls for "decolonizing the mind." But what imbues Fanon's writing with its distinctive force, its power to move readers born long after his death, is its mood of revolt, protest, and insubordination.

These qualities are visible in his face. In the few photographs of him that exist, Fanon rarely looks to be at ease. (To be Black in the West, he believed, was to experience a permanent sense of being out of place, of being seen through such a distorting prism of fears and fantasies as to be rendered invisible as an individual.) He was often described as an écorché vif, an ultrasensitive soul, someone who's been "flayed alive." Even as Fanon assumed his responsibilities as a professional militant, even as he assumed

the airs of a leader, even as he became ever more feverish in his vision of
Third World liberation, his writing continued to tremble with the anger
and passion of a young man seeking his rightful place in a world built to
deny him one. This is the spirit of Fanon, the intransigent grain of his
voice.

He did not use a typewriter or a pen; instead, he dictated his texts,
pacing back and forth, his body always in motion as he composed.
"O my body, make of me always a man who questions!" he exclaims in the
"final prayer" of *Black Skin, White Masks*. Fanon was an atheist; praying
to a higher authority would have struck him as ludicrous. And why pray
to his body? Did Fanon have some sort of mystical belief in the wisdom
of the flesh? Not at all. He was asking his body not to show him the path
of enlightenment but rather to rebel against any inclination toward complacency or resignation. The body, in his view, is a site of unconscious
knowledge, of truths about the self that the mind shies away from utter-
ing, a repository of desire and resistance. Fanon's relationship to reality is
fundamentally one of interrogation: "Anyone who tries to read in my eyes
anything other than a perpetual questioning won't see a thing—neither
gratitude nor hatred."

Yet Fanon's manner of interrogation was not that of a skeptic. "Man,"
he writes in *Black Skin, White Masks*, is not simply a "no," but "a yes that
vibrates to cosmic harmonies." His work is a celebration of freedom, and
of what he called "disalienation": the careful dismantling of psychological obstacles to an unfettered experience of selfhood that opens onto a
broader project for the mental well-being of oppressed communities. His
commitment to disalienation is especially poignant in his psychiatric
writings, which became available to the wider public only in the last few
years. Here we see Fanon the reforming doctor, determined to mitigate his
patients' suffering and to welcome them into the human community from
which they have been exiled. But Fanon came to believe that reform was
not just inadequate but also a lie—that, short of a revolutionary transformation, he would be complicit as a practicing psychiatrist in the culture
of confinement that sequestered Algerian bodies and souls. He was not
wrong. But the political choices he made in the world outside the hospital
were more troubled, and sometimes required a denial of the "man who

questions"—a tactical surrender of freedom that did not escape his notice or leave him without regrets. Being a fellow traveler in Algeria's independence movement—the great "yes" of his own life—made him a participant in a continental rebellion against colonialism. But the lived experience of the Algerian struggle was seldom harmonious, much less cosmic.

What's more, in Fanon's case, that experience generated nearly as many illusions as illuminations. I admire Fanon—his intellectual audacity, his physical bravery, his penetrating insights about power and resistance, and, above all, his unswerving commitment to a social order rooted in dignity, justice, and mutual recognition—but, as you will see, my admiration for him is not unconditional, and his memory is not well served by sanctification.

In this book, I will be exploring the questions that Fanon asked, and the questions he failed to ask, because both explain so much, not about the prophet but about the man. Fanon once said that all he wanted was to be regarded as a man. Not a Black man. Not a man who "happened" to be Black but who could pass for white. Not an honorary white. He had been all those men, in the eyes of others, but never just a man. He wasn't asking for much, but he might as well have been asking for the world—a different world.

"The Negro is not," Fanon wrote. "Any more than the White man." What he meant was that one isn't born a white man or Black man, just as one isn't born a woman: one must become one, as Simone de Beauvoir argued. In an odd way, the celebration of Fanon as prophet fixes him in an essence as surely as his race does. It treats him as a man of answers, rather than questions, locked in a project of being, rather than becoming.

THROUGH FORCE OF CIRCUMSTANCE Fanon came to see his work and his life as inextricably intertwined with revolutionary decolonization. But he was also impressionable, and his sense of his own identity was often quite labile. "'A man without a mask' is indeed very rare . . . Everyone in some measure wears a mask," the psychiatrist R. D. Laing reminds us. Still, it is striking how many masks Fanon assumed in his short lifetime: French, West Indian, Black, Algerian, Libyan, African, not to mention soldier and doctor, poet and ideologue, dismantler of myths and creator of myths. Some of these masks were imposed by circumstance, but others were the product of his own imagination, his passionate search for belonging, and, perhaps, his hope of becoming the "new man" he envisioned for the future of the developing world.

The American poet Amiri Baraka described James Baldwin, who was born a year before Fanon, as "God's Black revolutionary mouth." What Baldwin was for America, Fanon was for the world, especially the insurgent Third World, those subjects of European empires who had been denied what Edward Said called the "permission to narrate" their own histories. More than any other writer, Fanon marks the moment when colonized peoples make their presence felt as men and women, rather than as "natives," "subjects," or "minorities," seizing the Word for themselves, asserting their desire for recognition, and their claim to power, authority, and independence.

This was the beginning of a new world, the world in which we are living now, where formal colonialism has almost entirely crumbled but where inequality, violence, and injustice, exacerbated by the greatest epidemic in a century, remain the diet of much of the world's population, especially among the people whose conditions preoccupied Fanon. "The old is dying, but the new is not yet born; in the interregnum, a whole variety of morbid symptoms emerges," Antonio Gramsci wrote. Fanon, a medical doctor, was a trenchant diagnostician of those symptoms. He saw very clearly that people suffering from the traumas of racism, violence, and domination were not likely to reinvent themselves overnight—and that they had no choice but to continue fighting, if only so that they could continue breathing. The struggle for human freedom and disalienation was a constant battle between the wound and the will. Fanon bet on the latter, but his work is also a devastating acknowledgment of the former, even though pessimism was a luxury he could not afford. He had witnessed torture and death; he had languished in the zone of nonbeing. But he always placed himself on the side of life, and of creation.

# PART I

# NATIVE SON

———

# 1

# A SMALL PLACE

A FEW YEARS AGO, at *Soul of a Nation: Art in the Age of Black Power*, an exhibition organized by the Tate Modern, I came upon a reference, in a wall text, to a cultural conference in Lagos that Frantz Fanon was said to have attended in 1975—a remarkable feat for a man who had died fourteen years earlier. Then again, to be a prophet is to float free of the time and space coordinates that confine the rest of us. If you do a Google search on Fanon, you'll see him described variously as an African, a West Indian, an Algerian, and a Muslim. (He's almost never described as a French-man, although legally he was.) Fanon's fate has been to be remembered as a traveling ambassador for the wretched of the earth, if not a brother from another planet. But Fanon came from somewhere: the city of Fort-de-France, capital of Martinique.

Martinique is one of the islands in the Lesser Antilles chain, which runs from Grenada to the Virgin Islands. One of France's *vieilles colonies*, the "old colonies" acquired under the Ancien Régime, it had been a French possession since 1635, though it briefly passed into British hands on two occasions in the eighteenth century. It is a "small place," as Jamaica Kincaid has written of her own island, Antigua, where "the masters left, in a kind of way," and "the slaves were freed, in a kind of way." Martinique was a slave colony, based on the production of sugar, until emancipation came in 1848 and rum replaced sugar as its principal export.

Fort-de-France, where Fanon grew up, became the island's cultural and economic center in 1902 after the previous capital, the city of Saint-Pierre, was destroyed by an eruption from Mount Pelée that killed its thirty thousand inhabitants in a few minutes, burying them in hot volcanic ash and igniting the sugar and rum held in ships at the port. Originally known as Fort Royal or "Foyal"—locals still call themselves "Foyolais"—Fort-de-France had always been a poor cousin to Saint-Pierre. Although its population grew rapidly in the early twentieth century, it remained a sleepy town, plagued by "leprosies, consumption and famines," in the words of the poet Aimé Césaire. An American journalist infuriated the city's elites when he called it a "stinking pearl," but "oh how warranted" this was, Fanon's older brother Joby wrote, describing Fort-de-France as a "failed city . . . flat, sprawling, dirty, with drains that were nothing more than open sewers."

During Fanon's childhood Martinique was a French colony, where children descended from African slaves were taught about their "ancestors, the Gauls." The first three words Frantz learned to spell were *Je suis français*, "I am French." The administration was run by a Creole elite of mixed French and African ancestry; only a few thousand white descendants of the planter class, the *békés*, remained on the island. In March 1946, Martinique would become an overseas department of metropolitan France, represented by four deputies and two senators, after a campaign led by Césaire, then the mayor of Fort-de-France, who argued that his people's interests were best served by remaining a part of France rather than seeking independence.

Throughout his life, Fanon would express frustration that Martinique's people and their leaders had never taken their destiny into their own hands. Martinicans, as he saw it, were free but—as Kincaid wrote—only "in a kind of way." They had removed their chains only to submit to the more insidious domination of reflexes learned under slavery: intricate hierarchies based on skin tones and worship of the ways of the *métropole*. Prisoners of the white gaze they had internalized and made their own, they could no longer see themselves. They "looked at life with black skins and blue eyes," as the Saint Lucian poet Derek Walcott, who was born five years after Fanon, observed of West Indians of their generation.

Yet it was a stroke of luck to have been born in Martinique between the two world wars. Martinique fueled Fanon's sense of revolt and gave him his first taste of struggle. Its writers—Césaire above all—would supply him with a vocabulary for thinking about what it meant to be Black and colonized in a white-dominated world. Martinique was a small place, with all the constrictions and provincialism that implies. But it was also one of the centers of the revolution in Black thought known as Négritude. While Fanon would ultimately distance himself from most of Négritude's intellectual premises, he remained faithful to its most fundamental aspiration, the emancipation of Black humanity not only from political and economic domination but also from the tyranny of assimilation to white values.

Fanon benefited in another way from his early years in this backwater of empire. The islands of the Antilles are often parodied as places of languorous indolence, where those who can afford to do so pursue pleasure at the expense of reflection while the poor drown their suffering in rum. Fanon himself tended to think of Martinique in these terms: he never forgave it for not being Haiti, whose people had overthrown slavery in a violent revolution, rather than waiting for emancipation to be "granted" by their oppressors. Like most of his fellow islanders, he seems to have been unaware of the Martinican slave revolt of 1848, which immediately preceded emancipation, or of the sporadic slave uprisings that had rocked the island throughout its history.

But small places, by virtue of their isolation, can create, in some, an insatiable hunger for learning and travel. "The appetite for knowledge that agitates distant lands that have been newly brought into awareness of themselves is unimaginable," the Martinican writer Édouard Glissant remarks in his 1958 novel, *La Lézarde* (*The Ripening*). Glissant, who knew Fanon, described Fanon's decision to become an Algerian as the only real "event" in the modern history of the French West Indies. The hunger that would lead him to Algeria was nourished in Fort-de-France.

———

FANON IS WIDELY CELEBRATED as a tribune of the oppressed, but his childhood was, by Martinican standards, a privileged one.

Félix Casimir Fanon, his father, was a customs inspector, his mother, Eléonore Félicia Médélice, a shopkeeper who sold hardware and drapery. The Fanons did not mix with the *békés*, but they had impeccable middle-class credentials: servants, piano lessons for their daughters, even a weekend home outside Fort-de-France. They lived next door to a family of shopkeepers from Italy. Frantz's ancestors on his father's side were free people with property. His great-grandfather, the son of a slave, had started out as a blacksmith, a well-respected *nègre à talents* (Black man with skills), before purchasing a plot of farmland where he grew cocoa. Eléonore, Fanon's mother, had something even more precious than land in colonial Martinique: white ancestry. Her mother's forebears were originally from Strasbourg, in Alsace, where they had settled in the late seventeenth century, fleeing religious persecution in Austria. The name "Frantz" was probably an homage to her Alsatian roots. Like many members of the lower Martinican bourgeoisie, the Fanons were socialists who fiercely identified with the Republic that had ended slavery and allowed their family to prosper. They were, if anything, more French than the French, residents of the *vieilles colonies* who were horrified at the thought of being mistaken for the *nègres* in the African colonies that France had acquired in the nineteenth century.

Born on July 20, 1925, Frantz was the fifth of the couple's eight children. There has been much speculation about his troubles in the family. An early biographer claimed that he was stigmatized for being its darkest-skinned member, something Joby Fanon vehemently denied. Alice Cherki, a psychoanalyst who interned with Fanon, speculates that he "never had that imperceptible but very real core of serenity that is instilled in the sons of unconditionally supportive and loving mothers." Yet Fanon, in letters home during the war, expressed great devotion to his mother, while making no secret of his contempt for his often-absent father, who worked long hours and seemed to take little interest in his children. The accounts we have of his family life, superficial as they are, present no evidence of anything unusual, much less traumatic. Fanon would later argue that, insofar as colonized West Indians suffered from an "abandonment neurosis"—a term he borrowed from the psychoanalyst Germaine Guex—it derived not from dysfunctional parenting but from the neglect of their colonial masters, who had supplanted parental authority only to "inferiorize" children of the outre-mer. In Fanon's writing, the symbolic father represented by France would count much more than biological fathers such as Félix Casimir Fanon.

Fanon was something of a wild child—so turbulent that Eléonore Fanon sometimes joked that he must have been exchanged with her real son at the hospital. He got into brawls and at one point cut another boy with a razor blade. Nonetheless, most of his adventures were harmless. In his memoir of his younger brother, Joby Fanon describes how, after dusk, they would climb over the gates of the fruit and vegetable market and steal mangoes, apricots, and oranges, "more for the thrill of it than out of hunger." Frantz was a passionate footballer, and in early adolescence he became an even more passionate reader, devouring classic works of French literature at the Schœlcher Library. In Joby's reminiscence: "We were truly free."

Frantz, for his part, had no nostalgia for his childhood.

In her biographical portrait of Fanon, Alice Cherki writes of a conversation with him in which he recalled being perplexed—and then furious—when his teacher told him he owed his freedom to a dead white man. The white man in question was the French politician Victor Schœlcher, who drafted the 1848 decree announcing the abolition of slavery in all the *vieilles colonies* and was later elected to the National Assembly as a representative of Martinique and Guadeloupe.*

The son of a wealthy porcelain manufacturer, Schœlcher developed a loathing of slavery while on a sales trip to the New World in 1829. Traveling

---

* The decree was announced in 1848, the same year that France annexed Algeria and divided it into three departments, a decision that Schœlcher, like other liberal supporters of empire, including the diplomat and writer Alexis de Tocqueville, enthusiastically backed. He justified his support for both emancipation and Algeria's annexation on the same grounds: assimilation to the Republic. Victor Hugo, for his part, celebrated France's colonization of Africa as "a magnificent poem": "To be occupied by France," he wrote in 1849 in the newspaper he edited, *L'Evénement*, "is to begin to be free . . . To be burned by France is to begin to be enlightened." Quoted in William B. Cohen, *The French Encounter with Africans: White Response to Blacks, 1530–1880* (Bloomington: Indiana University Press, 1980), 273–74.

through Mexico, Florida, Louisiana, and Cuba, he was especially horrified by the racial character of slavery. On his return to France, he condemned the exploitation of slaves in an article titled "Des Noirs," but he stopped short of calling for immediate emancipation, suggesting instead a gradual process of manumission over some forty to sixty years. It was only when he learned that plantation owners refused to educate their slaves that he turned against gradualism and came out in favor of "the immediate abolition of slavery"—the subtitle of his 1842 account of his trip to the West Indies. Tireless in his advocacy of abolition, he served as undersecretary for the colonies and president of the Commission on Slavery, and became, in effect, the architect of the post-slavery order in the Antilles. The novelist Victor Hugo offered a telling description of the ceremony at which Schœlcher announced the final abolition of slavery, held in Guadeloupe on May 19, 1848: "When the governor proclaimed the equality of the white race, the mulatto race, and the black race, there were only three men on the platform, representing, so to speak, the three races: a white, the governor; a mulatto, who held the parasol for him; and a Negro, who carried his hat."

Not surprisingly, Schœlcher's vision of abolition revealed the limits of Black freedom under colonial capitalism. The old plantations were not broken up, nor were former slaves provided with land. Instead, slave owners received compensation for the loss of their property in slaves, while freed men and women remained on the land, producing cash crops. The hostility of white settlers to integration—they especially dreaded the prospect of having to accept people of mixed racial ancestry as equals—ensured the preservation of informal segregation in Martinique and other West Indian societies. Schœlcher himself discovered in 1881 that of the 138 government officials in Martinique, 99 were white, 38 colored (of mixed race), and only 1 Black: a policeman. As the historian Robin Blackburn has written, "While Schoelcher's humanitarianism and good intentions could never be in doubt, his paternalistic social republicanism became the integument linking the colored population to French colonialism."

Fanon, who later characterized the colonial world as a "world of statues . . . crushing with its stoniness the backbones of those scarred by the whip," visited the Schœlcher Monument when he was ten years old, on a class trip. The monument, built in 1887, was in La Savane Park, a grassy square where he played football on Sundays, which in *Black Skin, White Masks* he would bitterly describe as "lined by worm-eaten tamarind trees down each side," adding, "Yes, this town is a miserable failure. This life too." The centerpiece of the monument depicted Schœlcher standing on a pedestal as a freed slave looked up at him with gratitude. The inscription hailed him as a hero who had liberated the slaves from their chains. La Savane was also the site of the Schœlcher Library, an imposing, pagoda-like structure made of cast iron and glass, which had been first erected in the Tuileries Garden in Paris and then shipped in pieces to Martinique, where it was reassembled, its entrance lobby adorned with the names of Rousseau, Voltaire, and other philosophers of the French Enlightenment.

Why is Schœlcher a hero to us? Fanon remembered having asked his teacher. And why hasn't anyone told us about what existed prior to slavery? What, in other words, is *our* history?

Fanon would eventually come to see the history he had been taught as an invasive form of cultural colonization. He writes in *Black Skin, White Masks*:

In the Antilles, the black schoolboy who is constantly asked to recite "our ancestors the Gauls" identifies himself with the explorer, the civilizing conqueror, the white man who brings truth to the savages, a lily-white truth. The identification process means that the black child subjectively adopts a white man's attitude . . . Gradually, an attitude, a way of thinking and seeing that is basically white, forms and crystallizes in the young Antillean. [Once he grows up, he is] a crucified man. The environment that has made him (but which he has not made) has torn him apart.

To be Black and colonized is to inherit a world your ancestors haven't made, and to be condemned to mimicry. An impossible mimicry, because wearing a white mask will not make you white, much less set you free; on the contrary, it reinforces alienation and self-loathing.

It is hard to imagine the ten-year-old Fanon thumbing his nose at the Schœlcher Monument: the mask was on too tight for such acts of rebellion.

But one can easily imagine the older Fanon remembering, with horror and shame, that he hadn't.


ON SEPTEMBER 1, 1939, war broke out in Europe. That same day, Admiral Georges Robert departed from Brest on the cruiser *Jeanne d'Arc*, to take up his new post as high commissioner for the French West Indies and commander in chief of the West Atlantic Fleet. The destination of Robert's military flotilla was Fort-de-France, the base of France's West Atlantic theater of operations. As trenches were dug in La Savane and schools closed in preparation for air raids, panic spread among middle-class Martinicans that the war would reach the island. Fanon's mother had a more pressing concern: Frantz and Joby were wandering the streets and getting into trouble, in spite of her increasingly desperate efforts to impose discipline. (In one of her more fanciful attempts to keep them at home, she had forced them to wear their sisters' dresses.) In November, she sent her boys to study in Le François, a town on the Atlantic Coast where their uncle Édouard taught French. "Be irreproachable," she told them.

Casimir Fanon was furious that his wife had moved his boys without his approval, but Frantz adored his bachelor uncle, and Édouard was impressed by his nephew's writing skills. One of Frantz's first literary efforts was a school paper inspired by a story he had heard during a class trip to a plantation house. According to the guide at the plantation, the owner, a wealthy *béké*, had hidden his gold in the basement with the help of one of his slaves and then proceeded to murder the slave, burying him next to the gold so that the man's ghost would protect his treasure from thieves. Frantz's paper was a schoolboy's tale of buried treasure, of course. But it was also a striking anticipation of the mature Fanon's view that if you lifted the veil of European opulence, you were likely to find "the cadavers of *nègres*, of Arabs, Indians, and Asians."

In June 1940, France fell to the Germans, and Admiral Robert declared his allegiance to Marshal Philippe Pétain. An eighty-year-old hero of World War I, Pétain had signed an abject armistice with Nazi Germany, dividing France into an occupied northern zone and a southern "free" zone governed by a collaborationist regime based in Vichy. Fanon learned of the armistice just after his fifteenth birthday. The Allies, worried that the three hundred tons of gold taken to Martinique from the Bank of France would end up in Nazi hands, drew up plans to overthrow Robert's government, but in May 1942 they recognized his authority in exchange for a promise of neutrality. As a result of this agreement, the *Béarn*, France's only aircraft carrier, remained grounded, and the ships in the Fort-de-France harbor were immobilized under US supervision, leaving thousands of French naval personnel on shore. All of a sudden, Martinicans could no longer eat meat, since the cows were reserved for the white soldiers who, in Fanon's words, "submerged" the island. "We made practically everything in order to survive—soap, salt, copra oil, and shoes made out of old car tires and tiles," Joby recalled.

Opponents of Vichy's "national revolution" faced a wave of state terror during the Tan Robé—Creole for "Robert's Time." (Casimir Fanon fell under suspicion as a member of the Freemasons.) "Liberty, Equality, Fraternity," the motto on the facade of the Schœlcher Library, where Fanon would go to read, was changed to "Work, Family, Fatherland," the Vichyite catechism. In the town of La Trinité, on the Atlantic Coast, Victor Hugo Street was renamed Marshal Pétain Boulevard. Racism, of course, was by no means absent from Martinique before the Tan Robé: an awareness of skin color distinctions permeated everyday life. As Fanon wrote, when a mother described her child as "the darkest of my children," she meant the least white; indeed, for many Martinicans, "salvation . . . consists in magically whitening oneself." Black officials in starched white shirts were said to resemble "prunes in a bowl of milk."

But racism had been obscured, or at least somewhat blunted, by the fact that the island's affairs were largely run not by the white *békés* but by Creoles of mixed racial ancestry. Fanon himself had had few encounters as a child with the *békés* until the Tan Robé, when they mounted a political offensive with the backing of the occupation regime. While the regime stopped short of a complete purge of mayors of color, the political class became increasingly white. Members of the fleet flagrantly displayed their disdain for the local population. Sailors propositioned women in the street as if they were prostitutes. One sailor fell asleep in a movie theater on top of several Black audience members.

Glissant has described the Martinique of the 1940s as "a land that was learning the new violence of the world, after so much violence that had been forgotten." But the violence of slavery had been not so much forgotten as repressed, and memories of it rapidly resurfaced. Some Martinicans feared that slavery might be reinstated. After all, Napoleon had restored the peculiar institution in 1802, eight years after the French Revolution abolished it, at the urging of Empress Joséphine, the daughter of a Martinican planter with three hundred slaves.* It took another forty-six years before France definitively abolished slavery.

The language of resistance to the Robert regime reverberated with the metaphors of plantation society. Blacks who fled the island for Saint Lucia or Dominica during the Tan Robé called themselves "maroons," runaway slaves. The historian Julius S. Scott has observed that, ever since the late eighteenth century, the era of the French and Haitian Revolutions, there had been a "close symbolic connection between experience at sea and freedom" in the West Indies. To take to the sea was to become a masterless rebel, a potential importer of seditious ideas about freedom and self-determination. It was also to risk being drowned, and to join the millions of Africans who had been thrown overboard during the Middle Passage.

The *békés'* enthusiasm for Pétain's national revolution was hardly surprising: they were seeking to restore their power. But there were also Martinicans of color who sided with Vichy. One of them was Lucette Céranus Combette, a striking young woman from Fort-de-France who wrote an autobiographical novel under the pseudonym Mayotte Capécia. Combette came from a poor family; by the age of thirteen she was working at a chocolate factory. When a lieutenant in Admiral Robert's forces began courting her, she recognized an opportunity to escape her station. She embraced the Vichy social set with zealous calculation, attending its galas alongside her white partner and pouring scorn on the Black infantry units that would eventually help overthrow the Robert regime in July 1943—"*nègres* of the lowest category," she called them. Fanon would write damningly of Capécia's novel, *Je suis martiniquaise* (*I Am a Mar-*

* The statue of Joséphine in La Savane was symbolically beheaded by a group of protesters in 1991.

tinican Woman), in *Black Skin, White Masks*, in a chapter about Black women who take up with white men in the hope of "lactifying" themselves. Fanon's ridicule of Capécia and other "frenzied women of color, frantic for a white man" has long provoked justifiable charges of sexism from feminist scholars. But he had reasons other than misogyny to despise Capécia, a notorious symbol of "horizontal collaboration" in Martinique. By then he was a war veteran, and she had slept with the enemy.

ALISTAIR HORNE, IN HIS classic account of Algeria's decolonization, *A Savage War of Peace*, might well have had Fanon in mind when he remarked that "one of the more curious and less easily explained sidelights of the Algerian war was the presence in its more violent aspects, on both sides, of so many from a profession dedicated to saving human life." But Fanon became a soldier long before he gave any thought to a career in medicine.

It was in early 1943, on the night of their brother Félix's wedding, that he told Joby of his decision to join the Free French Forces. An increasing number of young men—known collectively as the Dissidence—had been fleeing the island at night in fishing boats rowed by *passeurs* (smugglers), to head for the British island territories of Dominica and Saint Lucia, to the north and south, respectively, of Martinique. More than four thousand Martinicans would take to the sea to join the Free French Forces under the command of Charles de Gaulle. Some never made it to their destination: the distance from Martinique to the other two islands was little more than twenty miles, but the waters were exceptionally dangerous, subject to fierce Atlantic currents, and full of sharks.

Aware of the risks involved, and "less carried away by patriotic declarations," Joby discouraged him, but to no avail. "I could not make Frantz see reason," he wrote. According to Joby, Frantz believed that the Vichy officials on the island were "false Frenchmen, indeed Germans in camouflage." In Frantz's thinking at the time, the representatives of a country devoted to liberty, equality, and fraternity couldn't be racist: France's official ideology was universalist and therefore intrinsically anti-racist. Joseph Henri, a Black professor of philosophy who taught both Frantz and Joby, strongly disagreed. When Henri, a radical pacifist, discovered that some of his students were preparing to join the Free French Forces in Dominica, he warned Joby and his classmates not to get mixed up in a white man's war. "Fire burns and war kills," he said. "The wives of dead heroes marry men who are alive and well. What is happening in Europe is no concern of ours. When whites are shooting each other, it is a blessing for Blacks." When Joby reported Henri's warnings to his brother, Frantz is said to have replied that when freedom is at stake, it concerns everyone, whatever their color. Or so legend has it, and legend is, frustratingly, often all that we have to go on. This noble rejoinder, which feels as if it were written for the stage, has been cited as evidence of Fanon's humanist universalism. Which, to be sure, it was. Fanon recognized that Nazism was the enemy of human decency and had to be defeated. But what's equally striking here is Fanon's impatience with—imperviousness to—his teacher's appeal to racial solidarity.

Fanon still didn't quite see himself as Black. Like most middle-class Martinicans of color, he had grown up thinking of himself as a French West Indian. When he watched *Tarzan*, he identified with the Lord of the Jungle, not the Africans—the real *nègres*. When his mother found fault with his behavior, she said, in Creole, "Ja nègre"—"You're already becoming a Negro." Like all French children, he had been raised on tales of the *tirailleurs sénégalais* (Senegalese riflemen)—the colonial infantrymen from Africa. "We knew about them," he wrote, "from what the veterans of 1914 had told us: 'they attack with bayonets, and when the going gets tough, they charge through the hail of machine gun fire brandishing their cutlasses . . . They cut off heads and make a collection of ears.'" He caught his first glimpse of the Senegalese riflemen shortly before the war, when a group of *tirailleurs*, stationed in French Guiana, passed through Fort-de-France. He saw these African soldiers much as white French children did: brave and savage, fascinating, and somewhat frightening. "We eagerly scoured the streets for a sight of their uniforms," he wrote, "the red tarboosh and the belt, that we had heard so much about." Casimir Fanon invited two of the infantrymen to dinner, much to his son's wide-eyed delight. As he would admit in *Black Skin, White Masks*, his racial self-understanding was not so different from that of Mayotte Capécia, who "saw herself as white and pink in her dreams." In colonial Martinique, this illusion was considered normal.

Unlike Capécia, of course, Fanon joined the resistance to fascism, rather than collaborating with the Robert regime. But his identification with France was equally strong. He simply looked to a different France— the "true" France of the Revolution and the Declaration of the Rights of Man and the Citizen, not the France of Vichy. His subsequent rejection of the motherland would be that of a disappointed son.

During the war, Fanon would act on his belief in the "real" France not once but twice. The first time he went to Dominica to enlist in the Free French Forces, he paid for his passage by selling a bolt of cloth he'd stolen from his father, who'd planned to make a bespoke suit from it. He left from the beach near Le Morne-Rouge, a town on the southeastern slopes of Mount Pelée; Joby accompanied him as far as Saint-Pierre, still trying to change his brother's mind. Frantz hoped to make his way, like other members of the Dissidence, from Dominica to Trinidad, and then to Britain, where he would join the Free French. But his trip turned out to be as short as it was perilous.

As Fanon began to undergo basic training on Dominica, Martinique revolted. A group of French troops stationed on the outskirts of Fort-de-France, many of them colonial infantry soldiers, launched a rebellion against Admiral Robert. They were led by Henri Tourtet, a pro-Gaullist officer. Joined by a local resistance organization, the Martinican Committee of Liberation, Tourtet's men overpowered Robert's army and forced him to flee the island, which subsequently came under the control of the Free French Forces. The Tan Robé was over.

A few weeks later, Fanon returned home to chants of "Long live de Gaulle" in the streets. But he was not content to rejoice in a local victory. As soon as the Fifth Antillean Battalion was formed under the direction of Lieutenant Colonel Tourtet, he enlisted again. Joby attributed his brother's decision to "a logic of stubbornness and morbid perseverance." But Fanon believed that he was fighting for his own people's freedom, too. In the words of Glissant, fighting in a colonial army was the "ultimate resort of a people whose domination by the Other has been concealed."

On the night of March 12, 1944, Fanon and his schoolfriend Marcel

Manville embarked for North Africa with a thousand other soldiers from
the West Indies on the *Oregon*, under Tourtet's command. Fanon told
Manville that they should fly the black flag, since not a single *béké* was on
board—only colonized Black men on their way to liberate their colonizers
from Nazism. "Hitler, we're going to knock you off your hilltop," they sang
in Creole as they set off.

# 2

# WARTIME LIES

---

IN APRIL 1945, FANON wrote to his family from France. At a battle two months earlier, he had been hit by shrapnel from an incoming mortar round and seriously wounded in the chest. The weather in Alsace, where he was stationed, was so cold that he thought he might die. "I was 20," the French novelist Paul Nizan wrote in his classic 1931 memoir of youthful rebellion, *Aden Arabie*. "I won't let anyone say those are the best years of your life." Fanon, who was just about to turn twenty, would have agreed. A year had passed since he had set sail on the *Oregon*, enough time for disillusionment. "I doubt everything," he told his family, "even myself." He continued:

> If I don't return, if you are informed of my death at the hands of the enemy, console yourselves but never say, "he died for a just cause." Say, "God called him to our side." Because we must no longer look to this false ideology, behind which secularists and idiotic politicians hide, as our beacon. I was wrong!

He then added, "Nothing here justifies that sudden decision I took to make myself the defender" of people who "couldn't care less" about efforts to free them from the German occupation.

Fanon's letter provoked a great debate among his family. "Frantz needs to grow up," said his father. But Frantz's youthful disenchantment was not a sign of immaturity. Nor was he alone in feeling that he had been betrayed. Fighting to free France from fascism, Fanon discovered that France was not as he imagined it. This would have been difficult enough for a young man who thought of himself as a member of a liberation army. What made it harder still was his realization that France did not see him as the fellow French patriot he imagined himself to be.

Fanon would suffer damage in the war, physically and mentally. It made him a different man, as it did millions of other soldiers. It's often said that wars shatter illusions—about human nature, about the limits of cruelty. But they also give birth to new visions in those who survive. The Second World War was not just a slaughterhouse but also a political dream factory for the men of color who fought against fascism in the armies of the countries that denied them citizenship rights and treated them as something less than white men—even when they were in uniform. After the war, they launched revolutions and revolts, turning their protests—and sometimes their guns—against the countries they had helped liberate. Fanon was one of them.

FANON'S UNSENTIMENTAL EDUCATION BEGAN during basic training at El Hajeb, a camp near Meknes, in Morocco. He was one of fifteen thousand soldiers. They included Frenchmen, European settlers from Algeria, Arabs, West Africans, and members of the Dissidence—West Indians like himself. The Free French Forces were fighting fascism, yet they were themselves divided and compartmentalized along distinct racial lines, reflecting their place in the imperial hierarchy. Martinicans and Guadeloupeans slept in a barrack separate from the *tirailleurs sénégalais* and were given different food. The African infantrymen wore fezzes and red flannel belts, while the West Indians wore European uniforms because they were judged to be more *évolué*—"evolved," or assimilated to Western values. Whites—French citizens from the *métropole* and Algeria—stood at the top of this racial hierarchy.

Fanon and his friend Marcel were considered *toubabs*—Europeans, or at least semi-Europeans. This was not a privilege that he relished; it violated the idea of fraternity that he'd been taught to believe was one of the Republic's most cherished values. He had joined the army to destroy a regime founded on white supremacy, not to defend another.

His discomfort grew sharper when his unit went east to Algeria, where, as part of Operation Dragoon, they would prepare to invade southern France in September 1944. Fanon could not have known that nine years later he would return to this country as a medical doctor, much less that he would join the Algerian rebels against France. But the experience left him with a disturbing image of French Algeria. While waiting to disembark in Oran, the coastal city in western Algeria where Albert Camus would set his 1947 novel, *The Plague*, Fanon saw a group of starving Arab children fighting in "rage and hatred" over bits of food that his fellow soldiers had tossed in their direction, as if they were feeding chickens. (Any European colony, he later wrote, resembled "a vast farmyard, one vast concentration camp where the only law is that of the knife.") This was France in its most treasured colony, so coveted that it had been annexed and divided into three departments of the *métropole*.

Not that Fanon felt an instinctive kinship with North African Arabs. He wrote later of what he and other Black soldiers felt: "We were astonished to see for ourselves that the North Africans detested Black men. It was truly impossible for us to have any contact with the native Arab population. We left Africa for France without understanding the reason for this animosity. Certain facts, however, were food for thought. The Frenchman doesn't like the Jew, who doesn't like the Arab, who doesn't like the *nègre*." He was becoming aware of what the Tunisian Jewish writer Albert Memmi, in his 1957 book, *The Colonizer and the Colonized*,* called colonialism's "pyramid of petty tyrants," in which members of each group measure themselves in relation to their distance from the dominant group and despise anyone below them in the structure.

Fanon was not the only Black soldier to remark on the colonial racism of France in Algeria. Two years earlier, Harold Cruse, a Black American soldier from New York City, had arrived in Oran during the Anglo-American landings. It was, he later wrote, the "beginning of my real

---

* Published in French under the title *Portrait du colonisé, précédé du Portrait du colonisateur*.

education about the reality of being Black." Among the French, he found, anti-Arab prejudice "was as intense as the American prejudice against Negroes." Black American soldiers attracted hostile stares from the French when they attempted to make conversation with Algerian Muslims. After more than a year in North Africa, Cruse returned home "a changed political animal." Two decades later, he would publish his classic study, *The Crisis of the Negro Intellectual*.

Cruse's experience led him to see Black Americans as suffering from a system of domination not unlike colonization. It enlarged his perspective on the workings of racism. Fanon's initial reaction was different because he was French—or at least he thought he was. He was also terribly sensitive—an *écorché vif*—as his mother knew well. Not for nothing did she ask his friend Marcel Manville to look after him. Fanon became increasingly demoralized in Algeria. The head of his unit described him as "an intelligent pupil but of difficult character and of doubtful military spirit," with a tendency to "make his own opinions known."


ON SEPTEMBER 10, 1944, a month into the Allied invasion of southern France, Fanon sailed from Algiers to the shores of Saint-Tropez on an American-flagged transport. The *tirailleurs sénégalais* of the Sixth Regiment, part of the Ninth Division of the colonial infantry, had fought bravely against the Wehrmacht and liberated the harbor town of Toulon, the main port of the French navy. On their arrival in Toulon, Fanon, Manville, and their fellow West Indian soldiers were incorporated into one of three *tirailleur* regiments. The Ninth Division took Aix-en-Provence and then headed north along the Rhône valley toward Grenoble. Fanon saw snow for the first time, and as the temperature dropped below zero, he slept in two-man tents only three feet high.

He was fighting alongside African soldiers who shared his skin color, against the defender of "Aryan" civilization, yet the heat of their common battle was not enough to melt the army's racial hierarchies, since West Indians like himself were considered honorary *toubabs*: Europeans, not Africans. In late October, as the weather grew colder, the High Command started to move the *tirailleurs* back to more temperate areas, on the grounds that they were not accustomed to freezing temperatures, and to replace them with European soldiers—a decision described in official documents as a *blanchiment* (whitening) of the division, now an officially European unit. Some of the African soldiers felt the decision had been made to deprive their regiments of the glory of crossing the Rhine into Germany. The differences in the army's treatment of African and West Indian soldiers, in the same regiment, were not lost on Fanon. Once, he would recall in *Black Skin, White Masks*, "a nest of enemy machine guns had to be wiped out," and the Senegalese riflemen were sent out by themselves three times, only to be forced back on each occasion. When one of them asked "why the *toubabs* didn't go," Fanon no longer knew who he was, "*toubab* or native." For many West Indians, however, this absurd situation seemed "completely normal. That would be the last straw, to put us with the *nègres*!" The European soldiers "disdained the African infantrymen, and the Antillean ruled over the *négraille* [the Black rabble] as the undisputed master."

But Fanon had not joined the army to become anyone's master. He wanted to fight and—contrary to his head of unit's report—he excelled in battle. On November 15, enemy mortar fire fell in all directions in the Valley of the Doubs near Besançon, and Fanon's fellow soldiers dug in. He was wounded after volunteering for the dangerous task of resupplying his unit. For this he received a Croix de Guerre with a bronze star. The general who pinned the cross on his lapel was Raoul Salan, who would later emerge as a ruthless defender of French Algeria.

While recovering in a hospital in the lakeside town of Nantua, in the Jura, Fanon wrote his mother that he was looking forward to a meal of "rice, chicken, red lentils, mangoes," and promised to "return, never to leave again." To his brother Joby he sent a more somber letter. "I'm older than you are now," he told him, and, shifting to Creole, added, "I made a mistake and I'm paying the price. Don't come to France before the end of the war. I'm disgusted . . . I could tell you certain things but I'm a soldier and you'll find them out later." Nonetheless, he was eager to return to the front, rejoining his unit in January 1945. In the letter he wrote to his parents in April suggesting that he might not return to them, he also noted that he was volunteering for a dangerous mission. But three weeks later, on May 7, the Germans surrendered.

After the war, Fanon and two other Martinicans in his unit, Marcel Manville and Charles Cézette, spent a month unwinding in a château in Rouen as guests of a local businessman who had been a member of the Resistance. Cézette met his wife in Rouen and never left. Manville discussed his plans to become a lawyer, a career path that Fanon briefly contemplated. Fanon never spoke in detail about what he had witnessed during the war, but he intimated to Joby that he had seen atrocities, alluding to the corpses of children massacred by German soldiers. He also said that many of the "farmers" he met—he probably meant small landholders, rather than poor agricultural laborers—seemed indifferent to the struggle being waged on their behalf. Yet the incident that seems to have hurt him most was returning to Toulon, during the celebrations marking the liberation of France, and finding that no Frenchwoman was willing to share a dance with him. White Frenchwomen preferred the company of American soldiers and recoiled when approached by their West Indian liberators, who discovered the bitter truth of their second-class citizenship.

Most of the soldiers in de Gaulle's army came from the colonies: the Republic was saved by the subalterns of France's vast overseas empire. De Gaulle himself was in no doubt as to the Republic's debt to soldiers from the colonies, which had rallied to his call in June 1940. "France is not alone," he declared in his first appeal to the nation. "She has an immense empire behind her." But during the liberation of Paris, de Gaulle capitulated to American demands to exclude Black colonial soldiers from the triumphal march into the capital, replacing them with Spanish Republican exiles in a process of *blanchiment*.* According to Joby, the rejection that Fanon suffered in France at the war's end left him "wounded to the core of his being." It aged him, too, and fed his sense of revolt. Manville felt similarly. "We had fought the war for the equality of races and

---

* As the historian Tyler Stovall acidly remarked in a comparative study of American and French history, the liberation of Paris was staged as a "white liberation." Tyler Stovall, *White Freedom: The Racial History of an Idea* (Princeton University Press, 2021), 235.

human fraternity," he wrote in his memoirs, only to suffer "solitude and contempt."

The principal target of Fanon's anger was not France, however. It was his father, Casimir, with whom he had never gotten along and who was still grumbling to his wife that "her son" had stolen his suit. In the same letter to his family in which he expressed his disillusionment, Fanon castigated Casimir: "You have at times been very inferior in your duty as a father. If I allow myself to judge you so, it is because I am no longer of this earth. This is the reproach of an inhabitant of the outer world." Which world was that? The world where life and death come into such close contact that survivors are never again sure they're still alive—the zone of war's survivors.

If the Fanon children had made something of themselves, he added for good measure, "the glory belongs to *maman* alone." According to Fanon's brother Joby, Casimir winced. "He tells us that he was mistaken in rushing to France's aid," Casimir said. "But his vision of each of our roles in the family is no more clear-sighted." Turning to his wife, he said, "Eléonore, from now on you'll wear the pants and I'll put on a dress." Two years later, Casimir would be dead, leaving Frantz to search for other fathers.

FANON CAME HOME AFTER the war and enrolled at the prestigious Lycée Schœlcher in Fort-de-France to prepare for the orals of his baccalaureate in philosophy. He studied under Monsieur Joseph Henri, the same professor who had discouraged him from fighting in a white man's war, a remark that must have left a sour taste for Fanon after his experiences in North Africa and the French countryside. Joseph Henri had also warned Fanon, "When you hear someone insulting the Jews, pay attention, because they're talking about you."

This line is often attributed to Aimé Césaire, who also taught at the Lycée Schœlcher. But Césaire, contrary to legend, never taught Fanon. After the war Césaire pursued grander ambitions, becoming Fort-de-France's mayor and Martinique's first deputy in France's National Assembly. (Fanon was in the audience for one of Césaire's speeches, and saw a woman faint under the spell of his oratory.) Thanks in large part to a campaign led by Césaire, the four *vieilles colonies*—French Guiana, Guadeloupe, La Réunion, and Martinique—became departments of France in 1946. "Departmentalization," as it was known, was an alternative path to decolonization, in which the overseas islands of the French West Indies acquired a status identical to the provinces of France proper. On paper, at least, there was no difference between an inhabitant of Fort-de-France and a resident of Paris or Bordeaux.

Fanon would later reject departmentalization as a form of neocolonialism and advocate territorial independence for the Antilles, but at the time he was an enthusiastic supporter of Césaire. He campaigned for Césaire during the elections, and embraced him as an intellectual model, speaking of his own dreams for Martinique's future in a lofty kind of poetry. "My cry," Fanon said, "will be that which the soldier hears on the battlefield; my cry will be that which the sailor lost in the night fog hears from the depths of the sea." This was a poor impersonation of Césaire, who virtually patented the "cry" or "shout" in his poetry. Still, it gives an idea of the hold that Césaire's writing exercised, and always would, on Fanon's imagination. The "inhabitant of the outer world" had returned to his native land and found a mentor in the poet, politician, and theorist of Négritude who had revolutionized French verse. Césaire was Fanon's first adoptive intellectual father, and we must take a brief detour to understand why.

AIMÉ CÉSAIRE WAS BORN in 1913 on a plantation where his father worked as a steward, in Basse-Pointe, in the north of Martinique. The plantation had been cultivated by Tamil laborers from Pondicherry who'd settled in Martinique in the mid-nineteenth century and helped shape what Césaire called the island's "métis* civilization." The Césaires lived near Mount Pelée, the volcano that had leveled Saint-Pierre in 1902. Césaire often characterized himself as *peléen*: volcanic, explosive, capricious, and violent—the qualities that define his hallucinatory, eruptive poetry. At age nine, he moved with his family to Fort-de-France, where he studied Latin, Greek, and French literature at the Lycée Schœlcher. He stood out in class

---

* The word "métis" refers to someone of mixed-race, or hybrid, origin.

as the boy from Basse-Pointe with precocious intellectual gifts and a very dark complexion. Stifled by the island's provincialism and pettiness, its racial and class hierarchies, he came to feel during his teens—as Fanon would a decade later—that "Martinique is shit."

In 1931, Césaire left for Paris to attend the Lycée Louis-le-Grand, a highly selective public school founded by Jesuits in the sixteenth century, in the heart of the Latin Quarter. One of the first people he met was a young African man standing in a student dorm in a gray jacket with a string belt holding up his trousers. Léopold Sédar Senghor, a student at the Sorbonne from a wealthy Catholic family in Senegal, seven years Césaire's senior, was writing a thesis about "exotic" motifs in Baudelaire's poetry. Césaire and Senghor began a deep exploration of French poetry; Husserl and Kierkegaard; and, above all, *The History of African Civilization*, an 1898 book by the German ethnologist Leo Frobenius that Senghor credited with restoring Africa's dignity and identity. (Frobenius also claimed to have discovered a lost Atlantis in North Africa.) Before long they were joined by Léon-Gontran Damas, a writer from French Guiana whom Césaire had met at the Lycée Schœlcher back home. Damas had briefly studied law and ethnology in Paris but was now living a down-and-out existence working at Les Halles, washing dishes and delivering newspapers.

Césaire, Senghor, and Damas were all members of the "evolved" elite, but otherwise they could hardly have been more different. Césaire, the youngest of the group, was attracted to communism, surrealism, and other forms of political and aesthetic revolt. His poetry was feverishly incantatory, a permanent insurrection against colonialism and the formal proprieties of literary French. Senghor, who went on to become Senegal's president, already carried himself as if he were a statesman for whom protest was a distant memory: serene, poised, his sensibility a syncretic mixture of Catholic mysticism and African spiritualism. "Do not say that I do not love France," he wrote in a poem about the *tirailleurs sénégalais*, in which he praised the French as a noble, freedom-loving "people of fire"; his was a love that survived disappointment.* Damas was at once the most

* And the discrimination he experienced in a French uniform: Senghor was enlisted in the Third Colonial Infantry Regiment of the French Army in 1939, with the insulting rank of

Parisian member of the group—a bohemian iconoclast and denizen of
jazz clubs and *boîtes de nuit*—and the least enamored of France. A moody
loner who struck Césaire as a "very bizarre man," he specialized in blunt,
gritty, often bitter poems, the kind of verse Céline might have written if
he'd been a working-class Black immigrant to Paris. In his 1937 collection *Pigments*, the first published work by a poet of the Négritude movement, Damas promised to "rub your nose . . . in all that capital letter shit/
Colonization/Civilization/Assimilation/and the rest," and lashed out at his
colonizers with their "masks of living chalk." (The French government
responded by banning *Pigments* in metropolitan France and in some of
its African colonies.) Fanon greatly admired the modernism and political
defiance of Damas's work, and in his mature voice there would be more
than a hint of Damas's ferocious irreverence and sarcasm.

For all their differences, Négritude's founders shared what Césaire
called a "stubborn refusal to alienate ourselves, to lose our attachment to
our countries, our peoples, our languages." They were increasingly persuaded that there existed, in Césaire's words, a "fundamental blackness"
and that the future of Black people lay in an unrepentant embrace of this
fact—and in the reappropriation of the word *nègre*, so that an "insult"
could be transformed into a "cry of identity." Fanon was one of many
young West Indians and Africans who rallied to Césaire's ideas.

The word "Négritude"—proudly capitalized—was first invoked in Césaire's poem *Cahier d'un retour au pays natal* (*Notebook of a Return to the
Native Land*), published in *Volontés*, a journal created by the avant-garde
writer Raymond Queneau and the novelist and translator Georges Pelorson, in August 1939. Césaire had written the poem a few years earlier on
holiday in Croatia, at the home of his friend Petar Guberina, a student
in linguistics. The landscapes and sea in Croatia reminded him of Martinique. He noticed an island from the window and asked Guberina its
name. Martinska, he replied. "It's Martinique!" Césaire thought. "I had
arrived in a country that wasn't mine, and its name, they tell me, is Mar-

---

private, in spite of his education. Captured during the Nazi invasion of France, he spent
the next two years in German prisoner of war camps—and on his release immediately
joined the Resistance.

tinique." He asked Guberina to pass him a sheet of paper—and began writing the work that would revolutionize French poetry and baptize a new movement:

> *My Négritude is neither a tower nor a cathedral*
> *It plunges into the red flesh of the soil*
> *It plunges into the burning flesh of the sky*

Césaire's verse, mythopoeic and incantatory, is driven by the desire not to mimeograph versions of Blackness but to invent and multiply its possible meanings. This, above all, is what Fanon would carry with him as he left Négritude behind. Even in the wake of his critical gaze, he would continue to pay homage to Césaire's influence.

In his emphasis on Blackness as invention, Césaire marked his distance from the Négritude of his cofounder Senghor, who believed that it consisted in turning toward Africa's ancient wisdom, like an eternal sun whose light would lift Black people up from their infernal "zone of nonbeing." For Senghor, like Frobenius, Blackness grew out of "the values and above all the spirit of Negro African civilization." He described the *nègre* as the quintessential "man of nature," a "sensualist," living "traditionally off the land and with the land, with and by the cosmos . . . The Negro is not deprived of reason, as some would have me say. But his reason is not discursive; it is synthetic." European reason, Senghor believed, was analytic, akin to a tool, while "Negro reason" was "intuitive" and participatory. A European racial theorist couldn't have put it better: in Senghor's writing, the Black man is a product of nature more than of history.*

Césaire, by contrast, stressed the historical "awareness of being Black," by which he meant "a taking charge of one's destiny as a Black man, of one's history and culture." Négritude was, for him, a dynamic force, a matter of living consciousness, forged in an imaginative recovery of the Black past, above all the horrors of the Middle Passage and plantation slavery. "So much blood in my memory!" Césaire declared, and his best-known

---

* The Nigerian writer Wole Soyinka would later mock Senghor's Négritude by remarking, "A tiger does not proclaim its tigritude, he pounces."

poem was written in memory's blood. Like C. L. R. James, who published his history of the Haitian Revolution, *The Black Jacobins*, in 1938, a year before *Notebook*, Césaire considered the slave plantation an engine of capitalist modernity. And as we read his epic, we realize that his "return" is a journey through historical memory as much as geography, and that the *pays natal* of the title refers not simply to Martinique but to every *pays* where Black people have endured slavery and exploitation.

The poem refuses the consolation of the otherworldly "vital forces" that Senghor believed it was African art's obligation to evoke; instead, the project is to align the energies of Blackness and revolution, and bring about the destruction of the old order. Césaire says that "the only thing in the world worth beginning" is "the end of the world, by Jove." In one of the poem's best known passages, he writes: "The work of man has only just begun . . . No race has a monopoly on beauty, or intelligence, or vitality, and there is room for all at the *rendez-vous de la conquête* [rendezvous of victory]." Fanon scarcely exaggerated when he wrote that "before Césaire, West Indian literature was a literature of Europeans."

Césaire was not the only writer in the family. His wife, Suzanne (née Roussi)—a métisse from a town in southern Martinique who would eventually acquire the nickname "the Black Panther"—was even more militant in her assertion of Blackness and had a more incisive sense of what racism had done to Black minds in the *pays natal*. According to their daughter, she "read Chekhov with her morning coffee" and "believed more in struggle than in tears." The Césaire marriage was a partnership of equals. When Vichy came to power in the Antilles, the Césaires decided that it was time to "pass from words to action," creating a Négritude literary quarterly, *Tropiques*. During its four-year run, the journal would publish essays, criticism, and poetry by some of the leading figures in West Indian writing.

Fanon never cited *Tropiques*, and it is not clear he ever saw the magazine, since he was mostly in Europe during its short existence. But he had met Césaire through school friends before he left for the war and had fallen under his spell; when the war was over, he rapidly familiarized himself with the journal's major contributors.

"The circle of shadow is tightening, amid the cries of men and the howls of wild beasts," Aimé Césaire announced in the first issue. "How-

ever, we are among those who say *no* to the shadow. We know that the salvation of the world depends on us, too." The anti-Vichy stance of *Tropiques*
was only lightly camouflaged: the strategy, in the words of Romuald Fonkoua, Aimé Césaire's biographer, was one of "obscurity in which, paradoxically, everything was clearly stated." Aside from Aimé himself, none
of the quarterly's contributors expressed their views with more daring and
power than Suzanne. When *Tropiques* was accused by the Vichy authorities of racist incitement, she replied that the journal was, indeed, guilty of
racism—"the racism of Toussaint Louverture, Claude McKay and Lang-
ston Hughes."

The Césaires were the Sartre and Beauvoir of Négritude: two brilliant
writers living, thinking, and agitating as a team. But, like Beauvoir, Suzanne Césaire left center stage to her famous male partner. While she refused the shadow of fascism, her husband's shadow was another matter.
Today, however, it is Suzanne who seems more like our contemporary. She
published only seven essays in *Tropiques*, from 1941 to 1945, but to read
them is to see Négritude developing into a more coherent critique of Western domination and its impact on the consciousness of the colonized—
themes that Fanon would take up in the 1950s. In an essay titled "Malaise
of a Civilization," she drew on the idiom of psychoanalysis, as he would, to
argue that "after the emancipation of people of color," the "collective consciousness" of West Indians had been contaminated by an erroneous faith
in the cultural "superiority of the colonizers." The Martinican had come
to believe that "liberation means assimilation" and was now so expert at
"mimicry" that "he honestly does not KNOW he is mimicking. He is unaware of his true nature, which exists all the same. In much the same way,
the hysteric is unaware that he is only imitating an illness, but the doctor
treating him ... knows it." Anticipating Fanon by more than a decade, she
reserved particular scorn for the "flower of human baseness, the colored
bourgeoisie." To her mind, the members of that social class could neither
"accept [their] Négritude" nor "whiten [themselves]."

Crucially, these essays took stock of the cost of assimilation for the inner lives of the island's inhabitants. "The psychoanalyst," Suzanne wrote,
"reveals to us that the effort required of a Martinican in adapting to an
unfamiliar life style" produces "a state of pseudo-civilization that one

can describe as abnormal." That state was also unsustainable, and ultimately explosive. "Millions of Black hands, across the raging clouds of world war, will spread terror everywhere," she wrote in "1943: Surrealism and Us," published the same year Fanon made up his mind to fight in Europe. "Roused from a long, numbing torpor, this most deprived of all people will rise up, upon plains of ashes . . . It will be time to transcend the sordid contemporary binaries: Whites-Blacks, Europeans-Africans, civilized-savage . . . Colonial idiocies will be purified by the welding arc's blue flame. The mettle of our metal, our cutting edge of steel, our unique communions—all will be recovered."

Fanon would cite many of the writers whose work appeared in *Tropiques*, but Suzanne Césaire was not among them. He was too focused, as he would be when it came to Beauvoir, on her more illustrious male partner to acknowledge her influence. But her psychoanalytic critique of colonial mimicry, her ridicule of the "colored bourgeoisie," her apocalyptic vision of a world remade, and redeemed, in violence find unmistakable echoes in his own writing. If he was Aimé's "son," he was also Suzanne's.

Fanon differed from the Césaires in one fundamental respect: he still had his eyes on the *métropole*. His encounters with racism in France had not dissuaded him from returning. After all, France owed him an education: as a demobilized soldier who had just passed his baccalaureate, he was entitled to a government grant that would subsidize his studies. He was still unsure about his academic plans: having decided against law, he was now considering dentistry. After receiving his scholarship, he set sail with his sister Gabrielle in 1946, a twelve-day journey across the Atlantic. They disembarked in Le Havre, where they parted. Fanon made his way to Paris. His stay in the capital lasted only a few days. Édouard Glissant, who met him for the first time in Paris, said that he appeared to be closely following political developments back home, but Fanon gave the overall impression of wanting to distance himself from his fellow Martinicans. "There are too many *nègres* in Paris," he joked. "Moins man wè yo pli man bien"—"The less I see them, the better I feel." In search of somewhere more "milky," he packed and headed for Lyon, where he enrolled as a student at the school of medicine.

# 3

## BLACK MAN, WHITE CITY

---

WHY WAS FANON SO averse to Paris, with its vibrant Black community? Why did he choose Lyon, a city notorious for its suspicion of outsiders?

It's possible, of course, that Fanon held himself aloof from other Black people; that, as a war veteran, he now saw himself as having completed an exalted life "cycle," as he would write mockingly of West Indians returning home from their studies in France. But if that had been the case, Paris would have made more sense, since the French capital would have given him the opportunity to show off to other expatriates from the islands—to engage in that highly competitive and sometimes cruel game of comparison that he would later diagnose as a peculiarly West Indian affliction. But Fanon didn't want to be part of a group, not even (or particularly not) the only group in France that would have welcomed him as one of its own—the West Indian diaspora. He wanted to invent himself, and to be known first and foremost as a self-made man: an illusion, to be sure, but a common one. He also relished a challenge, and Lyon was a challenge to any outsider. He would have to prove himself to the French, and see how they reacted when faced with compatriots of color like himself, without the sanctuary, or the angle of repose, that a West Indian community might have offered. He had not yet given up on France, and he wanted to assert his claim to—and to be fully recognized by—the country he had defended. The war was over, but Fanon's battle spirit was intact. It always would be, even as the target shifted.

Lyon was a lonely and rather desolate city, still reeling from the effects of the war. Housing was in short supply, and Fanon had to room in a former brothel that the Ministry of Education had requisitioned. The Black population was tiny, but there were a few thousand Algerian workers, most of them single men, living a dozen to a room in the Guillotière quarter, on the eastern bank of the Rhône. Not long after his arrival, police mistook Fanon for an Algerian and stopped him. Fanon was allowed on his way when the officers realized their mistake. "We know full well that a Martinican is different from an Arab," they would apologize. (In fact, most of those in Lyon who were thought to be Arabs were actually Kabyle Berbers, who had found work in the city's factories because of the severe economic crisis in the region of Kabylia, in northern Algeria.) It was the first of many such encounters with the police in Lyon.

Fanon took no more comfort in not being an Arab than he had in not being an African; wherever he went, he felt he was being watched. His looks were enough to attract unwelcome attention of one sort or another. In medical school, he was one of only a few Black students in a class of four hundred. The first question his professors asked him was invariably where he was from. When he told them, the reply was usually an expression of paternalist praise for his beautiful island, sometimes followed by praise for his mastery of French, as if it weren't his native language. One of his professors, he would later tell Sartre and Beauvoir, gave him "a five out of ten when he deserved a nine" on his exam. But, he added triumphantly, the professor finally addressed him with a formal second-person pronoun *vous*, rather than the familiar *tu*. Michel Colin, one of Fanon's professors in Lyon, remembered him as "touching and full of curiosity, extremely romantic, but also rather distant, sometimes even mistrustful." Although obviously brilliant, Fanon lacked scientific precision and was "not gifted at the practice of autopsies."

Fanon was known by some of his fellow students as "Blanchette"— "Whitey." When another professor remarked during an anatomy class that the corpse being dissected had a "Negro head," one of his classmates shouted across at him, "Did you hear that, Whitey?" The room filled with laughter; Fanon grabbed a scalpel and lunged across the desks between them; no one bothered him after that.* Some of them began to check the unconscious racism transmitted in phrases that, over centuries, had become idiomatic expressions in French. "We really worked like—" one of his classmates said, stopping himself. But Fanon implored him to finish his sentence. "Say it!" he shouted. "Like *nègres*."

The praise he received from white students troubled him almost as much as the casual racism he encountered. He wasn't *really* Black, they said, because he spoke French so well. "You're really one of us," he was told, since "you think like a European." In *Black Skin, White Masks*, he would describe his fury at reassurances that there was "no difference between us." The Black man, he explained, not only "knows there is a difference" between himself and the white man, "he *wants* it. He would like the white man to suddenly say to him, 'dirty *nègre*' . . . The former slave wants his humanity to be challenged; he is looking for a fight . . . But too late: the Black Frenchman is doomed to hold his tongue and bare his teeth." Fanon envied the clarity of the Black American struggle against segregation, in which nothing was "given free" and Blacks had no choice but to fight for their freedom.

What bothered Fanon more than anything wasn't so much being mocked, or even being the subject of condescending praise, as simply being *noticed* for his color: being seen (as a member of a racialized collective), and at the same time not seen at all (as an individual). Among strangers he wanted to be an invisible man. Whatever he did—take a stroll, dissect a corpse, make love, speak French—he did *while being Black*. It felt like a curse, or a time bomb in his head. The novelists who spoke to him most powerfully during his years in Lyon were the Black American writers Richard Wright and Chester Himes, whose work he discovered in translation in *Les Temps modernes*. Wright and Himes captured what he called "feelings of not existing" and the violent rage that gathers momentum in the minds of those who are consigned to the "zone of nonbeing." Fanon was fascinated by Bigger Thomas, the protagonist of Wright's 1940 novel, *Native Son*, a poor, alienated Black man from a Chicago slum

---

* Fanon decided that he could never become a surgeon because he had recoiled from dissection; the incident of the "Negro head" may well have contributed to his decision.

who accidentally kills his employer's daughter and then murders his Black girlfriend. In claiming responsibility for his killings, Thomas experiences a new sense of freedom and selfhood. Fanon was a medical student from a middle-class family, yet he was beginning to identify with the rage of a character from the South Side of Chicago and his liberating wish to acknowledge his own violence.

AS A BLACK STUDENT in France, Fanon was a conspicuous traveler on the public transit system, which he used almost daily. He knew what it was to be looked at or significantly ignored. But one freezing day in winter, he took the train and was appalled to find himself an object of fascination—and terror—for a little boy in the same carriage. "Look, *maman*," the child said to his mother, "a *nègre!*" The full force of his otherness struck him like a blow, and he never fully recovered. In his essay "Stranger in the Village," James Baldwin writes of a similar experience a few years later in Switzerland, where he was met by children shouting *"Neger! Neger!"* as he walked down the street. His appearance, he realized, was "nothing less than miraculous—or infernal—in the eyes of the village people . . . I was simply a living wonder." This sense of wonder, experienced by children with "no way of knowing the echoes this sound raises in me," merely confirmed to Baldwin that he was "a stranger here." Back home, where he was not a stranger, "the same syllable riding on the American air expresses the war my presence has occasioned in the American soul."

In "The Lived Experience of the Black Man," the central chapter in *Black Skin, White Masks*, Fanon would describe the incident on the train in very different terms. He explained that he had felt "fixed, in the same way you'd fix a preparation with a dye." He recalled that he tried and failed to laugh. (Baldwin, for his part, had managed a smile.) Under the unbearable weight of the boy's gaze, he became aware of his body as someone else's phobic object, returned to him "spread out, disjointed, worn down, draped in mourning on this white winter's day."

Fanon's agony lay in the fact that he "wanted to be a man, and nothing but a man," only to discover that such a modest aspiration was out of reach on account of his appearance, and that "there was no room whatsoever for any mistake." He continued: "The Black physician will never know how close he is to being discredited. I repeat, I was walled in: neither my refined manners nor my literary knowledge nor my understanding of the quantum theory could find favor . . . I was up against the irrational." Eventually, his anguish turned to fury when the boy's mother reassured her son, "Look how handsome the *nègre* is."

"The handsome *nègre* says, fuck you, madame," he replied. For a moment he felt free: "At last I was liberated from my rumination . . . I was identifying my enemies and I was creating a scandal. Overjoyed. We could now have some fun."

Here is the primal scene in Fanon's understanding of how Blackness is constructed in the white imagination, or rather the white "gaze"*—a term he borrowed from Sartre. It scarcely matters whether it took place: it crystallizes his sense of being othered in the French motherland, and his refusal to be anyone's *nègre*. To be spurned on a dance floor by peasant girls who mistook him for an African was one thing. To be hailed as a *nègre* by a child, to be a little boy's waking nightmare, was another. This scene has generated a small library of commentary, yet, strangely, it has seldom been asked why Fanon should have been so shaken by a child's reaction.

The child, in his innocence, precisely embodies the hypocrisies of a republic that claims not to see race yet instills racial "expertise" in its youngest citizens. (Baldwin wrote of America's glorified self-image, "It is the innocence which constitutes the crime.") In a passage reminiscent of one of Gertrude Stein's nursery rhymes, Fanon imagines a chain of associations with violence, terror, and cannibalism running through the boy's mind as he looks at Fanon (and as Fanon anxiously looks at himself, as if he were another person, a fearful racial other): "The *nègre* is an animal, the *nègre* is bad, the *nègre* is trembling because it's cold, the little boy is trembling because he's afraid of the *nègre*, the *nègre* is trembling from cold, this cold that chills the bones, the beautiful little boy is trembling because he thinks the *nègre* is trembling with rage, the little white boy throws himself into his mother's arms: *maman*, the *nègre* is going to eat me." On

---

* Sartre uses the term *le regard*, "the look" or "the gaze," to evoke the oppressive weight of being seen, and thus defined, by another person (the so-called other).

this bitter-cold day, Fanon says, "all this whiteness burns me." Burned by whiteness, he decided to assert himself "as a BLACK MAN," and to make himself known. The suggestion of snow in the city—it is a "white winter's day"—compounds his impression of creeping frostbite, with its fiery pain at the extremities of the body producing a countervailing rage of the will as numbness sets in. "I exploded," he writes. "Here are the broken fragments put together by another me."

In Lyon, Fanon's reconfigured "me" never let whites forget that he was Black. He recited Césaire's poems from memory, and devoured issues of *Présence africaine*, the flagship journal of the Négritude movement, launched in 1947. He became involved in anti-colonial activism in the orbit of the Communist Party; he was clubbed by the police during a demonstration in support of Paul Vergès, a Communist leader from La Réunion who had been arrested on a murder charge. And with the few West Indian and African students at the university, Fanon briefly published a magazine called *Tam-Tam* (no copies of which survive). But he also hungered for a more mystical kind of Blackness. Not surprisingly, he found it in the writing of Senghor. "This race," Fanon imagined, "staggered under the weight of one basic element: *rhythm*! Listen to Senghor, our bard." In *Black Skin, White Masks*, Fanon would look back on his infatuation with Senghor with a cold eye.

FANON NEVER WROTE EXPLICITLY about his years in Lyon, and little is known about his time there, or the friendships he formed. But if his essay on his encounter with the boy on the train is any indication, it was a period of intense and painful isolation, compounded by a sense of personal loss. In the first week of February 1947, not long after his arrival, he received a telegram informing him that his father, Casimir Fanon, had suddenly died in late January, at the age of fifty-six. He took a night train to Rouen to comfort his sister Gabrielle, and to talk her down from her decision to move back to Martinique to support their mother. It would be a help to no one if she abandoned her pharmaceutical studies, he told her; under his counsel, she stayed in Rouen until she finished her degree. Fanon had never been close to his father, but in a letter to his mother, he wondered what Casimir had thought of him and speculated that knowing his father's opinion might help him focus on his daily tasks. In Lyon, he wrote to a friend, "I became accustomed to detaching myself, to detesting everything, to hating everything." In choosing to become a psychiatrist, he had settled on a career that would afford him a middle-class life back home, but he dreaded what he called "that larval, stocky, obsolete life that awaits me once I've finished my studies. I don't want 'marriage,' children, a home, the family table." When he moved out of his student dorm and into his own apartment at 29, rue Tupin, Joby found him living in bohemian squalor, books "piled everywhere, even on the floor . . . A small mountain of clothes stood in the corner."

One of Fanon's responses to his feelings of drift and ennui was to write a series of plays, depicting youthful protagonists at war with their surroundings, in search of love and transcendence. Fanon's theatrical works evoke an overwhelming sense of oppression without naming its source; race is never explicitly mentioned in them. He had been reading Nietzsche's *Birth of Tragedy*, and there is more than a whiff in his plays of the German philosopher's swaggering rhetoric about individual will and action, the creative destruction of inherited values. The first, *The Drowning Eye*, was about two brothers at war with each other over a woman; the second, *Parallel Hands*, was a tale of parricide set on the fictional Lébos, a Greek-sounding island engulfed in darkness. (The third play, *The Conspiracy*, has vanished.)

Fanon sent one of the plays to the director Jean-Louis Barrault, whose productions in Lyon he had admired. He never received a reply. Fanon was hurt, but Barrault's lack of interest was hardly surprising. His plays, as sterile as they were grandiose, could have been written by any number of melancholy young literary men in France. Fanon himself may have suspected as much; he would later ask Joby to burn the manuscripts (a request Joby ignored). None of the characters is identified by race. But one of the brothers in *The Drowning Eye*, whose name is François (the French equivalent of Frantz), is assaulted on a "white bed" by a group of men who invade his room. Ginette, the woman he and his brother are pursuing, tells him that his body "has the audacity of the coconut tree and the muted brutality of a Negro tom-tom." As François Maspero, who became Fanon's editor in the late 1950s, pointed out, his plays were works of "personal exorcism," reflecting his struggles with his father and, even more so, the difficulties of his early relationships in Lyon.

James Baldwin once remarked that "love takes off the masks that we fear we cannot live without and know we cannot live within." Fanon's experiences with white women in Lyon left him more cautious and perhaps less optimistic than Baldwin. His first major love affair was with a woman named Michèle Weyer, a fellow student in psychiatry from a family of Russian Jewish immigrants. In 1948, she became pregnant and Fanon proposed marriage. But the family was against the match, and the relationship quickly fell apart. He acknowledged paternity but avoided seeing his daughter, Mireille. (His brother Joby always felt that "his position as an absent father gnawed at him.")

A year later, he noticed a young woman waiting in line outside a movie theater; after buying his ticket, he followed her inside and sat beside her. Marie-Josèphe "Josie" Dublé, the woman he would marry in 1952, was nineteen years old at the time and still finishing lycée. A gamine with thick dark hair and large brown eyes, she was of mixed Romani-Corsican descent and had a "way of speaking under her breath" that "evoked mystery and sex," according to the American activist Elaine Klein Mokhtefi, who would befriend the couple toward the end of Fanon's life. Josie was a passionate reader of literature, with left-wing politics and a streak of melancholia. Her parents welcomed Fanon into the family. They were staunch trade unionists who had given their daughter a radical political education; there was no objection to her marrying a Black man. But when the courtship began, Frantz and Josie were hauled into a police station on suspicion that, as a mixed-race couple, they were probably connected with sex trafficking, or white slavery.

FANON'S WORKS FOR THE theater turned out to be little more than a rehearsal for his life as a writer, even if they were a necessary detour. His literary future lay not in philosophical love triangles, much less the kingdom of Lébos, but in the world of the damned, among the mentally ill, the outcast, and the colonized. Psychiatry would point the way forward.

It's not clear precisely when, or how, he chose his field. In his 2000 biography of Fanon, David Macey speculates that he settled upon his discipline sometime in the late 1940s because it enabled him to explore his ideas about society (not least about his own experiences as a Black man in France) in "ways that would not have been possible in other areas of medicine." But psychiatry's relevance to the larger intellectual world—much less the mental health of the racially oppressed—was not something Fanon could have studied at the conservative University of Lyon, a "psychiatric desert," according to one of his peers.

His supervisor on the faculty of medicine was Jean Dechaume, a stolid neuropsychiatrist who'd lost an arm in World War I and wielded his stump to direct his assistant during surgeries. Dechaume believed that every psychiatric condition had an organic cause and could be treated with a combination of drugs, confinement, and electroconvulsive therapy, of which he was a committed (and, it seems, indiscriminate) practitioner. Fanon put up with Dechaume for the sake of his degree, but he was already being led in a different, more heterodox direction by the psychiatric and psychoanalytic literature he'd begun to read in his spare time—and by his first experiences as a general practitioner.

In 1948, Fanon's fellow student Nicole Guillet, a friend of Michèle Weyer, took him to dinner at the home of the psychiatrist Paul Balvet, where she was living at the time. Guillet's father was the bursar at the Saint-Alban asylum, a center of radical psychiatry that Balvet had helped found. Situated in the Lozère, an agriculturally rich part of southwestern France, Saint-Alban had acquired a reputation for its innovative methods of group therapy and its record of wartime resistance. Fanon instantly warmed to Balvet, who was working at the Vinatier Hospital in Lyon, a short walk from the university, and came back frequently to talk about psychiatry and surrealism, another interest they shared. Balvet had recently published a paper titled "La valeur humaine de la folie" (The human value of madness) in *Esprit*, a journal of the Catholic left that Fanon was beginning to read attentively. Describing madness as an "extraordinary mine," perhaps even "a new mode of knowledge," Balvet compared it to both mystical conversion and falling in love. Like religious ecstasy and romantic passion, he argued, madness was "a blossoming, a new birth"

whose *Erlebnis*—a German philosophical term for "lived experience"—
had to be grasped from the inside and reconstructed phenomenologically.
The psychiatrist who dwells on the "outside of madness" is like "the art
critic who can easily give us the date of a painting and tell us about its
vicissitudes, but who never gives us back the colors." If madness was the
"monstrous and disturbing resurgence" of a patient's entire life, it "must be
felt"—above all, at its "moment of crystallization," when "neurosis turns
into psychosis." Madness, for Balvet, was inseparable from the human
condition. "Madness is within us," he wrote, "and reveals us."

*Erlebnis* was to become one of Fanon's central concepts. And though
he remained skeptical of Balvet's somewhat romantic account of madness,
he shared his view that mental illness has much to tell us about the societies
in which it arises, and that without an understanding of a patient's lived experience, a complete diagnosis is impossible. Indeed, Fanon seems to have
understood this well before his psychiatric training had even begun, thanks
to the work he'd been doing among North African laborers in Lyon—men
whose faces were familiar to him from his wartime experiences.

As a young doctor, he often found himself responding to emergency
house calls in the Algerian neighborhood around the rue Moncey and
the Guillotère quarter, close to the city's historic center on the east bank
of the Rhône. Fanon would later evoke the grim ambience of his work in
this neighborhood: "It is two o'clock in the morning. The room is dirty,
the patient is dirty. His parents are dirty. Everybody is crying. Everybody
is screaming. The strange impression that death is not far away." Most of
the patients he treated during these house calls were Algerian Muslims
with French citizenship—their official designation was *Français musulmans d'Algérie*—but they cast their votes at home in an electoral college
separate from Algerians of European origin, in which a single European
vote in Algeria had the same weight as roughly nine Muslim votes. They
suffered from poverty, inadequate housing, and racism. They were also under intensifying surveillance, thanks to the French state's anxieties about
the growing force of Algerian nationalism.

Algeria's struggle for independence arose in large part in the French
diaspora, among expatriates who had often identified more strongly

with region, locality, tribe, or ethnicity (Arab, Kabyle, Chaoui, etc.) than with a unified Algerian nation. Once they were in France, they came to think of themselves as Algerians, and in the 1920s the idea of an independent Algeria began to gain ground in the industrial cities of the *métropole*. In 1951, at the urging of the Ministry of the Interior, the Paris police began to report on all eating and drinking establishments operated "by Muslims native to North Africa."

Fanon observed that most of his colleagues spoke to North Africans in an infantilizing language that he knew all too well: the pidgin French called *le petit nègre*. (*Le petit nègre*, Fanon wrote, meant only one thing: "Stay in your place.") They did so without thinking, as if they were speaking to children; they also addressed them with the familiar second-person pronoun *tu*. Fanon was determined not to "indulge in any form of paternalism," but even he felt himself "lapsing" at times, having been an honorary *toubab* in the colonial army. Over and again, he witnessed scenes of misunderstanding and failure: communication had almost entirely broken down between French doctors and their North African patients. North Africans who clearly felt themselves to be deathly ill appeared to be "enveloped in vagueness," unable to identify the physical site of their pain. In the absence of a "lesional" component—an identifiable physical symptom on which both patient and doctor concurred—"the North African's pain" was "judged to have no consistency, no reality." It was seen instead as a form of hysteria, the imaginary anguish of a "man who fancies himself to be ill," as in a Molière play—or simply as an excuse not to work.

French doctors, Fanon came to believe, were trained to regard "every Arab" as "a man who suffers from an imaginary ailment." He explained, "The young doctor or the young student who has never seen a sick Arab knows . . . that 'those fellows are jesters.'" When a North African entered a medical office, he was not approached as an individual case, since he bore "the dead weight of all his compatriots." Instead of seeing this unexplained pain as a challenge, doctors took it as proof of the North African's essentially deceitful and lazy character; he was considered a "simulator, a liar, a malingerer, a sluggard, a thief." Rather than attempt to uncover the causes of the patient's illness, they described it as a case of "North African syndrome" and washed their hands of it. This was considered an "objective" diagnosis by the medical profession.

In the February 1952 issue of *Esprit*, Fanon published "The 'North African Syndrome,'" a ferocious critique of this concept—and of his profession and society. He admitted that it was not easy to treat North Africans who suffered from pain without lesions. When one of his patients said his stomach hurt but then pointed to his liver, it was easy to dismiss the patient as suffering from North African syndrome and leave it at that. But Fanon refused to accept this diagnosis; he saw it as a racist barrier to understanding, a complacent flight from humanist ethics. "Who are they," he writes, "those creatures starving for humanity who stand buttressed against the impalpable frontiers . . . of complete recognition? Who are they, in truth, those creatures who hide, who are hidden by social truth, beneath the attributes of *bicot, bougnoule, arabe, raton, sidi, mon z'ami?*"*

In his description of North African life in France, Fanon summoned an unusual passion, eloquence, and lyricism; in attaching himself to the real, to the "concrete," he achieved powerful effects that had eluded him as a playwright. North Africans, he writes, are "alone": they are isolated people who have been deprived of the benefits of sociality and "seem absurd to us." And only dimly visible to the French: "From time to time one sees them working on a construction site, and yet one does not *see* them, one perceives them, one gets a glimpse of them. Associates? Relations? There are no contacts. There are only collisions. Do people realize how much that is gentle and polite is contained in this word, 'contact'?" Fanon was a middle-class Frenchman of color, several notches above these men in the colonial pyramid of privilege. But he identified with their loneliness, their sense of being outcasts, their invisibility.

They live, he writes, in a "perpetual state of insecurity," exploited by employers and landlords, ridiculed as primitive, accused of lusting after prostitutes (often the only women available to them). At the same time, they were belittled for not knowing their rights as French citizens. He continues:

* Racist epithets for North African Muslims, especially Algerians, most of which originated in the colonies and crossed the Mediterranean to the *métropole*.

Rights, Duties, Citizenship, Equality, what fine things! The North African on the threshold of the French Nation—which is, we are told, his as well . . . What connection does this have with the North African in a hospital setting? It so happens there *is* a connection . . . Threatened in his affectivity, threatened in his social activity, threatened in his membership of the community—the North African combines all the conditions that make a sick man.

Living in a society that fails to recognize him as a man, Fanon explains, the North African "will feel himself emptied, without life, in a bodily struggle with death."

It is no wonder, Fanon suggests, that North Africans can't identify a particular lesion: the pain they experience is often diffused throughout the body; they cling to it "volubly," almost as a point of honor. The North African "*is* his pain," not because he's making it up but because it's the one thing he owns, in his state of generalized dispossession. His pain signifies his body's protest against a life that is a "daily death," an unending humiliation.

Even as North Africans were denied the right of self-determination— "something for which not so long ago you were ready to give up everything, even your life," Fanon pointedly reminded his French readers—they were "told they were French. They learned it in school. In the street. In the barracks . . . On the battlefields. They have had France squeezed into them . . . in their bodies and in their soul. Now they are told in no uncertain terms that they are in 'our' country. That if they don't like it, all they have to do is go back to their Casbah." France, he writes, would not be worthy of his love until it treated the North African as "more than a body, more than a Mohammed." Identifying as a Frenchman himself, Fanon was arguing that the North African syndrome said more about France and its dehumanization of North Africans than it did about the hysteria it purported to diagnose.

The dehumanization of patients, especially those suffering from mental illness, was a widespread problem in French hospitals, where they were subject to what Michel Foucault, in his 1963 history, *The Birth of the Clinic*, would call "the reductive discourse of the doctor." But what Fanon

observed with North African workers and their doctors was a more specific problem: the way in which the colonial gaze obstructed careful diagnosis and proper medical care. He also suggested how easy it was to
acquiesce to the process; he felt tempted, he admitted, to throw up his
hands when confronted by some of his patients. Colonialism, he was beginning to realize, was a system of pathological relations masquerading
as normality. It was predicated on racist conceptions of the colonized and
their limited capacity for equality, sovereignty, self-governance—an in-
complete "personhood," as we'd say today. These conceptions were rooted
not only in hierarchical power relations but also in academic research by
doctors and anthropologists who relied on their expertise to explain why
the colonized were inferior and therefore predisposed to being colonized.
There is good reason to believe that Fanon's decision to become a psychiatrist grew directly out of his encounters with Algerians on the rue Moncey.

   Fanon was contributing to a sweeping reappraisal of the profession
by left-wing psychiatrists, many of them veterans of the Resistance. In the
words of Lucien Bonnafé, a Communist psychiatrist at the Saint-Alban
asylum, "madness was never a personal affair." Rather, it had to be grasped
as a "historical and dialectical phenomenon," in light of the "entire historical fact": an allusion to what the ethnologist Marcel Mauss called the "total
social fact," the intricate web of relations, institutions, and beliefs that constitutes social reality. For radical psychiatrists like Bonnafé, the distress of
their patients spoke to unresolved beliefs and conflicts in society at large.
In his 1943 study, *Essai sur quelques problèmes concernant le normal et
le pathologique* (Essay on some problems regarding the normal and the
pathological), the historian of science Georges Canguilhem, who went
into refuge at Saint-Alban while serving in the Resistance, argued that
the distinction we draw between normality and pathology is itself a social
construction, not a medical reality. Critics of "organic" neuropsychiatry
and Marxist psychiatrists who read Canguilhem drew radical conclusions
from these insights. They imagined a new and more democratic micro-
society emerging inside the asylum, a kind of decentralized psycho-utopia
where the lines blurred between caregivers and care receivers. A generation of radical psychiatrists—notably the British iconoclast R. D. Laing—
came to celebrate madness as a visionary mode of perception, much like

artistic inspiration. The hugely influential French psychoanalyst Jacques Lacan was intrigued by surrealism and its intimation that insanity spoke a kind of truth.

Fanon shared Lacan's belief that mental illness could not be reduced to neurological disorders in the brain; even when its underlying causes were organic, the forms it assumed were shaped by patients' social and familial relationships. He admired Lacan's 1932 thesis on paranoia, which argued that because madness had no single origin, it should be examined in the light of sociology and psychoanalysis, as well as neuropsychiatry and medicine. In his 1951 doctoral thesis on Friedreich's ataxia, a hereditary neurodegenerative condition often accompanied by psychiatric symptoms, Fanon called Lacan the "logician of madness." But this characterization was also subtly mocking, hinting that Lacan had supplied a rationale for the irrational.

Fanon could never bring himself to endorse the surrealist fantasy of madness as—in Rimbaud's famous expression—the "disordering of all the senses." Mental illness, he argued, was not freedom's extreme edge but rather a "pathology of freedom." This pulverizing alienation from the self, Fanon believed, presented an almost insurmountable obstacle to normal relations with others. The enforced solitude of the mad, prisoners of their delirium, held no romance for Fanon. That Fanon repudiated the Lacanian defense of madness—that he emphasized the vulnerability, suffering, and loss of freedom experienced by the mentally ill, rather than the "visionary" nature of their perception, or the ecstasy of hallucination—is a reminder of the value that he always placed on self-determination. To be mentally ill was to relinquish all control over one's mind and therefore one's body and destiny. For a descendant of slaves in a former sugar colony, it was impossible to confuse the condition of mental and physical disintegration with emancipation from an oppressive social order.*

---

* Nor would Fanon ever endorse the sweeping critique of "reason" as an instrument of Western domination: reason was also a weapon the weak could turn against their oppressors.

# 4

# TOWARD A BLACK
# EXISTENTIALISM

---

DURING HIS YEARS IN LYON, Fanon's phantom city was Paris, the heart of the country's intellectual life, where talk of freedom and overcoming alienation was in the air. He became a reader of little magazines in the vanguard of postwar critical thought and attended plays by Sartre and Camus at Lyon's edgiest theater, Les Célestins, located on the former site of a Celestine convent and church. In existentialism, Fanon found a new and seductive language that promised to supersede Négritude. The question was where, or whether, they intersected, and how they might enrich his thinking about psychiatry and about his own experience as a Black man.

Existentialism, with its fundamental conviction that "existence precedes essence," ran counter to the essentialism of Senghor's version of Négritude, with its evocation of an eternal, immutable African spirit. (Césaire's version was far more user-friendly to existentialists.) It proposed that we are not determined by biological or cultural destiny: human subjects create themselves by the decisions they make, as they assume the burden of their freedom. "A genuine rebellion of the intellectuals," Hannah Arendt wrote in 1946, "whose docility in relation to modern society was one of the saddest aspects of the sad spectacle of Europe between the wars," existentialism found a passionate following among young people who had known war and were impatient to remake their world after its devastation. The movement flourished outside the universities: its center was the Café de Flore on Paris's boulevard Saint-Germain, where Sartre, existentialism's unofficial but undisputed leader, held court with Beauvoir. Both had been relatively "docile" during the German occupation, but they had emerged from it as champions, and icons, of the Resistance.

By the time Fanon arrived in Lyon, their alliance with Albert Camus, whose celebrity as a novelist and philosopher was nearly equal to theirs, was becoming a casualty of the Cold War. Camus, a member of the Communist Party as a young man in Algeria and a heroic *résistant*, repudiated communism as a new and brutal form of tyranny, upholding instead the ideal of individual revolt in an absurd society. Sartre and Beauvoir, for their part, sought to promote a radical socialist politics independent of both the French Communist Party, whose intellectuals assailed existentialism as a reactionary nihilist doctrine, and the capitalist West. Neither of them joined the party, but in the early 1950s they became fellow travelers of the Soviet Union, in their judgment still a "revolutionary" state, whatever its flaws.* In October 1951, when Camus published *The Rebel*, a critique of revolutionary pursuits of "absolute justice," the tensions with Sartre and Beauvoir escalated into an official parting of ways. Yet for all their intense quarrels (and however much Camus rejected the label), the existentialists were united by their belief in the contingency of existence, their refusal to accept the world as it is, and their insistence upon freedom, even in the direst of circumstances ("extreme situations," in Sartre's terminology). At its core, existentialism was a somber, often tragic, ever vigilant mood of refusal: the philosophical continuation of the ethics of the wartime Resistance.

The movement's house journal was *Les Temps modernes*, edited by Sartre and Beauvoir. In its pages, Fanon—who would at last meet them both in 1961—discovered an adventurous model of intellectual practice that

---

* Sartre, who would break with the Soviet Union over the 1956 invasion of Hungary, famously defended his silence about Communist horrors by saying, "Il ne faut pas désperer Billancourt" ("Billancourt should not be made to despair"), an allusion to the workers in Boulogne-Billancourt, a suburb in Paris's "red belt."

encouraged speculative thinking and rejected specialization. Existentialism was never an exclusively philosophical movement; Sartre, Beauvoir,
and Camus were at home with art, fiction, and theater: their novels and
plays were rich in philosophy, their philosophical works highly literary. The
existentialists also took a keen interest in the United States, especially its
"race relations," the euphemism of the time. In *Les Temps modernes*, Fanon
read Bernard Wolfe's essay on racial minstrelsy and became aware of Richard Wright and Chester Himes, the Black American exiles in Paris whose
novels were championed by Sartre. Maurice Merleau-Ponty, who had just
published his magnum opus, *The Phenomenology of Perception*, was the
movement's most innovative philosopher and an enormously influential
figure at *Les Temps modernes*.

Fanon attended Merleau-Ponty's lectures in Lyon but never spoke to
him; he later told Sartre and Beauvoir that he had been too intimidated to
introduce himself. But Merleau-Ponty's ideas are central to Fanon's development as a psychiatrist and a writer. "We are in the world through our
bodies, and insofar as we perceive the world with our bodies," Merleau-
Ponty wrote in *The Phenomenology of Perception*. He did not mean the
physical, objective body so much as our experience (and psychological perception) of the body we inhabit, which he called the "phenomenal body."
He illustrated this point with the example of the phantom limb, which
intrigued Fanon. "A war-wounded man still senses in his phantom arm
the shrapnel that tore into his real arm," Merleau-Ponty wrote. The amputee is not hallucinating; rather, he is experiencing through his phenomenal
body, which, in spite of the loss, remains his orientation to the world. For
Merleau-Ponty, the world is not something that can be grasped by an individual. "The phenomenological world is not pure being," he wrote, "but
rather the sense that shines forth at the intersection of my experiences
with those of others through a sort of meshing into each other." Crucially,
these experiences must be *lived* in the body: there is no such thing as a
disembodied apprehension of the world. As Sartre put it, Merleau-Ponty
had no patience with thinkers who overlooked the body's experience and
knowledge, and "whose philosophy soared above the earth, forgetting that
we are bogged down in it from birth."

Fanon had not lost a limb in the war, but he knew perfectly well from his shrapnel wound the difference between a physical body and a phenomenal body. He had also grown up on an island whose economy had been based on slave labor, where the brutalization of Black bodies was the norm, and amputation among the punishments for theft and resistance. Could Fanon have had a "flesh memory" of this violence? In his first book, *Black Skin, White Masks*, he would suggest as much, likening his experience of racism to being threatened with the loss of a limb, and declaring, "I refuse this amputation." (The word "amputation" recurs in all his writing.) This refusal, like the insistence of the phantom limb, was the phenomenal body's rebellion against the violence that had been inflicted upon the objective body.

Fanon was also drawn to Merleau-Ponty's emphasis on *le vécu* (lived experience)—a French translation of *Erlebnis*, the term he'd discovered in Paul Balvet's essay on madness—and by his notion of a "bodily schema." Here was a philosophy brimming with potential psychological applications. But as Fanon began writing in earnest about what he called "the lived experience of the Black man" in a white society, with thoughts of making it the subject of his medical thesis, he found that he could not accept Merleau-Ponty's arguments to the letter; Black people, he was convinced, lacked something that Merleau-Ponty considered essential to human freedom: physical anonymity. Whites could pass without notice on the streets or on public transportation because their bodies were unmarked. Black people, however, were marked and could not avoid being seen even if their deepest wish, as Fanon would write in *Black Skin, White Masks*, was "to be anonymous, to be forgotten." Under the white gaze, they were simultaneously hypervisible (as members of a stigmatized collective) and invisible (as individuals).

Fanon came to believe that through a largely unconscious process, Black people "epidermalized" the white gaze, absorbed it into their bodies, and felt it as a burden, another obstacle to their freedom. Their "bodily schema"—the way they experienced their bodies in public spaces—was different from that of whites because beneath it lay "a historical-racial schema." As a result, a "genuine dialectic" between the Black person's body and the world was foreclosed. This is why Fanon described himself as being "locked in a crushing objectivity" by the gaze of the white boy in Lyon.

In a racist society, Black people are always on guard, because their bodies are "surrounded by an atmosphere of certain uncertainty." To this extent, Merleau-Ponty still engaged in the "high-altitude" thinking he disparaged: the kind of color-blind philosophical universalism that implicitly assumed the human subject to be white. Here was part of the reason Fanon turned to Sartre, who seemed to be speaking more directly to his concerns about racism than Merleau-Ponty was.

IN HIS EARLY PHILOSOPHICAL WORK, notably *Being and Nothingness*, Sartre's frame of reference was the individual consciousness. In that work, the "other"—one of Sartre's central concepts—is anyone who is not the self. But after the war—chastened, perhaps, by the Holocaust and by guilt over his less-than-heroic record of wartime resistance—Sartre began to reflect on the specific experiences of marginalized "others" such as Jews, Black people, Arabs, and gays. In Sartre, his most important influence after Césaire, Fanon found not only a political ally but also a thinker of extraordinary sensitivity. Sartre, whose roots were unimpeachably bourgeois, not only paid tribute to the struggles of the oppressed; he incorporated their struggles into his work and used them to broaden and even recast his philosophical project. He did not abandon universalism, but he realized that universality was an aspiration of critical thought, rather than its premise; it represented a future to be fought for and over, rather than assumed, because human experience was inherently plural, unequal, and divided. People who had been persecuted or oppressed by the West could scarcely be expected to recognize themselves in, much less exalt, a philosophical tradition that had denigrated and often denied their humanity. Long before the arrival of Jacques Derrida, the founder of "deconstruction," Sartre wrestled with the question of "difference" and what it meant for Western philosophy, especially what Derrida would call "white mythologies."

In 1946, the year that Fanon began his studies in Lyon, Sartre published a short book called *Réflexions sur la question juive* (published in English two years later as *Anti-Semite and Jew*), which examined the psychology of the antisemite and the way in which this "involvement of the mind" not only affected the object of his phobia, the Jew, but also, in a sense, created the Jew as a stereotype and scapegoat. The consequences of antisemitism had been exposed during the war, not least in France, where the Vichy authorities had deported seventy-six thousand Jews to concentration camps, only 3 percent of whom survived the war. Yet Sartre hardly discussed this history. He wanted instead to show how antisemitism limited the physical and mental freedom of Jews *after* the defeat of fascism, when their rights had been restored. The Jew, he argues, is "overdetermined" by the antisemite's phobic projection: "*marked* as a Jew" and thus stamped with a stigma that, for both Jew and antisemite, "extends to the physiological realm, as happens in cases of hysteria." Bearing this stigma as if it were a second skin, he subjects himself to "endless self-examination," developing "a phantom personality, at once strange and familiar, that haunts him and which is nothing but himself—himself as others see him."

In a passage reminiscent of Fanon's encounter with the boy on the train (and that Fanon would cite in a footnote in *Black Skin, White Masks*), Sartre writes that eventually all Jewish children experience the stigma that is their cruel inheritance:

> Some day they must learn the truth: sometimes from the smiles of those who surround them, sometimes from rumor or insult. The later the discovery, the more violent the shock. Suddenly they realize that others know something about them that they didn't know; that people apply to them an ugly and upsetting term that is not used in their own family. They feel themselves separated, cut off from the society of the normal children who run and play tranquilly and securely around them—those lucky children who have no *special name*.

The Black American intellectual W. E. B. Du Bois described a similar complex in his 1903 book, *The Souls of Black Folk*: "It is a peculiar sensation, this double-consciousness, this sense of always looking at one's self through the eyes of others, of measuring one's soul by the tape of a world that looks on in amused contempt and pity." Fanon never read Du Bois, but he found in Sartre a vivid and all-too-familiar account of the phantom personality, or "double-consciousness," created by racism. Sartre's pages on the lived experience of antisemitism, he would write later, were among "the most beautiful we've ever read. The most beautiful, because the problem they express hits us in the guts."

Yet anti-Black racism was not lived in quite the same way as anti-semitism. Jews could often pass unnoticed because they were white, which made it easier for French Christians to overlook their record of anti-semitic persecution, those "minor episodes in the family history," as Fanon called them. The Black man's visibility made this forgetting impossible: "I am a slave not to the 'idea' that others have of me, but to my appearance." Black people, moreover, were attacked in their physical being for their imagined "mind-blowing sexual potency": "Just think! With the liberty they have in the jungle. It seems they fornicate everywhere, and at any moment. They are genitals. They have so many children they can't count them. Be careful, they'll inundate us with mulattos." Antisemites, he goes on to say, "would never think of castrating the Jew. The Jew is killed or sterilized. The *nègre*, however, is castrated . . . The *nègre* represents bio-logical danger. The Jew, intellectual danger."

Nonetheless, Fanon was inspired by Sartre's analysis of antisemitism, and by the implication that it might apply to other racialized minorities. (He had taken to heart his lycée teacher's warning that "the anti-Semite is inevitably a Negrophobe.") In the conclusion to *Anti-Semite and Jew*, Sartre called for a "concrete liberalism" in which rights would be based not on "human nature" but rather on "active participation in the life of society." French Arabs and Black people as well as Jews, he wrote, "have a right in that enterprise; they are citizens. But they have these rights as Jews, Blacks and Arabs—that is, as concrete persons." Fanon had no desire to assimilate if it meant renouncing his identity, and thanks to Négritude, he was already affirming himself as a "concrete person," as a Black man. Now he appeared to have Sartre's imprimatur as well.

Yet it was not so simple, as he discovered when he read Sartre's 1948 es-say "Black Orpheus," a beautiful and fiery tribute to the poets whom Fanon also loved: Senghor, Damas, and, above all, Césaire. Sartre's essay was pub-lished as the preface to a collection that Senghor had edited of African and West Indian poetry, *Anthologie de la nouvelle poésie nègre et malgache de* *langue française.** "Black poetry in the French language," Sartre declared, "is, in our time, the only great revolutionary poetry."

He was not the first white Frenchman to write in praise of Négritude. The surrealist writer André Breton had hailed Césaire as a "great Black poet"—a phrase that grated on Fanon—in his preface to *Notebook of a Return to the Native Land*. But Sartre believed that Négritude heralded a revolution whose implications went far beyond poetry, and beyond the concerns of any specific "race." It embodied a world-historical challenge to the self-understanding, the language, and the values of the West. Its ultimate aim, he claimed, was not to make room for Blackness in the cathedral of white Western culture but to demolish the cathedral altogether.

"Black Orpheus" begins with a remarkable passage in which Sartre imagines the astonishment of his white French readers as they encounter Négritude poetry for the first time:

> When you removed the gag that was keeping these black mouths shut, what were you hoping for? That they would sing your praises? . . . Here are black men standing, looking at us, and I hope that you—like me—will feel the shock of being seen. For three thousand years, the white man has enjoyed the privilege of seeing without being seen . . . Today, these black men are looking at us, and our gaze comes back to our own eyes; in their turn, black torches light up the world and our white heads are no more than Chinese lanterns swinging in the wind.

The direction of the gaze had been reversed: the new Black poets were indifferent to the reactions of white readers, since they were "addressing themselves to Black men about Black men," emboldened by a "heightened awareness of racial difference and pride." Having been stigmatized as *nègres*, Sartre argued, Black poets had no choice but to embrace their identity, to close ranks among themselves: "This anti-racist racism is the only road that will lead to the abolition of racial difference." By "anti-racist racism"—a term that would sow considerable confusion—Sartre did not

---

* Anthology of the new Negro and Malagasy poetry in the French language.

mean anti-white prejudice so much as an early foreshadowing of identity politics, with its focus on what distinguishes members of an oppressed group from others. In the case of Négritude poetry, this meant a return to the Black self and Black culture. But where were these to be found? Thanks to centuries of racial domination, the Black writer—above all the Black writer in the West Indies, uprooted from Africa—had "become split." His desire to "reveal himself" as Black was itself an indication that he "was already exiled from himself," already haunted by a white "phantom personality." To reclaim his Blackness, he has to carry out a "tireless descent into himself," much as Orpheus descended into Hades to rescue his wife, Eurydice—hence Sartre's title.

Like Fanon, Sartre was beguiled by Césaire's interpretation of Négritude, which privileged an existential self-invention over Senghor's romantic return to the self within an "objective ensemble of Negro-African traditions." Césaire's poetic modus operandi was, of course, reminiscent of the subversions of surrealism, but here it was not "a matter of some gratuitous game" but rather a matter of the poet "discovering and becoming what he is." At the same time, Césaire's poetry, Sartre argued, contained the seeds of a new universality, where "race is transmuted into historicity," and Blackness "is no longer a state, nor even an existential attitude, it is a 'Becoming.'"

"Black Orpheus" was more than an exercise in sympathetic literary criticism: it was an homage, in Sartre's mind, to the revolutionary force of Blackness. It would become one of the Négritude movement's signature documents—certainly its most important manifesto by a white European writer. Several of its themes would reappear in Fanon's work: Black resistance to the white gaze, the centrality of language to the workings of racial oppression, the way in which cultural or ethnic self-assertion serves as preparation for collective struggle.

Yet, as Fanon would explain in *Black Skin, White Masks*, his initial response to Sartre's essay was to feel slighted, even betrayed. In the very act of praising the Négritude poets, Sartre had pulled the rug out from under their feet by suggesting that their movement's role was to catalyze a more "universal" revolution led by the proletariat, and once this was underway, to accept its own dissolution into a greater whole. A "means and not an end," the Blackness of Négritude was, in Sartre's words, a "weak phase of a dialectic progression," the antithesis of white supremacy. "But this negative moment is not sufficient in itself" since it requires a new thesis, which socialism alone supplies. Blackness, Sartre declared with his keen eye for paradox, was "an absolute that knows it is transitory." This, for him, was the "tragic beauty" of Négritude. It might "color the sea into which it flows," but in the end, he decided, it "does not matter."

Fanon was incensed. Sartre had hailed the vitality of Négritude only to declare it a tragic passion, destined to die once it renounced ethnic particularism—"anti-racist racism"—in the name of universal emancipation. By inscribing Négritude within the Hegelian dialectic, Sartre had written it off as a flickering, subaltern interlude in a greater historical process. What had become of Sartre's wish for a "concrete liberalism" in which Jews, Blacks, and Arabs would be welcomed as "concrete" people, rather than raceless individuals? Sartre was at least consistent, whichever way you looked at it. In *Anti-Semite and Jew*, he had criticized Jewish nationalism, even as he argued that Jews were forced to identify as Jews when they were attacked as Jews. Ethnic particularism had no place in the "universality" of the socialist future that he envisioned.

But, for Fanon, there was no consolation in Sartre's even-handedness. He was convinced that "Black Orpheus" had robbed Négritude of its "foundational blackness." Négritude, Sartre had written, "seems racial" but "is actually a hymn by everyone for everyone." Why couldn't it be both Black *and* universal? And why was Blackness a condition that a Black person had to transcend? Fanon had recently begun to proclaim his Blackness in the white city of Lyon only to see it belittled by a philosopher he revered. He experienced the essay as an attack on his own phenomenal body: "I sensed my shoulders slipping from the world, my feet no longer touched the ground. Without a Negro past, without a Negro future, it was impossible for me to live my Blackness [*nègrerie*]. Not yet white, no longer black, I was damned."

Fanon's argument with Sartre could be dismissed as the narcissism of small differences or an act of Oedipal rebellion: the son grudgingly accepts the father's wisdom but still has to slay him. And Fanon would often exaggerate his differences with his mentors, as if it were his only way of asserting himself. Nonetheless, he had good reason to take issue with Sartre's universalism. Sartre, he wrote, had "forgotten that the *nègre* suffers in his body differently from the White man." What set Black people apart from whites, for Fanon, was not their African spirit (as in Senghor) or their foundational Blackness (as in Césaire), but their lived experience of being Black: above all, their experience of what Merleau-Ponty called the phenomenal body. Fanon placed great value on this experience, however agonizing it had been for him in France: for all his belief in "man," he was not prepared to repudiate his Blackness as a tragic passion. So long as white supremacy persisted, the Black absolute—the consciousness of inhabiting a Black body in a white world—would be a necessary weapon. To hear Négritude described as a collective rite of passage reminded him of being lectured by an elder: "You'll change, my child; when I was young, I was like that, too . . . You'll see, everything passes."

In a brash footnote in *Black Skin, White Masks*, Fanon suggested that Sartre's entire framework for understanding alienation "reveals itself to be false" when applied to Black consciousness, because for the Black person, "the White is not only the Other, but the master, whether real or imaginary." But while Fanon resented Sartre at the time, the essay clearly left him unsettled. Whenever he wrote of Négritude, he would hear Sartre's voice.

Today, Fanon is often seen as a champion of Blackness. But in the course of his reflections on racism, Négritude turned out to be a passing phase. He would emerge as its most eloquent, and often scathing, detractor.

IN THE MAY 1951 issue of *Esprit*, Fanon published a lengthy essay titled "The Black Man's Lament: The Lived Experience of the Black Man," which included his reflections on Sartre and race. In a daring mélange of memoir, philosophy, psychoanalysis, and literary criticism, he wrote hauntingly of his psychological torment in white Lyon. The real battle of being Black in a white world, he suggested, is a struggle less against "a feeling of inferiority" than "a feeling of not existing," compounded by guilt and fear. It was the most autobiographical essay he ever wrote.

It took no little audacity for a twenty-six-year-old unknown from the outre-mer, studying medicine in a provincial city, to openly challenge the country's most celebrated philosopher. But Fanon appears to have been fearless, or at least determined to overcome his fears by taking on members of the intellectual establishment. (This would be a pattern throughout his life.) Significantly, he chose to publish both his first essay and "The 'North African Syndrome'" in *Esprit*, a journal founded by left-wing Catholics known for their fierce anti-colonialism, rather than in the Négritude tribune *Présence africaine*. He had a connection to an editor at *Esprit*, Jean-Marie Domenach, via Domenach's brother-in-law Michel Colin, one of Fanon's professors in the faculty of medicine in Lyon. More to the point, he may have either considered *Présence africaine* too accommodating toward France or wished to signal his distance from Césaire and Senghor.

"The Black Man's Lament" would become the fifth chapter of *Black Skin, White Masks*. The book grew out of Fanon's experiences as a doctor in Lyon, although it is neither a memoir nor a clinical study, but rather an unusual mixture of genres and discursive registers: analytic and poetic, despairing and hopeful, solemn and sarcastic. He seems to have originally conceived it as his doctoral thesis in psychiatry. Here, too, Fanon exhibited an audacity that bordered on self-sabotage, since he must have known that his conservative mentor Dechaume, whom he privately held in contempt, would never approve as his official thesis a genre-blurring, often polemical essay on racism, garlanded with citations of Sartre and Césaire. But Fanon seems to have desperately needed to write the book, not only to convey the lived experience of race for Black people but also to expose the blindness of the medical establishment in France, which treated this experience—*his* experience—as irrelevant to psychiatry.

He had begun to collect material for the book in the late 1940s in Lyon, and completed the manuscript in 1951, most likely during his internship at the Saint-Ylié Hospital in Dôle, two hours north of Lyon in the Jura. His supervisor in Dôle, Madeleine Humbert, would complain years later that her Martinican intern was "as disagreeable as possible" and that he behaved toward the nurses "like a colonialist"—a provocative charge to level at a Black anti-colonialist from a former French colony. What she disliked in Fanon, however, may have been his pride, his formality, his refusal to smile and express gratitude for being accepted, in the manner of a well-trained *noir évolué*. She took particular umbrage at his failure to take notes during consultations with patients, mistaking it for sloppiness. In fact, Fanon considered notetaking in consultations to be intrusive and inquisitorial. Patients, he felt, should be addressed with respect and compassion. Far too many were treated as specimens, especially if they were Black or Arab.

Outside office hours, however, Fanon was taking copious notes, except that they reflected social and political interests far afield from those of mainstream psychiatry. One of the cases that drew his attention involved a nineteen-year-old female patient who suffered hallucinations of "savage and cannibal" Black people, dancing around a pot and preparing to make a meal of a middle-aged white man; as it turned out, her father was a veteran of the colonial army in West Africa, and her fears could be traced back to memories of her father listening to radio broadcasts of "Negro music." Another patient, a prostitute, told Fanon that the very idea of having sex with a Black man brought her to orgasm, even though her sexual encounters with Black men were "no more remarkable than having sex with a white man." What excited her was thinking of "all the things" a Black man could do to her. Myths about Black male sexuality were so pervasive, Fanon discovered, that a Black gynecology student he knew refused to perform vaginal exams. What's more, these myths were impervious to logical refutation. "Isn't the superiority of the *nègre* real?" Fanon writes in *Black Skin, White Masks*. "Everyone knows it isn't. But that's beside the point. The prelogical thought of the phobia has decided it is."

A psychiatrist of a more conservative disposition might have dismissed the particular *content* of these phobias as secondary to their *essence*, but Fanon, a West Indian Black man whose illusions about French color blindness had been shattered in the war and on the streets of Lyon, could not. Racism, for him, was not merely the incidental expression of a pathology; it *was* a pathology, born of slavery and colonization. His interest in the architecture of racial fantasy and fear led him to conduct free association tests with a group of about three hundred French whites, to whom he gave questionnaires in which the word *nègre* was inserted among dozens of other words.\* Nearly 60 percent of those surveyed associated *nègre* with words such as "biological, sex, strong, athletic, powerful, boxer, Joe Louis, Jesse Owens, Senegalese infantrymen, savage, animal, devil, sin." When white colleagues posed the same questions to white patients, the percentage of such responses was even higher.

"Negrophobia," he found, was widespread among his West Indian patients as well. They had absorbed a sense of being inferior into their skin, by an "internalization or rather epidermalization"; the struggle to overcome it was almost indistinguishable from a desire not to be Black. "It's normal for the West Indian to be a Negrophobe," Fanon would write in *Black Skin, White Masks*. "In his collective unconscious, the West Indian has made all the European archetypes his own." In their nightmares of rape and sexual aggression, Creole women, the "almost white," invariably imagined a Senegalese or "so-called inferior." It was nearly always "in reference to the essence of the white man" that West Indians perceived one another's skin color, even their character. Fanon was also struck by the fantasies of violence, domination, and revenge that racism appeared to inspire in its Black victims. He interviewed a Black medical student who had enlisted in the army as a medical auxiliary after becoming convinced that his European patients would never accept him. But the student refused to join a unit in which he would have treated soldiers from the colonies. He wanted to treat whites, and to make them "adopt a Black attitude toward him," so that they would experience the indignities that he had undergone, and he would be "avenged for the imago that had always obsessed him: the frightened, humiliated *nègre*, trembling in front of the white master."

As Fanon mapped the psychic landscape produced by racism, with a focus on what we now call "implicit bias," he came to believe that Black men like himself had "a function" in the white West, and in color-conscious colonial societies like Martinique: "to represent shameful feelings, base instincts, and the dark side of the soul," especially the "biological" or sexual

---

\* It is not clear whether he gave these questionnaires in the context of formal research, or as an individual initiative, during consultations.

side. (James Baldwin would later make a similar observation: "The white man's unadmitted—and apparently, to him, unspeakable—private fears and longings are projected onto the Negro.")

"The analysis of reality is a delicate task," Fanon would write in *Black Skin, White Masks*. A scientist could limit himself to a description, especially if "his research always focuses on others and never on himself." He recalled being told to pretend that he was dissecting a cat during "several nauseating attempts" at performing an autopsy. But here he was facing a question that could not have concerned him more directly: "Can the white man behave in a sane manner toward the Black man and can the Black man behave in a sane manner toward the white man?" Fanon did not deny the neurological underpinnings of mental illness: his argument was not that racism alone drove people mad. But he believed that the "pathological" racism of his patients provided a window onto "normal" French and Martinican society, and that its symptoms were exaggerated versions of fantasies and beliefs engendered by racism and colonialism, and deeply embedded in society at large.


FANON WAS FAR FROM alone in his preoccupation with the psychology of race and colonialism. In 1950, while Fanon was at work on *Black Skin, White Masks*, the psychoanalyst Octave Mannoni published an influential study titled *Psychologie de la colonisation*. (The title of the English translation is *Prospero and Caliban*.) It provoked a wave of attacks from opponents of colonialism, Fanon among them.

Mannoni, whose father ran a correctional facility for young offenders in France, spent two decades working as a functionary in the colonial administration in Madagascar, before returning to France to train under Lacan. A liberal anti-colonialist, he condemned the racism and violence of the settlers, and expressed support for the 1947 nationalist revolt, in which tens of thousands of Malagasy were killed by French troops—many of them Senegalese infantrymen. Settlers in Madagascar had called for his expulsion. He was not an obvious target of anti-colonial wrath.

In his book, Mannoni argued that the French settlers in Madagascar suffered from an inferiority complex in relation to the *métropole*, and projected their fears of inadequacy onto the Malagasy—an idea that would find wide expression in the literature of anti-colonialism. But he also suggested, more controversially, that the Malagasy met them halfway, with their own "dependency complex." In Mannoni's description, colonization resembled an abusive relationship that both parties had willingly entered. Fanon was furious. Mannoni's book, he would write in *Black Skin, White Masks*, led him to "wonder if [colonial administrators] know what they are doing in the colonies. For twenty years, they persist in their program of turning the *nègre* into a White man. In the end they give up and tell him: you definitely have a dependency complex toward the White man."

Fanon argued, "What Monsieur Mannoni has forgotten is that the Malagasy no longer exists; he has forgotten that the Malagasy *exists in relation to the European*." The Malagasy was, in other words, a creation of the colonial system, just as the Jew was a creation of the antisemite, and the *nègre* a creation of whites: "Let us have the courage to say: *it is the racist who creates the inferiorized*." If the Malagasy had "been made to ask the question whether he is a man, it's because his reality as a man has been challenged" by the colonizer. Whatever Mannoni's insights into the everyday relations and reciprocal fantasies of colonizer and colonized, he had utterly ignored the "total social fact" that produced them.

That total social fact included the bloody repression of the Malagasy revolt two years before the publication of Mannoni's book—a necessary guide, in Fanon's view, to the Malagasy collective unconscious. Many of Mannoni's patients reported having dreams in which they saw dark and frightening images: shadows, black bulls and oxen, but also the Senegalese soldiers called in by the French to put down the rebellion. Mannoni saw these images as representations of the phallus. But Fanon argued that a Malagasy nightmare about a Senegalese infantryman had to be placed "*in its time*, and this time is the period during which 80,000 natives were killed, i.e., one inhabitant out of fifty; and *in its place*, and that place is an island with a population of 4 million among whom no real relationship can be established, where clashes break out on all sides, where lies and demagoguery are the sole masters." To understand why the Malagasy had nightmares about Senegalese soldiers, knowing that one of them was an infamous torturer at the police headquarters was more important than

"Freud's discoveries," Fanon wrote, "which are of no use to us whatsoever." The soldier's gun in these dreams "is not a penis, but a genuine 1916 Lebel rifle." Far from being psychic displacements, the images in these dreams are "genuine irruptions during sleep" of the brutal reality to which the sleeper wakes every morning.

Fanon—who would later meet Mannoni in the offices of Seuil, their common publisher—was not the only writer to attack him for "blaming the victim."* Nor is it surprising that he objected to the idea of a convergence, or complicity, between a European inferiority complex and a native dependency complex, which suggested that colonialism was a consensual relationship—and that people could only be colonized if they were already "colonizable." But, perhaps out of the same need that led him to amplify his differences with Sartre, Fanon overlooked the anti-colonial resonances of Mannoni's argument, which rested on the implicitly subversive suggestion that it was the European colonizer, not the non-European colonized, who suffered from an inferiority complex. For Mannoni, the prototype of the colonizer was not a conquistador like Christopher Columbus but · rather a shipwrecked man, like Robinson Crusoe, who finds himself surrounded by "savage" men and women. Afflicted by a sense of inferiority, menaced by castration anxiety, he seeks to establish his superiority by an act of psychic projection, depicting the colonized as his weak, effeminate, inferior opposite so that he can feel like a man again. In making this argument, Mannoni leaned not on Freud but on Alfred Adler, a dissident member of the Vienna Circle who argued that the principal drive among Europeans is not the libido but rather the need to overcome an inferiority complex rooted in childhood fears of physical vulnerability. This need, he suggested, resulted in a compulsive affirmation of superiority, and a dangerous will to power. Colonial domination, he argued, provided perpetually insecure European colonizers with a kind of collective therapy, a means of exorcising their fears of inferiority and castration. Unruly natives paid the price, in the acts of "fabulous sadism" through which Europeans reminded them of their total power.

---

* In his review for *Esprit*, Alioune Diop, the editor of *Présence africaine*, made the same point.

For all his hostility to Mannoni, Fanon shared his interest in Adler. In *Black Skin, White Masks*, he would apply Adler's ideas about the inferiority complex to the West Indian male, who, he writes, is *comparaison*—"conceited," in Creole. "Constantly preoccupied with self-assertion and the ego ideal," Fanon explained, the West Indian male has no sense of self-worth and must constantly prove his superiority over others: "It's on the ruins of my entourage that I must build my virility." The West Indian's drive to overcome his inferiority complex is aimed not at the French, or even at the *békés*, but at his own peers of color, whom he seeks to dominate, a bleak reminder of how colonial oppression is internalized and reproduced, after the formal end of colonialism. The Adlerian themes in Mannoni—the colonizer's fears of inferiority, the psychic pleasure of domination, colonial repression as narcissistic and spectacular exhibitionism—would later find even more powerful expression in *The Wretched of the Earth*. But Fanon historicized the pathologies of colonial psychology by situating their formation in the structures of racial and economic domination, rather than in parent-child relations.

There was a certain crudeness—and, arguably, a certain evasiveness— in Fanon's dismissal of classical Freudian psychiatry. It did not occur to him that the rifles in Malagasy dreams could have been both real rifles *and* phallic symbols. In *Black Skin, White Masks*, he would claim that "97 percent" of West Indian families were incapable of producing an Oedipal complex—"an incapacity that we highly welcome," he added proudly.* It was, to say the least, a curious remark coming from a man who adored his mother and had often expressed disdain for his father. "I am afraid the Caribbean is the least promising scenario in which to try to prove the absence of the Oedipal drama," the Jamaican-born British theorist Stuart Hall wrote in an essay on Fanon. "With its son-fixated mothers and mother-fixated sons, its complex paternities common to all slave societies of 'real' black fathers and 'symbolic' white ones, along with its deeply troubled, assertively heterosexual and often homophobic black

---

* He also claimed that homosexuality did not exist in the West Indies; while noting the presence of gender-fluid Martinican men who wore skirts and dresses, he insisted that "they have a normal [i.e., heteronormative] sexual life."

masculinities, the Caribbean 'lives out' the loss of social power by substituting an aggressively phallo-centred 'black manhood.'"

It is remarkable that a man as perceptive as Fanon, a trained psychiatrist and a reader of Lacan, did not see—or chose not to see—the complex affective dynamics of Martinican families like his own. But in a visceral sense, he may have believed that fathers like Casimir Fanon had been so emasculated by colonialism that they were incapable of performing their symbolic role, which was filled instead by the absent white father or master. A partial blindness, in any case, is often the price paid for insight, and Fanon was making a powerful argument for the significance of what he would call "sociogeny," the idea that some forms of psychological suffering have their roots not in an individual's psychic constitution but in oppressive social relations.

For the West Indian philosopher Sylvia Wynter, sociogeny was Fanon's most revolutionary discovery. But it was by no means a radical departure from Lucien Bonnafé's position on mental illness, and although he was unaware of it at the time, Fanon was now aligned with an international movement of psychiatrists and thinkers influenced by psychoanalysis who were applying themselves to the problem of racism.


ONE OF THE WRITERS Fanon most admired had reached conclusions similar to his own about the relationship between racism and mental disorder. Richard Wright was often characterized simply as a protest writer, but he was also one of the most psychologically penetrating novelists in American letters. "I'm convinced that the next great arena of discovery in the Negro will be the dark landscape of his own mind, what living in America has done to him," Wright wrote in his diary. His interest in psychology was sparked by his study of the convulsive impact of the Great Migration of Black southerners to northern cities. A Mississippi native who had fled the Jim Crow South and moved to Chicago in his late teens, Wright wrote in his 1945 memoir, *Black Boy*, that he was intrigued by "the frequency of mental illness, the tragic toll that the urban environment exacted of the black peasant." He came to believe that fear was "the fundamental emotion guiding black personality and behavior," even if it sometimes ap-

peared in the "disguise that is called Negro laughter." If Black people "unleashed physical and psychological violence on one another," he argued, it
was because they were "unable to retaliate" against their white oppressors.
He described his novel *Native Son*, published five years earlier, as a book
that offered "the psychoanalytic point of view" on race relations.

Fanon certainly agreed. In *Black Skin, White Masks*, he would draw
on the tragedy of Bigger Thomas, the protagonist of *Native Son*, as if it
were one of his case studies. "Bigger Thomas is afraid, but of what is he
afraid? Of himself," he writes. "We don't yet know who he is, but he knows
that fear will inhabit the world once the world finds out."

But Wright was not only a writer of psychological fiction; he was a
precocious advocate—unbeknownst to Fanon—of anti-racist psychiatry.
In this, his principal ally was the left-wing psychiatrist Fredric Wertham, a
German Jewish refugee who had published a probing essay on *Native Son*.
In 1946, the two men joined forces to create the Lafargue Mental Health
Clinic in Harlem. It was the first outpatient mental health clinic in a community where 400,000 Black people lived in a space designed for 75,000;
it was named after the French Cuban socialist Paul Lafargue, Karl Marx's
son-in-law and the author of the 1880 manifesto *The Right to Be Lazy*. The
Reverend Shelton Hale Bishop, who housed the clinic in the basement of his
parish church, had previously asked the New York Department of Hospitals to establish a mental health center in Harlem, only to be told, "Negroes
don't need psychiatry; they simply need bread." As Wertham put it, "Negroes are not allowed the luxury of neuroses," since "the official view is that
they are just unhappy, or they need housing, or they feel downtrodden."
The implicit premise of this view was that social misery was their natural
state. But Wertham, like Wright, saw in his patients' conditions the collective trauma of forced migration from the South, and racism and oppression
in the North. He referred to his patients as America's "displaced persons," a
phrase that evoked the Jews who had ended up in displaced persons' camps
after the war.

The Lafargue Clinic served Harlem residents for twelve years. It sought
not only to heal the wounds of racism but also to challenge the racist biases
of American psychiatry. As Wright noted, psychiatric court reports often
characterized Black people as "'pleasure-loving', 'lazy', 'shiftless', naturally

inclined toward crime, slow of comprehension, and irresponsible"—the American version of the North African syndrome. Wright himself had been rejected for military service on the grounds of his supposed "psychoneurosis." It is all the more remarkable, then, that he came to embrace social psychiatry as a weapon for liberating oppressed people. In his 1946 essay "Psychiatry Comes to Harlem," he hailed the "extension of the very concept of psychiatry into a new realm, the application of psychiatry to the masses, the turning of Freud upside down." His friend Ralph Ellison visited the clinic and paid homage to it in his 1948 essay "Harlem Is Nowhere," which linked the experience of Harlem's *aliénés* to their plight elsewhere in America. "Negro Americans are in desperate search for an identity," he wrote. "Rejecting the second-class status assigned them, they feel alienated and their whole lives have become a search for answers to the questions: Who am I, What am I, Why am I, and Where?"

When Ellison's picaresque masterpiece, *Invisible Man*, with its cerebral narrator and absurdist plot, was published in 1952, it was often contrasted with the grim proletarian setting and inarticulate hero of Wright's *Native Son*. But Ellison was equally sensitive to the psychological effects of racism—to what Fanon called sociogeny in *Black Skin, White Masks*, which appeared the same year. In the novel's famous opening passage, Ellison evokes the fear of "not existing" in white people's eyes, captured so powerfully by Fanon:

> I am invisible, understand, simply because people refuse to see me . . . When they approach me they see only my surroundings, themselves, or figments of their imagination—indeed, everything and anything except me.
>
> Nor is my invisibility exactly a matter of a biochemical accident to my epidermis. That invisibility to which I refer occurs because of a peculiar disposition of the eyes of those with whom I come in contact. A matter of the construction of their *inner* eyes, those eyes with which they look through their physical eyes upon reality.

Those same inner eyes hold Fanon captive, replacing his "corporeal schema" with an "epidermal racial schema," and leave him feeling

cursed, exploded into a pile of "fragments put together by another me."
For the little boy on the train, he is a cannibal, a slave, a "grinning *Y a bon
Banania*"—an allusion to the *petit nègre* spoken by the smiling *tirailleur
sénégalais* on posters for Banania, a chocolate drink for children. "For
a man armed solely with reason," Fanon writes, "there is nothing more
conducive to neurosis than contact with the irrational," and he feels "the
knife blades sharpening" within himself.* The narrator of *Invisible Man* is
gripped by a similar impulse when a white man on the street curses him
with an "insulting name." He is about to slit his throat but is stopped by a
realization: "It occurred to me that the man had not *seen* me, actually: that
he, as far as he knew, was in the midst of a walking nightmare . . . He was,
let us say, lost in a dream world. But didn't *he* control that dream world—
which, alas, is only too real!—and didn't *he* rule me out of it?"

While Ellison wrote his novel in Harlem, Fanon was in Lyon studying
the dream world of race, illusory but "only too real," and the violence that
simmered in it and sometimes spilled over into the physical world. The two
men never met, but their books speak to each other across what the critic
Paul Gilroy has called the "Black Atlantic," in a kind of *rendez-vous manqué*. Both books explore the relationship between the absurdity of racism,
the violent and phantasmagorical passions it arouses (not least in white
women who both desire and fear Black men), and the crippling agony
and self-doubt it induces in its victims. Each book tells a bittersweet story
of disillusionment with ideologies of racial nationalism, the romance of
what Ellison calls the "blackness of blackness." For the invisible man, this
is embodied by the Brotherhood, an organization inspired by the back-
to-Africa movement of Marcus Garvey. For Fanon, it is the "great black
mirage" of Négritude.

---

* "The individual who has been liberated by reason," Hannah Arendt writes in her study of
the nineteenth-century German Jewish *salonnière* Rahel Varnhagen, "is always running
head-on into a world, a society, whose past in the shape of 'prejudices' has a great deal of
power; he is forced to learn that past reality is also a reality."

# 5

# REFUSAL OF THE MASK

---

STILL REELING FROM HIS encounter with the boy on the train, Fanon began to dictate the manuscript of *Black Skin, White Masks* to his fiancée, Josie Dublé. He never had the chance to present it as his thesis: he showed his work in progress to his adviser, Jean Dechaume, who made it plain that Fanon would have to find a more suitable topic. (Nursing his wounds, Fanon claimed that he had not submitted his book as his thesis because "the dialectic forced me to take a much firmer stance.") The seventy-five-page thesis that he ultimately turned in on Friedreich's ataxia was written in a wholly different register: understated, even cautious in tone, always respectful of his elders.

Still, if we read between the lines, we find Fanon cutting through the compartmentalizing assumptions of his profession: the "systematic indifference" of neurologists toward the "psychiatric symptom," the calcified opposition of mind and body, the physical and the mental. Although he draws short of calling for a politicized psychiatry, the influence of the Saint-Alban school can be felt in his insistence on seeing the patient as "a whole, an indissoluble unity," and on the need to investigate Marcel Mauss's "total social fact." The thesis, dedicated to his mother and the memory of his father, was accepted in November 1951. In the copy that he gave to his brother Joby, he wrote: "The greatness of a man is not to be found in his acts but in his style . . . I do not agree with those who think it possible to live life at an easy pace. I don't want this. I don't think you do either."

Meanwhile, thanks to Jean-Marie Domenach, the deputy editor at *Esprit*, Fanon's unpublished thesis on racism found its way into the hands of a young editor at Éditions du Seuil, a prestigious publishing house in Paris with strong ties to the Catholic left. Three years older than Fanon, Francis Jeanson was a philosopher close to both *Esprit* and *Les Temps modernes*, the journal Fanon read most avidly. Although Jeanson was a white Frenchman from a petit bourgeois family in Bordeaux, he and Fanon had much in common, and their lives would intersect in striking ways over the next decade. Like Fanon, Jeanson was an existential radical driven primarily by a sense of ethical obligation, a thinker who gave priority to commitment over contemplation. Thin and handsome, with wavy hair and dark, piercing eyes, he had a lifelong hunger for action, and a resistance résumé that rivaled Fanon's. In 1943, at age twenty, Jeanson had fled to Spain to escape his *service du travail obligatoire*—forced labor in Germany, a joint program run by the Nazis and the Vichy government. Captured by the army of Francisco Franco, he spent six months in prison, after which he joined the Free French Forces in North Africa, later taking part in the liberation of Alsace. A case of tuberculosis prevented him from completing his studies in philosophy, but he managed to impress Sartre, who made him an editor at *Les Temps modernes*. When Sartre and Camus fell out over the left's relationship to the Soviet Union, it was Jeanson who took down Camus on Sartre's behalf, in an article titled "The Rebellious Soul," a sneering allusion to Camus's book *The Rebel*.

Jeanson was not a member of the Communist Party, but, like Sartre, he considered anti-communism a greater threat than Stalinism to the fortunes of the French left. The crimes that obsessed him were not those of communism in Russia but those of his own government in Algeria. In 1948, he had spent several weeks in Algeria, on vacation with his wife, Colette, and emerged as a fierce opponent of what was then euphemistically called the "French presence." Algeria appeared to be "conquered and pacified," he wrote in *Esprit*, but only thanks to a "regime of repression, at times even of terror." Denied equal citizenship by racism and poverty, a rigged electoral system, and state violence, Algerians were organizing themselves into nationalist parties of various ideological outlooks, from the fiery Islamic populism of Messali Hadj, through the liberal republicanism of Ferhat Abbas, to the religious conservatism of the Association of Algerian Muslim Ulama.

As Jeanson saw it, Algeria was witnessing the birth of an authentic movement for national independence, and it was an illusion to think—as the Communist Party persisted in doing—that its demands would be defused by political and economic reform. The "decisive" problem was the "racial alienation" of the colonized, who hungered for national sovereignty and freedom, not just bread and education—still less, "assimilation"—under French domination. If the *Français d'Algérie* (the French-speaking settlers who considered Algeria their home) hoped to stay, they would have to become *Algériens français* (French-speaking Algerians) in a decolonized, independent country with indigenous majority rule. As Jeanson put it, nine million Algerian men and women were fighting to become part of the "democratic world of the Rights of Man"—a world "that was ours without them, and which henceforth will no longer be ours *except with them.*" France's very survival as a democratic republic depended on Algeria's emancipation from French rule.

Fanon, who had become increasingly aware of the "Algerian problem" in his encounters with North African patients, was one of Jeanson's readers. Aside from Sartre, few white intellectuals in France were as sensitive to racism and colonial violence as Jeanson, for whom the struggle for Algerian independence would soon become a consuming cause, as it would be for Fanon. Both took inspiration from Sartre's work, and if Fanon was a psychiatrist drawn to philosophy, Jeanson was a philosopher attracted to psychiatry. When he read the manuscript of *Black Skin, White Masks,* Jeanson was overwhelmed (as he wrote in his twenty-three-page preface to the first edition) by Fanon's portrait of "a Black man plunged in a white world," the "obstinacy" and "vehemence" of his language, and his evocation of the "troubling thickness of experience." Not only had Fanon described Blackness as a "limit experience" that could be grasped only by descending to hell itself—an allusion to Sartre's preface to "Black

Orpheus"—but he had "magically" reproduced for the reader the explosive experience of being "hit by the absurd" in the form of racist injury.

"To be sure," Jeanson observed some years later, "Sartre, Freud, and Marx had helped him," but those thinkers "hadn't had to overcome a past defined by slavery or the color of their skin." And while "white philosophy hardly seemed anxious to put the world back together," Fanon wrote as if "the only truths that found grace in his eyes were those that passed through his body and burned his flesh." Reading Fanon, Jeanson was reminded of the transgressive gay novelist and playwright Jean Genet, another "pariah writer who had to reinvent an ethics to respond to the racist contempt of our moralism and said that he could only accept an idea if it had already run through him from his head to his toes."

At their first meeting in the offices of Seuil at 27, rue Jacob in the Sixth Arrondissement of Paris, Jeanson told Fanon how much he admired his manuscript, whose working title was "The Disalienation of the Black Man." What Jeanson really meant, Fanon responded, was that "for a *nègre* it's not so bad." The two men never became friends. But Fanon came to respect Jeanson and agreed that his suggestion for the title—*Black Skin, White Masks*—was an improvement on his own. They worked together closely to turn the manuscript into a book. At one point, Jeanson asked Fanon to clarify a particularly opaque passage. Fanon admitted that the passage was difficult to parse but said he wanted to touch his readers "irrationally, almost sensually." Quoting Aimé Césaire, he compared the experience of writing to the "bewildering lava of words the color of hectic flesh." In the same letter, he told Jeanson that he believed, in spite of his own rationalism, in the "magic of words." This reply is revealing. Fanon had come to disdain Senghor for saying that emotion was African, and reason Greek—a remark that crystallized the kind of racial essentialism he abhorred, and that surrendered the miraculous weapon of reason to the oppressors of Black people.* Yet he remained attached to a West

---

* Derek Walcott, in his 1970 essay "What the Twilight Says," would remark of Négritude writers: "The romantic darkness which they celebrate is thus another treachery, this time perpetrated by the intellectual. The result is not one's own thing but another minstrel show."

Indian poetic tradition, which—like the surrealism that tried to annex it—drew on sublime or ecstatic modes of expression that appeared to be at odds with reason. The figure who best embodied that tradition was, of course, Césaire, whose verse and prose are quoted throughout *Black Skin, White Masks*.

PUBLISHED BY SEUIL IN April 1952, *Black Skin, White Masks* was the first and last book in which Fanon fully identified himself as a Frenchman. Not yet twenty-seven years old, he was the very model of assimilation: poised for a successful career in medicine and engaged to a Frenchwoman. (He and Josie would marry a few months later.) His sense of national belonging had been bruised by his encounters with racism, but he was not yet fully disabused. "What's all this about Black people and a Black nationality?" he asked in a skeptical allusion to Négritude. "I am French. I am interested in French culture, French civilization, and the French. We refuse to be treated as outsiders; we are well and truly part of French history and its drama . . . I take a personal interest in the destiny of France, the French nation, and its values. What am I supposed to do with a Black empire?" But if *Black Skin, White Masks* was a protest on behalf of inclusion, rather than a defense of Black separatism, its author was not arguing on the old assimilationist terms that required Black people to downplay, conceal, or even renounce their identity. Black people, he insisted, must be recognized not merely as citizens but as *Black* citizens of a country that belongs to all its citizens. Universality, for Fanon, begins with the recognition of difference at the foundation of what Sartre had called concrete, rather than abstract, liberalism.

Difference, however, was precisely what the French Republic's rigid self-understanding—and its passionate belief in the universality of its model—could not countenance. In France, Black citizens like Fanon were ostensibly no different from other citizens in status and rights: their appearance as people of visible African ancestry, descended from slaves and colonized subjects, was widely thought to be of no real significance and may as well have been invisible. "Equality now proclaims you brothers," ran the lyrics of "La liberté des *nègres*," an old abolitionist song. "The color disappears, and man remains." *Black Skin, White Masks* took apart the myth of French color blindness with ferocious precision, in the language of psychiatry. By drawing on his clinical studies, Fanon revealed that whites persisted in seeing their fellow Black citizens as racialized others, while French West Indians were condemned to impersonate white people, having absorbed the idea that, notwithstanding their skin color, they *were* white for all intents and purposes. The "white mask" of Fanon's title is not a matter of code-switching or even of shifting from Creole to French; rather, the white mask has been figured and assumed in the depths of the collective Black psyche, forming the prism—or prison—through which West Indians see, and misrecognize, themselves.

A work of fewer than 190 pages in the original French, *Black Skin, White Masks* is organized into seven chapters: "The Black Man and Language," "The Woman of Color and the White Man," "The Man of Color and the White Woman," "The Supposed Dependency Complex of the Colonized" (Fanon's response to Mannoni), "The Lived Experience of the Black Man," "The *Nègre* and Psychopathology," and "The *Nègre* and Recognition." Walter Benjamin wrote that "all great works of literature found a genre or dissolve one." Fanon's first book does both, turning the genre of psychiatric analysis into a weapon of radical political critique while interweaving clinical observations with passages of scalding humor and with declamatory interludes in which he addresses the reader directly. It is a strange, sometimes disorienting, but always compelling combination of cool, detached observation rendered in a highly specialized psychiatric jargon and visceral, expressionistic monologue. It is not a "Black cry," but certainly one Black man's cry of rage.

Many readers, both Black and white, Fanon admits, "will not recognize themselves" in his case studies of mentally ill patients, but he adds, "The fact that I feel alien to the world of the schizophrenic or of the sexually impotent in no way diminishes their reality." The cases provide him with extreme expressions of the racial pathologies that course through French society. But many of Fanon's other examples are from novels, Hollywood films, folklore, comic books, and personal anecdotes. In its eclectic range of reference and flair for decoding representations of race in popular culture, *Black Skin, White Masks* anticipates Roland Barthes's 1957 collection of newspaper columns, *Mythologies*—and, indeed, the academic field that would become known as cultural studies. Yet this is the work of a psychiatrist, not a cultural critic. Like Freud, Fanon is a visionary scientist of the modern soul, unafraid to generalize on the basis of clinical observations. *Black Skin, White Masks* is a study of a racist civilization—the French variety in particular—and its discontents. "The explosion will not happen today," he declares in the book's opening line, just below a citation about colonial humiliation from Césaire's *Discourse on Colonialism*. "It is too early . . . or too late." What kind of explosion? He does not say, but the Césaire passage leaves little to the imagination, and throughout his first book, Fanon seems gripped by the sense of an impending crisis that will bring about nothing less than "the end of the world"—a phrase lifted, this time without attribution, from Césaire's *Notebook of a Return to the Native Land.*

BLACK SKIN, WHITE MASKS was part of an anti-racist wave sweeping French intellectual life in the early 1950s, brought on by the vast destruction visited on Europe by Hitler's Germany, with its doctrine of Aryan supremacy—and by the stirrings of independence movements in the colonies after the war. In *Race and Culture*, a 1951 paper commissioned by UNESCO, the writer and ethnographer Michel Leiris warned against the temptation of imagining, after the defeat of Nazi Germany, that "racism was dead." Most whites were still convinced of "their congenital superiority"—including, he added, those who did not consider themselves racists. This belief had been sustained by two powerful forces. One was the legacy of Enlightenment thinking about race, which had encouraged the notion that humanity could be "subdivided" into "racial" groups "equivalent to botanical 'varieties,'" and that those groups could in turn be differentiated on the basis of intelligence, physical beauty, morality, and capacity for self-governance. The other was Western imperialism, which had used the idea of race, and of "civilized" and "primitive" cultures, to "excuse violence and oppression by decreeing the inferiority of those enslaved or robbed of their own land and denying the title of men to the cheated peoples."

The anthropologist Claude Lévi-Strauss, in his own 1952 paper for

REFUSAL OF THE MASK

UNESCO, "Race and History," went further, pouring scorn on the "ethno-centrism" and "false evolutionism" of an arrogant West, which saw other societies as backward versions of itself, destined either to catch up and become more like "us" or to face subjugation, if not extinction. An anti-racism worthy of the name would have to go beyond "tolerance" and em-brace the "diversity of human cultures," or as James Baldwin put it a year later, "The world is white no longer, and it will never be white again." This would have profound consequences for the global distribution of power, as well as ideas about culture and identity, aesthetics, knowledge, and val-ues. Not only would the white man no longer rule the world; he would no longer have the exclusive authority to describe and define it.

*Black Skin, White Masks* fit comfortably within this critique of racism and Eurocentrism. Yet it also felt different—not least because its author was a Black psychiatrist of a decidedly philosophical bent, armed with an intimate knowledge of his subject. The book it resembled most strongly in form and sensibility was Simone de Beauvoir's 1949 study of the fe-male condition, *The Second Sex*. Like Fanon, Beauvoir wrote not just about the lived experience of an oppressed group but also from the standpoint of that group, exploring the ways in which the social construction of "woman" prevented women from experiencing authentic freedom—and the ways in which women internalized patriarchal ideology and became complicit in their own oppression. She shared Fanon's admiration for Maurice Merleau-Ponty's writings about the bodily nature of perception. Her famous phrase that "one is not born, but rather becomes, a woman"— that is, one only becomes a woman under the force of social convention and oppression—would lend itself to any number of groups whose identity had been made to feel like a straitjacket.

There is little doubt that Fanon read Beauvoir. In his essay "The Gender of Race: Fanon, Reader of Beauvoir," the French scholar Matthieu Renault has shown that the Nietzsche citation in *Black Skin, White Masks*, which Fanon scholars had failed to chase down—"Man's unhappiness is that he was once a child"—is, in fact, a line from Descartes, and that Fanon is al-most certain to have come upon a paraphrase in Beauvoir's 1947 treatise, *The Ethics of Ambiguity*. Yet, Renault writes, Fanon "erased any trace of Beauvoir" from his writing, even as he wrote about her partner, Sartre. By doing so, he effectively put himself forward as the interlocutor of a "great man," consigning that man's female partner to oblivion. Today, the parallels between Fanon and Beauvoir seem obvious, but few of their contemporaries remarked on them, a sad tribute to the disregard of Beauvoir's work among her male peers, even at *Les Temps modernes*.

Césaire was another "great man" to whom Fanon paid extensive homage in *Black Skin, White Masks*—while overlooking that man's gifted wife. Fanon's relationship with his fellow Martinican was more intimate, and therefore more complicated, than his relationship with Sartre, whom he would not meet until several years later. In 1952, Césaire was no longer a rebellious young poet; he was Martinique's deputy in France's National Assembly, having campaigned successfully for the island to become a department of metropolitan France six years earlier. Fanon had supported the campaign but later reconsidered his position: as he came to see it, Martinique's status as a French overseas department perpetuated colonial domination by the white *békés* and their Creole allies, even if the deputy representing Martinique in the National Assembly was Black.

Still, Césaire remained a hero for Fanon, not only because of his poetry, which had made it possible for a generation of West Indian intellectuals to embrace their Blackness, but also because of his increasingly outspoken attacks on colonialism. He had joined the French Communist Party and cut his ties with the journal *Présence africaine*, distrusting the anticommunism of its editor, Alioune Diop. In 1950, he published his *Discourse on Colonialism*, a withering assault on Western imperialism that shocked many readers with its claim that colonization had turned the colonizers into brutes, even as they claimed to be spreading the benefits of civilization to "primitive" societies. (It was a surprising echo of Mannoni.) Colonization, Césaire claimed, "works to decivilize the colonizer, to brutalize him, to degrade him, to awaken him to buried instincts, to covetousness, violence, race hatred and moral relativism." Anticipating Hannah Arendt's *Origins of Totalitarianism* by one year, he argued that colonial violence laid the necessary groundwork for the racism, persecution, and mass murder that Nazism had inflicted on the European continent. The "Christian bourgeois of the twentieth century," he wrote, "has a Hitler inside him," and "if he rails against him, he is being inconsistent." He continued:

What he cannot forgive Hitler for is not the crime in itself, the crime against man, it is not the humiliation of man as such, it is the crime against the white man, the humiliation of the white man, and the fact that he applied to Europe colonialist procedures which until then had been reserved exclusively for the Arabs of Algeria, the coolies of India, and the *nègres* of Africa.*

Many of the ideas and rhetorical figures of *Discourse on Colonialism* are present in *Black Skin, White Masks*: the fury at the idea that colonized Black people should be grateful to France; the debasing impact of the colonial system on perpetrators and victims alike (a theme on which Fanon would later expand in *The Wretched of the Earth*); the overlapping histories of colonialism and Nazism, and anti-Black racism and antisemitism. We can also hear Césaire's voice in the flashes of prose poetry that appear at various points in *Black Skin, White Masks*, when Fanon seeks to affect his readers in a more "sensuous" way.

But Fanon's ultimate aim, unlike Césaire's in *Discourse*, was not to condemn colonialism, whose barbarism he simply took for granted. In a vague allusion to political revolution, Fanon observes that an "authentic disalienation" will take place only once "things, in the most materialistic sense of the word . . . have been restored to their proper place." But in *Black Skin, White Masks*, he offers no prescriptions for this disalienation; instead, he limits himself to *diagnosing* the pathological symptoms of racism in everyday life. His research as a medical professional, he tells us at the outset, has led him to conclude that Blacks and whites interact "along neurotic lines" with one another: "The White is locked in his whiteness. The Black in his blackness." Indeed, it is partly from these patterns of neurotic behavior, Fanon suggests, that race is reproduced and becomes naturalized. Race, for Fanon, is a product of what the historian Barbara

* Césaire was not the only writer to make this argument before Arendt's book appeared. In his 1947 book, *The World and Africa*, W. E. B. Du Bois wrote that "there was no Nazi atrocity—concentration camps, wholesale maiming and murder, defilement of women or ghastly blasphemy of childhood—which the Christian civilization of Europe had not long been practicing against colored folks in all parts of the world in the name of and for the defense of a Superior Race born to rule the world."

Fields calls "racecraft": it exists in our minds, and forms us as racialized individuals, not because it is real but because we act as if it were.


BUT WHY THEN DO we act as if race were real—as if the terms "Black" and "white" have any value other than as vague and imprecise descriptions of complexion and physiognomy in people of African and European descent? According to Fanon, it's partly because these values are so fully embedded in language, the subject of the book's first chapter. He is not simply referring to the connotations of "black" (evil, sin, malice, filth, ugliness, enslavement) and "white" (beauty, innocence, purity, light, honesty, intelligence, freedom), but to the way language is deployed to enforce hierarchy in everyday social interactions. "Yes, I have to watch my diction," he writes, "since that's how they [the French] will judge me. He can't even speak French properly, they will say." The West Indian who masters French is, in turn, feared by his fellow West Indians as a quasi-white. "In France they say: to speak like a book," Fanon explains. "In Martinique: to speak like a White." And "the more the Black West Indian makes the French language his own, the whiter he gets—that is, the closer he comes to becoming a true human being."

One of Fanon's primary examples of racism in France is the use by French whites (and some assimilated West Indians like himself) of *le petit nègre* in addressing Black people and Arabs.* The effect of *le petit nègre*, he writes, is at once to "imprison" Black people and infect them with "extremely toxic foreign bodies." *Le petit nègre* was, of course, a creation of colonial rule in Africa. And it was common for liberal French writers such as Octave Mannoni to argue that racism was in essence a colonial problem, in no way constitutive of French society in the *métropole*. Fanon, however, dismisses the argument that republican France was "less racist" than its colonies, which could never have existed without it: no Maginot Line had prevented colonial racism from entering the Republic. Mannoni, he argued, had contributed to a complacent myth of separate regimes that

---

* In spite of its numerous references to anti-Arab racism, *Black Skin, White Masks* is often discussed as if it focused exclusively on anti-Black racism.

absolved the Republic of its sins by suggesting that racism was enacted "over there" in the violent passion of insecure settlers living thousands of miles overseas. "European civilization and its agents of the highest caliber are responsible for colonial racism," Fanon writes. "Every time we see an Arab with that hunted, evasive look of distrust, draped in those long-ragged robes that seem to have been made for him, we tell ourselves that Monsieur Mannoni was wrong." Colonial racism, he insisted, "does not differ from other forms of racism." At its core, every version of racism was an assault on the notion of a shared humanity.

Nonetheless, Fanon conceded, each form of racism had its distinctive features, its defining preoccupations. The all-consuming obsession of anti-Black racism, he asserted, was the Black body. And though he did not attempt to defend his thesis by citing the historical literature, he had good grounds for a case. In the early days of colonial conquest, the historian William B. Cohen observes in his classic study, *The French Encounter with Africans*, French writers on race were preoccupied by the question of skin pigmentation. Many argued that Blackness was a form of physical degeneration, caused by unnatural ecological conditions. Pseudoscientific speculation of this sort soon came to underwrite the notion that Africans were driven by instinct, incapable of reason. These ideas—which received a pseudobiological imprimatur with the emergence of scientific racism in the nineteenth century—served an obvious purpose in the plantation societies of the West Indies, providing a justification for the permanent enslavement and exploitation of African captives and their offspring.

"Scientific" theories of Black inferiority were embraced by many thinkers of the Enlightenment, including Kant, who described Black people as "lazy, indolent and dawdling," and claimed that "all Negroes stink" because of "the evaporation of the phosphoric acid" in their epidermis. The French philosophes Voltaire, Diderot, and Montesquieu, for their part, attempted to reconcile their anti-Blackness with their belief in equality and universal humanity by arguing that Africans weren't inherently inferior; they were merely savage. Thus the *mission civilisatrice*, or "civilizing mission," in France's overseas colonies was preparing future generations of enslaved or colonized subjects to emerge from "savagery" and eventually accede to citizenship. The idea of African savagery, in Cohen's account, provided the French with "a screen onto which they projected their own fears about themselves and their world." In Fanon's account, the *nègre* came to embody the "immoral impulses, the unmentionable desires" that Europeans loathed in themselves. While the West defined itself as a bastion of "progress, civilization, liberalism, education, enlightenment, and refinement," Black people were an "oppositional brute force"—a "biological" category of persons who remained to be mastered and assimilated.

As Fanon discovered in his work as a psychiatrist, the same ideas were in circulation more than a century after the fall of slavery. "For the majority of whites," he writes, "the Black man represents the (uneducated) sexual instinct. He embodies genital power beyond the reach of morals and taboos." For the white women he treated in Lyon, the Black man was "a phobic object," both repulsive and exciting, with sexual powers their "husbands or occasional lovers did not possess." He had almost certainly encountered these myths in his own life. His first great love affair in France, which led to the birth of his daughter, Mireille, had been torpedoed by Michèle Weyer's parents, who objected to her marrying a Black man, and he was now engaged to another white woman, Josie Dublé. Two of the early chapters in *Black Skin, White Masks* explore the disfiguring effects of racial fantasies on mixed relationships.

Fanon never discusses his own relationships. Still, it is striking that, in the chapter titled "The Man of Color and the White Woman," he chooses to focus on Black men who want not merely to be loved by their white partners but to be loved in the same way they would have been if they were white. He draws on a 1947 novel by the Martinican writer René Maran, *Un Homme pareil aux autres* (A man like everyone else). The main character, Jean Veneuse, is a West Indian man living with a white lover in Bordeaux. One of Veneuse's white friends assures him that he only appears to be Black: "You think like a European; hence it's natural for you to love like a European." (Fanon had heard similar things from white friends at medical school.) Veneuse's anxieties are not assuaged, however, and he becomes obsessed with proving himself, less to others than to himself. Invoking the analysis of the Swiss psychoanalyst Germaine Guex in her 1950 study, *The Abandonment Neurosis*, Fanon interprets Veneuse's condition as that of an "abandonment neurotic." It is a consequence of abandonment not by his mother, but by the colonial motherland. Veneuse refuses to believe that his white lover *really* loves him; it is only by making her suffer, and finally by abandoning her, that he can satisfy his "need for revenge."

The desperate flight from Blackness prevents Veneuse from forging a love relationship, just as it sends the Creole woman Mayotte Capécia—the subject of Fanon's chapter "The Woman of Color and the White Man"—into the arms of a white man in the hope of making herself white. Fanon is scathing about this mimicry of whiteness, yet he also depicts it as an understandable reaction to being Black in a society where every conceivable value has been coded as white. And to be a mimic, of course, is to be in a relationship of alienation to one's own self. This is what Fanon means when he remarks that the destiny of the French Black man is to become white: it is his only way of being recognized as a man. But it is a Sisyphean labor that will leave him feeling thwarted—whiteness remains forever out of reach. "Another situation is possible," Fanon hints, but the solution to a collective pathology cannot be individual; rather, "it implies a restructuring of the world."

IN THE CHAPTER "The *Nègre* and Psychopathology," Fanon attempts to explain why whiteness continues to have such power in the majority-Black societies of the West Indies. The answer, he suggests, lies in intergenerational trauma, lodged in the collective psyche of West Indians—their sociogeny. The authority he cites here is the Marxist Martinican poet René Ménil, who, in an essay on the situation of poetry in the Caribbean, published in 1944 in *Tropiques*, argued that the "repressed spirit" of African slaves had been replaced by an "authority symbol representing the master, a symbol planted in the core of the collective group and charged with maintaining order as a garrison controls a conquered city." For Ménil—a founding member of a circle of West Indian surrealist revolutionaries known as Légitime Défense—the internalized symbol of the master explained the persistence of "a certain masochism among Caribbean people." Fanon goes further, arguing that the failure to revolt against the master during the era of plantation slavery had condemned the societies of the *vieilles colonies*—French Guiana, Guadeloupe, La Réunion, and Martinique—to a "neurotic" present. Because slavery ended without a fight, West Indians remained subordinate to their former oppressors, captives of mental if not physical slavery.

Fanon's account of his island's history was not quite accurate: there were numerous slave revolts in Martinique, the first in 1678. Slaves in the Antilles, an early missionary recorded, were "ready to revolt, to do anything and commit the most horrible crimes to win their freedom." Those accused of disobedience were severely punished, and sometimes killed, but Fanon's ancestors were not passive, much less complicit, in their oppression.

Even so, he cannot forgive his fellow West Indians for failing to overthrow slavery, as Haitians did, by force of arms. In Martinique, he sees only a deceptive mirage of freedom, unredeemed by the culture of Négritude—a weak substitute for political struggle—or even by the emergence, after the war, of leaders like Césaire in France's National Assembly. He recognizes that Martinique is no longer enslaved, or even formally colonized, but neither is it independent. In the West Indies, Fanon writes, "the Black Man was acted upon . . . He went from one way of life to another, not from one life to another." This remark appears in a section called "The *Nègre* and Hegel," which is inspired by the analysis of "the lord and the bondsman" in Hegel's *Phenomenology of Spirit*. In Hegel's account, the roles of *Herr* (master) and *Knecht* (servant) are assigned in the midst of a life-and-death battle. The man willing to risk his life becomes the master; the one who chooses life over death and submits becomes the servant. Only through work, and by an act of self-possession, can the bondsman achieve self-consciousness and see that he no longer needs a master.

Some philosophers have understood the master-slave dialectic as a dramatization of the struggle between individual subjects for recognition, others as a struggle within one and the same individual. Transposed to large groups of persons, or indeed societies, it acquires a political, even a revolutionary, significance. It was this broader reading that the Russian émigré Alexandre Kojève advanced in a series of widely attended lectures on *The Phenomenology of Spirit* in Paris in the 1930s. Kojève's masters and slaves were the bourgeoisie and the proletariat under industrial capitalism; the master-slave dialectic was the motor of history, in which subaltern groups fight for recognition from their oppressors by waging a violent, revolutionary struggle whose outcome is a world without masters or slaves.

Long before they were published in a single volume in 1947, Kojève's Hegel lectures were legendary, attracting admiration from Sartre,
Merleau-Ponty, and Lacan. But the most creative application of Kojève was
made by Beauvoir in *The Second Sex.* "Woman . . . gives Life," she wrote,
"and does not risk *her* life; between her and the male there has been no
combat." Rather than fight their subordination, much less try to establish separate values and institutions, Beauvoir argued, women had sought
recognition from their male oppressors and failed as a consequence to
achieve self-consciousness.

Fanon makes a strikingly similar argument about West Indians. In
Hegel, he suggests, the slave "turns away from the master and toward the
object," but in the West Indies "the slave turns toward the master and aban-
dons the object." What Fanon means by this obscure formulation is that
enslaved West Indians in the French Antilles never took part in the life-
or-death battle that would have allowed them to seize their freedom—"the
object"—with their own hands. Instead, they received freedom as a gift,
with the decree of abolition in 1848, when "the White man, as master, told
the *nègre*: now you are free." The implication here, as in Beauvoir, is that
they remain trapped because they have never had a proper confrontation
with their oppressors. The descendants of slaves continue to seek recognition on the basis of the master's values, instead of creating their own.
Fanon points up "the imposing number of statues scattered around France
and in the colonies representing white France caressing the frizzy hair of
that brave Negro whose chains have just been broken." No doubt thinking
of his own experience on the battlefields of France, he writes that "from
time to time" the West Indian "fights for freedom and justice, but it's always for a white freedom and justice." That freedom is the facile one offered by Victor Schœlcher, rather than the hard-won freedom of Toussaint
Louverture.

The unequal relationship between the French *métropole* and its overseas departments in the West Indies remains, for Fanon, an inescapably
colonial one, designed to make Black West Indians forget who they are:
descendants of enslaved Africans, with languages and cultures of their
own, not descendants of the Gauls (as they were told in school) who
merely happen to have black skin. It is no accident that, in popular cul-

ture and even in school textbooks, "the Wolf, the Devil . . . and the Savage
are always represented by a *nègre* or an Indian." West Indian children,
he argued, were still encouraged to channel their aggression toward the
same demonized objects as their counterparts in France. As a result, "the
West Indian does not see himself as Black; he sees himself as West Indian.
The *nègre* lives in Africa." Indeed, it is only when the West Indian goes to
France and is subjected to the force of the "white gaze" that he "feels the
weight of his melanin."

Fanon, who grew up identifying with Tarzan and fearing the Senegalese riflemen, could be speaking of himself. And he is scathingly funny
about the efforts of his fellow West Indians to emulate the ways of the
*métropole*, depicted in scenes of colonial mimicry reminiscent of V. S.
Naipaul's early fiction. "The Black man who enters France," he writes,
"changes because for him the *métropole* represents the holy of holies . . .
The Black man who leaves for one week in the *métropole* creates a magic
around him where the words Paris, Marseille, the Sorbonne, and Pigalle
represent the keystones." Once he's back home, he talks about the Paris
Opera House, "which he has probably seen only from a distance"; he "answers only in French," pretending not to understand Creole, his native
tongue. Fanon illustrates this point by citing a West Indian folktale about
a young farmer who returns home after several months in France and, on
seeing a plow, asks his father what it's called. "By way of an answer," he
writes, "his father drops the plow on his feet, and his amnesia disappears.
A singular therapy."*

Indeed, the effect of the father's action is to remind his son that he is
not French and to strip off his white mask. But this is a folktale, and in the
real world, Fanon argues, the mask is not so easily removed, disalienation
not so efficiently achieved. He understood not only the mask's coercive
force but also its consensual appeal, since he, too, had longed for nothing
more than to be accepted as merely another Frenchman, even after the
broken promises of the war and the encounters with racism in Lyon.

Fanon was wrestling (not for the last time) with a question that many

---

* This is perhaps the only example of Fanon's endorsing a West Indian father's wisdom
against his son.

of his contemporaries in the colonial world were forced to ask: What, if anything, lies behind the mask? Is there a collective culture, a history, a stable identity uncontaminated by colonialism, waiting to take its place? Fanon's initial response, after his reading of Senghor, is to look for affirmation and belonging in the worship of Blackness. "On the other side of the white world," he writes, remembering Senghor's effect on him, "there lies a magical Black culture. Negro sculpture! I began to blush with pride. Was this our salvation? I had rationalized the world, and the world had rejected me in the name of color prejudice . . . I was made of the irrational; I wade in the irrational. Irrational up to my neck." He imagines himself as possessing a unique "poetical power," with a closer and more sensuous relationship to the world, which the white man can only "enslave."

Fanon's decision to lose himself "totally in Négritude" would seem to be a logical reaction to the anti-Blackness he has experienced and, in some fashion, epidermalized. (Many of his formulations, read out of context, could be interpreted in support of this conclusion, which explains in part why Fanon is still often read as an exponent of Négritude.) But Négritude turns out to be the antithesis of the thesis of whiteness, rather than a destination. For all the protection it provides him against a hostile white world, Black self-consciousness is a necessary component of freedom, rather than an end in itself. "We will speak of black genius," he writes, only "when man has regained his true place." And though Fanon clearly feels closer to Césaire's vision of Black self-invention than he does to Senghor's primordial African spirit, he is not persuaded that Black unity can provide a lasting foundation for a politics of liberation. A "doctor in Guadeloupe," he remarks, does not face the same set of problems as a "nègre who works in construction in the port of Abidjan." The doctor's "intellectual alienation," after all, is a "creation of bourgeois society." In contrast, he writes, "The few worker comrades I've had the chance to meet in Paris never raised the problem of discovering a Negro past. They knew they were Black, but, they told me, that didn't change a thing. And damn right they were."

IN THE LAST FEW PAGES, Fanon sketches out a vision of what he understands by the term "disalienation." It is addressed not only to the Black man who remains "locked in his body" but also to the white man who "is both mystifier and mystified." The dismantling of the master's house is, it turns out, a task for everyone—former slave and former master. "Every time a man has brought victory to the dignity of the spirit, every time a man has said no to an attempt to enslave a fellow man, I have felt a sense of solidarity with his act," Fanon writes. But celebrating a racial-cultural heritage will not rescue people from what he calls the "substantialized tower of the past." And once again he takes aim at Négritude, now with reference to Vietnam, where Ho Chi Minh's rebels were fighting for their country's independence in a guerrilla war with French troops: "It is not because the Indochinese discovered a culture of their own that they re-volted. Quite simply this was because it became impossible for them to breathe, in more than one sense of the word."* Fanon mentions a fellow soldier who had gone on to fight in Vietnam and who was startled by what he mistook for the fanaticism of the rebels—evidence, to many in France, of an Asian indifference to death. "It wasn't so long ago," he reminds us, "that this Asian serenity could be seen in the 'vandals' of Vercors and the 'terrorists' of the Resistance."

Fanon would shortly encounter this "serenity" in Algerian national liberation fighters facing death, but the notion already moves him in a way that racial solidarity for its own sake does not. "It is not the black world that governs my behavior. My black skin is not the repository of specific values," he writes, and then proclaims:

> I am a man, and I have to rework the world's past from the very be-ginning . . . In no way does my basic vocation have to be drawn from the past of peoples of color. In no way do I have to dedicate myself to reviving a black civilization unjustly ignored. I will not make myself the man of any past.

Suddenly, we are no longer reading the work of a psychiatrist; we are read-ing that of an orator, a rebel. "Scientific objectivity had to be ruled out for

* The second line is often cited, but almost never the first.

me," he writes, "since the alienated and the neurotic were my brother, my sister, and my father."

More surprising, perhaps, is his reluctance to make demands on others. On the contrary, he says he has no right to "wish for a guilt complex to crystallize in the white man regarding the past of my race," to look for "ways . . . of trampling on the pride of my former master," to "shout my hatred at the white man," or to "demand reparations for my subjugated ancestors."* He is not even confident of his "right to be Black," although he says that a white man who "challenges my humanity" will be told in no uncertain terms that "I am not this grinning *Y a bon Banania* figure that he persists in imagining I am." He says that his only duty is not to renounce his liberty through his choices. Self-invention, once again, takes precedence over any sense of belonging conjured from the past: "In the world I am heading for, I am endlessly creating myself . . . I am not a slave to the slavery that dehumanized my ancestors . . . The density of History determines none of my acts. I am my own foundation."

This burning wish to achieve freedom from history—a distilled expression of the existentialist ethos of the era—is startling to twenty-first-century sensibilities, but it has less to do with Fanon's opposition to financial compensation for past injury than with his distrust of the Négritude movement's imaginative focus on the crimes of the past. As he sees it, the triumph of disalienation—over the racial complexes from which both Black and white people suffer asymmetrically—depends on the future, not on the old universalism, in which freedom is white and whiteness is freedom. Nor does it depend, for that matter, on a fantasy of Black supremacy. The challenge is to create a new universalism, in which Black and white coexist on the basis of equality, recognition, and solidarity. "On the battlefield," he writes, "marked out by the scores of Negroes hanged by their testicles, a monument is slowly rising that promises to be grandiose, and at the top of this monument I can already see a white man and a black man *hand in hand*." For the Fanon of *Black Skin, White Masks*, Black and

---

* The refusal of reparations is especially striking in the light of contemporary anti-racist sensibilities; Fanon's relationship to those sensibilities will be explored at the end of the book.

white people in France are—as Martin Luther King Jr. would put it in his 1963 "Letter from Birmingham Jail"—"caught in an inescapable network of mutuality, tied in a single garment of destiny."

Fanon's grand aspiration—and his optimism about overcoming the injustices and absurdities of race—is hard to square with the anatomy of racism he provides in the rest of the book. Not surprisingly, his summary rejection of retroactive justice is rarely discussed by contemporary Fanonians, who prefer his analysis of anti-Black oppression and his pan-African politics. Yet in its assertion of independence, it is one of the most eloquent expressions of the freedom impulse that runs through Fanon's work, fusing the poetics of Négritude with existentialism's emphasis on self-creation.

WRITING IN *ESPRIT,* the phenomenologist Maxime Chastaing hoped that *Black Skin, White Masks* would shake the "good colonial conscience" of French readers who consoled themselves with the thought that, thanks to France, West Indians had long enjoyed the freedom that Black Americans were still fighting to achieve. But Georges Balandier, a renowned sociologist of Africa whom Fanon admired, raised substantive criticisms. In his review for *L'Année sociologique,* Balandier praised the "rare emotive value" of Fanon's chapter on the Black man's lived experience but faulted him for overlooking the "ever-present link between racial inferiority, economic exploitation, and enslavement." He added that the emphasis on "the relationship of Self and Other" and the "reliance on Hegel and psychoanalytic literature" had "led Monsieur Fanon to lose sight of the specific characteristics of the Black condition." It was a fair point: Why focus on the psychological injuries of racism if, as Fanon himself indicated, racism itself could only be dismantled by social and political change? Whether or not he agreed with Balandier's critique, Fanon would gradually lose interest in the psychological dilemmas of middle-class people of color like himself. Nor would he ever again be accused of losing sight of the brute facts of colonial oppression.

The three major French dailies—*Le Monde, Le Figaro,* and the French Communist Party newspaper *L'Humanité*—ignored *Black Skin, White Masks.* Most of the coverage in the popular press was dismissive, if not hostile. "Mr. Fanon is sick from being black the way others have measles," a right-wing writer complained. "He has thin skin and boiling blood . . . His neurosis is certainly a very bad neurosis. Physician heal thyself!" One of the few reviews of the book in his homeland accused him of being an ingrate for attacking colonization "without ever taking into account what the France of the Rights of Man and the Citizen—republican and secular France—has done for the country he came from: the French West Indies, for Fanon is Martinican." But the principal reason the book failed to attract a wide readership was its use of psychiatric jargon and its elusive, even cryptic language—decades later, a source of fascination for his academic exegetes.

Black activist circles in France found the book perplexing, since it was neither a Marxist pamphlet nor a pan-Africanist (or nationalist) call to arms. Much of it was composed in an abstruse psychoanalytic idiom, and for all its indictments of racist whites, it did not reflect well on Black people, either. It was particularly unflinching in its anatomy of Fanon's Martinique: its masochistic obsessions with color, class, and status. The Guadeloupean novelist Maryse Condé was a student at the Sorbonne when an excerpt from *Black Skin, White Masks* appeared in *Esprit*. She shot a letter of protest off to the editors. "The piece shocked and revolted us," she recalled in her memoirs. "We felt that Frantz Fanon had not only failed to understand our societies, but that he had maliciously insulted them." (Years later, however, she would come to think of herself as a "Fanonian.") As Fanon himself admitted in his introduction, no one had asked for this book, and no one seemed particularly keen on it—least of all the French West Indians to whom it was addressed. Had it not been for his later notoriety as an anti-colonial revolutionary, and the international success of *The Wretched of the Earth*, Fanon's first book might have remained a curiosity. Today, *Black Skin, White Masks* is widely recognized as an essential—arguably unsurpassed—reflection on the Black condition in France. But at the time of publication, it was an insurrectionary text in search of an insurrection that it proved powerless to spark. The first edition of *Black Skin, White Masks* sold only a few thousand copies in France.* Yet its ruthless, unsparing self-analysis would liberate the man who wrote it.

---

* *Black Skin, White Masks* became a worldwide bestseller only after its American translation, in 1967, six years after Fanon's death.

# 6

# THE PRACTICE
# OF DISALIENATION

---

IN HIS WRITING, FANON had already landed upon one of his great themes, even his life's project: the disalienation of the racially oppressed and dispossessed. Yet for all his interest in the *ideas* of progressive psychiatry, he'd had little opportunity to apply them with patients. His own training could hardly have been more traditional, and his early experiences as a doctor were mostly unhappy. His first residency was at a miserable hospital in eastern France, where he was the sole psychiatrist for 150 patients. Then, in February 1952, on a visit home with his brother Joby for carnival, he set up a clinic in the seaside town of Le Vauclin, twenty miles southeast of Fort-de-France. He rented a villa that belonged to a friend of his mother's and practiced for about two months—long enough to witness what Joby called "the cynicism and rapaciousness of the local elite." The native son was now a rather suspect returnee. He acquired the nickname "the witch doctor" because he performed autopsies. And he learned things about Martinique that he may have preferred not to know: above all, the pervasiveness of domestic violence. He told Joby of a woman whose rib cage had been smashed, her spleen ruptured, by blows from the flat of a cutlass. The witch doctor's work led to the arrest of some men for murdering their wives.

For all his scathing remarks about Martinique in his first book, Fanon found that being home was not without its pleasures: swimming in the ocean; playing football with his brother; seeing his mother, now a widow, for what turned out to be the last time. But it had never been his intention to stay; he was merely making some money while visiting family. Césaire's *Notebook of a Return to the Native Land*, inspired by a trip to the Balkans, had led the poet to go back home and serve his people. *Black Skin, White Masks* would turn out to be a farewell.

In late March, a few weeks before his book was published, Fanon returned to France; practicing psychiatry in Martinique, he told a friend, was "out of the question." (He did not elaborate on why, but it's possible he feared becoming one of the puffed-up, culturally alienated returnees he described in *Black Skin, White Masks*: "Many West Indians, after a fairly long stay in the *métropole*, return home to be deified . . . The Black man who has lived in France for a certain time returns radically transformed. Genetically speaking, his phenotype undergoes an absolute, definitive mutation.") The next month, he and his fiancée, Josie, arrived in Saint-Alban-sur-Limagnole, a town in the Lozère department of southern France. He would spend the next year and half at the Saint-Alban asylum, soaking up the methods of the new "institutional psychiatry," a collective approach to care that fused the insights of Freud and Marx, breaking down the hierarchies that separated patients and medical staff, giving the mentally ill a new sense of power over their lives.

Housed in a feudal castle high in the hills, Saint-Alban had been an asylum since 1821. It had nearly been destroyed by a fire in 1914 and ravaged by typhoid two decades later. When Paul Balvet became director in 1936, he devoted himself to improving the asylum's deplorable hygiene and infrastructure. Under Balvet, whose work Fanon had yet to encounter in *Esprit*, the asylum would become a center of resistance activity and progressive psychiatry during the German occupation. A practicing Catholic of conservative temperament, Balvet had initially welcomed the Vichy regime. But as his sympathies shifted to the Resistance, his reputation as a Pétainist allowed him to provide discreet cover for doctors working with the maquis—and for others at risk of persecution by the Occupation authorities. Throughout the war, in the words of one historian, "politics slept with madness" at Saint-Alban. Jews, maquisards, and dissident writers—including the Dadaist writer Tristan Tzara, the surrealist poet Paul Éluard, and Georges Canguilhem—all found sanctuary there.

Thanks to the ingenuity and determination of Balvet and his colleagues, Saint-Alban avoided the fate of other psychiatric hospitals during the war: the so-called *extermination douce*, or "soft extermination." Between forty thousand and forty-five thousand psychiatric patients—about half of those in France—died from hunger, malnutrition, cold, and other afflictions. Conditions were so desperate that some patients ate grass, insects, even their own hands. Neither the Vichy government nor the Nazi occupiers tried to save them; the mentally ill were considered subhuman, like the Jews. (The landscape of mental hospitals in wartime France has often been likened to the *univers concentrationnaire* of the camps.) By hoarding food, by training patients to gather edible mushrooms in the nearby forests, and by artful interventions in the black market, the doctors at Saint-Alban turned what would surely have become a morgue into a symbol of defiance and survival.

Saint-Alban also became a laboratory of radical psychiatry, giving birth to a new politics, even a poetics, of care. The revolution that unfolded at Saint-Alban had the imaginative freedom, the flair for spontaneity, of surrealism, but it was rooted in the unglamorous, mostly grinding labor of treating people suffering from extreme, often irreparable conditions—of restoring a sense of meaning and purpose to lives that had been stripped of both. It combined utopian dreams and reformist pragmatism. And it proved itself during the hardest test of all, war and occupation: hardly any of Saint-Alban's patients died of unnatural causes, and not a single person was denounced to the Germans. After the war, an almost angelic aura surrounded the castle in the arid hills of the Lozère.

Fanon had first heard about the psychiatric resistance in the Lozère at one of his dinners with Balvet in Lyon, but he was ultimately attracted to Saint-Alban by another figure, Balvet's colleague François Tosquelles, who had arrived at the asylum in January 1940 after spending several months in a camp for refugees from Spain.

Tosquelles was born in 1912 in Reus, outside Barcelona. The son of lower-middle-class shopkeepers with intellectual leanings, he read Marx

at an early age and developed an enduring sympathy for Catalan nationalism. An insatiable raconteur with a penchant for hyperbole, Tosquelles
claimed that by the age of ten he already knew what he wanted to do:
"bring Marx to the asylum." At age fifteen he began his studies in psychiatry in Barcelona, where he became a protégé of Sándor Eiminder, an
exiled Hungarian Jewish psychoanalyst who had been part of the Freud
circle in Vienna, and who had been analyzed by Sándor Ferenczi, one of
the first psychoanalysts to study the traumatic effects of war. Tosquelles's
other mentor, Emilio Mira y López, introduced him to Jacques Lacan's
1932 thesis on paranoia and fired his imagination with stories about "geo-
psychiatry," a practice of care that took place outside the walls of the hospital, in the homes of the mentally ill.

In his early twenties, Tosquelles practiced psychiatry at the Institut
Pere Mata in Reus and formed a clandestine group called the Bloque Obrero y Campesino (Workers and Peasants Bloc), which promoted a decentralized, libertarian kind of Marxism in opposition to Moscow. As a
proud Catalan, Tosquelles distrusted universal formulas, suspecting the
hand of a domineering, arrogant authority. As an anti-Stalinist with a pro-
nounced streak of anarchism, he rejected what he called the *tout-pouvoir*,
the "all-power."[7]

In 1935, Tosquelles took part in the creation of the Partido Obrero
de Unificatión Marxista (Workers Party of Marxist Unification, POUM).
When the civil war broke out a year later, he joined the POUM militias on
the Aragon front and created its psychiatric services. The war radicalized
his understanding of medicine. The people least accustomed to "normalcy,"
he realized, were often the best equipped to confront its collapse. He found
it easy to train prostitutes to become nurses; some "converted" and never
went back to their old trade. Members of his own profession found it more
difficult to adjust to the exigencies of war because they were all too wedded
to social conventions. One of Tosquelles's challenges during the war was
to help his fellow doctors overcome not only fear but also "something even
more important than fear": their sense of being "all-powerful" and their
attachment to "bourgeois, individualist ideology." Years later he would
remark that "a good citizen is incapable of doing psychiatry."

Condemned to death by Franco, Tosquelles fled Spain in April 1939.

After crossing the Pyrenees on foot, he was detained in the Camp de Judes in the town of Septfonds, north of Toulouse, one of the internment camps where some 450,000 Spanish refugees were held after the exodus known as the Retirada. (A few years later, Jews would be detained at Septfonds, before being deported to death camps.) The conditions were harsher than on the Aragón front: the camp was surrounded by barbed wire and monitored by surveillance posts; inmates slept in the cold in haystacks. But Tosquelles flourished at Septfonds, providing psychiatric care "in the mud," in his words, to "militants, painters, and guitarists."

When Balvet heard about the twenty-seven-year-old Catalan psychiatrist at Septfonds, he contacted the authorities, arranged for his release, and recruited him to work at Saint-Alban. But if Balvet imagined that Tosquelles would be a grateful, timid refugee, he was in for a surprise. A psychiatrist, Tosquelles believed, "must be a foreigner or pretend to be a foreigner." He never lost his Catalan accent, which made his French almost inscrutable, but he wasn't ashamed of it and even thought it had clinical advantages. "The sick person—or the normal type—has to make an effort to understand me; they are thus obliged to *translate* and take an active position toward me," he said.

Tosquelles had a playful, subversive side; with his wire-rim glasses, handlebar mustache, and impish grin, he looked like a bit of a clown. But he was also a visionary and diligent institutional reformer. When he arrived at Saint-Alban-sur-Limagnole, he had two books in hand: his old copy of Lacan's thesis and the German psychiatrist Hermann Simon's 1929 study of the Gütersloh asylum. Simon, an occupational therapist, insisted that "one must first of all take care of the hospital in order to take care of the patients." Tosquelles shared this conviction, describing the hospital as a *collectif soignant*, a "healing collective," in which doctors were no more important than other members of staff. His critique of medical hierarchies wasn't simply political; it was psychoanalytic. In effect, he reinterpreted—and collectivized—the psychoanalytic concept of "transference," the unconscious bond the patient develops with the analyst. Freud believed that transference was the key to understanding the patient's other relationships, but he applied the concept narrowly to those suffering from neuroses like anxiety, melancholia, and hysteria. In Tosquelles's view, psychotic patients suffering from hallucinations and delusions—radical breaks with reality—also forged relations of transference, but these were with every member of the healing collective, not just the doctor; he called this network *transfert éclaté*, or "exploded transference."

To illustrate how exploded transference worked, Tosquelles liked to tell the story of a schizophrenic patient who arrives at a hospital and begins chatting with the concierge. "I'm not a psychiatrist," the concierge replies, interrupting his monologue. "I'll take you to see the nurse." The patient is so taken with the nurse that he confides in her in even greater detail, until she tells him, "You really need to talk to the psychiatrist." But as soon as he lays eyes on the psychiatrist, he decides, "I don't like this guy's face. I'm not telling him anything." And so for the next hour he sits in the doctor's office, mute and defiant. "If the psychiatrist thinks that just because he's the doctor, he's the center of the world," Tosquelles concluded, "he's suffering from a megalomanic delirium." Instead, doctors, nurses, guards, and other members of staff had to work together in an almost artisanal manner, discussing their impressions of the patient, creating a network of transference. And patients, too, would have to become involved in the creation of a microworld approximating their lives outside the asylum, taking part in activities such as farming, art-making, theater, dance, and writing. They might not be cured of their pathologies, much less rendered "normal" (something Tosquelles never much valued, anyway), but even the most delusional patients could still participate in the productive and creative life of their institution. If they remained alienated from themselves, they did not have to be alienated from the healing collective of which they were a part—or deprived of the respect and recognition they deserved as fellow human beings. The individual, Tosquelles insisted, does not exist alone; therefore, madness is never merely a "personal affair." Here lay the foundations of what Tosquelles would call "institutional therapy" and what Fanon would later call "social therapy."

Tosquelles launched his reforms as soon as he arrived. The front doors were opened; the bars around patients' cells were removed. No longer physically confined, the *aliénés* could at last move from one space to another. "The right to vagabondage," Tosquelles believed, "is the first right of the sick person." But his project was vastly accelerated, as it had been in Spain, by war. In June 1940, France fell to the Germans. Dissidents and Resistance fighters soon began to arrive at the hospital, in search of a different kind of asylum. One of the first was the psychiatrist Lucien Bonnafé, who left a post in Paris so that he could continue his activities in the maquis, and who eventually replaced Balvet as the asylum's director. In Spain, Bonnafé and Tosquelles would have been rivals, if not mortal enemies: Bonnafé was a Communist, a member of a Stalinist party that had liquidated Tosquelles's party, the POUM. But the two men became the closest of allies at Saint-Alban, united by their commitment to psychiatry, their hatred of fascism, and their passion for surrealist poetry. Bonnafé wrote, "When poetry was called to the Resistance, it chose to share its life with a psychiatric hospital where the love of differences and the denunciation of an absurd order came together." In 1943, Bonnafé's friend and fellow *résistant* Paul Éluard found sanctuary at the hospital, having become a target after publishing a poem in praise of freedom, titled "Liberté."*

Under the leadership of Tosquelles and Bonnafé, a house of confinement turned into a place of welcome and hospitality, where the mentally ill could become active participants in their own recovery, and where, under the shadow of Nazi occupation and wartime rationing, they could live to see another day. When Fanon learned of the story of Resistance psychiatry at Saint-Alban, he began dreaming of working with Tosquelles.

TOSQUELLES WAS STANDOFFISH WHEN Fanon first walked into his office in the spring of 1952. "Fanon came from Lyon, from the Faculty of Medicine," he recalled, ridiculing the school as "a caricature . . . of analytic Cartesianism applied to the pathological event." In Lyon, he said, "the treatment can be summed up in a line. What am I saying? Not a line. A word will do . . . Here it is in capitals: TREATMENT: COMMITTAL. Nothing more, nothing less."

Fanon, in other words, had been trained by the enemy, the psychiatric

---

* Éluard paid homage to Saint-Alban in a 1945 suite of poems, *Souvenirs de la maison des fous* (Memories of the madhouse).

establishment Tosquelles disdained.* Still, he was curious about Fanon. "I noticed," he wrote, "the radical difference between the color of his skin and that of most of the men with whom I'd been accustomed to working." He asked Fanon what he could do for him. Fanon replied that he'd heard rumors in Lyon that, at Saint-Alban, doctors had invented a psychiatry "attentive above all to the complexity of difference—maintained and sometimes tragically reinforced—that bound the men in our care."

Tosquelles confirmed the rumors but stressed that "certain similarities" applied to all his patients. When Fanon handed him a copy of *Black Skin, White Masks* and shared some of his stories of the racism he'd encountered in Lyon, Tosquelles pushed back again, harrumphing that "whatever the color of our face or skin, we all advance masked when we encounter others." Curiously, Tosquelles, the Catalan nationalist, the self-described native of an "occupied country," was accusing Fanon of asserting a narrow ethnic particularism. Fanon was hardly a stranger to defensive reactions; still, the lecture must have gotten under his skin.

Tosquelles himself admitted, "The abstract character of these early exchanges didn't fool either of us. The discreet reference to the contrast in the color of our skins was at the center of our interviews." Old-fashioned masculine rivalry was another likely subtext. Fanon was twenty-seven, the same age as Tosquelles had been when he went into exile in France. He, too, was an outsider, from the outre-mer. As a critic of French racism, he struck Tosquelles as a self-styled representative of his race—"the ambassador of the singularity of his history." Much like Tosquelles, Fanon insisted on being recognized on his own terms. Yet Fanon, an assimilated Black man whose French could hardly have been more elegant, was in some ways more of a cultural insider than the stubbornly unassimilated exile who, with a playful absence of tact, likened his own speech to *petit nègre*.

The two men were talking past each other, sizing each other up. Nicole Guillet, who had introduced them, overheard the conversation and said it sounded like a bullfight. After their initial clashes, however, Tosquelles became as close to Fanon as he had been to Bonnafé, who had left Saint-Alban a few years after the war. He admired Fanon's physical grace, his

---

* Not that Fanon would have disagreed.

polemical zeal, and—perhaps above all—his lack of what Tosquelles called the "so-called virtue of patience." In other words, he recognized in Fanon a fellow rebel who shared his disdain for bourgeois etiquette. While Fanon's taste in poetry ran more to Césaire and Damas than to Breton and Éluard, he, too, had a powerfully literary imagination that often seeped into his work. At one point, during a meeting with patients and their families, he launched into an impromptu lecture about classical theater, underscoring the tragic dimensions of psychiatry.

Fanon threw himself into the life of Saint-Alban, organizing film screenings and musical evenings, impressing patients with his compassion and sense of humor (at one soirée he helped move a piano in a dainty pair of white gloves, gesturing like an actor in a silent film). He wrote short, philosophical essays for the in-house literary journal, *Trait d'union*, in a vaguely existential register, about the "therapeutic role of engagement," the need to "invent a new mode of living," and the creativity that can arise from the quotidian. And from Tosquelles—a war veteran and revolutionary who approached psychiatry as if it were an extension of politics by other means—he discovered a set of ideas and practices that he would apply, and refashion, in Algeria and Tunisia.

In 1953, Fanon and Tosquelles coauthored a series of papers on the Bini method of electroconvulsive therapy (ECT), named after the Italian doctor Lucio Bini. (Throughout his career, Fanon would remain a fierce believer in the virtues of ECT.) The participants in their research were profoundly troubled individuals whose conditions were caused by, or interwoven with, the histories of war and colonialism. One was a woman of twenty-eight who had gone into delirium, becoming violent and suicidal, after witnessing the deaths of her mother and father, in her presence, under aerial bombardment in 1944. Another was a forty-five-year-old nun who had developed schizophrenia after her brother's suicide. She spent her days walking through the garden, refusing to speak to other patients, and fulminating against the "naked" and "dirty" natives of Gabon, a French colony where she had been a missionary.

In their paper, Fanon and Tosquelles reported that the nun was able to return to her community after a hospitalization of three months, thanks to seventeen electroshocks and forty sessions of insulin therapy. Their conclusions are expressed in a neutral, pragmatic tone; they do not comment upon, much less judge, the racist content of the nun's ravings about the *nègres* in Gabon. But these could not have failed to make an impression on Fanon, after all his research on racist psychoses. In his first article for the *Trait d'union*, he cited an unnamed philosopher: "If you want to go deeper into the structure of a particular country, you have to visit its psychiatric hospitals."

After seven years exploring the hatreds and phobias that lay behind the French Republic's veneer of color-blind universalism, the problem of racism remained very much on his mind. On January 6, 1953, he wrote a letter to Richard Wright, declaring his intention to embark on a study of the "human dimensions" of the novelist's work. (Alioune Diop, the editor of *Présence africaine*, had given him Wright's address in Paris.) "My name must be unknown to you," he wrote. "I have written an essay, *Black Skin, White Masks*, in which I set out to show the systematic misconceptions that exist between Whites and Blacks." It would have been a fascinating exchange between a young West Indian critic of France's claims to anti-racism and an older Black American expatriate for whom France was as close to heaven as he'd ever gotten. But Wright, who said he enjoyed more freedom on a single block in Paris than in all of the United States, seems never to have replied, and the book was never written.

In September 1953, Fanon left Saint-Alban to become the interim head of a hospice in Pontorson, a small town near the Atlantic coast in northwestern France. The doctors, it transpired, were frightened of their patients, and he provoked an outcry by proposing a shopping expedition for a group of twenty-nine patients—in effect, applying the methods he'd learned from Tosquelles. When the administrative director refused to approve the trip, the patients went on strike. Fanon began to cast about for other jobs, writing to Senghor about working in Senegal; Senghor, whose work he'd mocked in *Black Skin, White Masks*, never replied. He also applied for work in Guadeloupe, having already ruled out Martinique. As he waited for a posting, he felt like "the little Indian boy in the Buñuel film *Los Olvidados*, who waits for his father the whole day in the face of all evidence that his father has deliberately forgotten about him."

Late that year, he was hired as the director of the Blida-Joinville

Psychiatric Hospital in Algeria—the homeland of many of the workers he had treated in Lyon, the men whose strange, seemingly inexplicable anguish had supplied him with the subject of his memorable essay on the North African syndrome. Fanon had last set foot there as a soldier for France and observed the misery of Algerian children fighting over scraps of food. "I'm going to Algeria," he wrote to his brother Joby. "You understand: the French have enough psychiatrists to take care of their madmen. I'd rather go to a country where they need me." Admirable sentiments. But the truth is that Fanon was worried about his prospects in metropolitan France. He had passed the *médicat des hôpitaux psychiatriques*, the competitive exam to become a *médecin-chef*, but had ranked thirteenth out of a class of fifty-four. (Josie, his wife, had done far better on her examination in Latin philology.) He had also developed a reputation for being difficult.

Because of the extraordinary turn that his life was to take in Algeria, Fanon's decision to go there is often portrayed as a political act, even a prefiguration of destiny. In his 1965 afterword to *Black Skin, White Masks*, Francis Jeanson writes: "I insist that in 1952 Fanon was an authentically revolutionary spirit, and that he remained so. Fanon the Algerian kept the promises of Fanon the West Indian; *The Wretched of the Earth* was the confirmation of *Black Skin, White Masks*." Perhaps. Fanon was undoubtedly an *écorché vif*, as Édouard Glissant observed, always on guard, ready to do battle. But he had yet to find a revolution he wanted to join, and—aside from Jeanson—few people in France imagined at the time that a war of national liberation was imminent in Algeria. As far as he knew, awaiting him on the other side of the Mediterranean, in France's most prized colonial possession, were a good job and the chance to start a family: the things that led other French people to settle there. The future anti-colonial warrior arrived in Algeria as an improbable beneficiary of colonial privilege and a representative of colonial authority.

# PART II

# THE ALGERIAN

# 7

# A WORLD CUT IN TWO

---

IN MAY 1954, Joby Fanon, who was in Paris studying for the entrance examination for the École Nationale d'Administration, flew to Algiers to pay
his brother a visit. Frantz was waiting for him at the airport with the hospital's pharmacist, Dr. Sourdoire, who drove them to Blida, about twenty-
five miles southwest of Algiers, where Frantz had settled into his new
position. After dinner, Frantz took Joby to the garage, turned on the light,
and revealed a shiny new Simca Aronde. Teasing his younger brother, Joby
remarked that he now understood why Frantz hadn't picked him up in his
own car. Frantz admitted that he wanted to surprise him, but he was also
showing off a bit. "I still have a big debt to pay off," he added, as if embarrassed by his good fortune.

At twenty-eight years old, Fanon was already a *fonctionnaire*, a civil
servant in charge of an important institution. A year later, he and his wife,
Josie, would have a son, Olivier, their only child. The idea of a Black West
Indian running a hospital in a French-ruled colony with a Muslim majority may strike contemporary readers as peculiar. But France had a tradition
of sending assimilated citizens from the old colonies in the West Indies to
serve as administrators in the new colonies of North and sub-Saharan Africa, where they were meant to provide an example of the glories of French
civilization. The Martinican novelist and poet René Maran, a native of

Fort-de-France, Fanon's hometown, had worked for nearly a decade as a French official in Ubangi-Shari (now the Central African Republic) when he published his 1921 novel, *Batouala*. Promoted, oxymoronically, as a "true Negro novel," *Batouala* won the Goncourt Prize, France's most prestigious literary award, but Maran provoked an outcry with his preface, which bitterly denounced the colonial system as a "kingdom [built] on top of corpses" and "mired in lies." Fanon, who discussed Maran's novel *Un Homme pareil aux autres* in *Black Skin, White Masks*, would go much further, and not just in writing.

Fanon's life in French-occupied Algeria would transform him. But in his first year in Blida, Algeria's "capital of madness," Fanon's ambitions were confined to the psychiatric ward. The Blida-Joinville Hospital belonged to the so-called second line of psychiatric wards, receiving patients who had not been cured of their illness at the Mustapha Pacha Hospital in Algiers. Many were Muslim men, unshaven, dressed in impersonal hospital-issued uniforms, listlessly wandering about the asylum like prisoners—and treated much the same. Fanon found some of them tied to their beds, others to trees on the grounds. Patients suffering from both schizophrenia and tuberculosis were tethered naked to iron rings in isolated cells with straw-covered floors. There were fifteen hundred patients and half as many beds. Here was the *univers concentrationnaire* that had characterized French psychiatric wards under Vichy, with the remarkable exception of Saint-Alban.

The day after Joby arrived, Fanon showed him around the hospital, starting with the section for patients who were considered dangerous. Noticing a look of horror on his brother's face, Frantz assured him that "all of this will come to an end." Determined to apply Tosquelles's methods of disalienation, he had already set up a playground and a football field on the grounds of the hospital, and female patients were putting on plays. But Blida was far from Saint-Alban, and Frantz would become increasingly circumspect about his chances of narrowing the gap.

WHEN FANON SET OUT for Algeria in December 1953, he was not leaving France; he was merely crossing an ocean. Algeria had been conquered in

1830 and administered as an integral part of France since 1848, when it was divided into three departments: Algiers in the center, Oran in the west, and Constantine in the east. (The Sahara was ruled by military government.) Tunisia and Morocco, which became French-ruled protectorates in 1881 and 1912, respectively, had small populations of settlers. In Algeria more than a million European settlers lived as French citizens. They were *chez eux*, "at home": according to a popular saying, the Mediterranean, separating France from Algeria, was much the same as the Seine in Paris, which divided the Left Bank from the Right Bank. If modern Israel had Theodor Herzl, Algérie française (French Algeria) had the ideologue Louis Bertrand, who, after seeing the Roman ruins in Tipaza, developed a hypothesis that Algeria was a lost Latin province, now rightfully restored to France. "For me, Latin Africa shows through the trompe l'oeil of the modern Islamic décor," Bertrand wrote in 1939 in a preface to a new edition of his 1920 novel, *Le Sang des races* (The blood of races). "The Africa of the triumphal arches and the basilicas rises before me: the Africa of Apuleius and St. Augustine. That is the real Africa." Algeria's Muslims were merely "contemporary shadows of those edifices"; French settlers were, by definition, the true natives.

There are echoes of this perversity even in a scrupulous writer like Albert Camus, who rejected the explicitly chauvinistic aspects of "Latin Africa." ("The only nationalism at issue here is the nationalism of the sunshine," he said.) Yet he, too, emphasized Algeria's Latin and Mediterranean ancestry, almost to the exclusion of its Muslim heritage. Camus's writings gave the impression that Algeria's history began with the arrival of settlers from Europe, who populated its empty cities and filled them with reinvigorating memories of the Old World. In his fiction, "the Arab" appears as a spectral, often threatening presence on the margins of European society. In *The Plague*, Arabs and Berbers are almost entirely absent; in his journalism, they are objects of pity and compassion, rather than protagonists with an identifiable history of their own.

That Algeria was, and would remain, French was accepted by even its most liberal citizens. Fanon would write that "colonialism imposes itself in the perspective of eternity." The long periods of peace that followed the wars of conquest of the nineteenth century led the French to imagine that they had won over native hearts and minds and been welcomed, and that Muslims wanted to remain a part of French Algeria. And until the war of independence broke out in 1954, most Muslim leaders worked to reform the existing system, not to overthrow it. But, as the Algerian political activist and historian Mohammed Harbi has written in his memoir, Muslims saw their uninvited guests as "foreigners with whom history had forced us to coexist, but who would leave one day." For as long as the French were in Algeria, Muslims would often refer to them as *roum* (Byzantines or Romans) or *ennasara* (followers of Jesus of Nazareth). "The colonist always remains a foreigner," Fanon wrote. "It is not the factories, the estates, or the bank account which primarily characterize the 'ruling class.' The ruling species is first and foremost the outsider from elsewhere, different from the indigenous people, 'the others.'"*

The "others" first landed in Algeria as an unpopular monarch's payback for a diplomatic slight. In 1827, Hussein Dey, the Ottoman ruler of Algiers, told the French consul that he expected to be repaid for loans made to the French government during the Napoleonic wars. When the consul general refused, the dey struck him with a fly swatter, calling him a "wicked, faithless, idol-worshipping rascal." On June 14, 1830, King Charles X dispatched thirty-seven thousand troops to the beach of Sidi-Ferruch, west of Algiers. He claimed to be restoring order to a "nest of pirates," but the Marseille business community had long had its sights on Algeria, which had always been subject to foreign occupations (Roman, Vandal, Byzantine, Arab, Turk). Since the Arab and Muslim invasions, it was argued, the country had descended into tribal anarchy. This was debatable. Alexis de Tocqueville, a strong supporter of conquest, observed in his 1847 report on Algeria, "We have rendered Muslim society much more miserable, more disordered, more ignorant and barbarous than it was before we encountered it."

The French, who entered Algiers on July 5, conquered Algeria in three weeks, with only four hundred deaths among their soldiers. But it would take another four decades to "pacify" the territory. The first challenge to

---

* The last line is probably a sly, anti-colonial gloss on Sartre's famous line "L'enfer, c'est les autres" (Hell is the others).

French rule came in 1832 from Emir Abdelkader, a twenty-five-year-old Arab from a family that descended from the Prophet Muhammad. "Ravage the country" was Tocqueville's advice to the army, which stamped out Abdelkader's jihad by destroying harvests, rounding up families, and razing entire villages until his surrender fifteen years later. One of the army's tactics was to light fires at the mouth of caves where Algerian families had found sanctuary, asphyxiating everyone inside—the so-called *enfumades*. After one *enfumade*, a French colonel remarked that "returning from the expedition, several of our horsemen carried heads at the end of their spears, and one of them served, it is said, a horrible feast." Fanon would later write, "The colonist is an exhibitionist. His safety concerns lead him to remind the colonized out loud: 'Here I am the master.'" In 1871, another mass revolt broke out, this one led by a Kabyle Berber named Cheikh El-Mokrani. The French responded by confiscating all the fertile land in Kabylia, reducing the Berbers to penury.

In its effort to "pacify" Algeria, a mountainous terrain four times the size of France, the French government was ultimately forced to populate it with immigrants from Italy, Corsica, Spain, and Malta, since few French citizens were inclined to move there. ("We have despoiled, pursued, and hunted down the Arabs in order to populate Algeria with Italians and Spaniards," Anatole France remarked.) The *français d'Algérie*, many of whom had never set foot in the *métropole*, came to think of Algeria as their home and of themselves as Algerians. A minority of the settlers were *grands colons* who lived on large estates in the coastal plains and in the west, on land that had been violently confiscated, often from the very Muslims they employed as cheap labor. The *grands colons* produced corn, alfalfa, and above all wine, a beverage that, as Roland Barthes noted, symbolized colonial dispossession, since Muslim grape pickers were forbidden to drink it. Yet even the poorest Europeans—the so-called *petits blancs*, or "down-at-heel whites"—enjoyed considerable advantages by virtue of their French citizenship. To become full French citizens, Algerian Muslims had to renounce being governed by Islamic law courts in matters of personal status (marriage, divorce, inheritance) and subject themselves instead to the French Civil Code. For most Muslims during the colonial era, such an act meant symbolically severing themselves from the

Muslim community, indeed renouncing their identity as Muslims, and was considered tantamount to apostasy: naturalized Algerians were vilified as *m'tournis*, "turncoats," who had defected to the occupier's camp. Only a few thousand became citizens before 1946, when citizenship was granted to all inhabitants of France's overseas colonies. That resistance to "integration" reinforced Muslims' disenfranchisement was an unintended consequence of the civil code, but not an undesirable one from the vantage point of most Europeans.

According to Mohammed Harbi, who grew up in a prosperous Arab family in Skikda (formerly Philippeville) in the 1930s and '40s, colonial Algeria "was not the Warsaw Ghetto, nor was it apartheid." In their everyday relations, middle-class Europeans and Muslims often treated one another with respect and even exuded, in Harbi's words, a "certain Mediterranean warmth." Nonetheless, Muslims and Europeans inhabited an "unequal and, above all, colonial space." The signs on the beaches of Algiers and Oran read "No dogs or Arabs."* Racist contempt for Algerians—often exemplified by slurs such as *bougnoule*, *bicot*, and *sale raton* (dirty little rat)—ran deep among Europeans. Marriages between Muslim men and European women were rare (and invariably contracted in the *métropole*); marriages between European men and Muslim women almost nonexistent. European and Muslim children were mostly educated in different schools—if the latter were educated at all: more than a century into France's *mission civilisatrice*, only one in ten Muslim boys attended school, and one in sixteen girls; more than 90 percent of Algerians remained illiterate in French. Neither Arabic nor Berber was taught in French schools since both were "foreign" languages; the writer Kateb Yacine compared his French education to a "second breaking of the umbilical cord."

There were efforts to integrate Muslims into the republic, but settler resistance scuttled each one of them, no matter how modest. In 1936, the Blum-Viollette Project, which would have granted citizenship and voting rights to twenty-one thousand members of the Muslim elite, went down to defeat. The elections held in Algeria by the French in 1948—in which

---

* That Meursault, Camus's protagonist in *The Stranger*, encounters an Arab walking on a beach where Arabs were all but forbidden is among the novel's many implausible features.

one European vote was equal to nine Algerian votes under the double electoral college—were rigged to deprive Algerian nationalists of their victory. In an ultimately self-destructive display of short-sightedness, no French government was sufficiently willing or able to challenge the settlers, a powerful voting bloc in France. "Algiers is not Paris," the settlers insisted. Fanon would often hear such sentiments of obstinate pride echoed among French Algerian doctors as they excused the mistreatment of their Muslim patients. But, as the settlers knew all too well, Algérie française could not have survived without French military protection. The continued stifling of reform—and Paris's endless capitulation to Algiers—would ultimately convince most Algerians that their only hope lay in independence.

The first Algerian leader to explicitly call for independence was Messali Hadj, the son of a shoemaker from Tlemcen, near the Moroccan border. A World War I veteran, Messali, as he was known, wore a long beard, dressed in a djellaba and a red fez, and reminded some of a Muslim Rasputin. He first attracted a following among Algerian workers in France in the late 1920s, when he created the Étoile Nord-Africaine (North African Star), an anti-colonial organization linked to the French Communist Party. But he broke with the party's tutelage in the 1930s to form his own party, the Algerian People's Party, later renamed the Mouvement pour le triomphe des libertés démocratique (MTLD). Skillfully interweaving revolutionary slogans with a nostalgic embrace of Algerian culture and tradition, Messali created a passionate and flexible synthesis of Islamic populism, socialism, and Jacobinism; at its core was an insistence on Algerian dignity and *nif*, "honor." For many of his followers, he was a messiah-like figure, but by the time Fanon came to Blida, some of the younger Messalists were growing frustrated by his cult of personality—and increasingly impatient to launch an armed insurrection.

The reason for their impatience could be summed up in a single word: Sétif. On May 8, 1945, Algerians had raised the banned flag of the MTLD at the VE Day celebrations in Sétif, a city in the east. As the gendarmes forced their way into the crowd, seizing flags, clashes broke out, and a twenty-year-old Algerian man was killed. Protesters attacked European bystanders, killing dozens, including the town's socialist mayor. Some recited chants of holy war, as if they were picking up the battle led, a century earlier, by

Emir Abdelkader. A similar revolt erupted in nearby Guelma. More than a hundred Europeans were killed, some of them dismembered—breasts slashed, throats slit, genitals stuffed inside the mouths of their victims. It was a shockingly intimate kind of violence: the killers and their victims were often neighbors.

Over the next few weeks, the army and settler militias presided over a campaign of terror that stirred collective memories of the original conquest. In Guelma, a quarter of the Muslim adult population between the ages of twenty-five and forty-five was killed. As many as fifteen thousand Muslims—the precise number will never be known—lay dead by the end of May. Some of the soldiers who suppressed the revolt were Senegalese infantrymen with whom the Muslims—and Fanon—had fought to liberate Europe from Nazism. "I have given you peace for ten years," General Raymond Duval said. "But if France sits idle, everything will start again for the worse and probably in a terminal way." His prediction was off by a year, but accurate in every other way.

"We heard very little about what had happened at Sétif," Simone de Beauvoir recalled. Even the Communist Party—which denounced the revolt as "Hitlerian"—accepted the official figure that only a hundred or so Algerians had been killed. But the Muslims of Algeria knew better. The liberal nationalist leader Ferhat Abbas, a pharmacist from Sétif, said the massacre had "taken us back to the days of the Crusaders." Kateb Yacine, who was sixteen at the time, was arrested and tortured in Sétif; his mother suffered a breakdown and had to be committed to a psychiatric institution. "I never forgot the shock which I felt at the pitiless butchery that caused the deaths of thousands of Muslims," Yacine recalled. "From that moment my nationalism took definite form." Two years later, a group of young MTLD militants formed the Organisation Spéciale, the first armed independence group and the precursor to the Front de libération nationale (FLN), which Fanon would later join.

For Messali's radical sons, reform was dead and attempts at it would soon be declared treasonous, along with any form of political resistance outside the FLN's authority. The hour of revolution had come. Younger, educated Algerians like Harbi, who had learned French and assimilated the ideas of republicanism and freedom—and whose fathers had cobbled together a modus vivendi with their uninvited French guests—increasingly chafed at being occupied by foreigners. After the sacrifices they had made to free France from the German occupation—and the blood they had spilled for raising the Algerian flag in Sétif—they would accept nothing less than complete independence. In their spirit of intransigence and revolt, in their rebellion against the fathers who'd raised them and the colonial motherland that claimed to be civilizing them, Fanon would see a mirror image of himself.

BLIDA, WHERE FANON ARRIVED in 1953, was founded in the sixteenth century by Sidi Ahmed el Kebir, a marabout from the Western Sahara, with a group of Muslim refugees from Spain. The name comes from *boulayda*, "small city" in classical Arabic. El Kabir preferred to call it *Ourida*, "Little Rose," and the nickname stuck. But Blida wasn't a very picturesque city. It was a garrison town, originally occupied in 1839 by French troops. They built their first military base there, later adding an airbase, a communications and posting center, and a military hospital. In the early 1950s, a quarter of the town's European population was linked to the military. Otherwise, Blida was known for little else besides the rich farmlands of the Mitidja Plain, which the French had created out of malarial swamps, and its abundant supply of what André Gide dreamily described as "Arab boys as beautiful as bronze statues."

In Blida, Fanon encountered what he would later describe as the "compartmentalized" world of colonialism, a "world cut in two," where the border between settler and native zones was "marked by barracks and police stations" and statues of the nineteenth-century conquerors of Algeria provided constant reminders to the indigenous population that "we are here by the force of bayonets." It was a mixed town of sixty thousand inhabitants: there were wealthy settlers and *petits blancs*, and both poor and middle-class Muslims. There was also a small but significant population of Jews—former *indigènes* (natives) who had been granted French citizenship by the Crémieux Decree of 1870, and whose attachment and gratitude to the Republic had grown only fiercer thanks to the trauma of having lost their citizenship for two years under the Vichy government. On the surface, Blida gave the impression of being less segregated than Algiers. But this was misleading. While Blida's boarding schools welcomed both Europeans and Muslims, the children were housed in separate dormitories. On the place d'Armes in the European center of town, people drank in cafés on streets lined with lemon trees, while in the Casbah, 100,000 Muslims were packed into an area of a square kilometer called *le village nègre*—"Negro town."

Doctors had been present at the creation of this compartmentalized world: the expeditionary force at Sidi-Ferruch included 167 surgeons and other medical professionals. Psychiatry, Fanon's specialty, had played an important role, not only in providing treatment but also in explaining and diagnosing the mysterious and often frustrating workings of the native mind—at least as seen by its rulers. The field's most influential figure in North Africa was Antoine Porot, who had created the first modern psychiatric ward in Tunisia in 1912, four years before being named the head of psychiatry at the Mustapha Pacha Hospital in Algiers. Although only one of Fanon's colleagues had studied with Porot, the Blida-Joinville Psychiatric Hospital, founded in 1938, had been built under his direction and was shaped by his work. Porot was a reformer who emphasized the importance of "understanding" native society; he was also a passionate exponent of the ideas of Arthur de Gobineau, an aristocratic theorist of white supremacy and "scientific" racism. The Algerian Muslim, in Porot's description, was hysterical, predisposed to criminality, and intellectually inferior: "a primitive being" driven by instinct and incapable of rational thought.

Fanon was well aware of Porot's work, and of the thread that linked his views on Algerian Muslims to anti-Black racism: "on the psychophysiological level, the Black African greatly resembles the North African—the African is a unity." His work with his Muslim patients in Blida would be a daily struggle against Porot's legacy. But in his research papers he was careful not to challenge Porot by name. His only published attack on Porot, in the anti-colonial magazine *Consciences maghrébines*, was unsigned.

The medical space in which Fanon worked at Blida was a grim tribute to Porot's legacy. The unit for which he was personally responsible was divided into separate pavilions for 220 Muslim men and 165 European

women. Porot himself had devised the segregation of the hospital's patients on the grounds that "in disturbed minds, differences of moral or
social conception, or latent impulsive tendencies, can disrupt the necessary calm at any moment, can fuel delusions, and trigger or create dangerous reactions in an eminently inflammable milieu." The reasoning was
racist, but the argument contained a grain of truth: as Fanon would soon
discover, relations between Europeans and Algerians *were* potentially
inflammable.

IN *A FORTUNATE MAN*, his 1967 portrait of a poor people's doctor in rural
England, John Berger writes:

> An unhappy patient comes to a doctor to offer him an illness—in the
> hope that this part of him at least (the illness) may be recognizable. His
> proper self he believes to be unknowable. In the light of the world he is
> nobody; by his own lights the world is nothing. Clearly the task of the
> doctor—unless he merely accepts the illness on its face value and in-
> cidentally guarantees for himself a "difficult" patient—is to recognize
> the man. If the man can begin to feel recognized—and such recogni-
> tion may well include aspects of his character which he has not yet
> recognized himself—the hopeless nature of his unhappiness will have
> changed: he may even have the chance of being happy.

This was the task—humble, but in fact quite formidable—that Fanon
set for himself in Blida. He was a Black man, from an old colony in the
West Indies, but he was also French and therefore a European in the eyes
of his Muslim patients. And since he spoke neither Arabic nor Berber, he
often depended on interpreters—Algerian nurses, for the most part—to
communicate with his patients. (He began to take Arabic lessons only in
1956.) His work with Algerians was a work of constant translation.

His closest ally in Blida was his intern Jacques Azoulay, for whom he
developed great affection. Two years younger than Fanon, Azoulay was the
son of a Jewish tailor in Algiers whose three children all became doctors.
A man of the left, close to the Communist Party, he shared Fanon's passion

for philosophy and his acute sensitivity to racism and antisemitism. They began to set up meetings at which the entire staff could discuss the day's events, with an eye to making Blida more responsive to the needs of its patients.

Another intern, Charles Geronimi, a European Algerian of Corsican origin who arrived somewhat later, remembered that under Fanon's leadership, "debate was permanent." Anything and everything was up for discussion—even the quality of the food served at the hospital. Fanon wrote to his staff:

> Eating is not inferior to thinking. The person who is concerned with what he or she eats, who requests that the dishes . . . be better prepared, who points out that the food is being served cold, that the fish is always covered in sauce, that the vinaigrette is often only vinegar, who bemoans that dessert is such a rare event, who notes that some dishes are repugnant . . . is . . . developing the sense of a taste for nuance.

Geronimi himself was interviewed by Fanon at one of Blida's posher establishments, and sensed that he was being tested on his gastronomic taste.

The strange ideas of their new Martinican boss did not endear him to all his colleagues; nor did the zeal with which he pursued them. Even before Geronimi arrived in Blida, he had heard rumors in Algiers about "this new director who's pissing us off with the new psychiatry." The often racist chatter about him among psychiatrists in Algiers—one of Porot's protégés called him "a pretentious idiotic Martinican with a complex"— may explain why Fanon developed a dislike, even a suspicion, of the capital. In Algiers he had sought out psychiatric experts on Arab culture, only to discover that those who spoke Arabic were often the most racist toward Algerians. Algiers struck him as provincial and chauvinistic, a fortress of French Algeria.

Some of Fanon's colleagues in Blida ridiculed him as a naïve "Arab lover," but their resentment stemmed as much from complacency and resignation as from racism. (As he would later reflect, "Not even the civil servant transferred for two years to a colonial territory fails to feel himself psychologically changed in certain respects.") For doctors who had grown accustomed to the siestas and the sluggish pace of colonial life, his energy must have been a provocation, if not a humiliation. He always arrived at work before his interns, dressed in fastidious shirts with cuff links, and sometimes changed his tie twice a day. After dinner, he would often meet with staff to discuss Freud's clinical studies or the latest developments in psychiatric research. In a letter to a friend written a few months after his arrival, Fanon complained, "Here, you have the impression that each doctor tries to form a cell, a block, an absolute . . . At the start of meetings everyone is already tired as if all dialogue were simply in vain. It seems that this is something specifically North African and that I, too, will be exhausted before too long." The other doctors, he added, "do not budge and cast a dreamy eye on my restlessness." He heard doctors compare their patients to animals; he saw others inject their patients with distilled water, claiming it was penicillin or vitamin B. None of the doctors was Muslim; only three of the Muslims on staff held positions of authority, working either as head nurses or assistant head nurses.

But Fanon soon found that he could rely on his nurses and interns, and they in turn grew to admire him, even if he pushed them nearly as hard as he pushed himself. The nurses belonged to the Confédération gé-nérale du travail (CGT), a trade union federation linked to the French Communist Party that was open to both Europeans and Muslims. Some of Fanon's junior colleagues were active in the Communist Party, while others supported Messali's nationalist organization, the MTLD. Their po-litical commitments outside the hospital's walls inflected the treatment they provided inside, working as a militant *collectif soignant*, much like Tosquelles's at Saint-Alban. When the war of independence broke out, sev-eral of Fanon's colleagues would join him in the resistance. Some would pay for their involvement with their lives.

One of Fanon's earliest innovations at Blida was to establish a newslet-ter modeled on Tosquelles's *Trait d'union*. He decided to call it the *Journal de bord* (On-board journal, or Ship's log), explaining:

> On a ship, it is commonplace to say that one is between sky and water; that one is cut off from the world; that one is alone. This journal, pre-cisely, is to fight against the possibility of letting oneself go, against

that solitude. Every day a newssheet comes out, often poorly printed, without photos and bland. But every day, that newssheet works to liven up the boat . . . The boat, though isolated, keeps contact with the outside, that is to say, with the world. Why? Because in two or three days, the passengers will meet up again with their patients and friends, and return to their homes.

Writing itself provided a means of overcoming isolation, of advancing mutual understanding: "Writing is certainly the most beautiful discovery, since it allows man to remember, to present things that have happened in order and above all to communicate with others, even when they are absent."

In the end, however, the newsletter was called *Notre journal.* Taking to its pages, Fanon emphasized his favorite themes: the need for vigilance among the staff, and the goal of disalienation. The hero, he wrote, is not someone who "performs a dazzling feat and goes to bed thinking he's done enough." Rather, he is someone "who gets through his or her task with conscientiousness and love," and never succumbs to the illusion that "the work undertaken, if it is abandoned even for a moment, remains intact." The worst mistake in therapy, he argued in another article, is to "adopt an attitude of punishment," rather than understanding. "If care is not taken," he warned, a hospital can degenerate into "a barracks in which children-boarders tremble before parent-orderlies." Every effort should be made to "keep intact the links that unite the patient with the outside world," since "the patient ought not to endure hospitalization as a kind of imprisonment."

In a striking commentary published in April 1954, he questioned the spatial isolation of the modern asylum, anticipating Michel Foucault's 1961 *Folie et déraison* (*Madness and Civilization*):

Future generations will wonder with interest what motive could have led us to build psychiatric hospitals far from the center. Several patients have already asked me: Doctor, will we hear the Easter bells? . . . Whatever our religion, daily life is set to the rhythm of a number of sounds and the church bells represent an important element in this

symphony . . . Easter arrives, and the bells will die without being reborn, for they have never existed at the psychiatric hospital of Blida.
The psychiatric hospital of Blida will continue to live in silence. A silence without bells.

Restoring the symphonic order of everyday life was the aim of social
therapy, and Fanon pursued it with his customary vigilance, introducing basket weaving, a theater, a film club, a record-collecting society, ball
games, and other activities. This experiment was a great success with the
European women, but an utter failure with the Muslim men, who would
drift off and go to bed, claiming they were tired, while the nurses became
increasingly "irritated by their lack of will." Conversations between Fanon
and Azoulay and their Muslim male patients—for whom movies and theater meant as little as the sound of church bells—would often come to a
sudden end, since they had no common reference points, or even a language: "As Merleau-Ponty said, 'to speak a language is to bear the weight
of a culture.'" Whatever their political sympathies, Fanon and Azoulay
represented France for their Muslim patients, and "we were obliged to
recognize our failure."
    The older European doctors appeared to relish the failure of the "Arab
doctor." "When you've been in the hospital for fifteen years like us, then
you'll understand," they said. But Fanon refused to "understand." He suspected that the failure lay in his use of "imported methods"—Western
practices of recreation and culture—and that he might achieve different
results if he could provide Muslim patients with forms of sociality that resembled those they knew in their lives outside the hospital. Working with
a team of Muslim nurses, he created a café maure, a traditional Moorish
café where men drink coffee and play cards, and later an "Oriental salon"
for the hospital's small group of female Muslim patients. Muslim musi-
cians and storytellers came to perform; Muslim festivals were celebrated;
and, for the first time in the hospital's history, the mufti of Blida paid a
visit during the breaking of the Ramadan fast. This time the results were
noticeably different. After a few months, it was as if the hospital's Muslim
patients had awakened from a long slumber. (According to Azoulay, there
was also a marked decline in the number of injuries to caregivers.)

Later, when Geronimi asked Fanon—author, after all, of "The 'North African Syndrome'"—to speculate about his initial failure, he replied that "you can only understand with your guts." He added that he refused to simply pursue "external methods more or less adapted to the 'indigenous mentality'"—an allusion to the Porot school, no doubt. His purpose, rather, was to demonstrate that "Algerian culture had values other than colonial culture," a legitimacy of its own, and that "those structural values should be embraced without a complex by those who are bearers of them: Algerian care givers or those receiving care."

In a joint paper on their experiment, "Social Therapy in a Ward of Muslim Men," Fanon and Azoulay attributed its original shortcomings to a "policy of assimilation," the premise of which was that "the natives do not need to be understood in their cultural originality. It is the 'natives' who must make the effort and who have every interest in being like the type of men suggested to them." France's approach to assimilation, they argued, "does not presuppose a reciprocity of perspectives. It is up to one entire culture to disappear in favor of another . . . A revolutionary attitude was essential, because it was necessary to go from a position in which the supremacy of Western culture was evident, to one of cultural relativism." Psychiatry in a colonial society had to draw on the lived experience and the values of the colonized; it could not impose a foreign culture as a universal one. Fanon was coming to suspect that the incidence of mental illness among his Muslim patients was directly related to their experiences of dehumanization under colonialism.

Since many of his Muslim patients had been farmers, he encouraged them to grow vegetables, and gave them spades and picks to plant a garden in a soccer field. This was part of his effort to insert them into a world similar to the one they knew outside the hospital, and it wouldn't have raised an eyebrow at Saint-Alban. But in Blida there were still memories of the anti-European violence in Sétif, and Fanon found himself accused of supplying Muslims with potential weapons. A senior administrator who considered him "madder than the madmen" called the gendarmerie, and a barbed wire fence was erected around the field until Fanon forced them to take it down.

But in a sense, Fanon *was* arming his patients with a powerful new weapon, a growing sense of selfhood and dignity, and they became increasingly assertive about their rights. One patient, Ahmed Noui, diagnosed with paranoia, asked why the men hadn't been invited to perform in an all-female production of Molière's play *Le Bourgeois gentilhomme.* "Why . . . make things abnormal through such separation," he asked, not unreasonably, "while many patients are reproached for not being sociable?" In *Notre journal,* Fanon praised Noui's question about gender separation but insisted that "mistrust is not the issue here. The truth is that we have no common theater space in the hospital in which we can gather all the patients together." He then promised, "The day that this theater exists, there will be no difficulty . . . Do not say that the society of which we speak is only a dream; on the contrary, it is very real, but demands to be built with calmness, prudence, and measure."

For all his talk of adopting a revolutionary stance, Fanon remained a painstaking, diligent reformer in his day-to-day practice as the director of a mental hospital. His innovations did not take the place of more conventional cures, such as ECT and insulin therapy. (He was apparently convinced of ECT's "magical virtues," and boasted of having shocked one of his female patients at Saint-Alban ten times in a single day.) He recognized that many of his patients were hard cases whose chances of reintegration into normal life were slim. But he never showed any trace of disdain or condescension toward them.

Much of the work that Fanon was doing at Blida he had learned from Tosquelles. But he was adapting his mentor's theories of institutional psychiatry and disalienation to a colonial setting, and infusing them with an awareness of identity and culture that he had absorbed from Négritude. A universalist method, based on French culture, was no antidote, he realized, to Porot's racist ethno-psychiatry: while Algerians were not different biologically from Europeans, they did not share the same history as his European patients. If they were to be disalienated as men, they had to be disalienated as the "concrete" individuals they were: Muslim Algerians with traditions of their own.

When the French psychiatrist Albert Gambs came to Blida-Joinville for an inspection in late 1954, he was struck by Fanon's use of institutional therapy, especially the Moorish café—"an excellent terrain for relearning gestures of the outside world," he wrote in an admiring description of his visit. Obviously proud of the impression he'd made, Fanon reprinted Gambs's letter in *Notre journal* and responded with existentialist musings of his own: "*To relearn.* I find this expression very beautiful ... It is a matter of enabling the inpatient to reprise, to begin again by helping him or her to understand better, to grasp things better, that is to say, to grasp him or herself better again ... to *rediscover* what has existed. It is necessary to induce the inpatient to rediscover the meaning of freedom, which is the first milestone on the way to responsibility."

FANON'S CURIOSITY ABOUT "what has existed"—about the Algeria that France had attempted to "pacify"—led him far outside the hospital's gates. He made several trips to the mountains of Kabylia, the crucible of El-Mokrani's uprising in 1871, accompanied by either Jacques Azoulay or François Sanchez, another intern. (Azoulay admitted that before these expeditions, it had hardly occurred to him that Algerian Muslims *had* a culture of their own, an indication of the European community's breathtaking ignorance with regard to Algerian Muslim life, even among its progressive members.) It is unclear how Fanon was received by people in the douars, the villages where most rural Algerians lived, but he was aware that he was stepping into a world very different from the mixed city of Blida, a place where, as he wrote, "the stranger is also the other, the one who comes from Elsewhere, the one who has lived under different skies. Hence the presence of the traveler ... can engender a feeling of malaise: he represents the unknown, mystery."

Fanon and his fellow psychiatrists visited communities where marabouts practiced exorcisms based on a belief in djinns, genies thought to have control over the personality of a mentally ill person. Deep in the *bled* (outback), they attended late-night ceremonies where people suffering from hysteria were healed in "cathartic crises" during dances in which djinns were welcomed so that the possessed could be separated, and freed, from the spirits that besieged them. In these ceremonies, Fanon discovered a more merciful attitude toward mental illness: Algerians blamed madness not on the sufferer, but on possession by djinns. An Algerian mother who had been violently attacked by her son would "never dream of accusing him of disrespect or murderous desires," because she knew that if her son were free of the djinns he would be "unable to do her any harm." Far from being a sign of their backwardness, he argued, Algerian attitudes about mental illness represented an admirable alternative to Western medicine, and not only to the racist psychiatry of the Algiers School. The mentally ill person, Algerians believed, had to be "protected, fed, maintained, looked after by his own within the realm of possibility," Fanon wrote, adding, "Madness itself does not command respect, patience, indulgence; instead, it is the human being impaired by madness, by the genies; the human being as such."

In his writings on these practices, Fanon never used the word "superstition." To describe "certain behaviors" as "primitive," he wrote, is merely a "value judgment . . . which hardly allows us to progress in our knowledge of the Muslim population . . . In Algeria it's normal to believe in genies." A doctor, he believed, could scarcely practice medicine among Algerian Muslims without knowing what medicine meant to them—without, indeed, knowing what they understood to be "normal." Yet even as he insisted on the integrity of North African culture, he was careful to avoid the essentialism of the Algiers School. He wanted to pierce the frozen, apparently natural surface of reality. "This society, which is said to be rigid," he wrote, "is fermenting from the base."

The "fermentation" of Algerian rural society was a subject of acute interest to French ethnographers, including Germaine Tillion, who in the 1930s spent three years among Chaoui Berbers in the Aurès, Algeria's highest range of mountains, and Pierre Bourdieu, who did his fieldwork on Kabyle Berbers in the late 1950s. Bourdieu first arrived as a conscript and then stayed on to examine the collisions between the traditions of Algeria's peasants, the *fellah*, and the capitalist economy imposed by the French—the subject of his first book, *Sociologie de l'Algérie* (The sociology of Algeria). As studies of rural Algeria, Fanon's reports from the countryside, a mix of inspired psychoanalytic speculation and anthropological observation, lack the richness, density, and precision of this work. Still, he was making a careful study, on his forays into the *bled*, of Algerian society, taking notes on gender and power, ethnic divisions between Kabyle

Berbers living in the mountains and Arabs living in the plains and cities, and the disruptive transformations that colonization had wrought in land ownership. He was educating himself about the people to whose liberation he would soon dedicate himself.


FANON WAS ESPECIALLY INTRIGUED by the role played by Algerian women in the villages he visited. At first glance, he noted in a paper written with Azoulay and Sanchez, they seemed like captives of an implacable rural patriarchy, members of "a closed society that remains in the shadow of men, who alone are permitted to participate in a truly public society." Yet he realized that women also represented "the world, the others, the unknown" since the destiny of a woman in a traditional society was to marry into another person's family. "Her situation is ambiguous: on the one hand she is subordinate," he wrote, "and on the other, she is someone who causes a man's power to fail." Algerian patriarchy was inherently fragile, because women had recourse to traditional magic to render their husbands impotent if they were suspected of philandering. Impotence was an especially serious problem in a society in which "all deficits of virile potency are experienced as a major personality disorder, as if the man rendered impotent had been targeted in his essential attribute." A Kabyle man afflicted with impotence did not go to a Western doctor; rather, he consulted a marabout, or a taleb, a traditional healer versed in the Quran. Fanon and his coauthors described a number of the cures, based on the writings of the medieval scholar Jalal Eddin El Suyuti: consuming a mixture of Indian spices (ginger, pepper, cloves); ingesting the penis of a fox or wild donkey, for a period of seven days; rubbing the genitals with oil from a vase inscribed with cabalistic verses. "The taleb," they wrote, "combats magical sorcery by a sort of counter-magic—on the one hand, he seeks to replace the sex by a member of an animal that serves as a product of substitution. On the other, he responds to magical formulas by incantatory formulas."

Life in the douars demonstrated the enduring power and resilience of Algerian tradition under colonialism. Far from producing a "harmonious mixture" of European and Muslim cultures, Fanon observed, the

French presence had led to "their simple coexistence, the Muslim citizen often remaining at the margins of Western civilization." To spend time in rural Algeria was to see that it was not, would never be, France. Although he did not predict a revolt, he became increasingly aware of the national awakening that his editor, Francis Jeanson, had discerned in his report in *Esprit*. He could hear it in the "short, acute and repeated modulations" of Muslim women at Blida, as they applauded a visiting orchestra performing Arab-Andalusian music.

The papers Fanon wrote at Blida were couched in a more cautious, dispassionate language than *Black Skin, White Masks*, but they were political interventions all the same, demolishing the mythologies of a racist psychiatry by revealing what lay beneath the ostensible pathologies of Algerians: a stubborn psychological resistance to colonial domination, rooted in an attachment to national identity and tradition. For all his skepticism about Négritude, his suspicion that *racial* identity was an expression of mysticism (if not worse), Fanon was coming to recognize that an identity long repressed could become a powerful source of collective self-assertion.

In one of his most arresting papers, co-written with Raymond Lacaton, another of his colleagues at Blida-Joinville, Fanon reflected on why Algerian criminals refused to confess, even after overwhelming evidence of their guilt was presented. In a 1938 essay, Porot had blamed this refusal on the "tenacious and insurmountable obstinacy" of Algerian Muslims. This "primitivism" was not, he claimed, the result of a "lack of maturity" but of something "far more deep-seated," an inability to distinguish between truth and lies. Fanon and Lacaton rejected the racist assumptions of this theory, pointing instead to the defiance behind the refusal to confess, and to what (in a nod to Merleau-Ponty) they called the "lived experience of the act." In French law, the *aveu* (confession) is not only a signed declaration of guilt; it is also a moral recognition of wrongdoing. The *aveu* is a "way of initiating a reintegration within the social group." But in a colonial society, "there can . . . be no reintegration if there has been no integration." If Algerian criminals do not "feel bound by a social contract," it is because they do not belong to the social group represented by France; they belong to a subjugated nation.

In Camus's 1942 novel, *The Stranger*, a book that Fanon was surely

aware of, the protagonist Meursault, in the trial that precedes his execution, assumes his responsibility for murdering an Algerian Arab on the
beach. But Meursault is a European, and therefore a member, despite his
alienation, of the dominant settler community. The Algerian criminal
who refuses to confess is a man who has been made to feel a stranger in his
own country, so denying responsibility for his crime in a French court of
law becomes his final expression of revolt. "The accused Muslim's refusal
to authenticate the social contract proposed to him by confessing to his
act," Fanon and Lacaton wrote, "means that his often profound submission to the powers that be . . . cannot be confused with an acceptance of
this power."

In a mocking aside about Négritude in *Black Skin, White Masks*,
Fanon had sneered at the idea that people revolt in defense of their cultural heritage; they revolt, rather, when they can no longer breathe. He had
not changed his mind, and throughout his short life he would continue
to belittle Négritude's vision as a "black mirage," a mystical search for
ancient African kingdoms and the fading sounds of tom-toms. But his
experiences with the mentally ill in Algeria suggested that culture and the
ability to breathe were inextricably connected—that cultural belonging,
even clinging to seemingly outmoded traditions, could be a way in which
the colonized body continued to draw breath, and affirm its will to live.
Perhaps Césaire and Senghor, in their celebration of the emancipatory
powers of Black culture and consciousness, had been onto something. And
yet what Fanon observed with growing admiration in Algeria was not the
bookish, willful search for a lost past that alienated him from Négritude.
It was a living culture, lodged in the body, and distinguished by the refusal
to adapt to the conqueror's civilization: the refusal of the mask.

The Algerians, as Fanon saw it, with more than a touch of romanti-
cism, weren't like the West Indians, who aspired to whiteness and mea-
sured themselves—their achievements, their speech, their worth—by the
white man's standards. After more than a century of domination, they
persisted in saying no to the French: to their medicine, to their lifestyle,
to their food, to their judicial system—to the amputation of their identity
that colonialism sought to inflict. Even the lethargy of his Muslim patients
impressed him as a weapon of the weak, a sign of their rejection of assimi-

lation, their insistence on being recognized as Algerians. While he had no desire to restore the lost unity, the phantom limb, of precolonial cultures in Algeria—the ambition of the Association of Algerian Muslim Ulama and other religious currents in Algerian nationalism—he could hear the rumblings of a people who, even in defeat, refused to surrender to their conquerors.

"L'Algérie montait à la tête" (Algeria went to the head), the French statesman Louis Joxe said in 1961. It went to Fanon's. On the eve of Algeria's war of independence, and after nearly a year of working among colonized Arabs and Berbers, he arrived at a deeper and more sympathetic understanding of culture as a bulwark of psychological resistance. He was also developing an increasingly passionate attachment to the Algerian people. When the explosion came in November 1954, Fanon was already rushing toward the flames.

# 8

# THE ALGERIAN EXPLOSION

---

IN AUGUST 1956, at a conference of psychiatrists in Bordeaux, Fanon met the left-wing psychoanalyst Jean Aymé. They spoke about the war in Algeria, realized they were on the same side, and decided to travel back to Paris together. On the train, Fanon told him about his work with the FLN and recounted what Aymé called "the story that would change his destiny." A year earlier, during Ramadan, Fanon had been in his car smoking a cigarette, when an Algerian man passed by and, mistaking him for a fellow Muslim, warned him that if he continued to smoke, he would have "serious troubles." This was an allusion to the FLN's boycott of cigarettes produced in France: first-time violators had the tips of their noses, or their lips, cut off; a second offense could result in execution. (The nose, in Kabyle tradition, is the seat of a man's *nif*, his "honor.") Aymé claimed that it was "at this moment of recognition" that Fanon reimagined himself as an Algerian. "I felt that I'd been designated as one of them," he reportedly told Aymé.

The story has an appealing symmetry. It's as if Fanon, who had been brutally made aware of his Blackness when a white child called him a *nègre* on the train, embraced his mission as an anti-colonial revolutionary when a Muslim stranger *misidentified* him as an Algerian. In fact, well before this incident occurred, Fanon was already providing care and refuge for wounded fighters in the FLN's armed wing, the Armée de libération nationale (ALN). Nevertheless, the anecdote conveys a visceral truth about Fanon's absorption in Algerian politics: his sense that he was personally implicated—that, as a child of French colonialism, he was compelled to side with the colonized.

The Algerian war of independence was launched in the early morning of November 1, 1954, All Saints' Day, a holiday for European Algerians, when small units of poorly armed fighters carried out a series of seventy attacks throughout Algeria. Their stronghold in the east was the rugged terrain of the Aurès, which had never been occupied, even by the Romans. FLN fighters burned crops; cut telephone wires; set off bombs in radio stations, gasworks, and petrol depots; torched granaries laden with cork and tobacco; and raided barracks and gendarmeries. (Insurgents made a failed attempt to seize weapons from the barracks in Blida.) The material damage ran to about 200 million francs. Nine people were killed, and four wounded. The fighters had been under strict orders not to harm any European civilians—a restraint that, as the war became more brutal, would be lifted and come to seem almost quaint. But one European civilian, a liberal-minded French schoolteacher just back from his honeymoon, was killed in the crossfire. Guy Monnerot and his wife were traveling from Biskra to Arris, in eastern Algeria, when their bus was held up by ALN fighters. On board was Hadj Sadok, a caid* who tried to thwart the assault, declaring that he would not speak with "bandits." In the burst of gunfire aimed at Sadok, who was killed, the Monnerots were both shot. Guy Monnerot was left by the side of the road, where he bled to death from his wounds before he could be taken to a hospital.

In pamphlets distributed on November 1, the leaders of the FLN took the opportunity to introduce themselves—not just to their French enemies but also to the Algerian people, who were unaware of their existence. (The FLN had no more than a thousand fighters at the time, and little in the way of money or guns.) They described themselves as "a group of responsible young people and dedicated militants, gathering about it the major-

---

* Caids were local Muslim administrators who were chosen by, and answered to, the French authorities, serving as the eyes and ears of the colonial regime in the countryside.

ity of wholesome and resolute elements." Their purpose was to "take the National Movement out of the impasse into which it has been forced by conflicts of persons and influence"—a message directed at Messali Hadj and his organization, the MTLD—and to undertake "the true revolutionary struggle at the side of Moroccan and Tunisian brothers." Their goal: "national independence through the restoration of the Algerian state, sovereign, democratic, and social, within the framework of the principles of Islam." All fundamental freedoms would be protected, "without distinction of race or religion." French citizens could either remain in Algeria as foreigners or adopt Algerian nationality.

Aside from the FLN's criticism of Messali's leadership, this founding communiqué was a variation on themes that he himself had composed. Not surprisingly, the authorities assumed that Messali, who was living in western France, was responsible for the events of November 1, and placed him under house arrest. Messali, for his part, was furious that another group—created by dissident members of the MTLD's own central committee, the so-called Centralists—had launched a war without his approval. This was nothing less than a coup against his leadership. But he was also jealous and did nothing to dispel the rumors that he was behind the uprising. A month later, he formed his own guerrilla army, the Mouvement national algérien (MNA). The MNA never developed into a significant anti-colonial insurgency, but the FLN regarded it as a mortal adversary, and for much of the war, in both Algeria and in France, the two groups were engaged in ruthless factional warfare, in which thousands of militants were killed by their fellow Algerians. From the outset, the FLN made clear that it, and only it, spoke for the Algerian people, and that anyone who wished to participate in the cause of national liberation would have to accept its authority. In the early years of the war, the FLN's principal victims were other Algerians: caids, MNA members, Algerians accused of collaboration; and, above all, the *harkis*, Algerians fighting alongside the French.

Fanon seems to have needed little convincing to side with the FLN. The FLN was led by young, impatient men like himself, men who felt that their humiliated "fathers" should step aside. Three of its founders (the so-called *chefs historiques*), including independent Algeria's first president, Ahmed

Ben Bella, had served in the Free French Forces in the Second World War. In their decision to break the impasse of Algerian politics, to launch a war against one of the world's most powerful militaries, and to declare themselves the sole representative of the Algerian people, they were certainly brazen, even reckless. Their authoritarianism and their penchant for settling problems by violence were undeniable. Yet by bringing themselves into existence as a movement, they also exemplified what Hannah Arendt called "natality," or the capacity to initiate something new. In *Black Skin, White Masks*, Fanon had sung the praises of natality and of radical initiative, reserving his highest praise for the soldiers of the Vietminh who were fighting the French in Indochina. Now, six months after the French defeat at Dien Bien Phu, the FLN had set Algeria on a new path, rejecting the electoral road to independence and proclaiming its determination to liberate the country by force of arms. The FLN's revolt was not only against the French; it was a challenge to an entire generation of Algerian Muslim politicians and activists who had placed their hopes in peaceful protest and political reform. These men and women were not collaborators; they were patriots, educated in French schools, who believed that the secular, democratic Republic of metropolitan France would ultimately be won over to their arguments in favor of Algerian self-determination. When the liberal nationalist Ferhat Abbas was elected to the second of the two electoral colleges in the constituent National Assembly in 1948, he declared in his first speech, "We have been waiting 116 years for this moment." The second college, representing Algerian Muslims, was inherently unequal, yet, like many of his colleagues, he remained hopeful that Algerian participation in French politics was the beginning of the end of settler domination. Now the FLN—a group no one had heard of—was telling them to step aside. Bullets, not the ballot, would decide Algeria's future.

Fanon had seen enough of French rule to know where he stood. Here was the heroic leap of invention that he had rhapsodized about, and he was electrified. At first, he even considered seeking out the ALN in the maquis and offering his services; after all, he was a decorated soldier, with a Croix de Guerre.

As it turned out, Fanon would aid the FLN inside Algeria not as a fighter, but as a doctor. But to make himself useful, he first needed to establish contact with this clandestine and highly secretive organization. According to a myth spread later by his admirers, Fanon made the connection while treating ALN fighters. But ALN fighters did not simply show up at the Blida-Joinville Psychiatric Hospital. They knew that an active sympathizer was practicing there. And they knew this not because of his pioneering work with Muslim patients, much less because he was Black, but rather because he had been assigned this role by the FLN. Fanon had little love of Algiers, but it was in the capital that he first met FLN supporters, who introduced him to the organization. Most of those supporters were not Algerian Muslims or even European Communists. They were left-wing European Catholics, many of them with links to *Esprit*, the journal that had published his first essays.

IN *THE WRETCHED OF THE EARTH*, Fanon would describe the Catholic Church in Algeria as "a Church of the Whites, a foreigners' church. It does not call the colonized to the way of God, but to the way of the White man, to the way of the master, the way of the oppressor." Yet the church also had its dissidents, who believed that colonial oppression was a betrayal of Christ's teachings. And those dissidents were freer to rebel against colonialism than members of the Communist Party, because they were guided by a moral vision unfettered by party directives: a liberation theology *avant la lettre*. Since the end of the war, they had formed a *groupuscule* of anti-colonial militancy. Their leader was a young, iconoclastic scholar of Latin, André Mandouze, who in 1946 had boarded a ferry in France to take up a post at the University of Algiers.

Mandouze's political outlook was shaped by the Catholic Worker movement, which was deeply critical of Church hierarchy, and by his involvement in the Resistance. During the war, he had helped to rescue Jews, while publishing the anti-fascist Catholic magazine *Cahiers du témoignage chrétien*. His decision to go to Algiers was partly inspired by his love of Saint Augustine, who had lived there. He soon made a name for himself on campus by taking his students on trips to the Roman ruins, the subject of Camus's lyrical essay "Nuptials at Tipaza." But Mandouze was not a follower of Louis Bertrand, or a believer in Algeria's essential Latinity. As a former *résistant*, he felt as if he had "landed on another planet" in colonial Algeria, a place where Pétain was more popular than de Gaulle. When he mentioned Algeria's problems to the chaplain of students at the university, he was told they could all be solved with a machine gun. Even the young Communists he met were hostile to Algerian nationalism.

Algeria's Communist Party was active in defending the rights of the Muslim community, and a few of its leaders were Muslims. But the official position of the French Communist Party, formulated by its leader, Maurice Thorez, in the late 1930s, was that Algeria was a "nation in formation" and had been "forged through the mixing of twenty races." Thorez's melting-pot formulation was originally put forward in response to European Algerian racists, who identified themselves—but not the country's Muslims—as "Algerians." But Thorez glossed over the settler-colonial nature of French Algeria and strongly indicated that the still immature Algerian nation's "evolution" should be overseen by France. The "right to divorce," he said, did not mean that divorce was desirable. Muslim nationalism, the party warned, would divide the country's working class, and play into the hands of fascism. In a socialist future, Muslim Algerians would be free; until then, their role was to fight alongside the European working class.

But Algerian Muslims suffered from colonial and racial oppression, not merely from class injustice, and they didn't see why they should wait for a socialist revolution (led, as usual, by Europeans in the *métropole*). Neither did Mandouze, whose deepest conviction was "the equality of all men." Since the Algerians were "the weakest, those whose humanity and dignity were undermined," his solidarity with them was "automatic." Within a year of his arrival, he had published a lacerating critique of French rule in *Esprit*: "Impossibilités algériennes ou le mythe des trois départements" (Algerian impossibilities, or the myth of the three departments). As he would often put it later, the logic of his convictions had led him from one resistance to another, from anti-Nazism to anti-colonialism.

In 1950, Mandouze created a journal, *Consciences algériennes*. "Algerian conscience," he declared in his opening editorial, "is not possible without a definitive liquidation of racism, and of all racisms," and "without a definitive commitment to democracy." The journal folded, but in early 1954 Mandouze presided over the launch of another anti-colonial maga-

zine, *Consciences maghrébines*. His collaborators were a group of students
at the university who, two years earlier, had created the Association de la
jeunesse algérienne pour l'action sociale (AJAAS), an organization of European and Muslim students opposed to colonial rule; their aims were to
"enrich each other's lives with our mutual differences"; to "move past reactions that have been conditioned by our own race or caste prejudices"; and
to create a space for joint action against poverty, illiteracy, and inadequate
health care in Algeria's shantytowns, and other forms of colonial injustice.
Several of the AJAAS's founders would become leaders in the FLN.

One of Mandouze's protégés at *Consciences maghrébines* was a young
Catholic radical named Pierre Chaulet, an intern in epidemiology at the
Mustapha Pacha Hospital, where Antoine Porot taught. Born in 1930,
Chaulet was from a French family that had settled in Algeria in the nineteenth century, but his work in the AJAAS with Algerian children in the
Casbah had awakened him to the cruelties of French rule and led him
to become a fervent supporter of Algerian independence and one of the
FLN's few European members. His sister, Anne-Marie, who was also an
activist in the AJAAS, shared his convictions and would marry one of
their Algerian colleagues in the group, Salah Louanchi, secretly a member
of the FLN. In March 1955, Chaulet, Louanchi, and another FLN activist, Mohamed Drareni, went to a dinner in Algiers with Frantz and Josie
Fanon. Fanon had spoken at AJAAS events in Algiers and was known to
be sympathetic to the rebellion. Chaulet had read *Black Skin, White Masks*
when it was published in 1952 and had given a copy to Louanchi, his future brother-in-law, with the inscription "So that the masks fall one day."
Chaulet and Fanon spoke all night about Algeria's history, the racism of
the *grands colons*, and the promise of the national movement. "That night
marked the debut of a long friendship and of Fanon's commitment to the
Algerian liberation struggle," Chaulet recalled in a memoir he wrote with
his wife, Claudine, an equally impassioned anti-colonial activist. No less
impressed, Mandouze, the Chaulets' mentor, praised Fanon as a poet, "in
the classical Greek sense of someone who knows how to get something
done, and not merely someone who knows how to write, and more precisely someone who acts in writing, the word being a kind of action."

Through Chaulet, Fanon met Mustapha Bencherchali, the son of a wealthy tobacco grower from Blida with ties to the FLN. While pretending to undergo therapy at the hospital, Bencherchali introduced Fanon to nationalist leaders in Blida. The FLN had divided the country into six *wilayas*, or "zones"; Blida belonged to Wilaya 4. This was Fanon's great fortune. The leaders of Wilaya 4 were among the most open-minded and progressive people in the FLN, a front that included a wide variety of political tendencies: liberal republicans, conservative nationalists, Marxists, and Islamic traditionalists. Fanon was especially impressed by Colonel Si Sadek (Slimane Dehilès) and the commanders Si Azzedine (Rabah Zerari) and Omar Oussedik, Marxists who believed that national liberation would not be worthy of the name unless it led to social revolution and a dramatic improvement in the lives of Algeria's poor, especially in the countryside.* All three of these men were Kabyle Berbers, with close ties to their fellow Kabyle Abane Ramdane, the most influential leader in the Algerian interior.

These men came, in turn, to admire Fanon, who was entrusted with running a covert day clinic inside the Blida-Joinville Psychiatric Hospital, open at all hours to fighters in need of both physical and psychological care. This was an indispensable task: at other hospitals wounded Algerians faced the risk of being turned over to the police. (Pharmacists were forbidden to provide penicillin, streptomycin, or even cotton wool without a prescription, and strongly encouraged to inform on Algerian purchasers.) Here the Algerian wounded were safe: Fanon even prevented the police from entering the hospital grounds with loaded guns. Many of the nurses were Algerians he himself had trained. For them, as for Fanon, the provision of proper medical care was a part of national liberation. By overseeing the care of the Algerian population, the FLN was building a health ministry of its own—the institution of a future state.

A number of Fanon's young interns were active sympathizers of the

---

* Wilaya 4, with its unusually inventive command structure, was also more welcoming of women in the maquis, although female "combatants" were not allowed to fight and were instead designated auxiliary tasks like food preparation and medical care.

FLN. One of them was Alice Cherki, born in Algiers in 1936 and expelled from her nursery school as a Jew in 1940. As a teenager, she had discovered the misery of Algerians living in shantytowns, and joined Pierre Chaulet's group, the AJAAS. "I acquired the conviction that the independence was an inevitable necessity," Cherki said. "It wasn't a utopian belief." She was studying psychiatry.

In 1955, Cherki went to hear Fanon speak at a psychiatric conference in Algiers. The subject of his talk was fear and anguish. She was transfixed. "I'll say this despite how it might come off, because it's true: listening to him speak, I forgot that he was Black," she told me. "He spoke the most impeccable French—more French than the French. And this was also fascinating." (When she told him later that she had somehow failed to notice he was Black, he burst out laughing.) She was struck, she wrote in her own portrait of Fanon, by "the sparkle in his eyes, of a brown so clear as to be transparent." His arrival in Algeria also cheered up young intellectuals opposed to colonialism. Since many of Algeria's best minds were leaving the country—the great Jewish journalist from Blida, Jean Daniel, for instance—Fanon was, Cherki said, among the "very few people we could talk to."

When Cherki expressed her frustrations with the way psychiatry was taught at the University of Algiers, Fanon invited her to come to Blida. There she would meet her first husband, Charles Geronimi, and observe the transformation underway at the hospital. She was thrilled to see patients becoming "more aware of their bodies," among the many liberating effects of social therapy. Fanon introduced her to the music of the bebop revolutionary Charlie Parker, to Freud's first five lectures, and eventually to Sándor Ferenczi's writings on war trauma. She also learned to listen for the unexpected knock at the door in the middle of the night, in case an FLN fighter turned up in need of help.

By putting himself and his institution at the service of revolutionary war aims, Fanon became to the ALN fighters of Wilaya 4 what his mentor, François Tosquelles, had been to the POUM fighters in Catalonia. As early as February 1955, three months into the war, leaders of Wilaya 4 were holding meetings at the hospital. Fanon never explained his decision to cast his lot with the revolution. He simply did his work, as Blida-Joinville, the house of the mad, evolved into a laboratory of revolutionary ferment and innovation.

THE YEAR THAT FANON went into active resistance against French rule, 1955, began with a personal tragedy. In January, his sister Gabrielle, a pharmacist living in a small town on the north coast of Martinique, went into premature labor in the seventh month of her pregnancy, fell into a coma, and never awoke. She was thirty-three. In a long letter to his family, Fanon paid tribute to Gabrielle as "one of the few people in whom I never perceived despair." He continued:

> Even when all the challenges had combined at the same time, she remained solidly focused on the future. There was no scorn of others, no hatred, no pettiness, only that abundant sap from which flowed a balanced life . . . I found out from Joby that during labor, she had an accident. Of course, it would be easy to identify certain errors here and there. But perhaps my proximity to Islam is having an effect on me. What explanations suffice when it comes to death? Is not each death absurd, illogical, grotesque, inexplicable? . . . Gabrielle's death is not just that of a sister. In her I've lost one of the rare women who trusted me, pure and simple.

Eight months after Gabrielle's death, Fanon became a father for the second time, when Josie gave birth to their son, Olivier, at a hospital in Lyon. For all of Fanon's anger at the injustices of French rule in Algeria, he wanted to be sure his son was born in France, to French parents. This decision may seem surprising, but Fanon believed in fulfilling his responsibilities as a father, as his own, in his estimation, had not. And for all the traumas he'd experienced in Lyon, he may have felt, even if in some obscure way, that the son of a Black father and a white mother would have better prospects with a passport showing that he was born in the *métropole*.

At the time of Olivier's birth, the war in Algeria was still mostly confined to the rural east. The French government claimed that it was facing *hors-la-loi*, "outlaws," rather than rebel soldiers or patriots; the "events" would soon pass, like bad weather, and "order" would return. "Algeria is France," the interior minister François Mitterrand declared in November 1954, and France couldn't be at war with itself. (Not until 1999 would the French state admit that it had fought a war in Algeria.) For the first ten months of the war, France could sustain this fiction without too much strain—and with only sixty thousand soldiers on the ground, of whom just three thousand were combat trained. Most of the FLN's attacks targeted other Algerians suspected of disloyalty (or insufficient obedience), not the French. Encircled by the French army, the FLN had arrived at a crippling impasse: Algerians hadn't rallied to their side, and more moderate politicians appeared to be gaining ground, pushing for a peaceful settlement with France.

All that changed on August 20, 1955, when two FLN leaders in Wilaya 2, Youcef Zighoud and Lakhdar Bentobbal, launched a new uprising in the harbor town of Philippeville (modern-day Skikda), in eastern Algeria. To recover the initiative, Zighoud and Bentobbal organized peasant militias and told them that the Egyptian army would be providing air cover. Armed with grenades, knives, clubs, axes, and pitchforks, the militias descended on some thirty cities and towns. Over the next few days, they killed 123 people: 71 Europeans, 31 soldiers and police officers, and 21 Algerians. As they carried out the killings, some cried, "Revenge for Sétif." At the mining center of El-Halia, Algerian workers went from house to house, killing 37 Europeans, 10 of them children. Among the Algerian victims were two leaders of Ferhat Abbas's liberal nationalist party: the municipal councilman Alloua Abbas (Ferhat's nephew) and Chérif Hadj-Saïd. Abbas was murdered by an FLN commando. Hadj-Saïd survived and immediately joined the FLN.

France's governor-general, Jacques Soustelle, had arrived in Algeria in January with a reformist vision of "integration," which recognized the specific cultures of the country's different communities but sought to narrow the social and economic gap between them. A left-wing Gaullist and Resistance veteran, he had lectured on Aztec and Mayan civilization at the Musée de l'homme in Paris, and considered himself a liberal reformer. He doubled spending on education, made Arabic an official language in Muslim schools, and eliminated the oppressive *communes mixtes* (Muslim-majority municipalities governed directly by French administrators, flanked by loyal caids approved by the governor-general). He also created the Sections administratives spécialisées (SAS), a "hearts and minds" program designed to improve conditions in the countryside, hiring as his chief adviser the ethnologist Germaine Tillion, a renowned authority on the tribes of the Aurès. Known as the *képis bleus* because of their blue-tipped hats, SAS members traveled to remote sections of the Algerian *bled* to talk to Algerian Muslims about their local needs and to provide remedies, much like Peace Corps volunteers. The settlers were suspicious of Soustelle. Whether or not he was a Jew, as the rumors had it, he struck most of them as an untrustworthy "Arab lover," promoting reforms that would lead to the demise of French Algeria.

That was before he saw the carnage in Philippeville. "When you see hundreds of people cut into pieces, young girls raped, heads cut off and so on, it makes an impression on you," he said. Soustelle swerved to the side of the settlers, launching a ferocious campaign of repression. More than ten thousand Algerians were killed, once again stirring memories of the massacres of Sétif and Guelma. The Muslim middle classes, who had held themselves aloof from the insurrection, rallied behind the FLN, since they, too, were targeted by the counterinsurgency. A group of sixty-one moderate nationalists in the Algerian Assembly condemned the "blind repression" of the army and championed the "Algerian national idea." As Soustelle himself later conceded, he had helped dig "an abyss through which flowed a river of blood."

Philippeville was a grisly affair. It was also a psychological victory for the insurrection. Before Philippeville, the Algerian war had been a low-intensity battle between maquisards and soldiers in the mountains of rural Algeria. After Philippeville, it became a war between two violently opposed communities: European settlers and colonized Muslims. As Mohammed Harbi has argued, the "social axis" of Algerian nationalism began to shift away from the cities, where French-speaking liberal nationalists had forged alliances with liberal Europeans, and toward the countryside, where the rural masses saw the "physical suppression of the foreigner" not as a crime but as revenge for the humiliations they had suffered over a

"century of colonial despotism." In its appeals to rural Algerians, the FLN
downplayed the idiom of secular anti-colonialism—a language spoken by
intellectuals and militants—in favor of populist Islam, describing its fighters as *moudjahidine* (Islamic guerrillas) engaged in a holy war. This was in
part a matter of practicality, but it would slowly chip away at the pluralist
ideals of some of the movement's leaders by suggesting that the enemy was
not simply French *colonialism* but the French themselves, and that the
revolt's ultimate goal was the expulsion of all foreigners.

Attempts to cobble together a provisional entente—or even an agreement not to target one another's civilians—came too late and were met with
ridicule. In late January 1956, Albert Camus held a meeting in Algiers to
promote a "civilian truce" between people on both sides. To Simone de
Beauvoir, he "had never sounded hollower than when he demanded pity
for civilians," since "the conflict was one between civilian communities."
For all his apparent evenhandedness, Camus opposed negotiations with
the FLN, waiting for an *interlocuteur valable*, a more malleable third force
with whom France could negotiate a political settlement protecting the
interests of the European community.

Camus's political vision for Algeria was hardly distinguishable from
Soustelle's integration project, with its cocktail of liberal reform and counterinsurgency: "The Arab personality will be recognized by the French
personality but in order for that to happen, France must exist. 'You must
choose your side,' cry the haters. Oh I have chosen it! I have chosen my
country. I have chosen the Algeria of justice in which French and Arabs
will associate freely." The "Algeria of justice" that Camus had chosen, however, remained firmly under French authority; any separation of the two
peoples, he warned, would result in "a mass of ruins."

"We expected that Camus would take a clear position on the Algerian problem," said Fanon's colleague Charles Geronimi, who attended the
event. "What we were treated to was a sweet sister speech. He explained to
us at length that the innocent civilian population must be protected, but
he was categorically against fund-raising in favor of the innocent families
of political prisoners. We in the hall were dumbfounded."

Yet even Camus's cautious proposal for European-Muslim dialogue—

and for sparing the innocent—was too much for the "ultras," the most fanatical defenders of Algérie française. A mob of right-wing settlers— shouting "Camus to the gallows!"—broke up the meeting, and the civilian truce project was stillborn. What Camus did not realize was that the Algerians protecting him from the mob were FLN members who had infiltrated the movement. They had hoped to sway its leader, the country's most famous novelist, to their side. But Camus was unwilling, or unable, to accept the idea of Algerian independence and fell into a stubborn, bitter silence.

Meanwhile, French repression—and the FLN's attacks on "traitors"— led most Algerian politicians to align themselves with the FLN. Ferhat Abbas, the liberal nationalist whose nephew had been murdered by the FLN in Philippeville, fled to Cairo in 1956 to join the FLN leadership in exile. Abbas was an Algerian patriot, but—as a product of French schools, married to a Frenchwoman—he had long believed that self-determination could be achieved without provoking a violent rupture between the two communities. Now it seemed that his efforts had come to nothing. "The methods that I have upheld for the last fifteen years—co-operation, discussion, persuasion—have shown themselves to be ineffective," he told a Tunisian newspaper.

For assimilated Algerians who supported independence, the deepening chasm between Europeans and Muslims was sometimes an excruciating ordeal, because to turn against France was to turn against a part of themselves. The case of the poet Jean Amrouche, a leftist Kabyle Berber, is revealing. Amrouche, whose parents were Christian converts, taught French literature and was a friend of Camus. But his middle name was El Mouhoub, and he was an ardent supporter of the independence struggle. In a 1956 journal, Amrouche wrote:

Each day, El Mouhoub hunts down Jean and kills him. And each day, Jean hunts down El Mouhoub and kills him. If my name were only El Mouhoub, things would probably be easy. I would embrace the cause of all the sons of Ahmed and Ali . . . If my name were simply Jean, it would also probably be easy. I would adopt the reasoning of all the

French who hunt down the sons of Ahmed. But I am Jean, and I am El Mouhoub. The two live in one and the same person. And their ways of thinking are at odds. Between the two, there is an insurmountable distance.

Amrouche's predicament was unusual, but the inner conflict that he described was not. Jacques Berque—an Algerian-born sociologist of North Africa and a supporter of independence—observed, "We have not intertwined for 130 years without this descending very deeply in our souls and in our bodies. The depth of the French impact here has gone beyond the usual alienations of colonialism." But when the FLN forced them to choose between the resistance and the French army, French-speaking Muslim intellectuals had no trouble deciding. Mouloud Feraoun, a Kabyle novelist born in 1913, wrote extensively in his wartime journals of the FLN's brutality against other Algerians; he also taught French at one of the "social centers" that Soustelle established to improve the lives of Algerians, as part of his integration project. Yet Feraoun, too, experienced the insurgency as a long-awaited national awakening. In December 1955, he wrote:

Why is it that all of a sudden, an entire population recognizes the existence of a sizable rift and stands ready to make it even larger? . . . The truth is that there has never been a marriage. No, the French have remained aloof. Scornfully aloof. The French have remained foreigners. They have always believed that they were Algeria. Now that we feel that we are rather strong or that we see them as a bit weak, we are telling them: No, gentlemen. We are Algeria. You are foreigners on our land.

While Feraoun was disgusted by the thuggery of some ALN soldiers, he noted with pride that their orders were now "as welcome as any official decree":

There are no cigarettes on the shelves; smokers give up tobacco and no longer have any desire to smoke on the sly at home. Everybody has deserted the French cafés, and you no longer see any drunks stumbling in the streets . . . The mind takes giant steps; the most frustrated among us discuss politics or strategy or combat. We talk about the past and envision the future. We finally feel like men . . . We feel that we are free or in the process of freeing ourselves.

They no longer felt like members of a subjugated, colonized race. This is what Fanon meant when he described the violent drama of decolonization as the creation of a "new man."

FRANCE'S REPRESSION IN PHILIPPEVILLE marked, in Fanon's words, "the point of no return," and it shaped his understanding of decolonization as an inherently violent process. It may also have shaped his (often overlooked) reservations about the indiscriminate use of violence. The massacre had not been spontaneous. It had been deliberately orchestrated by the leaders of Wilaya 2. But the fact that both Algerian peasants and mine workers could be so easily roused into slaughtering unarmed civilians—some of whom they personally knew—was a disquieting indication of the "insurmountable distance" between Algeria's communities, and of the "atmospheric violence" that, as he put it, lay "just under the skin." He would later write, "The very same people who had it constantly drummed into them that the only language they understood was that of force, now decide to express themselves with force . . . To the expression: 'All natives are the same,' the colonized reply: 'All colonists are the same.'"

Given the brutality of colonization, episodes of explosive violence by the oppressed were, in his view, inevitable in the opening phase of a liberation war. He would write in *The Wretched of the Earth*, "For the colonized, life can only materialize from the rotting cadaver of the colonist . . . At the individual level, violence is dis-intoxicating.* It rids the colonized of his inferiority complex, of his passive and despairing attitude." Like Feraoun, Fanon could see that Algerians were acquiring a taste of their own power now that the FLN had taken up arms on their behalf. Violence provided,

---

* The English translation of *la violence désintoxique* as "violence is a cleansing force" is somewhat misleading, suggesting an almost redemptive elimination of impurities, whereas Fanon's more clinical word choice indicates the overcoming of a state of drunkenness, the stupor induced by colonial subjugation.

he thought, a kind of shock therapy for the colonized mind—an exhilarat-
ing rush of self-confidence and energy that exploded the North African
syndrome of depression and helplessness.

Thanks to the liberation war, common crime by Algerians against
other Algerians nearly disappeared; so did folk rituals such as the possession ceremonies Fanon had witnessed. The aggressive impulses of
Algerian society seemed to have been channeled in a single direction:
liberation from France. But violence in itself was no long-term political
strategy, especially if it was anarchic or blind in its application, treating
all members of the settler population as existential enemies. Fanon wrote:

> Racism, hatred, resentment, and "the legitimate desire for revenge"
> cannot nurture a war of liberation. These flashes of consciousness
> which fling the body into a zone of turbulence, which plunge it into
> a virtually pathological dreamlike state where the sight of the other
> induces vertigo, where my blood calls for the blood of the other, where
> my death through mere inertia calls for the death of the other, this
> passionate outburst in the opening phase, disintegrates if it is left to
> feed on itself . . . Leaders will come to realize that hatred is not an
> agenda . . .
>
>   The people who, in the early days of the struggle, had adopted the
> primitive Manichaeism of the colonizer—Black versus White, Arab
> versus Infidel—realize en route that some Blacks can be whiter than the
> whites, and that the prospect of a national flag or independence does
> not automatically result in certain segments of the population giving
> up their privileges and interests . . . The people discover that the iniqui-
> tous phenomenon of exploitation can assume a Black or an Arab face.

They will also discover, he added, that some members of the colonizing
population—he may have had in mind his friend Pierre Chaulet—"prove
to be closer, infinitely closer, to the nationalist struggle than certain native
sons." Violence would have to be "organized and guided by the leadership." It could not remain a murderous rampage.

Thanks both to the Philippeville uprising and France's ferocious response, violence increasingly became the language by which Europeans

and Muslims addressed one another. In their campaign to crush the insurgency, the French army practiced torture, extrajudicial execution, and other "Gestapo tactics," as the journalist Claude Bourdet, a survivor of Buchenwald, called them in 1955. They "disappeared" Algerian activists, raped women, and dropped napalm on civilians. The FLN, meanwhile, tried to organize and channel the anger of its supporters, as Fanon recommended. Even so, the line between resistance and revenge, between justice and murder, was seldom clear. Nor did the French have a monopoly on the use of torture and extrajudicial execution. The FLN's struggle was at once a heroic insurgency against the French army and a dirty war waged against civilians—many of them fellow Algerians.

In his writings on the FLN, Fanon would never explicitly question its tactics. But he was no stranger to the moral ambiguities of the liberation struggle, or to the psychological costs of the war, on both sides. As a psychiatrist at Blida, he bore witness to what he later called the "pathology of the entire atmosphere in Algeria": the dehumanization of the other side, the lifting of taboos against cruelty. Among his patients were two Algerian adolescent boys, thirteen and fourteen years old, who had murdered their best friend, a European. The fourteen-year-old asked Fanon if he had ever seen a European arrested and punished for the murder of an Algerian (an inadvertent summary of the surreal plot of Camus's novel *The Stranger*). Fanon replied that he hadn't. "And yet there are Algerians killed every day," the boy said. "How do you explain that?" Fanon replied that he couldn't but asked him why he had murdered his friend. The boy explained that two members of his family had been killed in a village outside Algiers where French militias had dragged forty men from their beds and murdered them. He and his friend killed their friend, a European, because the French were determined, they said, to kill all Algerians. The conversation went on:

"But you are a child and the things that are going on are for grown-ups."

"But they kill children too."

"But that's no reason for killing your friend . . . Did this friend do anything to you?"

"No, he didn't do anything."

Another of Fanon's patients at Blida was a European police officer who had tortured Algerians, and who could identify "just which stage the interrogation has reached by the sound of the screams." Fanon put him on sick leave, and agreed to treat him as a private patient. One day, Fanon was in the ward, tending to an emergency, when the man came to his home for his appointment. Josie told him that he could wait until her husband returned, but he said he preferred to go for a walk, in the hope of finding Fanon on the hospital grounds. A few moments later, Fanon found him "leaning against a tree, covered in sweat," in the full throes of a panic attack. He drove the man home; on the sofa, the man explained that he had stumbled upon an Algerian who had been tortured at police headquarters. Fanon learned afterward that the officer had himself tortured the patient in question and that, after the encounter, the patient had gone missing. "We eventually discovered him hiding in a bathroom where he was trying to commit suicide," Fanon wrote in his case notes. The Algerian victim was convinced that his torturer had come to the hospital to arrest him.

The psychological devastation of the war left Fanon feeling both necessary and helpless: How could he dress these psychic wounds? How could he fight against alienation in such dehumanizing conditions? And what was his responsibility when he treated torturers—men who had tortured other patients at the hospital? As a doctor, Fanon did not discriminate between Algerians and Europeans: all, in his view, deserved compassion and care. He described only one case in which he broke off treatment: when a sadistic torturer who was also beating his wife and three children asked Fanon to train him to suppress his feelings of guilt while continuing to torture. Fanon knew that some of his professional colleagues were performing a similar service at torture centers like the Villa Sésini in Algiers. This was where he drew the line.

Yet soldiers, and even torturers, were entitled to counseling. Whether victims or perpetrators, Fanon's patients suffered from what he later called the "mental disorders of colonial warfare." Many were survivors of interrogation cells, where they were exposed to a repertoire of torture techniques: waterboarding, rape with bottles, blows from billy clubs, forced immobility, and, above all, the *gégène*, an army signals magneto from which electrodes could be applied to various parts of the body, especially the genitals. They reported a variety of physical symptoms, including stomach ulcers, disturbed menstrual cycles, impotence, muscular stiffness, and fitful sleeping. But the worst effects were often mental: nightmares, feelings of murderousness or despair, a paralyzing sense of depersonalization. Some survivors of the *gégène* were terrified of electrical appliances; others felt as if "their hands are being torn off, their heads are bursting, and they are swallowing their tongue." No wonder Fanon described the Algerian struggle for independence as "the most hallucinatory war that any people has ever waged to smash colonial aggression." At Blida, the war felt like a factory of hallucinations. Fanon's clinical observations confirmed his belief that colonial violence was a far better guide to understanding his patients' illnesses than Freudian psychoanalysis or traditional psychiatry—to say nothing of Antoine Porot's theories about the North African personality. The "triggering event" of the psychoses he treated, Fanon wrote, was "mainly the bloody, pitiless atmosphere, the generalization of inhuman practices, the tenacious impression that people have of witnessing a real apocalypse."

Shaken by the traumas he observed in that bloody, pitiless atmosphere, Fanon wrote in early 1956 to Daniel Guérin, an anti-colonial activist in France. "Every passing hour is an indication of the gravity and imminence of the catastrophe," he warned. "The days to come will be terrible days for this country. European civilians and Muslim civilians are really going to take up the gun. And the bloodbath no one wants to see will spread across Algeria." Fanon's prophetic horror at Algeria's descent into carnage is striking, since he is often assumed to be an uncritical champion of violence, not just by his critics but by some of his admirers. Simone de Beauvoir, for example, would claim in her memoirs that Fanon helped to train bomb-carriers for their missions.

In fact, there is no evidence of Fanon's being directly involved in violent operations. He did, however, act to *prevent* a violent conspiracy against Guy Mollet, France's socialist prime minister. Mollet's Republican Front won the legislative election in January 1956 on a campaign for "peace in Algeria," a slogan that stirred fears of betrayal among European Algerians. And though he emphasized the "indissoluble unity of Algeria and metropolitan France," Mollet promised to pursue complete equality for all the country's inhabitants. One of his first decisions was to replace Soustelle, whose dramatic turn to repression had won him the support of the settler community, with Georges Catroux, who had negotiated the return of the exiled Mohammed V to Rabat in the run-up to Morocco's independence.

When Mollet announced that he would visit Algiers, angry settlers began preparing a hostile reception. One of Fanon's patients, a European woman, told him that her husband was plotting an attack on the prime minister. André Achiary was a violent settler who had been a member of Charles de Gaulle's secret service during the war and had taken part in the Sétif massacre in May 1945. Along with a group of the settlers known as ultras, he intended to hire criminals from the North African underworld to do the job so that the violence could then be blamed on the *fellagha*—an Arabic word for "bandits," used by the French to refer to the FLN.* After learning of the plot—and in a rare violation of doctor-patient confidentiality—Fanon reported it to André Mandouze, who had just returned from meetings in Paris with Pierre Mendès-France, Mollet's minister of state. Mandouze took the first plane back to Paris and briefed Mendès-France. When Mollet arrived on February 6, some sixty thousand Europeans turned out on the streets demanding Soustelle's return, and rioters pelted him with tomatoes while he laid a wreath at a World War I memorial. Had it not been for Fanon and Mandouze, he might have been greeted with machine-gun fire.

But the cries of "Mollet to the gallows!" were enough to leave the prime minister chastened. "From February 6 onwards," Fanon wrote, "we could no longer turn our eyes to France." No sooner had Mollet returned to Paris than he capitulated to the settlers, announcing his decision to increase French forces in Algeria to 500,000, nearly ten times as many as in Algeria on November 1, 1954, and withdrawing Catroux's appointment in favor of Robert Lacoste, who would quickly side with the settlers against the FLN. He also introduced a bill requesting "special powers" against the FLN. "France will fight to remain in Algeria," Mollet announced, "and she will

---

* The use of "fellagha" implied, of course, that the nationalist rebels of the FLN were no more than common criminals, without legitimate political demands.

remain there. There is no future for Algeria without France." Mollet's motion passed on March 12, by a vote of 455–76, with support from the French
Communist Party, which feared alienating the French working class in the
colony. The party would never entirely recover in the eyes of the Algerian
nationalist movement—or in the eyes of Fanon.

IT COULD NOT HAVE escaped Fanon's notice that one of those who voted
for special powers was the Communist deputy from Fort-de-France, his
old mentor, the poet Aimé Césaire. Césaire soon came to regret his vote,
and in October he resigned from the party, in a long and eloquent letter
addressed to its leader, Maurice Thorez. He had joined the party, he said,
in the hope that Marxism would be put in the service of Black people, not
that Black people would be put in the service of Marxism.

Fanon and Césaire had crossed paths a month earlier, in September
1956 in Paris, when both men spoke at the First International Congress
of Black Writers and Artists, organized by the journal *Présence africaine*
with help from Richard Wright, and held at the Sorbonne. Wright had
recently published a book of reportage, *The Color Curtain*, on the Bandung Conference of Asian and African states, which had taken place in
April 1955 in Indonesia, and conceived the event as a pan-African sequel,
bringing together Black intellectuals from the motherland and the diaspora. The sixty-three delegates—not a woman among them, as Wright
fiercely lamented from the podium—came from twenty-nine countries
and included some of the most remarkable Black writers from around
the world: Wright and Césaire, Senghor, Alioune Diop (the founder of
*Présence africaine*), and the Barbadian novelist George Lamming. In a
telegram, W. E. B. Du Bois, whose passport had been confiscated by the
US government, urged the audience to follow the path of socialism "as
exemplified by the Soviet Union." Fanon attended as a member of a Martinican delegation along with Césaire and the gifted young writer Édouard
Glissant, three years his junior, whom he had met when he first arrived
in Paris, as a student. A group of Algerian writers, including the Kabyle
storyteller Mouloud Mammeri and the historian Mostefa Lacheraf, sent a
letter to the conference: "In the midst of the painful events that are unfold-

ing and from the heart of an atrocious war whose cost is being paid by our people, we Algerian writers assure our brother black writers and artists of our friendship and our hopes."

As James Baldwin noted in his report on the conference, Senghor began his speech by invoking the "spirit of Bandung," as several others did, but the focus at the congress was culture, specifically Black culture, and what it might look like with the advance of decolonization and African independence. Senghor celebrated, as usual, what he took to be the cultural particularity of people descended from Africa. For Black people, he said, *sentir c'est apercevoir*, "to feel is to perceive."

Césaire was less sanguine. The violence of colonization, he argued, had subjected Black cultures to a shattering dislocation that no amount of intuition could overcome: "Wherever colonization is a fact the indigenous culture begins to rot. And, among these ruins, something begins to be born which is not a culture but a kind of subculture, a subculture which is condemned to exist on the margin to which European culture consigns it," without any "chance of growing into an active, living culture." Returning to the "ancient civilizations" of Africa was impossible, because Black people in the diaspora were "too distant from them." Instead, they would have to create a "synthesis" of "the old and the new," so that "our people, Black people, make their entrance on the great stage of history."

Fanon was sympathetic to Césaire's position, but in his speech, "Racism and Culture," he all but ignored the subject that was the conference's ostensible raison d'être: the future of Black culture, both in Africa and the diaspora. Instead, he begins with an intriguing, typically opaque observation: "The apparition of racism is not fundamentally determining. Racism is not the whole but the most visible, the most day-to-day, and, not to mince matters, the crudest element of a given structure." What is "structural" about racism, in other words, is not that racism *determines* structures of inequality and oppression, but rather the reverse: racism is produced by those structures. Fanon put it as follows: "Race prejudice in fact obeys a flawless logic. A country that lives, draws its substance from the exploitation of other peoples, makes those peoples inferior. Race prejudice applied to those peoples is normal." Fanon made a similar argument in *Black Skin, White Masks*, especially in his discussion of popular culture, but his focus has shifted here from the white gaze and the lived experience of Blackness to the nature of colonial subordination and exploitation.

In the early era of conquest and plunder, Fanon argues, the colonizer seeks to "make of the native an object in the hands of the occupying nation." Eventually, however, the "occupier" is forced to take a "new attitude," with "the perfection of techniques of production." At this point, an outwardly more conciliatory dispensation toward the colonized arises, a "camouflage of the techniques by which man is exploited." A system of exploitation cannot be built on force alone; it requires collaboration from the indigenous population—hence the emergence of a "'democratic and humane' ideology," promoting cooperation between colonizer and colonized. What Fanon has in mind is France's "liberal" empire, in which colonized subjects could, in principle, acquire the motherland's language and culture, and become "evolved," thereby supplying proof of the universality of the French model.

As Fanon notes, liberal imperialism discarded the "primitive, oversimple racism" that "purported to find in biology—the Scriptures having proved insufficient—the material basis of the doctrine" in favor of the "more refined argument" of "cultural racism." This was grounded in the idea of Western supremacy, its object "no longer the individual man but a certain form of existing" at variance with the "Occidental values" held to be universal, and superior. This does not mean, however, that colonial powers seek to extinguish native cultures: "The aim sought is rather a continued agony than a total disappearance of the pre-existing culture." The colonizer may even express "concern with 'respecting the culture of the native population'"—the idea at the heart of Soustelle's program of "integration" in Algeria. But "this behavior betrays a determination to objectify, to confine, to imprison, to harden." In a remarkable anticipation of Edward Said's *Orientalism* (1978), Fanon argues that "exoticism is one of the forms of this simplification." The admiration of the culture of the oppressed, even an erudite fascination, becomes an insidious way of keeping them in their place.

Fanon mocks efforts by colonized intellectuals to oppose racism by embracing their native culture. In a sarcastic allusion to Négritude, an ideology espoused by many of those in his audience at the Sorbonne, he evokes a colonized person who "rediscovers a style that had once been devalorized" and goes into "ecstasies over each rediscovery." He continues: "The wonder is permanent. Having formerly emigrated from his culture, the native today explores it with ardor. It is a continual honeymoon. Formerly inferiorized, he is now in a state of grace." The problem is that, far from being "grasped anew, dynamized from within," that culture "is proclaimed." And "it is at this point," he adds, that "the incorrigible character of the inferiorized is wheeled out for commentary. Arab doctors sleep on the ground, spit all over the place, etc. . . . Black intellectuals consult a sorcerer before making a decision." In a racist society, racists are often quite comfortable with cultural difference, which can easily be offered as an example of the inferiority, or inadequacy, of the oppressed.

So long as racism exists as a "characteristic whole"—"that of the shameless exploitation of one group of men by another which has reached a higher level of technical development"—culture, too, will remain racist. The efforts of the colonized to reclaim their cultures, and to force their oppressors to recognize their value, are therefore no substitute for what he calls "total liberation." Only then can "the two cultures . . . approach each other, enrich each other," since "universality resides in this decision to recognize and accept the reciprocal relativism of different cultures once the colonial status is irreversibly excluded." Fanon never uttered the word "revolution" in this speech—the last time he addressed an audience in France—but it is the implicit message. Culture will be free of racism only when the structures of racism—colonial rule—are eliminated. Although Fanon could not openly advocate Algerian independence in Paris in 1956, the speech is a powerful illustration of the "Algerianization" of his perspective on racism. Decolonization, he believes, is the a priori condition of cultural reconciliation and cross-pollination.

Fanon's speech must have seemed out of place at the congress. Much of the debate revolved around the differences between the struggles of colonized Africans and Black people in the diaspora. As Fanon would observe in *The Wretched of the Earth*, although whites in America had not "behaved differently than those who dominated Africans," the Black American delegates soon realized that "the existential problems that confronted them" were different from "those faced by African Negroes."

Baldwin expressed an identical view in a skeptical essay on the event, but he never mentions Fanon's speech, and there is no record of the audience's reaction. But an Algerian audience would have had no trouble understanding Fanon's argument that crude, biological racism was being eclipsed by cultural racism, notably in the form of condescending affirmations of the superiority of Western values. Much as he loathed Antoine Porot's scientific racism, Fanon understood that it represented a nineteenth-century anachronism. When the French authorities defended the cause of Algérie française, they spoke not of the underdeveloped cortex of Algerians but rather of Western civilization, freedom, and, not least, the emancipation of Muslim women from Islamic patriarchy, a subject to which Fanon would turn in his 1959 essay on the veil.

Fanon's address would have made more sense if he had delivered it at a conference the FLN held a few weeks earlier in the Soummam Valley in Kabylia, a nationalist stronghold. The architect of the Soummam Conference was Abane Ramdane, whom he deeply admired. Born in 1920, Abane grew up in the Kabyle village of Azouza and attended high school in Blida. He was short, stocky, and possessed of a shrewd, analytical mind. When the war broke out in November 1954, he was in prison for his activities in Messali's MTLD. He had made good use of his internment, studying Marx and Lenin. On his release, in January 1955, he joined the FLN, after being courted by Krim Belkacem, the movement's leader in Kabylia (Wilaya 3), who had to overcome Abane's considerable doubts about the wisdom of an offensive: the decision to launch the war, he felt, was wildly premature.

Krim, whom Fanon would also come to know well, was an imposing figure, of ruthless, Machiavellian instincts. He had been in the maquis since 1946, developing, in the words of Mohammed Harbi, the restless, ever-suspicious personality of a "hunted man." Krim was especially severe toward fellow Kabyles who advocated an explicitly Berber—as opposed to nationalist, Arab Islamic—political project. In March 1956, a few months before the Soummam Conference, his comrade in Wilaya 3, Amar Ould Hamouda, a longtime advocate of the "Berberist" tendency, was condemned to death and executed under Krim's orders; he would not be the last. For Krim, any affirmation of Berber identity was a gift to the French, who had tried to exploit Arab-Berber tensions since the early days of colonization. In this, Abane and Krim were on the same page, and their Kabyle origins only strengthened their bond. Welcomed by Krim into the revolution's inner sanctum, Abane rapidly established himself as the FLN's senior leader inside the borders of Algeria, answerable to exiled leaders in Cairo and Tunis. By spring 1956, thanks in part to Abane, the ALN had nearly twenty thousand well-equipped fighters operating on Algerian soil.

The ALN was also increasing its regional presence, as a result of developments just across the borders of Algeria. In March 1956, Morocco and Tunisia both won their independence. As protectorates, they were destined to reclaim their sovereignty at one point or another, but the timetable was accelerated by insurrections in both countries—and, even more so, by the intensifying revolt in Algeria, which, as an integral part of France, mattered far more to the French government.* Withdrawal from the protectorates, it was hoped, would enable the army to devote all its resources to the Algerian campaign. Yet the loss of Morocco and Tunisia created, in the short term, a more favorable regional environment for the FLN. Both Mohammed V, the king of Morocco, and Habib Bourguiba, Tunisia's leader, would supply the FLN and the ALN with a base of operations. Exiled leaders of the FLN no longer had to go all the way to Cairo; they could slip across the border to a friendly North African neighbor.

North Africa stood united behind the FLN's war of liberation. But the ALN's expansion on the other side of Algerian borders would lead to the development of a vast bureaucracy, dominated by the military forces in Morocco and Tunisia; this so-called army of the frontiers saw the war very differently from the forces of the interior, which Abane Ramdane would lead until he was forced to escape. The split between the interior and exterior leadership would shape the movement's—and Fanon's—future.

The Soummam Conference, which took place in utmost secrecy in dense woodland on the eastern Mediterranean coast, was the opening volley in the struggle between the FLN's two branches. The founding act

---

* The talks that led to independence in Tunisia and Morocco were launched by Pierre Mendès-France, France's prime minister from June 1954 to February 1955. Three decades later, one of Mendès-France's sons would marry Fanon's daughter, Mireille.

of the modern Algerian state, the conference established the seventeen-member Conseil national de la révolution algérienne (National Council of the Algerian Revolution), providing the interior with a provisional government, as well as a five-man politburo, the Comité de coordination et d'exécution (Committee of Coordination and Execution), of which both Abane and Krim were members. The creation of these governing bodies was Abane's response to deepening French repression. But it was also a daring internal power play. Abane had sent messages to exiled FLN leaders in Cairo and Tunis, promising to provide them with passage from Italy to Tripoli, and then to Algeria, but by the time they arrived in Tripoli, they discovered that the conference was over—and that it had resoundingly affirmed the "primacy" of the interior branch of the struggle over the exterior.

Abane believed that civilians and leaders inside Algeria, rather than exiled members of the FLN bureaucracy and the growing army of the frontiers, should determine the direction of the movement. He also argued in favor of extending the war from the countryside to the cities, where most Europeans lived, as well as to metropolitan France: unless the French paid a price in blood, he insisted, they would never relinquish their control of Algeria. The shooting, he further insisted, could not stop until complete independence—including Algerian control of the Sahara, where oil and gas reserves had been discovered—was recognized.

At the same time, Abane stressed the need for alliances with trade unions, women's organizations, and Algeria's Jewish community, a largely indigenous* minority that had acquired French citizenship in 1870. He cultivated friendships with intellectual supporters of the movement, whatever their origins, notably André Mandouze, whom the French would accuse of having written the Soummam Platform. (As Mandouze remarked, the authorities "could not imagine that Algerians were capable of producing such a thoughtful and well-organized text.") "For Abane," Alice Cherki told me, "men like Fanon and Pierre Chaulet were citizens of a new

---

* Although most Algerian Jews could trace their roots back thousands of years, some were descendants of refugees from the Inquisition, while others were from settler families that had arrived in the nineteenth century.

society, a new Algeria that would be founded along pluralist lines." Soon after the conference, Pierre and Claudine Chaulet drove around Kabylia, distributing copies of the Soummam Platform, hidden in the diapers of their infant son.

Abane was an uncompromising militant who sought total authority over the forces of the interior. He had a sharp tongue, and he did not spare the leadership in exile: "If you cannot do anything for us outside, come back and die with us. Come and fight. Otherwise consider yourself as traitors." Some of his comrades—especially in the exterior—would come to fear him as a Robespierre in the making, but his strategic and political vision exerted enormous influence over his followers. Fanon was one of them, and his vision of Algerian liberation would always bear Abane's imprint.

Abane's military strategy, however, helped provoke an escalation of the war that would jeopardize the future of the interior—and force Fanon to leave Algeria. In June 1956, Abane decided to take the war to the cities after two FLN militants, Ahmed Zabana and Abdelkader Ferradj, were guillotined in the courtyard of the Barberousse prison in Algiers, which overlooks the densely populated Casbah. For every guillotined FLN member, Abane said, a hundred Europeans would be killed indiscriminately. ("One corpse in a jacket," he is said to have remarked, "is always worth more than twenty in uniform.") At Abane's urging, the FLN launched a campaign of urban terrorism in what is referred to as the autonomous zone of Algiers, targeting European men between the ages of eighteen and fifty-four. (Algiers had previously belonged to the FLN's Wilaya 4 but could now take initiatives of its own.) The campaign was organized by a baker from the Casbah, Yacef Saadi; strategy and policy were determined in collaboration with Ali La Pointe, a former criminal who had been recruited by the FLN in prison. Over three days—between June 21 and 24—FLN insurgents killed or wounded forty-nine people in the capital. Then, on August 10, a group of European terrorists, including members of the police, planted a bomb outside an FLN safe house on the rue de Thèbes in the Casbah. More than eighty people were killed, and both the safe house and neighboring buildings collapsed in a pile of rubble and ashes. Standing before the people of the Casbah as they grieved for their dead, Saadi promised that the atrocity would not go unanswered.

On September 30, 1956, ten days after Fanon returned to Algeria from the congress sponsored by *Présence africaine* in Paris, the FLN took its revenge in a variety of locations in the center of Algiers, all haunts of the European community: the Milk Bar at place Bugeaud, the Cafeteria in the rue Michelet, and the Air France terminal. The bombs were planted by three Algerian women: Zohra Drif, Djamila Bouhired, and Samia Lakhdari. They dressed in European clothes for the occasion and easily passed through checkpoints, sometimes flirting coquettishly with the soldiers who manned them. On arrival at their respective locations, they slipped their bags under tables or chairs before leaving. Three people died and fifty were seriously wounded at the Milk Bar and the Cafeteria; a faulty timer led to the failure of the attack at Air France. Mouloud Feraoun wrote in his diary:

> There are more and more stupid and atrocious attacks in the cities. Innocents are cut to shreds. But what innocence? Who is really innocent? The dozens of peaceful European customers in a bar? The dozens of Arabs lying all over the highway around a bus torn to pieces? Terrorism, counterterrorism, terror, horror, death, cries of despair, cries of atrocious suffering, and death rattles. Nothing more. Peace.

Daniel Timsit was a young Jewish Communist whom Saadi had hired to build the FLN's first explosives laboratory on the impasse de la Grenade in the Casbah. He had been led to believe that the bombs would be used in the countryside and was aghast at their use against civilians in Algiers.* Pierre Chaulet expressed his horror at the choice of targets, only to be lectured by Abane, who was hiding at the Chaulets' home, that he saw no difference between a "girl who places a bomb in the Milk Bar" and a French

---

* Timsit was arrested in October and spent the rest of the war in prison. He later published a memoir of his involvement in the FLN titled *Algérie, récit anachronique* (Bouchene, 1998).

aviator who bombards a village. ("The rue Michelet," he said, "will be our Dien Bien Phu.") Fanon is likely to have shared Abane's view. He was impressed by the growing involvement of women in the FLN, especially those who passed as Europeans on their missions, like Drif and Bouhired. As he would write in his 1959 study of the independence struggle, *L'An V de la révolution algérienne*\*:

> Carrying revolvers, grenades, hundreds of false identity cards or bombs, the unveiled Algerian woman moves like a fish in Western waters. The soldiers, the French patrols, smile to her as she passes, compliments on her looks are heard here and there, but no one suspects that her suitcases contain the automatic pistol which will presently mow down four or five members of one of the patrols.

In October, Fanon told Marcel Manville, his friend from Fort-de-France who was now a lawyer representing FLN suspects in Algeria, that he was fed up with some of his "intellectual friends, who claim to be humanists" but criticized him "for being totally involved in this struggle." Whatever his misgivings, he was now committed to revolutionary violence as a legitimate response to the everyday violence of colonial oppression.

Fanon's involvement in the Algerian struggle was by now so total, so all-consuming, as to rule out any sympathy for those whose ardor did not match his own. "When you told me you wanted to leave Algeria," Fanon wrote in a letter to a French friend, "my friendship suddenly assumed the cloak of silence." In announcing his departure, Fanon's friend had joked that while Algeria might see another Sétif, he and his wife would not be around to witness it. "Behind your laugh . . . I saw your ignorance of this country and its ways," Fanon wrote, accusing him of being concerned about humanity "but strangely not about the Arab." He continued, "You will leave, but all these questions, these questions without answers. The collective silence of 800,000 French men, this ignorant silence, this in-

---

\* The title literally translates in English as "Year 5 of the Algerian Revolution." The English translation of the book was published first under the title *Studies in a Dying Colonialism* (Monthly Review Press, 1965) and later as *A Dying Colonialism* (Grove, 1967). Both editions were translated by Haakon Chevalier.

nocent silence. And 9,000,000 men under this winding-sheet of silence." It was a harsh verdict, he conceded, but then added, with rhetorical flourish: "I don't want it to be beautiful, I don't want it to be pure . . . I want it to be torn through and through." He went on to evoke the unforgiving lives of Algeria's *fellahin* (peasants) in a kind of Césairean prose poem, while satirizing the justifications for French rule: "What would you do without us? A fine country this would be if we left! Become a swamp in no time at all."

AS IT TURNED OUT, Fanon's time in Algeria was about to end: the involvement of the hospital's staff in the resistance had been exposed. To stay was to risk arrest, possibly torture and execution. As the hospital's director, Fanon was especially vulnerable. Warned by Corsican cousins in the police that a raid of the hospital was imminent, Geronimi was the first to leave for France. At the time, Geronimi's wife, Alice Cherki, was in Algiers distributing pamphlets for the FLN aimed at the Algerian Jewish community, urging them to support independence and Muslim-Jewish unity against the *grands colons*. When her father discovered her cache of pamphlets, he told her to destroy them. "He knew independence was inevitable, but he hoped it would occur peacefully, and siding with the FLN was inconceivable for him," Cherki told me. She packed her bag and joined Geronimi in Paris.

On December 29, 1956, just before Fanon left for France, Pierre Chaulet arranged for him to meet Abane Ramdane and Abane's deputy, Benyoucef Benkhedda: the top leaders, along with Larbi Ben M'hidi, of the autonomous zone of Algiers. Abane had requested the meeting, having heard of Fanon's devotion to the cause from his FLN comrades, but their rendezvous had to be postponed by a day because of security risks: the FLN's assassination, on December 28, of Amédée Froger, the president of the Algerian Federation of Mayors, had set off riots by local Europeans. Chaulet drove Fanon to a location where he was received by Benkhedda and then presumably debriefed by Abane.

Having received the blessings of the Algerian interior, Fanon proceeded to fire off a blistering letter of resignation to Robert Lacoste, the country's new governor general:

For nearly three years I have placed myself wholly at the service of this country and of the men who inhabit it. There is not a parcel of my activity that has not had as its objective the unanimously hoped-for emergence of a better world.

But what can a man's enthusiasm and devotion achieve if everyday reality is a tissue of lies, of cowardice, of contempt for man? . . .

Madness is one of the means that man has of losing his freedom. And I can say, on the basis of what I have been able to observe from this vantage point, is that the degree of alienation of the inhabitants of this country appears to me frightening.

If psychiatry is the medical technique that aims to enable man no longer to be a stranger to his environment, I owe it to myself to affirm that the Arab, permanently an alien in his own country, lives in a state of absolute depersonalization . . .

There comes a moment when tenacity becomes morbid perseverance . . .

For many months my conscience has been the seat of unpardonable debates. And their conclusion is the determination not to despair of man, in other words, of myself.

Lacoste responded with an expulsion order, but Fanon was already safely in Paris. And in January, the Blida-Joinville Psychiatric Hospital was raided. François Sanchez, one of Fanon's colleagues, was imprisoned at the Lodi internment camp, southwest of Algiers. Raymond Lacaton, Fanon's coauthor of the paper on criminal confession, was assaulted by soldiers and tossed into a sty so that he would be devoured by pigs; he was lucky to survive. One of the hospital's Algerian interns, Dr. Slimane Asselah, died under interrogation.

The Battle of Algiers had begun. General Raoul Salan, who had decorated Fanon with his Croix de Guerre, had arrived in Algiers that December as the new commander of the armed forces. A month later came General Jacques Massu, with his paratroopers and a carte blanche to use any and all methods to defeat the FLN. The paratroopers' signature leopard-style fatigues were designed by General Marcel Bigeard, a specialist in "unconventional" warfare who also invented the so-called *crevette*

*Bigeard* (Bigeard shrimp)—the army's term for FLN suspects whose feet had been encased in buckets of cement: once it set, they were thrown into the sea from helicopters. Massu, Salan, and Bigeard were all veterans of France's failed campaign in Indochina who saw Algeria as another front in the war against international communism. They were determined not to allow the "Viets" (as they often called the FLN) to humiliate them again. Massu's men systematically hunted down opponents of French rule, including the FLN leader Larbi Ben M'Hidi and the nationalist lawyer Ali Boumendjel, both of whom were "suicided" in March 1957, and the young Communist mathematician Maurice Audin, who vanished in June—one of more than three thousand disappearances during the Battle of Algiers.* Nearly half of the male residents of the Casbah would be arrested between the spring and summer of 1957. Torture became institutionalized, often practiced by men who had experienced it firsthand in the chambers of the Gestapo during the occupation or as prisoners of war in Indochina. The ALN forces of the interior led by Abane would never recover from Massu's counterinsurgency, which gifted the exterior—the exiled leadership, and the FLN's formidable intelligence services—with the upper hand over the independence struggle.

The Algerian interior that had defined Fanon's experience of the independence struggle went into exodus. In February, the FLN leaders Abane Ramdane and Krim Belkacem fled Algiers in a Citroën driven by Claudine Chaulet. Both men headed to Tunis: Krim made his way overland, mostly by night, on mules; Abane and his deputy, Benyoucef Benkhedda, flew there after escaping via the Moroccan border. Pierre Chaulet was detained, then expelled by Lacoste, and headed to Tunis. The classics scholar and Catholic progressive André Mandouze, whose network had provided Fanon with his introduction to the FLN, was barred from entering his own church, where violent defenders of French Algeria told him that if he loved Arabs so much he should attend a mosque instead. He left for the University of Strasbourg under death threats. That autumn,

---

* The police chief in Algiers, Paul Teitgen, a survivor of torture by the Gestapo, resigned from his post in protest after discovering that more than three thousand people assigned to house arrest had simply vanished.

Yacef Saadi, the Casbah's leader during the Battle of Algiers, would be arrested by the paratroopers, and France would gloat over its—ultimately pyrrhic—victory.

The heroic days of the Algerian interior, Wilaya 4, and the psychiatric resistance against colonial alienation in Blida were over. But out of his memories of the revolt, Fanon would forge a lasting myth of the Algerian Revolution.

# PART III

# THE EXILE

# 9

# VERTIGO IN TUNIS

FANON HAD ARRIVED IN Algeria as a Frenchman; he left as an Algerian, citizen of a state that did not yet exist. Algeria's independence struggle had given him not just a mission but also a new identity. As soon as he landed in Paris, he began to make plans to leave again, this time for Tunis, where the exterior leadership of the FLN enjoyed the protection of Tunisia's leader, Habib Bourguiba. Algeria was now the only country in what had been called French North Africa to remain under French rule. But then, as countless French politicians, of virtually every political stripe, insisted, Algeria was France.

By early 1957, the reverse was also true, for the war had crossed the Mediterranean. Algerians had never been made to feel welcome in France, but now they had become grimly accustomed to arbitrary crackdowns, and sometimes brutal interrogations, in the north of Paris and in the *bidonvilles* (shantytowns) of the *banlieues*, the working-class suburbs on the outskirts of the capital. In this pervasive climate of fear and suspicion, not only Algerians but also any man who could be mistaken for an Algerian risked being arrested. One such case of mistaken identity was that of a young Colombian writer who became unexpectedly familiar with French prisons after his arrival in Paris in December 1955. Gabriel García Márquez's Algerian cellmates distrusted him at first, but "since they and I continued to be such assiduous visitors to the nocturnal lockups, we ended up reaching an understanding," he wrote. "One night, one of them said if I was going to be an innocent prisoner wouldn't it be better to be a guilty one, and put me to work for the Algerian National Liberation Front."

It was not until August 1958 that the FLN took the battle to France, with strikes against state targets, oil refineries, and police officers. But the movement had already designated France as the seventh Wilaya, the only one outside Algerian territory, and it was active on several fronts, especially student organizations and trade unions. There were 300,000 Algerians in France, and members of the FLN's French wing, the Fédération de France, visited the homes of Algerians in the shantytowns and slums to collect a war tax from every adult. (Failure to pay the tax could result in execution.) As in Algeria, the FLN was also fighting a bloody war with members of Messali Hadj's MNA, over the course of which roughly four thousand Algerians in France, belonging to both factions, were killed.

The *guerre sans nom*, "war without a name," appeared to be driving the *métropole* toward a civil war of its own. In June 1958, the crisis in Algeria would provoke the fall of the Fourth Republic, with General Charles de Gaulle returning to power as president. Whatever one called it—a battle with "bandits" and "outlaws," a campaign to restore order, "the events," or, heaven forbid, a war—it looked unwinnable. And it was leading France into increasingly reckless foreign adventures, notably the October 1956 Suez War, a joint expedition with Britain and Israel against Egypt's new leader, Gamal Abdel Nasser, in response to Nasser's decision to nationalize the Suez Canal. The French regarded Nasser, who had provided the exiled FLN leadership with a base of operations, as the puppet master of the Algerian uprising; Prime Minister Mollet compared him to Hitler. The war ended in a humiliating defeat and catapulted Nasser to even greater prestige in the Arab world. The long era of colonial complacency about the "three departments" on the other side of the Mediterranean was finally coming to an end.

Opposition to France's war in Algeria, fueled by reports of the army's use of torture during the Battle of Algiers, began to rise among intellectuals. One of the war's most eloquent critics was a brilliant young Jewish scholar of ancient Greece, Pierre Vidal-Naquet, whose parents had been murdered at Auschwitz. In the course of his campaign against torture and war crimes in Algeria, he would model himself on the French socialist Jean Jaurès, who had defended the innocence of the Jewish army captain Alfred Dreyfus, falsely accused in 1894 of handing over secret documents to the Germans. If French rule in Algeria did not end, Vidal-Naquet feared, the result would be the permanent moral corrosion of the Republic, possibly the return of fascism.

Not all the war's intellectual opponents in France were Dreyfusards like Vidal-Naquet, defending Republican values against their betrayal in the colonies. Some—notably Raymond Aron, a liberal philosopher of conservative temperament who made the case for withdrawal in realpolitik terms in his 1957 book, *The Algerian Tragedy*—simply considered the war an exercise in futility. And then there were intellectuals on the radical left who not only opposed the war but also embraced the members of the FLN as liberation fighters, at once heirs to the struggle against Nazism and architects of a new, emancipated future for the oppressed of *le tiers-monde* (the Third World).* For the most ardent *tiers-mondistes*, Algeria's revolution was a veritable force of salvation, not just for Algerians but also for other oppressed peoples, from the dominated nations of the Global South to the French proletariat, whose silence on the sufferings of the colonized appeared to have been purchased by the wages of imperialism.

The (unofficial) leader of France's *tiers-mondistes* was Fanon's former editor, Francis Jeanson, a supporter of Algeria's nationalist movement since the late 1940s. In December 1955, Jeanson and his wife, Colette, had published an admiring account of the insurrection, *L'Algérie hors-la-loi* (Outlaw Algeria). Taking nearly as many risks as Fanon had in Blida, Jeanson had created a network of activists to assist the FLN. They were known as the *porteurs des valises*, "suitcase carriers," and they worked closely with the FLN's Fédération de France. The *porteurs des valises* smuggled money

* The term *tiers-monde* had been coined in 1952 by a French demographer, Alfred Sauvy, to indicate the historic transformation of decolonization, as well as the impending emergence of a bloc of nations that, like the majority population of the *tiers état* (Third Estate) in France's ancien régime, were excluded from the privileges of the other two: nobility and clergy. The Third World belonged neither to the First World, led by the United States, or the Second, led by the Soviet Union.

and FLN documents, provided sanctuary and safe passage for Algerian activists in France and throughout Europe, and sometimes hid arms. Most of the *porteurs* were French, but a number were leftists from abroad. Jakob Moneta was a German Jewish Trotskyist who worked as a trade union representative at the West German embassy in Paris and used his diplomatic bag to transport FLN documents. The group's forger, Adolfo Kaminsky, was a Russian Jewish immigrant from Buenos Aires who had fabricated passports for the anti-Nazi resistance while still a teenager. In their secrecy, devotion, and internationalist ideals, the *porteurs* saw themselves as continuing the wartime resistance. Kaminsky described himself as using the only weapons he had—"technical knowledge, ingenuity, and unshakable utopian ideals"—to oppose "a reality that was too harrowing to observe or suffer without doing anything about it."

This, of course, is exactly what Fanon had done—with impressive modesty and daring—at the Blida-Joinville Psychiatric Hospital. And there is no reason to think he could not have served the cause in France, as a psychiatrist in the Algerian community, as a writer, or perhaps as an ally of Jeanson in the *porteurs de valises* network. It's tempting to imagine Fanon settled in Paris, meeting up with Sartre and Beauvoir at the Café de Flore, then wandering over to chat with Richard Wright and Chester Himes at the Café Monaco, before returning home for a quiet dinner with Josie and Olivier or going out for a performance of Genet's *Les Nègres*.

But the life of a left-wing Parisian intellectual would no longer suit Fanon, if it ever would have. (Remember his horror at the "larval, stocky, obsolete life" of the middle classes.) Nor did he have any interest in returning to Martinique, as his friend from back home, the left-wing lawyer Marcel Manville, urged him to do. The Algerian struggle—and his proximity to Abane Ramdane and other leaders of the interior—had opened a new and larger horizon than France or his native island could afford him. When Jeanson met with him, Fanon was even more brusque than usual, as if he saw Jeanson as occupying a lower floor in the house of revolution, where the help worked. He expressed disdain for people working in France, even those who'd helped with his passage from Algeria and were now organizing his passage to Tunis. "He was going to Tunis and we did not exist," Jeanson remembered. Fanon, he felt, had a "terrible need" to follow the most extreme path. (When the two men met by chance at the Madrid airport three years later, Fanon was dismissive, belittling Jeanson's work and saying—brutally, but not inaccurately—that Jeanson knew nothing of how the FLN was organized in France: behind the "political façade" was a military leader he "would never meet.")

The difference between Jeanson and Fanon lay in their relationship to France. Jeanson's clandestine support for the FLN was a kind of patriotism, a radical defense of the core principles of the French Republic— equality, liberty, and fraternity—that had never been honored in the colonies. Fanon had once shared that vision: it had led him to fight in the Free French Forces, and it permeated *Black Skin, White Masks*, a native son's call for the Republic to live up to its professed values. But in Algeria, Fanon had come to believe that a new chapter in history was being written, outside France, outside the West, and he wanted to be a part of it. He would write in *The Wretched of the Earth*: "So, my brothers, how could we fail to understand that we have better things to do than follow in Europe's footsteps? . . . Come, comrades, the European game is finally over, we must look for something else. We can do anything today provided we do not ape Europe, provided we are not obsessed with catching up with Europe." He had no reason to be in France when he could be working alongside his "brothers" in Tunis. He did not want to be a fellow traveler in the *métropole*; having been expelled from Algeria, he wanted to be as close as possible to its revolutionary flame.*

ON JANUARY 28, 1957, a day after he was officially expelled from Algeria, Fanon left France for Switzerland, then traveled to Italy, where, two months later, he flew to Tunis. He would never again set foot on French soil.

---

* Fanon's distaste for France was shared by his colleague Charles Geronimi, who, after passing through Paris on his way to Tunis, wrote: "The Parisians cared for nothing but their outings, their theatres, their vacations prepared three months in advance. I came to detest them, to despise all those French who were sending their sons to torture in Algeria and who could only be interested in their little boutiques." Simone de Beauvoir remarked in her memoirs that French soldiers' uniforms had the same effect on her that swastikas once did.

Fanon's departure from France was organized by an acquaintance from Algiers, Salah Louanchi, the husband of Pierre Chaulet's sister, Anne-Marie, and now a leader of the Fédération de France. (Louanchi was arrested a month later.) At the airport he was greeted by the FLN leaders Abane Ramdane and Benyoucef Benkhedda, whom he had met just before his flight from Algeria.

Within days he resumed his psychiatric practice, first at the hospital Razi de La Manouba, then at Charles Nicolle Hospital, where he oversaw the treatment of Algerian soldiers suffering from physical and psychological injuries. In June, he joined the FLN press office (based in its ministry of information at 14, rue des Entrepreneurs), and in September—thanks to an endorsement from Abane, his most powerful ally in the movement—he became a member of the editorial committee of the rebels' French-language paper, *El Moudjahid*, where he worked alongside Pierre Chaulet and Redha Malek, an Algerian from the Aurès, the heartland of the rebellion.

That Fanon went to Tunis because it was where he thought he could be most useful can hardly be doubted. The FLN needed people with Fanon's skills, both as a writer and as a doctor. His skin color would also turn out to be an unexpected asset when the FLN sought allies in sub-Saharan Africa. In his passion for the cause, he had few equals. But it would be a mistake to discount a more mundane, if less exalted, motive behind his decision to head to Tunis: ambition. After the Battle of Algiers, the center of gravity in the movement was swinging from interior to exterior, from Algiers to Tunis. If you wanted to rise in the movement, Tunis was where you went.

It was a gutsy decision. As he knew well, the life that he had chosen for himself in Tunis would be fraught with peril. In late October, just a few months before his arrival, five of the FLN's leaders, among them the man who would become the first president of independent Algeria, Ahmed Ben Bella, were on their way from Rabat to a conference in Tunis when their plane—the king of Morocco's private aircraft—was intercepted over the Mediterranean by the French air force and forced to land in Algiers, where Ben Bella and his colleagues were arrested and sent to La Santé prison in Paris. There was also the ever-present threat of *La Main rouge* (the Red

Hand), a terrorist organization run by French intelligence, whose purpose was to liquidate FLN members.

For the first time in his life, Fanon would enjoy the protection of a bodyguard, a Black Algerian from the south named Youcef Yousfi. A few years younger than Fanon, Yousfi was a veteran of the maquis. "We resembled each other physically, and everyone thought we were brothers," Yousfi recalled. "Since he called me brother . . . no one knew if he was a brother in arms or a blood brother." Some of Fanon's Algerian patients would ask Yousfi why his "brother" did not speak Arabic. Yousfi, who described Fanon as "humanity personified," took care of his car, picked up his mail, and sometimes even passed for him when Fanon couldn't make himself available. "The Tunisians won't be able to tell the difference between two Black men," Fanon said. They even carried the same fake passport, bearing the name Dr. Ibrahim Farès. As Fanon's profile grew and he became a target of French intelligence, it was Yousfi who opened his packages; if there were chocolates inside, he was the first to taste them.

FANON HAD FIRST COME to prominence as a young rebel, marking his distance from Senghor and Césaire, both men of renown in the world of Black politics, leaders as well as poets. But the further he drifted from Négritude, and the more Algerian he became, the more he saw himself as a leader. Algeria made him even more aware of something that Senghor and Césaire had always known: that words could translate into power.

But Senghor and Césaire were leaders of their own people, who revered them. Fanon's wager was riskier. He had enlisted in another people's revolution, in the hope that he would be recognized as one of their own. He was, by some; but true belonging would elude him since he was neither an Algerian nor a Muslim. He would achieve a measure of symbolic power, but he would never be a decision-maker. He was not a member of the FLN's ruling body, the Committee of Coordination and Execution, and was never provided with a diplomatic passport, traveling instead on short-term tourist visas. Nor was he ever a "theoretician" of the Algerian Revolution, whose direction was set by men with guns. His principal role was to represent the movement: to give public expression to its goals, especially for foreigners. (Most Algerians could not read French and got their news from the radio.) The power he acquired as a spokesman would flatter his ambition and nourish his pride; later it would burnish his legend. But it came with a price, since he was obliged to defer to the FLN's positions, even when he objected to them.

This did not come easily to him. For all his humility among the sick and the oppressed, he sometimes revealed a streak of volatility to his peers, an arrogance that he found difficult to suppress. Even in a people's revolution, Fanon was not a natural bureaucrat. And then there was the great prayer addressed to his body, which he could not have forgotten: "O my body, make of me always a man who questions." Fanon's questions had led him to make common cause with the maquisards of the Algerian interior. But in Tunis—the capital of the exterior—he was to learn that some questions had to be reserved for the page, and, even then, with considerable discretion, lest he arouse the suspicions of his comrades, his brothers-in-arms. In any people's army, let alone a people with whom he had no national affiliation, a man had to be a good soldier. Otherwise, he might be accused of treason.

In Tunis, and in his travels throughout Africa on behalf of the FLN, Fanon would write some of his most luminous pages: inspired analyses of Algeria's transformation, searing chronicles of decolonization that at times achieved the power of fiction. He would come into his own as a thinker and a prophet. He would become a hero of the revolution. But he would also become its captive.

WHEN HE FIRST LANDED in Tunis, Fanon was more of a free man than he'd ever been—or would ever be again. He was surrounded by comrades from Algeria: Omar Oussedik, the Kabyle Marxist from Wilaya 4; Pierre and Claudine Chaulet; his political mentor, Abane Ramdane; and, eventually, his interns Charles Geronimi and Alice Cherki, who worked with him for the FLN's medical services. He continued using the name Ibrahim Farès, for reasons of security. But he otherwise no longer needed to wear a mask. He could speak his mind about French rule in Algeria, without subterfuge. So could his wife, Josie, an equally committed anti-imperialist who took a job as an editor at the pan-African magazine *Afrique action* (later known as *Jeune Afrique*). Frantz and Josie had not only married each other; they had married the revolution itself. They moved into a modest apartment with a terrace on the outskirts of the capital, and they socialized among other anti-colonial activists.

Habib Bourguiba, Tunisia's leader, was a moderate nationalist, not a radical, but he was welcoming toward Algeria's rebels, his fellow North Africans, who now had offices in the capital and tacit approval to build training camps and smuggle weapons across the border. (He was also less intrusive in Algerian internal affairs than Egypt's leader, Gamal Abdel Nasser, who had tried to exert his control over the FLN in Cairo.) While Bourguiba ruled with a firm hand, in the early years of independence women made great strides in the workplace, non-Muslim minorities were protected, and Tunis retained its aura of cosmopolitanism and Mediterranean charm.

The Fanons would come to appreciate the pleasures the capital had to offer: the beaches, the superb grilled fish, the well-stocked Chez Lévy bookshop and the Rotonde art house cinema. They were frequent guests at the home of Pierre and Claudine, casually known as "Dar Chaulet," where sympathizers and fellow travelers of the FLN met after office hours. And they became especially close with several left-wing Tunisian Jews, among them the Communist lawyer Roger Taïeb and his wife, Yoyo, a pianist, who threw parties for anti-colonial intellectuals and activists at their weekend home in La Marsa, a coastal town outside Tunis; and their older friend, the sociologist Paul Sebag, who had been tortured by the French during the independence struggle.

Fanon was at ease with the Taïebs in ways that were not possible with his Algerian colleagues, with the exception of his friend Oussedik. (Fanon, who loved to dance, never did so in the company of his FLN colleagues.) In La Marsa, Frantz and Josie would listen to Yoyo play piano while their son, Olivier, played in the nearby cornfields with the children of Frantz's young French secretary, Marie-Jeanne Manuellan, and her husband, Gilbert, a Tunisian agronomist of Armenian origin, who were also friends with the Taïebs. "The Taïebs were older than we were," Manuellan recalled, "but they were old people whose lives struck us as respectable, admirable, and courageous. They were Tunisians, 'citizens of the world,' before being Jews. And despite the rigidity of the Communist Party, they had a certain freedom, compared to the conformist, narrow outlook of the Tunisian bourgeoisie."

Before long, Fanon acquired a reputation for being the most extreme exponent of the FLN's armed struggle, expressing his militant views at press conferences and in unsigned editorials for *El Moudjahid*. The substance of his remarks was the same as what other FLN officials said, but his incendiary rhetorical style made all the difference. So did his hauteur. For example, Fanon made no secret of his disdain for Western—especially French—journalists: "Even the most liberal of the French reporters never ceased to use ambiguous descriptions to characterize our struggle. When we reproach them for this, they reply in good faith that they're just being objective. For the colonized, objectivity is always directed against him." For the members of the so-called Maghreb Circus covering Algeria's revolution from Tunis—Thomas F. Brady of *The New York Times*, Jean Daniel of *L'Express*, Guy Sitbon of *Le Monde*—the FLN's new spokesman was a fascinating enigma: a Black West Indian, a child of the empire who'd turned against the mother country, a man who combined elegance and intransigence in equal measure.

Sitbon, who grew up in a Tunisian Jewish family in Monastir, a port town a hundred miles south of Tunis, often visited Fanon at the offices of *El Moudjahid*. Born Isaac Shetboun in 1934, Sitbon had gravitated to the Communist Party in his youth, seeking an escape from the closed and highly traditional Jewish society in which he'd been raised. While studying in Paris in the mid-1950s, he had developed strong ties with Algerian independence activists, including Mohammed Harbi, who had joined the FLN's Fédération de France in 1956. But Fanon did not see him as a comrade, and when Sitbon came over for dinner he launched into a lecture on the inhumanity of imperialism. Sitbon remembers:

> His formulations were original. He was fervent, seductive, and very theatrical—almost an actor. And he took a real interest in you if you were the audience. But he was also somewhat nervous, rarely serene, and intolerant of anyone he considered a bastard or a traitor. The other

people in the FLN weren't angry. Fanon was. It was as if he were possessed by his anger. I considered Fanon a Frenchman, a Lyonnais, but the essential thing *for him* was his skin—his color was his nationality, because that's how he was identified in Lyon, and he obviously suffered from this.

When the left-wing filmmaker René Vautier came to Tunis to discuss a documentary he had been making about the maquis of the interior, Fanon insisted that it be approved first by the ALN. "A French Communist," he said, could not be permitted to enter "the heart of the Algerian maquis with a camera and then make use of the images he was bringing out without the FLN's approval." Fanon had neither forgotten nor forgiven the Communist Party's vote on special powers.

A few months after he settled in Tunis, Fanon spoke to Jean Daniel while visiting an ALN base near Tétouan, a city in northern Morocco. Born Jean Daniel Ben-Saïd in 1920, Daniel grew up in a lower-middle-class Algerian Jewish family in Blida, yet he carried himself like a dignitary and always regarded himself as a writer, rather than a mere journalist, modeling himself on Albert Camus, his mentor. Daniel had fought with the Free French Forces, like Fanon, and had been among the first soldiers to enter Paris at the liberation. An early convert to the cause of Algerian independence, he had chronicled the horrors of French repression, including the assassination of his high school classmate, the nationalist lawyer Ali Boumendjel, in March 1957, during the Battle of Algiers. In spite of their disagreements about independence, Daniel was, like Camus, already melancholy about Algeria's future under FLN rule, and apprehensive about what it held in store for French-Muslim relations, for Europeans who were not *grands colons*, and for his own religious community. He was repelled by the FLN's violence against civilians, and by its ideological authoritarianism, especially the tendency of some of its leaders to see the French presence as a "parenthesis" that could be wiped away and forgotten. Algeria, he believed, had become a different country after more than a century of French rule, with an Arab, Berber, and Jewish elite that had undergone an extensive acculturation to French norms. Emancipation from colonial rule struck him as a somewhat tragic inevitability, not the revolutionary victory that Fanon championed as "the beginning of a new life, a new history . . . the dissolution of all the chains of the past." Daniel was impressed, but also intimidated, even frightened, by Fanon: "He revealed himself to be attentive, speaking with reflection, above all trying to sound me out, to ask questions, but the interview ended with his radical affirmation of a break with a certain world that for him I nevertheless represented."

That world was France, and the Western imperial order to which it belonged. On November 1, 1957, under the headline "Algeria and the French Crisis," Fanon wrote in *El Moudjahid*: "In the second half of the nineteenth century, one spoke of the 'sick man of Europe,' the Ottoman Empire. Today as well, Europe has a sick man: France . . . There is not an Algerian problem today, there is a French problem." (The paper was not to everyone's taste: Mouloud Feraoun described *El Moudjahid* in his diaries as written in "the pompously idiotic style of a certain regional weekly . . . Poor mountain people, poor students, poor young men, your enemies of tomorrow will be worse than those of today.")

A month later, in a three-part series, Fanon went still further, denouncing the French left for failing to unconditionally support the Algerian struggle, and arguing that in a settler colony such as Algeria, the colonized and the European proletariat did not have common interests, because all Europeans were beneficiaries of colonial privilege and therefore complicit. "The Frenchman in Algeria cannot be neutral or innocent," he wrote. "Every Frenchman in Algeria oppresses, despises, dominates." Did that mean every French citizen was fair game? Gilles Martinet, a left-wing French journalist, remarked that the anonymous author must be "a recent convert to the FLN," with a "taste for verbal outrages and psychological striptease." Taken aback by Fanon's language, his Algerian superiors deleted his reference to "a nation as perverted as France."

In fact, Fanon's accusations against the "beautiful souls" of the French left, and his claims about colonial privilege, were scarcely unprecedented. A similar set of arguments had been advanced by Albert Memmi, a Tunisian Jewish anti-colonialist writer who left Tunis for Paris in June 1956, less than a year before Fanon arrived. An acquaintance of the Fanons' friends in Tunis, Paul Sebag and the Taïebs, Memmi was in some ways Fanon's doppelgänger, although the two never met. Like Fanon, Memmi was an existential radical, an analyst of the concrete, "lived experience" of colonial domination and racism. "Injustice, injury, humiliation and insecurity," he wrote, "can be as unbearable as hunger." Memmi believed that the victims of racism should proclaim their right to be accepted as they are, "with their differences," rather than assimilate to the norms of their oppressors.

Their intimate lives mirrored each other's as well. Like Fanon, Memmi had married a Frenchwoman he met while studying in France, a Catholic from Alsace. The experience disabused him of any illusion that love conquered all in a colonial society. In his 1955 novel, *Agar*, a portrait of a mixed marriage like Memmi's own, an assimilated Tunisian Jew and his French wife settle in Tunis, only to find themselves bitterly at odds. The more she complains about his family's traditional ways and declares the superiority of France, the more furiously he rises to the defense of customs he'd prided himself on rejecting, and the more resentment he feels toward his adoptive French culture. As Memmi put it: "I discovered that the couple is not an isolated cell, a forgotten oasis of light in the middle of the world; on the contrary, the whole world is in the couple." That was, of course, Fanon's argument about interracial relationships in *Black Skin, White Masks*.

In the winter of 1956, against the backdrop of the Battle of Algiers, just before Fanon escaped from Blida, Memmi met with Sartre in Paris and gave him a copy of an essay, "Portrait du colonisateur de bonne volonté" (Portrait of the well-intentioned colonizer). The essay, an exacting critique of the European liberal who doesn't see himself as a colonizer yet refuses to embrace the revolt of the colonized, struck a chord with Sartre, who published it in *Les Temps modernes*. It's not hard to see why. Memmi's well-intentioned colonizer was guilty of what Sartre called "bad faith," opposing the symptoms (torture, injustice) but not the cause (French rule). Sartre may also have welcomed Memmi's essay as a swipe against Camus, who—out of loyalty to the *petits blancs* of Algeria and revulsion at the FLN's killing of civilians—refused to endorse independence, holding out for a federal solution that would leave the country attached to France. Camus, who had written the preface to Memmi's autobiographical novel, *The Pillar of Salt* (1953), evidently interpreted it that way, identifying a veiled portrait of himself in the liberal colonizer who "participates in and benefits from those privileges which he half-heartedly denounces." Memmi and Camus's friendship never recovered.

Yet Memmi didn't spare himself in his account of leftists horrified by the often ugly realities of the anti-colonial struggle they otherwise welcome. Formed by a Western Marxist tradition that condemns terrorism, Memmi wrote, the left-wing colonizer recoils from the violence of the colonized. He also fears that when liberation comes, the new government will impose Islamic law. To remain committed to the cause, he must "temporarily forget that he is a leftist." His choice is "not between good and evil, but between evil and uneasiness," the dilemma that Memmi himself faced—and that ultimately led him to resettle in France.

Fanon shared Memmi's impatience with the French left, but not his uneasiness about the revolt he'd adopted as his life's cause. This may have had something to do with where they stood in relation to Memmi's pyramid of colonial privilege. Memmi had grown up at the edges of El Hara, the Jewish ghetto of Tunis, but as a Jew he was considered closer than his Arab compatriots to the French; occupying a place between colonizer and colonized, he became a student of the subtleties of colonial hierarchy from an early age, and learned to turn them to his advantage.

Memmi's first intellectual model was his lycée professor Jean Amrouche, the Berber Christian poet from Algeria, who showed him that "it was possible to be born poor and African and to transform oneself into a cultivated and well-dressed man." But he came to see Amrouche, a man who felt torn between his Algerian and French selves, as paralyzed by his failure to break with the world of the East—the world of Memmi's own father. Memmi, for his part, looked to France and the West. The love was not always requited. While studying philosophy at the University of Algiers, Memmi was excluded under Vichy's antisemitic laws, as Fanon's colleague Alice Cherki had been from her nursery school. In *The Pillar of Salt*, Memmi's alter ego, Alexandre Mordechai Benillouche, reflects: "I wanted to reject with all my indignation this new image of France, but, after all, the gendarmes were as French as Descartes and Racine."

Later, at the Sorbonne, Memmi heard a rumor that, as a Tunisian "native," he might not be permitted to sit for the examination in philosophy. When the revolt against French rule in Tunisia broke out, Memmi be-

came a militant in the independence movement and founded the nationalist newspaper *Action*, edited from prison by Bourguiba. Yet his belief in
French republicanism and his conviction that he was ultimately better off
in the *métropole* than in an independent, Muslim-ruled Tunisia were un-
diminished. "As a Tunisian Jew of French culture on the left," he wrote in
his diary, "I belong to a French culture and it's too late for me to change
that . . . I neither wish to nor can I allow myself to espouse a hatred or pure
anti-French passion that I don't feel." He decided to "help the North Africans to win their freedom, even if this freedom not only doesn't benefit us,
but even risks hurting us." He observed that "historical responsibility and
interests don't always coincide." After taking part in Tunisia's liberation,
Memmi sold his home and settled in Paris.

   Fanon's upbringing was more middle-class, but he bore the stigma of
his color; the wound of betrayal by the Republic for which he had fought as
a young man would never heal. Not only would he never be mistaken for a
white Frenchman, but—as he learned while sitting in his car in Blida—he
could be easily mistaken for an Algerian Muslim. Unlike Memmi, he no
longer considered himself a member of an eternal minority, condemned
to search for the home that would best ensure his clan's security. Thanks
to the Algerian Revolution and the rise of other independence movements
against colonialism, he reimagined himself as part of a new majority—
Black, brown, and yellow—that would cleanse the world of racism and imperialism. The "damned" would one day inherit the earth; the last would
be first. While Fanon's understanding of colonial oppression continued to
be grounded in his psychiatric work, his vision of disalienation as a revolutionary politics would acquire an increasingly utopian—even messianic—
cast in his last years.

   Fanon manifested all the zeal of a convert or, perhaps more to the
point, of an *assimilé*. Just as his French was more perfect than that of the
French, so now he was more Algerian than the Algerians. According to
Harbi (who later came to know him in Tunis while working for the FLN's
foreign ministry), "Fanon had a very strong need to belong."

   The rhetorical fervor of Fanon's attacks on the French left reflected
his alliance with Abane Ramdane, who had been urging the editors of *El
Moudjahid* to adopt a harder line. Abane believed that the FLN should

form commandos inside Wilaya 7—that is, France—not only to reduce pressure on the interior but also to force the French of the *métropole* to pay a price for the war's continuation. The Fédération de France's leaders, including Harbi, opposed this move, not because they ruled out attacks in France but because the Algerian diaspora in France was simply not ready for the repression that was sure to follow. This was also the view of the FLN's historic leaders, whose plane had been hijacked the year before and who were now imprisoned in Paris. In a letter written from La Santé in the fall of 1957 to their colleagues in the exterior, Ahmed Ben Bella, Hocine Aït-Ahmed, Mohamed Boudiaf, and Mohamed Khider argued that such a decision failed to acknowledge the "economic, moral and human conditions in which Algerian migrants live." To launch a war inside France was to expose Algerian immigrants, living in "already precarious conditions," to the "chauvinist hostility of the entire country," possibly to anti-Algerian pogroms. The organization needed to sow division inside France and cultivate potential allies—whether or not they embraced the FLN's every move—not to turn the entire country against the Algerian cause. Armed struggle, by then, was only one part of the FLN's strategy for achieving independence, and the role the organization played after the Battle of Algiers would become increasingly symbolic. The FLN leadership knew that it could never defeat the French on the battlefield. It needed to wage a "diplomatic revolution," as the historian Matthew Connelly has put it, exploiting France's political weaknesses on the international stage. The main arena was the United Nations General Assembly, which opened the first debate on Algeria's future in February 1957.

One of the diplomatic revolution's most effective leaders was the FLN's representative at the United Nations, M'hammed Yazid, an amiable and garrulous native of Blida who worked out of the FLN's office on East Fifty-Sixth Street in New York City. Even as the French army dismantled the FLN during the Battle of Algiers, Yazid and his colleague Abdelkader Chanderli, both fluent English speakers, were wooing Senator John F. Kennedy. After Yazid and Chanderli's briefing, Kennedy gave an impressively informed address on the Senate floor on July 2, 1957, in which he came out in favor of Algerian self-determination and declared that the United States should not base its policies on "the myth of French empire."

The Algerian crisis, he concluded, "touches the most vital interests of all the free world—NATO, the emergent proposals for a common market for Europe, Euratom and the precarious growth of the new states of Africa. All of these great enterprises and visions will, I fear, come to nothing if we cannot close the Algerian wound."

Kennedy's speech infuriated the French; two days later, a bomb exploded outside the US consulate in Algiers. But it was a major victory for the FLN. Men like Yazid were, increasingly, the public face of the Algerian nationalist movement: sophisticated, urbane diplomats who favored suits over guerrilla fatigues. They were nationalists more than revolutionaries; their goal was to force France to withdraw, not to condemn it as a nation. While they were keen to court the support of newly independent nations in the former colonial world, they did so for a single, pragmatic reason: to secure Algeria's freedom from French rule. Once the French let go of Algeria, they saw no reason not to have good relations with their former occupiers. After all, they had known each other for more than a century: in Fanon's words, "The colonizer and the colonized are old acquaintances."

When the provisional government—the Gouvernement provisoire de la république algérienne (GPRA)—was formed in the fall of 1958, with Ferhat Abbas as president and Krim Belkacem as vice president, Yazid became its minister of information and replaced Fanon as the FLN's media spokesman. Although Fanon continued to write for *El Moudjahid*, his columns were closely monitored; in one case the paper was called back from the printer because of objections to his language. Yet he continued to rise within the movement: his incendiary rhetoric might be questioned, but not his dedication to the cause.

FANON WROTE IN *The Wretched of the Earth*:

> For the people, only fellow nationals are ever owed the truth. No absolute truth, no discourse on the transparency of the soul can erode this position. In answer to the lie of the colonial situation, the colonized subject responds with a lie. Behavior toward fellow nationalists is open and honest, but strained and indecipherable toward the colonists.

> Truth is what hastens the dislocation of the colonial regime, what fos-
> ters the emergence of the nation. Truth is what protects the "natives"
> and undoes the foreigners. In the colonial context there is no truthful
> behavior. And good is quite simply what hurts *them* most.

The elasticity of truth in conditions of colonial warfare was no abstract
matter for Fanon. As an FLN spokesman, he was entrusted with articulating the FLN's views, and he did so faithfully.

In his first public statement in Tunis, Fanon denied allegations that, in
May 1957, the FLN had been behind the killing of more than three hundred villagers in the small hamlet of Mechta Kasbah, outside the mountain
village of Melouza. In fact, no direct order from the leadership* was given
for the slaughter in Melouza, which was carried out by ALN soldiers at the
initiative of Mohammedi Saïd, the brutal head of Wilaya 3, who, like many
regional commanders, enjoyed considerable discretion, especially when
it came to the punishment of suspected traitors. But the rogue nature of
the operation was also a potential embarrassment, since it gave the lie to
the notion of a unified command structure. The victims, moreover, were
Algerian Muslims whose only crime had been to support a different rebel
group, Messali Hadj's MNA. Although only a small offshoot of the Messalists made common cause with the French, the FLN regarded all MNA
supporters as traitors, and so did Fanon.

The French press published horrifying spreads of the Melouza massacre, as it became known; the government cited the atrocities as evidence
of the barbarism of the *fellagha*. The FLN, in turn, blamed the French, but
its responsibility soon became clear, even to observers who supported the
rebellion. One of Fanon's acquaintances in Tunis, Mohamed Ben Smaïl—a
member of the Maghreb Circus writing for *Afrique action*, where Josie
Fanon worked—went to Melouza to investigate. Even though he blamed
the French in his report, he told his press colleagues that the FLN had
committed the massacre. Jean Daniel signed a petition on Melouza in *Le
Monde*, urging the FLN to renounce terror against civilians. As the French

---

* It is unlikely that the FLN's executive branch, the Committee of Coordination and Execution, had any prior knowledge of the attack on Melouza.

government and the FLN accused each other of responsibility, the novelist Mouloud Feraoun pleaded in his diary:

> Gentlemen of the FLN, gentlemen of the Fourth Republic, do you think that a drop of your blood is really worth anything more than a drop of anyone else's blood—blood that, because of you, is being shed on the soil of Algeria? Do you truly believe that, with your dirty hands, you are going to build the better future that you are promising with your hysterical speeches?

According to Charles Geronimi, Fanon knew that the FLN was responsible. And in *L'An V de la révolution algérienne* he would implicitly acknowledge the FLN's responsibility: "The French ministers Lacoste and Soustelle have published photographs with a view to sullying our cause. Some of these photographs show things done by members of our revolution." Yet he quickly alluded to "other photographs that show some of the thousands of crimes" committed by the French army's Algerian collaborators, and the "tens of thousands of Algerian men and women who have been and continue to be victims of the French troops. No, it is not true that the Revolution has gone to the lengths to which colonialism has gone." Still, he went on, "because we want a democratic and a renovated Algeria, because we believe one cannot rise and liberate oneself in one area and sink in another, we condemn, with pain in our hearts, those brothers who have flung themselves into revolutionary action with the almost physiological brutality that centuries of oppression nourish and give rise to." But the Melouza massacre was a case not so much of "revolutionary action" against colonialism as of score-settling in a civil war: a troubling reminder of lingering divisions among Algerians.*

At his press conference on June 5, 1957, Fanon performed his duty, disavowing the FLN's responsibility and denouncing the "foul machinations over Melouza, which are intended to discredit the National Liberation Front

---

* Mohammedi Saïd, the ALN commander who presided over the massacre, acknowledged his responsibility in the 1991 documentary *Les Années algériennes*: "Our first enemy wasn't the French soldier, it was the traitor among us."

in the eyes of the civilized world." The French, he argued, were exploiting the massacre to distract attention from their own atrocities in rural Algeria, where the army was waging a ruthless counterinsurgency. He was not wrong. Over the course of the war, more than two million villagers—nearly half the rural population—were forcibly evicted from their homes and moved into *camps de regroupement* (resettlement camps). Their villages were declared *zones interdites* (forbidden zones), where anyone who remained could be killed as a rebel; their governing councils, known as *djema'a*, were dismantled. Soldiers set fire to forests, raped women, destroyed harvests and livestock, and used napalm. In their letters home, some soldiers compared the scenes they had witnessed to the massacre at Oradour-sur-Glane, a village in the Limousin where the Germans had responded to the capture of one of their officers by killing almost all its inhabitants.

The official aim of "resettlement" was to protect villagers from the FLN, but the real purpose—as the sociologist Pierre Bourdieu and his Algerian colleague Abdelmalek Sayad wrote in their 1964 book, *Le Déracinement* (*Uprooting*)—was to disintegrate the native social order in order to subordinate it. Resettlement was a repetition of the nineteenth-century war of "pacification," a continuation of France's *mission civilisatrice*. Now France was brandishing the truth about Melouza in defense of a lie: the myth of Algérie française.

In wartime, truth is whatever hurts the other side most, and Fanon remained a good soldier. In any case, he had few other options: he was the spokesman of a secretive and authoritarian organization that did not hesitate to punish—and eliminate—members who disobeyed orders or were thought to threaten its unity. In his 1982 memoir, *Nour le voilé*,* the French radical Serge Michel, one of Fanon's colleagues at *El Moudjahid*, gave a vivid account of the paranoid atmosphere that spread through FLN circles in Tunis. Born Lucien Douchet in 1922 to parents of Polish origin, Michel had changed his name in homage to two of his heroes: the Russian-born revolutionary writer and dissident Victor Serge and the anarchist leader Louise Michel. Like Fanon, he was an "adoptive" Algerian, hav-

---

* Nour the Veiled One.

ing joined the FLN while living in Algeria in the mid-1950s and earned
the trust of its leaders. (Abane Ramdane described him rather poetically
as "sleeping on a cloud, fragile, without protection and belonging to no
clan.") Michel had fled to France after learning that the army was about
to arrest him; sheltered in Paris by Colette Jeanson, he was driven across
the border to Switzerland, where he edited the pro-FLN journal *Résistances algériennes* until he could make his way safely to Tunis. "Don't trust
anyone and watch your skin," an Algerian colleague told him when he
arrived. "Here everyone barricades themselves with a smile, the better to
show their teeth. Always ready to bite. There is no real power yet, but all
the chiefs, with the clients, are already on the lookout. Tunis was, and still
is in part, our sanctuary; but if we let them, it will be our common grave.
They will fight to throw the first shovelful on our corpses."

Even more than his Algerian brothers, Fanon had to constantly renew
his pledge to the organization. However often the words "we Algerians"
appeared in his articles for *El Moudjahid*, he remained an outsider, and
in the wake of Melouza his position in the movement was suddenly more
delicate, since Abane Ramdane had begun to lose ground in the intensifying power struggles that pitted the internal maquis against the exterior
leadership.* Abane's personal integrity, daring, and political modernism
had earned him a passionate following among left-leaning FLN militants,
Fanon among them. But he was also explosive—possibly due in part to an
undiagnosed ulcer—and did little to conceal his contempt for the military and intelligence officers based in Tunis who, since the defeat in the
Battle of Algiers, had gained the upper hand. The most influential of these
men was Abdelhafid Boussouf, who had been the commanding colonel
of Wilaya 5 (in western Algeria, including the coastal city of Oran) and
was now the head of intelligence. In Tunis, a group of powerful men—
including Boussouf's childhood friend Lakhdar Bentobbal, one of the
leaders of the uprising in Philippeville, and Abane's ally from the interior, Krim Belkacem—had closed ranks around him. They were known as
"Boussouf's boys." Boussouf, who wore a small mustache with a reddish

---

* Abane was still seen as a member of the interior, even though he no longer operated
inside Algeria.

tint and thick glasses, divided his time between Tunis; the FLN base in
Tripoli, Libya; and a clandestine arms factory in Morocco, built by the
Greek Trotskyist Michel Raptis, alias Pablo. A deeply conspiratorial and
secretive man with strong ties to the exiled military leadership, Boussouf
saw Abane, the charismatic architect of the Soummam Conference and an
unyielding champion of the interior, as a thorn in his side. At a meeting
of the FLN's central committee in August 1957, the two men clashed over
the movement's direction.

Abane reportedly complained to Ferhat Abbas that Boussouf's boys
were "Oriental despots in the making," "the negation of the freedom and
democracy we want to establish in an independent Algeria." He concluded,
"I will not march for such a future." Abbas urged him to calm down, suggesting that he spend some time in a spa in Switzerland. Abane replied
by tapping the butt of his pistol and threatening to return to the maquis.
"You are building a power based on the army," he said. "The maquis is
one thing, politics is another, and it is not conducted by illiterates or
ignoramuses"—a clear allusion to Boussouf.

But for all his bravado, Abane was arguing from a position of weakness. The interior had been devastated by Jacques Massu's paratroopers.
And in September 1957, just as the Battle of Algiers ended, the French
would complete the construction of the Morice Line, an eight-foot-high
barbed wire fence, named after France's defense minister, André Morice,
running along the entirety of Algeria's borders with Tunisia and Morocco,
and designed to prevent incursions and weapons shipments by the ALN.
It was guarded by eight thousand troops; on each side lay a minefield
forty-five meters wide. Within six months of its completion, six thousand
FLN militants would die trying to cross it. Thanks to these developments,
the center of gravity in Algeria's struggle for independence now lay with
the exiled military leadership, not Abane's legendary interior. Even Krim,
his fellow Kabyle, who had invited him to join the FLN, began to take his
distance from him.

Fanon admired Krim, whom he considered an authentic man of the
people, but he otherwise shared Abane's overall view of the leaders in
Tunis, disparaging them as "goat herders." He distrusted Boussouf and
Bentobbal. "The idea of a secular state, or of socialism, the idea of man,

for that matter, these are things that are entirely alien to them," he told Ferhat Abbas. But the left-wing maquisards of Wilaya 4, whom Fanon considered the vanguard of Algeria's struggle, were a minority current in the FLN. And they would be increasingly eclipsed by populists like Bentobbal and Boussouf, whose aim was the restoration of Muslim Algeria, not social revolution—especially if the latter led to changes in Algerian cultural practices, around gender and the family, that might challenge traditional mores.

In late December, Krim Belkacem and Mahmoud Chérif, a colonel in the ALN, accompanied Abane to Morocco, where Abane had been told there would be a summit conference with King Mohammed V. (Bentobbal gave his approval but chose to stay in Tunis.) They were picked up in Tétouan by Boussouf and two other men. The car drove toward Tangier but then stopped at a farm, where Abane was ordered out. Krim told Boussouf that Abane was to be imprisoned, on instructions from the central committee. "I haven't got a prison here," Boussouf replied. Abane was strangled to death.

The Boussouf boys took joint responsibility for the murder of one of their brothers—a man who, as they saw it, threatened to impose a cult of personality on a movement explicitly based on collective leadership. When Ferhat Abbas, who had learned of the murder from Mahmoud Chérif, confronted Abane's killers in Tunis a few weeks later, Krim and Boussouf both claimed that they had saved the revolution by eliminating a potential dictator. "Who made you judges?" Abbas asked. "I resign!" He did not. But he would be pushed aside in the leadership and eventually expelled from the FLN, which he went on to accuse of having confiscated Algeria's independence. (Many years later, Krim, who had gone into exile following the post-independence military coup in 1965, would be found strangled in a hotel room in Frankfurt.)

Five months after Abane's murder, Fanon's paper, El Moudjahid, announced that Abane had died in battle on the "field of honor." The leader of the interior no longer stood in the way. The exterior, also known as the army of the frontiers, would now evolve into a para-state, preparing to take power after independence; nearly half of Tunisia was occupied by ALN fighters. Fanon, who was close enough to the intelligence services to know of his friend's murder, was deeply shaken; shortly before his own death, he would confess to Sartre and Beauvoir that he felt personally responsible for Abane's. But in Tunis he remained silent. And in his remaining years he would develop an increasingly intense relationship with the army of the frontiers, for the sake of the revolution and, perhaps, to protect himself: according to Harbi, his name was on a list of those to be executed in the event of an internal challenge to the FLN leadership.* Fanon's dilemma was, of course, not his alone: in the Algerian struggle, as in most insurrectionary movements, the ultimate measure of commitment was the willingness to get one's hands dirty, even to betray one's most cherished ethical principles, for the cause.

By the end of 1958, the leadership would find a new assignment for Abane's protégé, the Algerian from Fort-de-France, but it would be far from North Africa.

Abane's death marked a turning point in the Algerian struggle for independence. But executions of this kind were not uncommon, and they were usually carried out by a group of people, not a single individual, so that responsibility was shared among les frères, the brothers, who never spoke of what they had done. In his memoir, the ALN signals operator Mokhtar Mokhtefi recalls that when two soldiers were accused of making plans to desert a base, trainees were obliged to take part in their killing. The result was a climate of fear, typical of the internal culture of revolutionary movements, that Sartre would later identify as "fraternity-terror"—a concept that resonated powerfully with Fanon.

---

* In his memoir, Une vie debout: Mémoires politiques (La Découverte, 2001), Harbi, who also knew the truth about Abane's death, remembers seeing Abane's baby boy, Hacène, in the arms of Krim, one of his father's murderers. "The vision of one of those responsible for Abane's assassination playing with his son," he wrote, "troubled me profoundly."

# 10

# DISALIENATING PSYCHIATRY

---

AS FANON WAS LEARNING, the life of an anti-colonial revolutionary meant an acceptance of revolutionary discipline, and therefore of secrecy, silence, and denial: repressive responses to trauma that most psychoanalysts would consider an obstacle to treatment, if not to mental health itself. Yet his time in Tunis turned out to be his most creative and innovative as a doctor. As Boussouf's boys took over the reins of the Algerian movement, Fanon pursued an ever more revolutionary course as a psychiatrist, carving out a space of autonomy and freedom that he had voluntarily renounced as an FLN spokesman.

His first position was at the Manouba clinic, a psychiatric hospital in a suburb of Tunis, founded by his old nemesis, Antoine Porot. It did not go well. While the Manouba was a handsome facility, with elegant lawns and flower beds, its long-term patients reminded Fanon of the gaunt, unshaven men he had seen when he arrived in Blida. Intent on introducing François Tosquelles's methods to Tunisia, Fanon made a request for funds for occupational therapy. When his request was denied by the hospital's director, Tahar Ben Soltane, he went to see Tunisia's minister of health.

According to Albert Memmi, Ben Soltane, who had replaced the hospital's French director at independence, was a "jovial and friendly" man, but he was also intellectually insecure, and intimidated by Fanon's expertise in

the new psychiatry. Having spent years waiting for a promotion, he bitterly
resented having his authority questioned by the new doctor from the West
Indies, whom he referred to as *le nègre*.* He eventually accused Fanon of
spying for Israel and of mistreating patients on Israeli orders: it was as
good as calling for his liquidation. The head of the FLN health services
promised that those involved in the "Zionist plot" would be executed.
Fanon was, indeed, closer to the Jewish doctors on staff, notably Lucien
Lévy, a Communist, than he was to the Arabs, but Ben Soltane's only
"proof" of Fanon's Zionist connections was his writing on antisemitism.
The charges were dismissed.

But by the end of 1957, Fanon had left Manouba for the psychiatric
services of the Charles Nicolle Hospital, in the center of Tunis, where
he was soon joined by a group of young doctors working for the FLN:
Geronimi and Cherki, his interns from Blida (now married to each other),
and the French surgeon Michel Martini, who had arrived in Tunis from
Algeria after spending nearly a year in prison for aiding the FLN. Fanon
grew especially close to Cherki, a small, elegant woman, half the height of
her tall, dashing husband, with (in Martini's words) "lively and brilliant
eyes, an allure of prying and curious smiles, with high cheekbones and a
slightly curved forehead."

The Charles Nicolle facility was less picturesque than the one in Manouba; Fanon's brother Joby described it as "run down and less well ventilated" than Blida. But Fanon had a highly motivated Tunisian and Algerian
staff, and a devoted and feisty secretary in Marie-Jeanne Manuellan, who
would soon play an important role in his writing life. Charles Nicolle became the laboratory of Fanon's most radical experiment yet: the creation of
Africa's first psychiatric day clinic, established with the blessing of the Tunisian authorities. The Centre neuropsychiatrique de jour (CNPJ) opened

---

* Anti-Black racism among North Africans, as Fanon had learned as a French soldier, was
not uncommon. Mohammed Harbi writes in his memoir, *Une vie debout*, of a Black Algerian doctor, a comrade in the movement, who decided to marry a Frenchwoman. When
his colleagues objected, he replied, "Who among you would allow me to marry your sister?" Only one of them said he would—and he didn't have a sister. "It was a shock for me,"
Harbi writes. "We reviled the racism of which we were victims, all the while forgetting to
sweep in front of our own door."

its doors in May 1958. Fanon saw it as a potential model for psychiatric care, especially in what he called underdeveloped countries. During the first eighteen months of its existence, the CNPJ would treat more than one thousand patients; almost none of them became inpatients. In the words of Martini, "Fanon literally swept away . . . the dust of classical Tunisian psychiatry and, in doing so, attracted the solid hatred of his Tunisian colleagues, about which he couldn't have cared less."

Martini was somewhat skeptical of Fanon, who, in his view, "was very ambitious and eager for glory, with a taste for giving orders." Although he admired Fanon as a doctor, the "courtesan side" of Fanon's relationship to the FLN's ideology—especially his populist odes to the wisdom of the masses—struck him as "a little undignified for a man of his stature." During an argument over circumcision, for example, Fanon passionately declared his willingness to perform it if it was "the people's desire," although he was personally opposed to it. "Nobody obliged him to attack the taboo of a community to which he aspired to belong," Martini wrote, "but nobody obliged him to support and defend it either, or to take openly regressive positions." Fanon seemed to be always playing a role, "a character that he really wasn't." Still, Martini developed a grudging admiration for Fanon. "I was aware," he wrote, "that I was looking at a 'Monsieur' with strong and original ideas as soon as he put on his psychiatrist's uniform or took up his pen."

Tosquelles had dreamed of something he called "geo-psychiatry," consisting of "breaking bread with the mentally ill in their homes." In Tunis, Fanon put this dream into practice, building on his mentor's work while also going beyond it. At Saint-Alban and in Blida, he had been a rigorous practitioner of social therapy, creating a microcosm of society inside the walls of the hospital, a "neo-society" where patients and caregivers worked together in a shared project of disalienation. But he had come to suspect that even the most well-intentioned neo-society ended up reproducing the "complacently punitive attitude" of the modern asylum. In a context of psychiatric confinement, he argued, "we create fixed institutions, strict and rigid settings, and schemas that are rapidly stereotyped. In the neo-society, there are no inventions, there is no creative, innovative dynamic. There is no veritable shake-up, no crises . . . The lived experience

of internment-imprisonment considerably limits the curative and disalienating value of social therapy . . . This is why we think today that the
true social-therapeutic milieu is and remains concrete society itself." (He
never mentioned his mentor by name in his writings on the clinic, but
he damned Tosquelles's work with faint praise: "Of course institutional-
therapy is far from being useless.")

That Fanon attributed positive therapeutic value to crises reflected his
belief in the beneficial qualities of shock, at least in some forms. "We do not
believe in the curative value of dissolutions of consciousness," he wrote in
his first paper on the clinic's work. "The service is oriented toward awareness, verbalization, explanation, and strengthening the ego." But he drew
upon some of the medical procedures that he and Tosquelles had used
at Saint-Alban, including insulin shock therapy (to induce sub-comas),
seismotherapy (mechanical vibrations produced by electroshocks), and
sleep therapy (in which patients were given heavy doses of neuroleptics).
The purpose of these measures was to prepare patients to return to their
lives—and, in the case of Algerian soldiers, to the battlefield.

To shield patients from the world, Fanon felt, was to encourage a
"thingification" of their condition—"and therefore of the patient," he
pointedly added. He advocated a more dynamic, confrontational approach
to care, in which patients were forced to reckon with "the violence of the
conflict, the toxicity of reality." To create a safer, sanitized "neo-society"
was, in his words, to "remain indefinitely at the level of magic," when what
was needed was a "syncopated dialogue between the overall personality
and the environment." Day hospitalization, he argued, provides families
with the means to avoid "amputation," reducing the "carceral or coercive"
dimension of treatment. Treatment would be more like performing a job
than serving time: patients at the CNPJ would arrive in the morning and
return home at 6:00 p.m.; they were no longer isolated from their families
and friends.

In his two papers on the CNPJ (the second of which was co-written
with Geronimi), Fanon advanced an increasingly radical critique of what
he called "classical hospitalization," which "condemns [the patient] to exercise his freedom in the unreal world of fantasy." In the day clinic, he
argued, the "master/slave, prisoner/jailer dialectic created in internment"

could be transcended, transforming the meeting of doctor and patient into "an encounter between two freedoms. That condition is necessary for all therapy, but especially in psychiatry." Since the psychiatrist is no longer "shutting himself in the asylum with his madmen," he loses his "phantas-magorical, mysterious and somewhat disturbing" aura, and becomes "just another doctor," approaching each case as "an illness as lived by a patient," in "a specific environment . . . This makes for a concrete, dynamic, in vivo examination of the illness." In Blida, Fanon had used psychiatry to bring about the disalienation of his patients. Now he was attacking confinement itself, proposing to transform—or disalienate—his own profession. That very Sartrian phrase, "an encounter between two freedoms," also encapsulated Fanon's vision of relations between Blacks and whites, Muslims and Europeans, in a decolonized society.

Fanon's critique of the profession, which anticipated the "anti-psychiatry" of R. D. Laing and Thomas Szasz, was unknown to most of his former colleagues. He was no longer giving papers at medical conferences in France or elsewhere in Europe, where he would have been at risk travel-ing under his own name because of his FLN activities. Some of his French colleagues lamented that he had abandoned psychiatry for politics, as if anti-colonial revolution were a deviation from Fanon's work as a doctor, rather than its ultimate expression. In fact, Fanon remained as passionate as ever about psychiatry, and in his work in Tunis in the late 1950s, he gave the impression of a mind on fire.

His lectures at the University of Tunis were, according to his students, inspired performances, in which Fanon improvised on ideas he had ex-plored in *Black Skin, White Masks*, while developing the arguments of his later work on the psychological drama of decolonization. His central theme was the lived experience of the outsiders, the oppressed, and the castaways of Western modernity: Black Americans, colonized Arabs, of-fice workers surveilled by unseen cameras, the mentally ill. He illustrated his argument about anti-Black racism's impact on mental health—in America, "the aggressiveness of the Black man is turned against the Black man"—with quotes from the novels of Chester Himes and from blues lyr-ics about suicide and murder. But the somewhat naïve vision of interracial protest that he had sketched in *Black Skin, White Masks* had, by then, given way to a bleaker appraisal of the tenacity of anti-Black oppression. Normal relations between Blacks and whites were impossible in America because of the "lie of the situation." He noted, "When a Black kills a Black, nothing happens; when a Black kills a white, the entire police force is mobilized." To be Black in the United States, he went on, is to undergo a "sort of conditioning by absurdity . . . The difficulty of defending one's pride devalues this pride."

If Black Americans were prisoners of what Fanon called "social definition," they were not alone. In the colonies, he pointed out, an unemployed person was not a worker without a job but rather a native "whose energy has not yet been claimed by colonial society." For the colonized, idleness was not a sign of laziness; rather, it was "a protection, a measure of self-defense, foremost on the physiological level." The mentally ill, too, were imprisoned by oppressive classifications, he suggested. Although Fanon had always shied away from the romanticization of madness by psychoanalysts like Lacan, he was beginning to see it as something other than a pathology of liberty. The "mad person," he said, "is someone who is foreign to society. And society decides to rid itself of this anarchic element." Psychiatrists, he went on, were complicit in this effort, structural allies of "the police, the protector of society *against*." In a kind of Socratic disquisition about the category of normality, he remarked: "People often say that a normal person is someone who doesn't make a fuss . . . But labor activists make demands and protest. Are they normal? What are the criteria of normality? For some the criterion is work. But a prostitute works!"

In the classes he taught at the University of Tunis, Fanon raised questions about normality that he was never able to fully develop in his writing, which had sometimes revealed the inherited biases of a midcentury heterosexual male, especially when it came to gender and sexuality. Understandably, perhaps, impotence and vaginism (fear of penetration) fell under the rubric of sexual disorders, but so did homosexuality. In *Black Skin, White Masks*, he had expressed revulsion toward male homosexuality and cast doubt on its existence in Martinique. Not surprisingly, Fanon's belief that homosexuality was an abnormality that had to be cured—along with his speculations about rape fantasies among white women—would inspire a small but passionate literature of denunciation. But, according to

Alice Cherki, Fanon's views on homosexuality evolved in a markedly less normative direction in Tunis, thanks in part to his work with a mentally disturbed gay man, one of the only patients with whom he attempted a traditional psychoanalytic treatment. While Fanon liked to hear himself talk, he was a keen listener in his medical practice, willing to change his mind in light of the lived experience of his patients. His students in Tunis were often the first to hear of Fanon's epiphanies in the clinic.

"His personality fascinated us," the Tunisian sociologist Lilia Ben Salem, one of his students, remembered. "He was imperious all the while being ready to listen to others; distant, passionate, and fascinating . . . We asked him questions, but he had a tendency to deliver monologues, reflecting out loud. It was not only the doctor expressing himself but, above all, the philosopher, the psychologist, the sociologist." Fanon would sometimes invite his students to accompany him to the ward after class. "We were enormously impressed by his ability to listen to his patients and his art of making them talk without fear," the sociologist Frej Stambouli recalls.

In the clinic, at least, Fanon remained a dissident and heterodox intellectual. Even as he adhered to the FLN's discipline, he rebelled against the confines of his own discipline—and in his warnings about the carceral dimensions of confinement and hospitalization, it is tempting to see a displaced protest against the FLN's authoritarianism. Most of his patients were Tunisians, but he also saw Europeans, Algerian refugees, and, not least, soldiers from the ALN. Soldiers treated by him were described by their fellow fighters, with affectionate mockery, as having been Fanonized. One ALN soldier who came to see Fanon, Abderrahmane Dridi, was faking mental illness: he'd spent years in the maquis running away from French airstrikes, he didn't think he was being heroic, and he didn't want to go back. Fanon quickly realized that Dridi was pretending, but he still took him on as a patient and never informed his superiors. He was moved by Dridi, an illiterate apprentice mason who'd grown up without a father in a small village near the Tunisian border. Sometimes Fanon would give him money and tell him to go to the cinema, but Dridi found the European art films he recommended very boring, so he went to see Westerns instead. Fanon knew that Dridi was lying when he claimed to have seen a film he had suggested, but he never said anything. In those silences, in that complicity, lay a great tenderness for the young men, mostly from poor rural backgrounds, who were fighting for Algeria's liberation.

There was, of course, an inescapably political dimension to the Fanonization of ALN soldiers. The FLN wanted its fighters to be cured so that they could reenter the field, and in spring 1959 it assigned him the task of reorganizing the ALN's medical services, nine hundred miles away on the Moroccan-Algerian border. One of his favorite techniques was "active hibernation," in which he used mild, nonaddictive sedatives, as he remembered Tosquelles doing, to put exhausted soldiers to sleep for long spells so that they could recover their strength and energy. In this period, Fanon often traveled with his bodyguard Youcef Yousfi to ALN bases in the vicinity of the Tunisian-Algerian border on weekends, and is said to have crossed the Morice Line into Algeria on clandestine missions. This was dangerous work, conducted under threat of aerial raids by the French air force. In early February 1958, a few days after an ALN attack on a French patrol in which fifteen French soldiers were killed and four captured, the French air force bombed the Tunisian border town of Sakiet Sidi Youssef, claiming that it harbored an FLN base; more than eighty civilians were killed, many of them children whose school had been flattened.* At least once in the course of these missions, Fanon reprimanded ranking officers when he saw them behaving cruelly toward young recruits. "Few Algerians would have dared" to express such criticisms, Yousfi remarked.

Fanon's role as a doctor in the FLN was similar to that of the British doctor W. H. R. Rivers, who treated soldiers suffering from shell shock during World War I, notably the poet Siegfried Sassoon. After the death of Abane Ramdane, this role may have offered him a measure of consolation: Fanon, who had always seen medicine as a form of politics, could now use his expertise to restore soldiers to health, and thereby serve the independence struggle. His work with ALN soldiers bound him ever closer to the army of the frontiers. No longer a ragtag band of guerrillas, the ALN

* The bombing of Sakiet Sidi Youssef drew condemnation from the Tunisian authorities and intensified international pressure against France—not least from the United States, which increasingly took the view expressed by Senator John F. Kennedy that Algeria would be lost to the Russians if the war continued.

was evolving into a highly professional organization, comprising former maquisards who had crossed over into Tunisia and Morocco, and, increasingly, Muslim deserters from the French army.*

Fanon developed an increasingly romantic attachment to the soldiers of the ALN, whom he revered as "warrior-philosophers." And during a trip in 1959 to the Ben M'hidi base (named after the assassinated leader Larbi Ben M'hidi) in Oujda, Morocco, Fanon was visited by their enigmatic leader, Colonel Houari Boumediene, one of Boussouf's closest allies. Born Mohammed Ben Brahim Boukharouba, Boumediene (his nom de guerre) was the son of a poor wheat farmer in Clauzel, a village near Guelma in eastern Algeria. He is said to have studied at Al Azhar, the center of Islamic learning in Cairo; he spoke only in Arabic, although he understood French. A slender but formidable man with reddish hair and green eyes, he was soft-spoken, modest, and almost never smiled. ("Why should I smile just because a photographer is taking the trouble to photograph me?" he asked.) He appreciated Fanon's work and took a liking to him.

On these visits to the army of the frontiers, Fanon forged an alliance with the *état-major* (general staff)—the FLN's exterior leadership, which had eliminated Abane and put an end to the primacy of the political over the military forces in the movement. But he got something precious in return. Fanon's unusual access to the soldiers of the ALN provided him with a rare window onto the lived experience—and the psychological disturbances—of anti-colonial rebels. The men he treated were young, sometimes still in their teens, mostly from rural backgrounds. Many of them told him about family members who had been killed, tortured, or raped by French soldiers. Some expressed feelings of guilt and shame, often about the violence that they themselves had committed against European civilians. They suffered from a variety of psychological and physical symptoms: impotence, fatigue, melancholic depression, acute anxiety, agitation, and hallucinations. Their disorders were caused, he came to believe, by "the bloody, pitiless atmosphere, the generalization of inhuman

---

* During the war of independence, more Algerians fought with the French, either as soldiers in the army or in auxiliary units known as *harka*, than with the ALN.

practices, of people's lasting impression that they are witnessing a veritable apocalypse."

Fanon also treated Algerian refugees in camps in Tunisia and Morocco, just over the border with Algeria. (There were roughly 300,000 on both borders, living in extreme poverty.) The refugees, he noted, "live in an atmosphere of permanent insecurity," ever fearful of attacks by French troops "applying the 'right to hunt and pursue.'" Incontinence, insomnia, and sadistic tendencies were widespread among the children. Female refugees, he found, were especially susceptible to puerperal psychosis—mental disorders following childbirth—ranging from "deep asthenic depression coupled with multiple suicide attempts" to "a delirious aggressivity aimed at the French, who want to kill the unborn or newborn child." Treatment proved extremely difficult: "Even after the patient has been cured, her predicament sustains and nurtures these psychological complications."

Working with fighters and refugees led Fanon back to the Hungarian psychoanalyst Sándor Ferenczi's writings on war trauma. "There is no need to be wounded by a bullet to suffer from the effects of war in body and soul," he realized. Some of the most serious cases of psychological trauma that he analyzed involved fighters who had never been injured. One of his patients was an FLN member suffering from impotence and depression because his wife had been raped by soldiers who had come to his house looking for him. At first the patient was enraged at what he perceived to be his wife's dishonor. Once it dawned on him that she had been raped because she had refused to reveal his whereabouts, he felt ashamed that he had failed to protect her. But while he resolved to take her back after the war, he still worried that "everything that had to do with my wife was rotten."

Another soldier, a nineteen-year-old Algerian whose mother had recently died, told Fanon of a woman who was "haunting, even persecuting, him" in his dreams, a woman he knew "very well" because he had killed her himself. He had attempted suicide twice, heard voices, and "spoke constantly of his blood being spilled, his arteries drained." At first, Fanon thought this might be a case of an "unconscious guilt complex after his mother's death," along the lines of Freud's account in his 1917 essay on grief, "Mourning and Melancholia." As it turned out, the soldier's guilt was genuine. A few months after he joined the FLN, he explained, he learned that a French soldier had shot his mother dead, and that two of his sisters had been taken to the barracks, where they were probably tortured, possibly raped. Shortly after, he took part in a raid of a large farm managed by a "notorious colonist" who had murdered two Algerian civilians. The owner wasn't home. "I know you have come for my husband," his wife said, pleading with them not to kill her. But as she spoke, the soldier kept thinking of his own mother, and before he even realized what he was doing, he had stabbed her to death. "This woman would come every night asking for my blood," he said. "And what about my mother's blood?" In his case notes, Fanon wrote that whenever the man "thinks of his mother, this disemboweled woman looms up disconcertingly in her place. As unscientific as it may seem, we believe only time may heal the dislocated personality of this young man."

These case studies would appear in one of Fanon's most powerful pieces of writing, "Colonial War and Mental Disorders," the final chapter of *The Wretched of the Earth*. In their sensitivity to concrete detail and psychological ambiguity, in their portraits of men and women in dark times, they suggest what a fine writer of fiction he might have been. They are the tales of a country doctor, like Chekhov, but they have the brutal irresolution of Isaac Babel's war stories in *Red Cavalry*. We do not know whether these people will ever be healed, much less liberated, when Algeria's freedom comes, but we are given strong reason to doubt it.

After the war, the unmastered memory of violence, rape, and torture—of barbarism suffered and inflicted—would supply Algerian novelists with their raw material, even as Algeria's leaders attempted to put this shameful history behind them, purging it from the revolution's official mythology: the fable of a virtuous people, united against the occupier. Fanon was among the first to break the taboos and to illuminate what he called "France's human legacy in Algeria." For all his utopian proclamations about Algeria's decolonized future—or his assertions about the disintoxicating effects of anti-colonial violence—he did not expect the psychological damage to be easily repaired. "Our actions never cease to pursue us," he wrote. "The way they are ordered, organized, and reasoned can be a posteriori transformed. It is by no means the least of the traps history and its many determinations set for us. But can we escape vertigo? Who dares claim that vertigo does not haunt every existence?"

In his role as a spokesman for the FLN, Fanon dutifully presented a heroic image of the Algerian Revolution. But as a doctor, he was dressing the psychic wounds of Algeria's soldiers, bearing witness to the kinds of horror that nationalist fables are designed to make us forget. It was a tightrope act.

# 11

# FANON'S "TAPE RECORDER"

FANON KEPT HIS BALANCE during his years in Tunis by absorbing himself in psychiatric research and—for the first time since *Black Skin, White Masks*—in writing for a general audience. He would distinguish himself both as an analyst and as the bard of Algeria's revolution—its theoretician, at least in the eyes of left-wing French readers. (Most of the Algerian brothers considered his writing propaganda directed at a foreign readership, whether they judged it useful or misleading.) But first he needed a typist. Josie, who had typed her husband's first book, was busy editing copy at *Afrique action* and hosting a program on contemporary fiction for Tunisian radio. Fanon had never written alone and wasn't about to start now. Like Aimé Césaire—who, as a young professor, would recite poetry to his students on top of his desk in Fort-de-France—he had to speak his thoughts aloud, to hear them take shape in another person's presence and imagination. Although he wasn't a poet and hadn't written a play since his student days in Lyon, he carried on the tradition of West Indian storytelling in his prose: an aspect of Négritude that he never renounced.

The person he chose as his amanuensis was his secretary, Marie-Jeanne Manuellan, who would become his friend and confidante, as well as his muse. Fanon's relations with his male peers—Frenchmen, above all—were often tense, distorted by suspicion and rivalry. Only with Joby and his closest West Indian male friends, notably Marcel Manville, did he really let his guard down, often chatting in Creole, although it annoyed Josie, who felt excluded from the conversation. With women, he set aside his armor and revealed a more fragile side of himself—including his battle scars.

Let's be clear: Fanon was in no way a feminist. While he considered Josie a political comrade in Algeria's struggle, the lion's share of home-making and parenting duties fell to her, even if she no longer took dictation. Fanon once told the surgeon Michel Martini that he couldn't bear not being a "god" to his wife, "a confession of a surprising frankness and lucidity, above all coming from the mouth of a man who advocated de-colonization by violence. He was clearly aware of the contradiction, but he accepted it without trying to justify himself." Nor does Fanon appear to have been a faithful husband—especially when he was on the road.

Some of Fanon's detractors have vilified him as a misogynist. Yet Fanon formed strong attachments with many of his female colleagues, such as Alice Cherki, his intern and future biographer, who would never cease to pay homage to his influence on her thinking as a psychoanalyst. And it is to Marie-Jeanne Manuellan that we owe the most intimate por-trait of him as a man: *Sous la dictée de Fanon* (As dictated by Fanon), a memoir she published in 2017, two years before her death in Paris.

She was born Marie-Jeanne Vacher in 1927, in the Corrèze, the south-ernmost department of the Limousin. Her father, a socialist, came to the aid of Spanish refugees, then rescued Jews and hid weapons for the Re-sistance during the war. "He was a terrorist," she would often joke about him. While training to become a nurse in Paris, she joined the Commu-nist Party, under the influence of her cousin Jeanne, a courageous young woman who had spent much of the war in detention camps. The day that she received her party card, she met the man who would become her husband. Gilbert Manuellan, a student in agronomy and a fine classical pianist, was a Tunisian of Armenian origin whose parents had fled the devastation of Smyrna by Turkish forces in 1922 for a refugee camp in Bi-zerte. Refused entrance at the École normale supérieure because his father wasn't French, Gilbert quit school and joined the Free French Forces, took part in the country's liberation from the German occupation, and became a Communist. Marie-Jeanne and Gilbert married in 1949 in Malakoff, a suburb outside Paris and a Communist stronghold, then settled in Tulle, the capital of Corrèze.

In 1956, after Nikita Khrushchev's revelations of Stalin's atrocities and the Soviet invasion of Hungary, they left the party and redirected their political passions toward the cause of anti-colonial revolution. "We had lost Communism," Marie-Jeanne wrote, "but we could believe in the Third World." Shortly after Tunisia's independence in 1956, Marie-Jeanne and Gilbert moved to the capital with their three small children. At first Marie-Jeanne missed the greenery of the Corrèze, but she soon came to love her new home: the fragrance of marigolds and orange trees, the beaches and dunes. "In Tunis," she wrote, "we were freer, even in our bodies."

While Gilbert worked for the ministry of agriculture, Marie-Jeanne cared for women in the shantytown of Djebel Amar, on the edges of Tunis. She was the only French employee. She had seen her share of horrors while working at a hospital in Tulle after the war, but never the misery she observed in Djebel Amar. When mothers didn't have enough milk in their breasts, they would feed their babies bread with a bit of olive oil, tinted red with harissa. "Djebel Amar became 'my' China," Marie-Jeanne, who had been reading about Mao's revolution in the countryside, recalled. Like Fanon's experiences in Blida, hers provided her with an apprenticeship in caregiving as a form of political solidarity. She distributed bottles with powdered milk to women whose breasts had dried up, sometimes accompanying them to the dispensary in the morning. When the doctor didn't show up, she piled into a taxi with a group of mothers to protest at the Ministry of Health. "Don't bring the women of Djebel Amar to the ministry," an official told her. But her patients welcomed her audacity and her commitment; some gave her their necklaces. The dirt of Djebel Amar's slums never disgusted her as much as the injustice. She was appalled by the contempt shown by doctors—Tunisian Arabs who treated poor women no better than the French doctors who had trained them did, as if "they weren't their compatriots or even human beings, but animals." France had left Tunisia, but the attitudes that Fanon had exposed in his writings on the North African syndrome had not: colonial forms of medicine, she learned, remained intact.

In early 1958, Marie-Jeanne Manuellan was transferred to Fanon's Centre neuropsychiatrique de jour. She was unhappy to leave Djebel Amar, and Fanon did not change her mind. He was "glacial, hardly shaking my hand, looking beyond me, as if I were a transparent and inconvenient object." Her "office" was a storage room. Fanon's colleagues—Cherki, Geronimi, and Lévy—ignored her; she felt "incongruous, useless and even disturbing" to them. For the next month, Fanon shut himself in his office, while Manuellan longed for Djebel Amar and returned home complaining to Gilbert about her boss, whom she nicknamed "the Sadist." Gilbert urged her to quit. But her Algerian friends told her about Fanon's courageous work in Blida with the FLN. "You might detest him now, but soon you'll come to love him," one of them said. She didn't believe it.

When Geronimi saw that Fanon hadn't given Manuellan anything to do, he invited her to work with him in the women's ward, which came as a great relief, since she was already feeling guilty about being an idle, salaried Frenchwoman in a poor country that had just won its independence from France. It was only when Fanon saw Manuellan chatting with Geronimi that he noticed her. Shortly after, he cornered her at the door of her office and said, in a gruff tone, "Do you want to work?" She replied that she did. He told her to "note down everything the patient says, and everything I say." She wrote words that were utterly new to her, medical terms that she was embarrassed not to know already and that she was afraid of misspelling. Fanon, after all, had "such a severe air." She made mistakes, but he never complained. What mattered to him was keeping a record. To her surprise, "he was not intoxicated by his status as the head of the service, or pretentious. What was important to him was efficiency."

For Manuellan, working with Fanon was not merely a job; it was an education in the methods of psychoanalysis, which her Communist indoctrination had taught her to frown upon as a "bourgeois science." (Although Fanon was not a psychoanalyst, he had read deeply and widely in the literature of psychoanalysis, and drew on its methods, especially transference.) She came to realize that no matter how sincere patients were, "another story" lay behind each of the stories they told about their lives. "Through what Fanon said, in his exchanges with his colleagues and his patients," she wrote, "I discovered the unconscious." He told her about

François Tosquelles ("the man who taught me my métier") and explained his mentor's theories about "disalienation," another word that she'd never heard before.

Fanon took a lively, if somewhat paternalistic, interest in his secretary's intellectual awakening. He sent her to Chez Lévy, his favorite bookshop on the rue d'Alger, instructing her to pick up Freud's *Interpretation of Dreams*, as well as books by Alfred Adler, Helen Deutsch, and other psychoanalysts. Later, he introduced her to Chester Himes's crime novels set in Harlem, on which he had been lecturing at the University of Tunis. "Read this, and then we'll talk," Fanon would say whenever he recommended a new book. Under his guidance, Manuellan wrote, her "own psyche began, unknowingly, to stir, and to function differently." She wrote down her own dreams and sometimes described them to colleagues at the hospital, until Fanon told her: "You must never tell your dreams to anyone." She should do so only with a professional. He hadn't discussed his dreams on the couch yet, but said he intended to do so. "As soon as I'm finished with this Algerian Revolution," he told her, "I will undergo analysis." If she wanted to become an analyst, he would train her in Algeria after the war.

Manuellan observed Fanon closely at work. He "had infinite respect for his patients," she wrote, exhibiting a kind of "delicacy, especially toward the humblest of people." He also understood the importance of touch. While treating a young Algerian woman immobilized by depression, Fanon sat by her bed, took her hand, and waited for her to speak. Surrounded by the entire team of the CNPJ, the young woman criticized her husband while praising her brother-in-law, as if she'd married the wrong man. The quiet but forceful way in which she expressed her lament suggested, to Manuellan, a melody. As the woman spoke, sometimes breaking into sobs, Fanon held her hand with both his hands, caressing it to "the rhythms of her lament, his eyes fixed on the patient." This went on, wordlessly, for some time. Suddenly Fanon said, in a muffled voice, "In front of the sick, we are filled with humility."

In that moment, Manuellan grasped the ethos of Fanon's practice: the patient's world "was also that of each of those who had listened to the lament," including the psychiatrist and his staff. They and their patients "shared the ingredients of the same humanity"; the only difference was that the caregivers "were still standing." The aim of treatment, she learned, wasn't making patients happy, but rather "transforming [their] hysterical misery into common unhappiness"—one of several of Freud's sayings that Fanon would often repeat—so that they could get back on their feet. Many of his patients came to see him as "something of a wizard, as he had been among the peasants in Saint-Alban."

Yet Fanon could also be impatient, and sometimes irritable, when others failed to defer to his counsel. One day, the director of the newly opened nursing school at Charles Nicolle asked for his help with a student, a nineteen-year-old Tunisian Jewish woman who had been exhibiting what appeared to be schizophrenic symptoms. To treat her, however, he would first need the authorization of her parents, and the father told him that his wife did not want her to see a psychiatrist. When Fanon insisted that he bring his wife over to the hospital, the man replied that she couldn't leave the house since she had been ill the last few months, beset by a strange case of compulsive belching. Suspecting that he had stumbled upon a "pathogenic and even pathological family constellation," Fanon raised his eyebrows. "If I understand correctly," he told the father, "it's your wife who wears the pants." The man returned with his wife, who announced that what their daughter needed wasn't a psychiatrist but a husband, and that she had already hired the services of a matchmaker. "But, madame," Fanon said, "you are married, and that hasn't stopped you from getting sick." The couple got up and left. Fanon tried to persuade them to allow him to examine their daughter, to no avail. For the next several days he held his temper in check, "thinking of that nineteen-year-old girl left without care."

Fanon also made no secret of his disdain for the arrogance of Tunisia's new ruling elite. One day a woman jumped in front of a long line of patients, complaining of a headache. The nurse explained that she was the mother-in-law of a government minister, and Fanon agreed to see her. But just as he was beginning his examination, he asked the assistant to tell her, "I am here to take care of the poor, not the mothers-in-law of officials." The woman understood French and had no need of a translator.

Vigilant with himself, he was equally vigilant with his staff, intolerant of "the least failure, the least negligence when it was avoidable." When one of his patients, a little Tunisian girl, referred to a "bird" hidden in her mother's stomach, she used a word that often designated the penis. Fanon leaned over Manuellan's notes, saw that she hadn't written this down, and reprimanded her for her omission. The next time the girl came to see him, she used clay to create "the most suggestive forms of the male and female sex, nestled one inside the other." Another patient asked Manuellan to put on his watch. At Fanon's insistence, she fulfilled the man's request. The patient went on to have dreams in which a "silent writing person held an important place." Only much later, when she went back to school in France to study psychoanalysis, did she realize that Fanon was using her as an object of transference for his patients. "Fanon worked like the first Viennese psychoanalysts grouped around Freud," she wrote. "He experimented and discovered, mobilizing his curiosity and audacity."

When Fanon wasn't seeing patients, FLN officials and representatives of the provisional government, the GPRA, would often stop by the office. Their faces were familiar to Manuellan from their newspaper photographs. His conversations with them took place behind closed doors, and Fanon never spoke to her of his political work. But she witnessed an incident that troubled her enough to write about in detail nearly sixty years later. One day, Fanon walked out of his office with a Black man his age, who had a complexion somewhat lighter than his. "My secretary will give you the letter because afterward I will have to go to the ward," he declared. Taking leave of the man, he brought Manuellan into his office and made her sit down to take dictation. In his letter—a request to an employer, or perhaps to the FLN—Fanon said that the man wanted to spend some time in France, before concluding abruptly: "I hope he will starve to death." He asked Manuellan to sign for him, sealed the letter, and told her to wait another five minutes before passing it on, so that he would have time to walk over to the ward. Manuellan was shocked by Fanon's coldness and told herself that the man must be "some sort of traitor," until she realized that this was the epistolary equivalent of electroshock therapy. Fanon knew that at some point the patient would read the letter, perhaps even before he'd left the hospital. His purpose was to rebuke him for his decision to leave for France, perhaps even to make him reconsider: for all his harshness, Fanon had not yet given up on the man.*

Fanon and Manuellan both appeared in a short documentary about the CNPJ, made for Tunisian television in 1959. The film is just three minutes and forty-four seconds long, and there is no sound in the only surviving copy. In one scene, Fanon is giving a speech as his listeners studiously take notes. In another, he strides down a hallway in white medical robes, followed by men in dark sunglasses, and flashes a rare smile, confident of being at the center of things—a leader, at least in his own hospital. As he lectures in front of a chalkboard, men take photographs of him. Paparazzi at the Charles Nicolle Hospital? The notion seems implausible yet eerily prophetic, since we know that the doctor will go on, after his death, to become an icon, almost a saint for his followers. Manuellan, meanwhile, sits in a room with a group of children who are happily making figures out of clay. Some turn out to resemble phalluses, a moment that gives the image a comic but also haunting innocence—what Roland Barthes would have called its "punctum," the detail that "pricks me (but also bruises me, is poignant to me)."

Not all of Fanon's patients were as welcoming of Manuellan's presence as these children. One Algerian fighter told Fanon that he didn't want to speak "in front of that woman." She got up to leave, but Fanon stopped her, and reassured the soldier: "This woman isn't a woman, she's a tape recorder, and I need her to do my work." The soldier went on to recall the imprisonment and torture he had suffered in Algeria before crossing the Morice Line into Tunisia. Manuellan was ashamed to be taking notes on his ordeal but continued to write. "If it's too much for you," Fanon told her, "you don't have to come anymore." But she decided that her discomfort—a case of wounded narcissism, she thought—was nothing compared to "what this man had endured," and she stayed for the remainder of his sessions. Still, she appreciated Fanon's gesture, since "he had demonstrated a certain humanity in my regard."

---

* Years later, Manuellan reflected that Fanon "had no pity for those who did not have his esteem," but that "to lose his esteem you had to have done, or be about to do, something serious."

A few months into their work together, Fanon learned that Manuellan's bus stop was on his way to work and offered to drive her. This became their morning routine. But he responded coolly when she invited him and his family to dinner at her home. "You know perhaps that I have responsibilities in the FLN and that I do not socialize with French people!" She felt humiliated and reported to Gilbert that Fanon was still "a pretentious sadist." The Manuellans had other friends in the FLN, Algerians who were perfectly content to visit their home. But "it was normal for him to mistrust French people," she wrote; after all, "I belonged to the enemy camp." Even so, she was slowly winning his trust. He confided in her about his daughter, Mireille, expressing frustration and sorrow that he could no longer visit her in France because of his FLN ties. He had recognized his paternity and still paid child support. Manuellan reported that he told her this "as if he were confessing . . . like a guilty child." He also revealed a hurt, still raw, at having never heard back from the director Jean-Louis Barrault, whom he had sent copies of the plays he'd written as a student in Lyon.

In the spring of 1959, Fanon was living with his wife and son in the center of Tunis on the avenue de Paris, in a large building behind the Monoprix department store. One day, he summoned Manuellan to his home with an urgent request.

"I'm going to need you," Fanon said.

"To do what?" Manuellan asked.

"To write a book."

François Maspero, a radical editor in Paris who had heard about Fanon from an Angolan revolutionary friend, had commissioned him to write a book about the Algerian independence struggle for the publishing house that bore his name. Manuellan went out to buy a light, portable Japy typewriter, and every morning at his office, from seven to nine o'clock, he would dictate the book to her. Fanon initially grew frustrated at Manuellan's slowness, and threatened to find another typist, so she proposed a solution: she would write down his words by hand, and then type up her notes at home, after putting her children to bed. They called these morning sessions "the ceremony of the book." Fanon "paced and 'spoke' his book as if from his steps, from the rhythm of his body on the move." He never sat down, and he never asked her what she thought, but "he said things that hit me in the gut." He often reminded her of an actor, reading his lines for dramatic effect. "Fanon could not have 'spoken' his books to anyone . . . He could have found another secretary. But he needed a suitable one . . . Fanon's words had to fall into the ear of another person to whom he felt close." Fanon's writing, which is often cited by French-language rappers, is a record of what were essentially spoken-word performances.

*L'AN V DE LA RÉVOLUTION ALGÉRIENNE* was written over a period of three weeks, and published in October by Maspero. Fanon's first book on the Algerian struggle, it is a passionate account of a national awakening, a celebration of the "victory of the colonized over their old fear and over the atmosphere of despair distilled day after day by a colonialism that has incrusted itself with the *prospect of enduring forever.*" The book is also a document of the utopian visions that Algeria's struggle aroused in Fanon, who had come to think of himself as an Algerian after three years in Blida. In his depiction, the Algerian Revolution was not simply an anti-colonial uprising but also a social revolution against class oppression, religious traditionalism, even patriarchy. As Fanon suggested in a strikingly existential passage, the "new system of values introduced by the Revolution" forced every Algerian to "define himself, to take a position, to choose." These new values were, in fact, deeply contested within the independence struggle; today, much of *L'An V* reads like a record of revolutionary hopes soon to be dashed by the socially conservative tendencies in the movement he had joined. Yet it is also an arresting example of his psychiatric thinking about the lived experience of decolonization, the way the independence struggle had substituted "awareness, movement, creation" for the "tense immobility of the dominated society."

Fanon considered *L'An V* to be a work of sociology. Each of its five chapters addresses a specific aspect of Algerian society: women's dress, the radio, the family, medicine, the European and Jewish minorities. What he revealed in each of these realms were shifts in both collective and individual consciousness under the impact of revolution, as Algerians became aware of themselves as historical actors, as members of a nation capable of taking its destiny into its own hands. But the book was also a revolutionary pamphlet aimed explicitly at French propaganda—especially with respect to gender.

In late 1956, as the historian Neil MacMaster has shown in his book *Burning the Veil*, the French government launched a campaign to "modernize" Algerian women, liberating them from what was perceived to be the backwardness of Muslim patriarchy and seclusion. The army's psychological warfare experts believed that if Muslim women were persuaded to accept European norms of family and gender relations, they would be won over to the French side, and their men would not be far behind them. Or, as Fanon saw it, "converting the woman, winning her over to foreign values, wrenching her free from her status, was at the same time achieving a real power over the man and attaining a practical, effective means of de-structuring Algerian culture." The great show of concern over the status of Algerian women confined to their homes also provided a welcome distraction from their oppression by colonialism (more than 90 percent of Algerian women were illiterate), by targeting their "real" enemies: their fathers and husbands. As Fanon noted: "In the face of the Algerian intellectual, racialist arguments spring forth with special readiness. For all that he is a doctor, people will say, he still remains an Arab."

France's emancipation campaign achieved its theatrical apotheosis in May 1958, days after extreme right-wing elements in the army carried out a bloodless coup in Algiers and installed a temporary "revolutionary" authority headed by the Committee of Public Safety under Generals Jacques Massu and Raoul Salan—the immediate prelude to Charles de Gaulle's return to power. On May 17, in a ceremony orchestrated by the army, Algerian women took off their *haïks** and set them on fire in front of the general government buildings in Algiers; the following day, hundreds of women from the slums marched into the center of the capital, where they removed their *haïks* or had them taken off by their European "sisters," while Muslim women speakers declared their desire for emancipation and modernity as full French citizens. The not-so-subtle message

---

* The *haïk* is a traditional white outer garment worn by North African women, which also conceals the hair and part of the face.

of these "fraternization" parades was that if Algerian women wanted to be free, they had to choose France, not the *fellagha*. These "test-women, with their bare faces and free bodies," Fanon observed, "were surrounded by an atmosphere of newness. The Europeans, over-excited and wholly given over to their victory, carried away in a kind of trance, would speak of the psychological phenomenon of conversion."

The first chapter of *L'An V,* "Algeria Unveiled," one of his most famous pieces of writing, was a direct response to the unveiling ceremonies, a demystification of the colonial trance. In May 1958, he wrote:

> Every veil that fell, each body that became liberated from the tradi-
> tional embrace of the *haïk*, every face that offered itself to the bold and
> impatient glance of the occupier, was a negative expression of the fact
> that Algeria was beginning to deny herself and was accepting the rape
> of the colonizer . . . Unveiling this woman is unveiling her beauty; it
> is baring her secret, breaking her resistance, making her available for
> adventure. Hiding the face is also disguising a secret; it is also creating
> a world of mystery, of the hidden . . . This woman who sees without
> being seen frustrates the colonizer. There is no reciprocity . . . The Eu-
> ropean faced with an Algerian woman wants to see. He reacts in an
> aggressive way before this limitation of his perception . . . The content
> of the dreams of Europeans brings out other special themes. Jean-Paul
> Sartre, in his *Reflections on the Jewish Question*, has shown that on the
> level of the unconscious, the Jewish woman almost always has an aura
> of rape about her . . . Thus the rape of the Algerian women in the dream
> of a European is almost always preceded by a rending of the veil . . . The
> European always dreams of a group of women, of a field of women,
> suggestive of the gynaeceum, the harem—exotic themes deeply rooted
> in the unconscious.

While the veil was worn by many Algerian women, he acknowledged, "because tradition demanded a rigid separation of the sexes," it was also worn "because the occupier was *bent on unveiling Algeria*." It was a protection from the occupier's aggressive attempts to possess women, to make them visible to the male European gaze.

Fanon's emphasis on the oppressiveness of this gaze was deeply Sartrian, but his account of the fantasies of the colonizer also revealed an unacknowledged debt to a thinker he had excoriated in *Black Skin, White Masks*: the psychoanalyst Octave Mannoni. In *Prospero and Caliban*, Mannoni had attributed the colonizer's violent exhibitionism to an inferiority complex that had to be constantly disproved by acts of domination and cruelty. Fanon's experience in Blida—not least his treatment of French soldiers who tortured Algerians and then brutalized their wives if their authority was questioned—led him to a similar view, even if he never recanted his criticisms. The difference, of course, is that the women in "Algeria Unveiled," unlike Mannoni's Malagasies, are not "colonizable"; they defiantly reject coercive attempts at their assimilation.

As Fanon argued, French colonialism had reignited the very Algerian traditionalism it sought to replace with European values, and given "a new life to this dead element of the Algerian cultural stock." Indeed, Algerian women "who had long since dropped the veil once again donned the *haïk*" after the symbolic unveilings of May, since the "dominant psychological feature of the colonized is to withdraw before any invitation of the conqueror's." Yet once this "dead element," the *haïk*, is wedded to the resistance, it ceases to be a sign of "modesty" or women's subordination; on the contrary, it expresses an attitude of cultural rebellion, like Négritude: "It is the white man who creates the Negro. But it is the Negro who creates Négritude. To the colonialist offensive against the veil, the colonized opposes the cult of the veil." The white cloth signified a refusal of the white mask, and the conqueror's culture.

Not surprisingly, perhaps, some of Fanon's devout Muslim readers, both in the Algerian movement and beyond, would embrace his account of the veil as a celebration of resistance grounded in the principles of Islam. One of them was an Iranian graduate student in Paris, Ali Shariati, who made contact with the FLN's Fédération de France in 1959 and helped to translate some of Fanon's writings into Persian the following year. Shariati, who went on to become a major influence on Iran's Islamic revolutionaries, shared his vision of Islam as an inherently revolutionary faith in a letter to Fanon. In his reply, Fanon acknowledged that the defense of Islam had been an important rallying cry in anti-colonial struggles in

Muslim-majority countries. But he criticized the idea of an Islamic politics as a "withdrawal into oneself" disguised as liberation from "alienation and de-personalization." He warned that to "reanimate the sectarian and religious spirit would hinder the necessary reunification—already difficult to achieve," and separate the emerging nation, "which is at best a nation in the process of becoming," from "its ideal future, in order to reconnect it with its past." He continued, "This is what I dread, and what causes me anguish in my efforts with the honorable men of the Association of North African Ulama"—an allusion to the Algerian religious scholars who understood independence as a "return" to the ways of Islam. Like the "great black mirage" of Négritude, the affirmation of Islamic identity was a stop along the way, not an ultimate destination.

In fact, the veil is a highly complex object, both in Fanon's writings (in which it is alternately a symbol of cultural rigidity and anti-colonial resistance), and for the historical role it played in the closing stages of colonial rule. Once the national liberation war began, Fanon argued, a "mutation occurred," as the FLN decided to involve women as "active elements," and "the veil was abandoned in the course of revolutionary action." Starting in 1955, Algerian women, often from middle-class families, became increasingly involved in the struggle. As he emphasized, this decision to allow women to join the maquis was not made lightly. Women's participation exposed them to the ferocity of the French army; it also challenged the gender conventions within Algerian society. But it was a necessary step if women were to perform essential tasks for the revolution, above all passing as Europeans and moving freely around the cities on FLN missions— liaison or lookout duties, handing guns to fighters, or indeed planting explosive devices themselves. Fanon's hope was that the courage and sacrifice they had demonstrated were leading irreversibly to an improvement in their status in Algerian society, indeed to the "birth of a new woman."

In a remarkable account of an anonymous Algerian woman who removes her veil, dresses as a European, and deposits a bomb in the European quarter of Algiers, Fanon evoked a process of revolutionary disalienation. "Each time she ventures into the European city, the Algerian woman must achieve a victory over herself, over her childlike fears," he writes. "She must consider the image of the occupier lodged somewhere in her mind and in her body, remodel it, initiate the essential work of erod-ing it, make it inessential, remove something of the shame that is attached to it." Because she was accustomed to confinement in her home, and to the protection of the veil, "her body did not have the usual mobility in a limitless field of avenues, unfolded sidewalks, of houses, people dodged or bumped into . . . The unveiled body seems to escape, to dissolve. She has the impression of being improperly dressed, even of being naked. She ex-periences a sense of incompleteness with great intensity." In a passage strongly marked by Merleau-Ponty's writings on the "phenomenal body," he continued:

> The absence of the veil distorts the Algerian woman's corporeal schema. She quickly has to invent new dimensions for her body, new means of muscular control. She has to create for herself an attitude of an unveiled-woman-outside . . . The Algerian woman who walks stark naked into the European city relearns her body, re-establishes it in a totally revolution-ary fashion.

This is not at all what the French imagined with their orchestrated veil burnings in the spring of 1958. By becoming a woman who can walk alone in the city by herself, without feeling naked, Fanon's Algerian woman is assuming the burden of freedom, both her people's and her own, and ar-riving at a "new dialectic of the body and of the world." Although she must pass as a European settler, "there is no character to imitate." Fanon continues, "On the contrary, there is an intense dramatization, a continu-ity between the woman and the revolutionary. The Algerian woman rises to the level of tragedy."

Fanon took the view, in other words, that unveiling as a revolution-ary tactic was allowing Muslim women ownership of their bodies. And now that "men's words were no longer law," Algeria's freedom would be "identified with women's liberation, with their entry into history." The co-lonial unveiling ceremonies of May 1958, far from being a moment of self-emancipation, were a spectacle of coercive "emancipation" stage-managed by the French authorities. In the years that followed, Fanon argues, women increasingly wore the veil as a gesture of pride and collective affirmation.

He claims nonetheless that it had been "stripped once and for all of its exclusively traditional dimension" since it "helped the Algerian woman to meet the new problems created by the struggle": by reassuming the veil, many militant women were confronting a new round of "problems created by the struggle." Where the French saw a covered woman subordinated to Islamic patriarchy, Fanon saw a determined anti-colonial warrior, wearing her *haïk* much as he had once worn his black skin—only with a message for one of the brothers, or a weapon, concealed inside it.

Fanon also hailed sweeping transformations in Algerian attitudes toward Western technology and medicine. Before the independence struggle, he noted, few Algerians had a radio; most saw it as a symbol of colonial power and exclusion, like wine, "an evil object, anxiogenic and accursed." Radio-Alger, "the voice of France in Algeria," was aimed at the European community, especially settlers on farms far from the cities, for whom it was "a daily invitation not to 'go native,'" not to forget the superiority of their culture. But with the outbreak of the war, and the creation of the FLN's radio broadcast, the *Voice of Algeria*, the purchase of a radio became "the only means of entering into communication with the Revolution, of living with it . . . Almost magically . . . the radio receiver lost its identity as an enemy object."

Western medicine, too, shed its hostile veneer. Under colonialism, doctors had been an "integral part of colonization, domination, and exploitation." Algerians experienced their visits to the doctor as "an opposition of exclusive worlds, a contradictory interaction of different techniques, a vehement confrontation of values." As a result, "the colonized person who goes to see the doctor is always rigid," often exhibiting the symptoms of the North African syndrome. Racist European doctors would quickly conclude that "with these people you couldn't practice medicine, you had to be a veterinarian." The colonized could only respond defensively, following up "every pill swallowed or every injection taken" with "the application of a preparation or the visit to a saint"—a marabout or healer. All this changed, Fanon argued, with the national liberation war, and the FLN's expansion of health-care services for ordinary Algerians. "The Algerian doctor," he wrote, "became a part of the Algerian body . . . A population accustomed to the monthly or biennial visits of European doctors saw

Algerian doctors settling permanently in their villages. The Revolution and medicine manifested their presence simultaneously." The result was a "remarkably creative atmosphere," in which Algerians overcame what European doctors had interpreted as fatalism and sought to "understand the explanations proffered by compatriot doctors or nurses." The rural religious practices that Fanon had described in his medical papers, such as the belief in *djinn*, "all the things that seemed to be part of the very physiology of the Algerian, were swept away by revolutionary action and practice."

To read *L'An V* is to feel like a vicarious witness to a traditional society in flux, fighting for its liberation not only from colonial oppression but also from the inherited weight of the past. All that is solid melts into air, as calcified traditions—paternal authority, the separation of the sexes, rural superstitions—are "knocked over and challenged by the national liberation struggle." In a chapter on the Algerian family, Fanon describes the revolt of nationalist sons against their timid fathers, who were forced to relinquish their authority "before the new world" in the making or face the consequences, including execution by the FLN for treason. "This defeat of the father by the new forces that were emerging," Fanon writes confidently, "could not fail to modify the relations that had formerly prevailed in Algerian society." In the maquis, marriage was no longer "an arrangement between families," and young men and women could choose their partners: "The united militant couple, participating in the birth of the nation, became the rule in Algeria."*

Fanon's rosy account of disalienation among Algerian women was exaggerated, but it was not altogether a fiction. Thousands of women participated in the war effort, as bomb-carriers, messengers, funds collectors, nurses, lookouts, and cooks, and their involvement challenged not only the restrictions of Algerian patriarchy but also their own inherited sense of what life had to offer them. Malika Ighilahriz, a member of the FLN underground in the capital, remembered the delicious frisson of putting on

---

* The contrast here with Fanon's depiction in *Black Skin, White Masks* of West Indian women like Mayotte Capécia, who "lactify" themselves by marrying white men, could not be starker.

red lipstick, getting into an American sports car, and shuttling back and forth between the Casbah and assignments in central Algiers. Safia Bazi, a maquisarde in Wilaya 4, read *L'An V* in prison. "[It] contained for me an exact analysis of what I'd personally lived," she wrote, the "radical transformation in women's behavior under the impact of the Revolution and their contribution to it." During the war and after independence, women fighters like Zohra Drif, Djamila Bouhired, and Djamila Boupacha became international icons of the Algerian resistance, even of decolonization itself.

But while the FLN projected these female bomb-carriers as examples of patriotism and self-sacrifice, it persisted in the strongly patriarchal idea of the "family-as-fortress," a bulwark against colonialism. Among the many problems that Fanon failed to acknowledge was that women who hoped to achieve emancipation from the strictures of Algerian patriarchy risked being attacked as "colonialist lackeys." Mouloud Feraoun worried that the only freedom the female maquisards were winning was the right to be arrested and tortured alongside their male comrades. "Perhaps a new world is being constructed out of ruins," he wrote, "a world where women will be wearing the pants, literally and figuratively, a world where what remains of the old traditions that adhere to the inviolability of women, both literally and figuratively, will be viewed as a nuisance and swept away." Among those who were swept away or vilified in the years following independence was Malika Ighilahriz's sister, Louisette, an FLN militant who, after her arrest by the French in 1957, was raped and tortured, before being rescued from a colonial military prison by a French military doctor who found her huddled in a pool of excrement and menstrual blood. Post-independence, the Ighilahriz sisters and other women veterans would find themselves fighting a losing battle to defend the fragile gains achieved during the war, which were chipped away by regressive legislation on matters of marriage, divorce, and child custody.

The opposition of Algerian men (and quite a few women) to Western conventions of gender equality was, in part, an expression of indigenous resistance to France's efforts to woo and co-opt Algerian women—to "save brown women from brown men," as the literary critic Gayatri Spivak has characterized colonial campaigns to "liberate" colonized women. What

Fanon refused to see was that hostility to Algerian women's empowerment was not merely a "dead element" of the past into which colonialism
had breathed new life: religious currents in the nationalist movement, especially those close to the Association of Algerian Muslim Ulama, were
keen to reinforce patriarchy and the traditional family, invariably in the
name of Islam. Fanon's belief in the revolution—and, possibly, his own
atheism—blinded him to the religious component of Algeria's struggle.
When Jacques Berque, the sociologist of North African Islam, met him
in Tunis, he found Fanon to be "a psychiatrist of great refinement" and
a master of "clinical observation"; he admired his "anger, his reason, and
his goodness," but added that "like almost all French supporters of the
FLN, he failed to grasp [its] Arab and Islamic dimension."

For all its appeals to Islam, Fanon insisted in L'An V, Algerian nationalism was a nationalism of the will, rather than of ethnicity or religion,
open to anyone willing to join the struggle. In the chapter about radio,
he argued that the FLN transmissions were "consolidating and unifying
the people" around a "non-racial conception" of the nation. By broadcast-
ing in Berber as well as Arabic, they were dismantling prejudices against
Kabyle Berbers, no longer seen by their Arab comrades as "the men of
the mountains" but as "brothers who . . . made things difficult for the enemy troops." And because the French language was also used to promote
the revolution—the French announcer on Voice of Algeria was Fanon's El
Moudjahid colleague Serge Michel—it was no longer identified with treason; according to Fanon, Francophone transmissions played their part in
"exorcising the French language." When liberation came, there would be
a place for everyone at the table, as Fanon's compatriot Aimé Césaire had
once imagined.

Many European men and women, he noted, had contributed to "our
units and our political cells"; under interrogation "the tortured European
has behaved like an authentic militant in the national fight for independence." Some of Algeria's Jews, too, had joined forces with the FLN, becoming the "eyes and ears of the Revolution." The relationship of Jews to
the revolution, he admitted, was complicated, by virtue of their own experience of racism: "The Jew, despised and excluded by the European, is
quite happy on certain occasions to identify with those who humiliate him

and humiliate the Algerian in turn." In the pyramid of colonial privilege described by Albert Memmi, Jews were only a few steps higher than Muslims. But Fanon added that Algeria's Jews, themselves former *indigènes*, tended to be more liberal than Europeans, and that "it is very rare . . . to see Jews, in broad daylight, affirm their membership in Algeria's extremist [European] groups." In the Soummam Platform of August 1956, he pointed out, the FLN had called upon Algeria's Jews, who "have not yet overcome their qualms of conscience, nor chosen sides," to "take the path of . . . Revolution" by "proudly proclaiming their Algerian nationality."

Fanon was friendly with a number of Algerian Jews, including Alice Cherki and Lucien Lévy, who had joined the FLN. He was no doubt aware of figures like Daniel Timsit, the FLN's Jewish bomb maker, who was in a French prison. Fanon wrote, with emphasis, that *"the Jewish lawyers and doctors who in the camps or in prison share the fate of millions of Algerians attest to the multiracial reality of the Algerian Nation."* But most of the country's 120,000 Jews were in no hurry to declare themselves Algerians if it meant giving up their French passports. The experience of having their citizenship revoked by the Vichy government in 1940 had only strengthened their attachment to the Republic, its language, and its culture. During World War II, the Europeans of Algeria had rallied to the cause of Vichy's National Revolution, applauding anti-Jewish measures such as the expulsion of Jewish children from French schools—an event that the philosopher Jacques Derrida, who was ten years old at the time, described as the "earthquake" of his childhood.

Meanwhile, Algeria's Jews had enjoyed the solidarity of their Muslim neighbors, most of whom rejected the appeals of the Axis powers. But once their citizenship was restored in 1943, few Jews wished to become *indigènes* again, or to align themselves with a nationalist, Muslim-led rebellion against France, a country they credited with ushering them into Western modernity. And though there was "almost no antisemitism in that period among Algerians," as Cherki remembers, Algerian Muslims increasingly identified with the Palestinians' struggle to recover their land from Zionist settlers—another growing source of tension between the two communities.

In *L'An V*, Fanon gave eloquent expression to the hopes of the FLN's revolutionary wing, those Algerians who breathed the revolution as if it were (in his words) the "oxygen which creates and shapes a new humanity." The future Algeria, he proclaimed, would be "open to all," including Europeans, so long as they renounced their colonial privileges: "What we Algerians want is to discover the man behind the colonizer." This vision of post-independence Algeria was not his alone. It represented the ideals and aspirations of Abane Ramdane and the Soummam Conference, at which the primacy of the interior was affirmed—and, even more so, of the progressives in Wilaya 4, whom Fanon had befriended in Blida.

By 1959, however, with the FLN's defeat in Algiers and Abane's murder, Fanon's portrayal of the Algerian Revolution had drifted even further from Algerian realities. Remarkably, Fanon never mentions that there were more fighters, many cooling their heels, in Tunisia and Morocco than in Algeria itself. Under Houari Boumediene's leadership, the army of the exterior had become increasingly professionalized, its vision of Algeria more narrowly Arab-Islamic. Those who envisaged a multiethnic, democratic Algeria, always a minority, saw their numbers diminish with each atrocity by the army or the settlers. While colonialism was dying, the structures of the colonial world—the rigid, hierarchical segmentation of Muslims, Europeans, and Jews; the divisions between Arabs and Berbers; the defensive customs of the indigenous majority—were withering at a much slower rate, and were in some ways being reinforced by the war and the resistance itself. Algerians in the FLN were less likely to speak of "multiracial" or "nonracial" Algeria than of "Muslim Algeria," and the appeal of "restoration" was stronger than that of any revolution *within* Algerian society. As his former student, the Tunisian sociologist Frej Stambouli, has observed, Fanon overlooked the "two decisive sinister legacies" of colonization in Algeria—mass illiteracy and the marginalization of Islam—both of which ensured the dominance of religious populism, rather than secular leftism, in the independence movement.

Fanon, of course, was not simply analyzing the Algerian Revolution; he was articulating a specific interpretation of its aims, one that he hoped would strengthen its progressive tendencies and raise its international profile. To spread this message, he urged his publisher, Maspero, to send copies of the book to Tunisia, Morocco, Guinea, Senegal, Sudan, Cameroon, the

French West Indies, Haiti, Switzerland, and Belgium. But it would find its most enthusiastic following among the radicals of the Jeanson network, who were fascinated by Fanon's highly existential account of the ethical dilemmas faced by Algeria's fighters: including young men forced to accept the revolution's decision to execute their fathers and the battle of conscience experienced by women as they placed bombs in public places. In Fanon's portrait, moreover, Algeria was not just liberating but also reinventing itself. *L'An V* was modernization theory for radicals, presenting revolution as a kind of shock therapy for a traditional society.

"Your book has represented, for me, everything that my collection should be: revolutionary and violent," François Maspero told him. Perhaps for this very reason, Aimé Césaire declined to write a preface. So did Albert Memmi, who felt that Fanon had stolen his ideas without attribution. (He later admitted his error in his journals, having discovered that *Black Skin, White Masks*, published in 1952, preceded *The Colonizer and the Colonized* by five years.) According to Maspero, Memmi advised him to keep his distance from Fanon. Finally, the GPRA leader Ferhat Abbas, who was living in the same apartment building as Fanon, agreed to preface it, something that made Fanon proud. But when he gave Manuellan a copy, she noticed that Abbas's preface wasn't there.

"Who told you I was going to have a preface by Abbas?" Fanon said.

"You did."

Fanon fell silent; he had obviously forgotten that he'd told her.

"It didn't matter to me," she recalled, "but I know that the absence of this preface greatly concerned some people." It is not clear whether Abbas withdrew or simply never wrote his preface. But the lack of an FLN endorsement was a reminder of Fanon's ambiguous status in the movement, and it hurt.

IN DECEMBER 1959, *L'An V de la révolution algérienne* was seized by the police in bookstores in France. But Manuellan, Fanon's "tape recorder," received a promotion for her efforts: she now worked beside Fanon in his office. The "ceremony of the book" had brought them closer, she recalled, and when Fanon heard that she and Gilbert were throwing a Christmas party, he wondered why he hadn't been invited.

"Because there will be a lot of French people," she replied.

"But if they're French the way that Jean-Paul Sartre is French, I'm fine with it."

"Fine, come!"

She was horrified at the idea, remembering how he'd turned down her last invitation. "Dance in front of Fanon? It wasn't possible . . . But how could I tell him, 'Stay home!' He was going to spoil our evening."

He asked if he could bring a friend.

"Bring whoever you like."

He arrived at their home in Mutuelleville, a suburb of Tunis, with Josie and Olivier, as well as his bodyguard, Youcef Yousfi; Bertène Juminer, a Guyanese parasitologist at the Pasteur Institute in Tunis; and both their wives. To Manuellan's great surprise, Fanon was the life of the party. "Smiling, truly happy, cracking jokes," he picked up a guitar, sang West Indian beguines, and even danced. The joyous, infectiously syncopated popular music of Martinique brought out a levity, a warmth, in Fanon that Manuellan was only beginning to notice.*

After that evening, they became regular visitors to each other's homes. She was surprised, and a little disappointed, that he never looked at her bookshelves, until she noticed he barely kept any books of his own. "He approached books like a doctor," she wrote. "He used them but had no special relationship to them." Food was another matter. He taught Manuellan how to improve her vinaigrette and emphasized "how important it was for a child to smell the fragrance of the jam made by his mother." (He spoke often, and tenderly, of his mother, but "seemed rather distant from his father" and accused West Indian fathers of neglecting their children.) When Manuellan's father visited Tunis, Fanon gave him FLN documents

---

* Fanon's childhood friend Marcel Manville writes in his memoir that whenever he visited Fanon in Blida or Tunis, Fanon would play him 78s by the great Martinican clarinetist Alexandre Stellio. "He got his wife, Josie," Manville recalled, "to make cod marinades for us, not always successful, but savoured a bit like Proust's madeleine." See Marcel Manville, *Les Antilles sans fard* (Harmattan, 1992).

to take back to France, since he sensed in this former resistant "a raw sympathy for our cause." The former maquisard did so without hesitation. Fanon was moved by the family tales of the Corrèze, its land, and its role in the wartime resistance. "What Martinique is for me, the Corrèze is for you," he told Manuellan. Both places represented, in her words, "the land of origins, of childhood, of ancestors, where we were born and grew up, but where we weren't obliged to remain as if we were attached like cabbages. On the contrary, we are curious about other lands, other cultures. We become 'rich' alongside others, we acquire multiple identities. We take part in a certain 'universal' . . . It was this status of composite beings that must have pleased Fanon, since it resembled him in some way."

Fanon had even more in common with Gilbert Manuellan, a war veteran who, like him, had fought in the Colmar Pocket in the winter of 1944 and received a Croix de Guerre. Both, as Marie-Jeanne put it, "believed in man." They went to the same tailor, an Italian supporter of the FLN. Even so, Fanon seems to have enjoyed provoking him.

"The *nègres* invented nothing," he once said, with a melancholy air.

"What about music?" Gilbert replied. "Blues, jazz!"

Marie-Jeanne couldn't tell if Fanon had just then rediscovered this Black invention, or whether he had deliberately "pretended to have forgotten," as a test of her husband's convictions. Then Fanon brought up the subject of white prejudices about Black people. Whites, he said, claim that Black people smell bad, but he took three showers a day. Marie-Jeanne was speechless:

> Obviously neither Gilbert nor I shared this way of seeing things. For us, there were only human beings, whatever their skin color. We knew about Aimé Césaire, Toussaint Louverture, Jomo Kenyatta. It was a provocative speech, and I don't know why he gave it. That day, Fanon asked if he could take off his shoes and walk around in slippers (which didn't bother us at all). And then the men went back to talking about music.

They often discussed Algeria's economic future after independence. Gilbert, the more sober of the two, stressed how long it took to add value to land, and warned that demographic growth would present a serious

FANON'S "TAPE RECORDER" 237

challenge to development. "This Manuellan is sapping my morale!" Fanon joked, turning to what he saw as the promising experiment in worker self-management that Tito had pioneered in Yugoslavia—a model briefly adopted in Algeria after independence.

One night in 1959, the Fanons and the Manuellans went to see Alain Resnais's new film, *Hiroshima Mon Amour*, at the Rotonde, near the Cathedral of Saint Vincent de Paul. Fanon, who suffered from myopia but refused to wear glasses because he found them to be an encumbrance, insisted on sitting in the front row. Josie declared that she wasn't going to ruin her eyes and sat farther back, leaving Marie-Jeanne beside Fanon. In Resnais's film, Emmanuelle Riva plays an actress who has come to Hiroshima to make a film about the impact of the bomb. There she falls for a Japanese man and finds herself flooded with memories of the war, when she had an affair with a German soldier: a clandestine relationship that led to her humiliating punishment, the public shaving of her hair, at the liberation.

Fanon asked Marie-Jeanne what she made of the film. She replied that its treatment of trauma and repression reminded her of psychoanalysis. To forget her experience, she explained, Riva's character must first remember and name it. "What's repressed is something we can't remember," Manuellan said, "and yet the repressed is there, alive, but only in our dreams." She compared the experience of repression to the amputation of a part of oneself. Fanon, who had always been drawn to the metaphor of amputation (and phantom limbs), was overjoyed by her explanations: "He said to me, 'You make me happy, I've taught you something.'"

Fanon also loved the film, but, in Manuellan's view, it resonated with him for another reason: its depiction of what he called "contingent" or "parallel" love—a somewhat grand, philosophical term for the kind of dalliances that Sartre and Beauvoir both permitted themselves, so long as those dalliances were not a threat to their own enduring bond. Fanon believed that jealous people were "dangerous paranoids" and that jealousy was "an evil to be eliminated so that humans could be truly adult." At one dinner at the Manuellans' apartment, Fanon said that he hoped to be able to approach a man and say, "I would like to share a slice of life with your wife, if she's in agreement, without this having any effect on what binds me to my wife, or what binds you to yours. It doesn't take away anything from you. On the contrary it's a 'gain,' since no one is anyone else's property. Everyone can live in liberty. Everyone is the sole proprietor of their freedom. This isn't easy, but this is true love." (Did he encourage Josie to pursue her own parallel loves? Marie-Jeanne didn't say, but Josie seems to have taken a lover, an official in the FLN, when her husband's absences grew more frequent.)

"We were all as serious as he was," Manuellan recalled, "weighing the pros and the cons while peeling our blood oranges at the table." Josie defended her husband's position, while the others objected that "not everyone could be Sartre and Beauvoir." Fanon replied that contingent love was, in any case, "impossible now to put into practice. We need to make the revolution first."

Fanon never approached Gilbert with such a proposal, but an attraction, if not a parallel love, had begun to stir between the doctor and his secretary. Marie-Jeanne did not find him handsome, but "he was naturally elegant and seductive," and one day her hand accidentally brushed against his cheek. His skin was warm, and Fanon responded to her touch, embracing her. They went to a hotel, but as soon as they arrived, he hesitated, and said he could not go in. Why? "Because I am Black," he replied, meaning that he would inevitably be seen, and noticed, quite possibly by one of Abdelhafid Boussouf's spies in the so-called Mobile Brigades. "They were all being watched," Marie-Jeanne recalled, and he could not take the risk. "It was not a question of power. He had none. But he didn't want his reputation to be sullied." They made one more attempt, a few weeks later, when they got into a car and drove to the Taïebs' empty house in La Marsa, to which Fanon had keys. "We didn't even have time to take off our clothes when there was a knock on the door," Manuellan recalled. It was the gardener. They took the interruption as an omen and drove home. Manuellan told me that they never had an affair, but added, mischievously, that even if they had, she would never reveal the secret. Whether or not a relationship ever materialized, a collaboration did. Fanon "spoke" his books; Marie-Jeanne Manuellan, his tape recorder, was the first to write them down.

# 12

# BLACK ALGERIA

---

ON NEW YEAR'S EVE 1959, having just published *L'An V de la révolution algérienne*, Fanon announced to Marie-Jeanne Manuellan that he had asked the FLN leadership in Tunis to send him across the Morice Line so that he could join the maquis. It was an extraordinary request. Although Fanon was no longer the FLN's spokesman in Tunis, he remained a man of considerable authority: a member of the editorial committee of *El Moudjahid*; the director of a pioneering day clinic at the Charles Nicolle Hospital; an increasingly influential author, particularly among the *porteurs des valises* in Europe, Jeanson's "suitcase carriers." He was also the father of a small child. Yet Fanon wanted to return to the interior, the field of honor where Abane Ramdane hadn't died, to fight for the cause where it mattered most in his mind—and, perhaps, to redeem himself for his silence after his friend's murder.

If he had been permitted to go, it's unlikely he would have lived to write *The Wretched of the Earth*. After being elected president in December 1958, Charles de Gaulle set out to destroy the resistance in rural Algeria. He was uncertain as to Algeria's ultimate status and would maintain a sphinxlike ambiguity as to his intentions almost until the end of the war, but he wanted to make his decision from a position of strength. To that end, in February 1959, he launched the Challe Plan (named after General

Maurice Challe) to recapture the Algerian countryside. Under the Challe Plan, the army used helicopters to move special mobile units composed of elite troops into areas where ALN fighters were hiding, on search-and-destroy missions (a strategy later adopted, with similarly destructive results, by the Americans in Vietnam). By the end of June 1961, when de Gaulle announced on live television that the fighting was virtually over, only five thousand maquisards remained in Algeria.

The Algerians refused to grant Fanon's wish. But less than a year later, he would embark on his last operation as a soldier with the FLN's blessings, in the heart of what the French still called *l'Afrique noire* (Black Africa).

"Each generation must discover its mission, fulfill it or betray it, in relative opacity," Fanon would write in *The Wretched of the Earth*. So it was with Fanon's growing involvement in Africa: a striking turn—and perhaps an imagined *return*, like Césaire's—toward the land of his ancestors. As a West Indian boy with a white mask in Fort-de-France, he had learned to associate Africa with the *tirailleurs sénégalais* and with the grinning Black man on advertisements for chocolate milk. In *Black Skin, White Masks*, he had claimed that the fate of the majority-Black world was of little concern to him, a Black citizen of the Republic. Yet now, on the eve of African independence, the Algerian Fanon would find himself making common cause with other Black people as a representative for the GPRA in sub-Saharan Africa. He had not rediscovered his Négritude, nor had he been suddenly seized by a desire to defend Black culture for its own sake. Taking up arms to defend a "race" or a "culture" remained an unfathomable idea as far as he was concerned. But he had come to see the destinies of sub-Saharan Africa and North Africa as inextricably linked. Both parts of the continent were subjugated by colonialism; both sought their freedom. And the Algerian struggle, he believed, showed the way for the rest of Africa, because of its commitment to total independence, without compromise on territorial sovereignty—and because of its willingness to use any means necessary, including violence. Algeria's liberation, he wrote in *El Moudjahid*, would be "an African victory," a "step in the realization of a free and happy humanity."

One person who did not need to be persuaded that the fates of Algeria and Africa were intertwined was de Gaulle. On September 28, 1958, a referendum was held in France and its overseas territories to determine whether voters approved the constitution de Gaulle had drafted for the Fifth Republic. At the same time, the inhabitants of thirteen of France's sub-Saharan African colonies* voted in a referendum on whether they wished to remain connected to France (yes) or whether they favored complete independence (no). As de Gaulle's biographer Julian Jackson has observed, the very term for the proposed new dispensation, "the French Community of Africa," illustrated his "gift for suggestive obscurity," since it "had the advantage of sounding generous while having no precise juridical meaning." With a yes vote, the African states in the French Community would be offered formal independence—except in the crucial areas of sovereignty, including foreign policy, defense, and finance, all of which would remain in French hands. It was a transitional—or counterfeit— independence, in which Africans would govern their internal affairs while French troops would remain stationed on their territory. To Fanon, it doubtless resembled a mid-twentieth-century sequel to the abolition of slavery in the West Indies, with de Gaulle cast in the role of Victor Schœlcher, granting the natives their freedom, the elusive prize that could be won only by struggle and probably violence.

For many French West Africans, however, de Gaulle's offer seemed a marked improvement over second-class citizenship within the French Republic. In the decade after the Second World War, forced labor was abolished and overseas inhabitants finally acquired French citizenship. Most African leaders saw the new arrangement with the *métropole* as an opportunity to further transform the empire—into a decolonized, multinational state based on equal rights. Léopold Sédar Senghor, who was elected to the National Assembly in 1945, argued that colonization itself was a "historical fact" whose legacy—in the words of the historian Frederick Cooper— would have to be "recognized and overcome, not by imitation or rejection of everything French but by a considered reconfiguration of the relationship." Senghor described his program as "the fight for Eurafrica," an arrangement that he said would be based on "vertical solidarity" between Africans and the metropolitan French, and "horizontal solidarity" among

---

* French Togo and French Cameroon were not included in the referendum.

French West Africans. If he was repudiating the African "nation," he was doing so to save the "African *patrie*"—homeland and culture.

In his belief that African identity and development were best fostered by a continued association with France, Senghor was in no way an outlier among his African peers. One influential manifesto of the time, proclaimed in 1946 by the Rassemblement démocratique africain, warned against "seductive" formulas such as "immediate, brutal, total independence." According to one of its signatories, Félix Houphouët-Boigny, a deputy from Côte d'Ivoire, French Africans had chosen "the difficult route of the constitution with the *métropole*, of a community of men who are different but equal in rights and duties." The ultimate goal of statesmen like Senghor and Houphouët-Boigny was not independence but rather—as the Malian leader Modibo Keïta put it in March 1958—"interdependence with France in a federal construction." This was a matter of realist calculation, as well as idealist vision. As Keïta explained, African governments needed French help to build roads and schools.

The French government looked favorably on the idea of association but rejected the idea of a federal republic based on equality, in which African votes would have equal weight in the French National Assembly. Otherwise France would "become the colony of its former colonies," a right-wing legislator warned, in language that would be picked up, many years later, by the theorists of the so-called great replacement. Senghor understood that the French Community of Africa fell far short of his vision of Franco-African unity. But when de Gaulle took his appeal directly to African voters on a tour of the thirteen colonies, in late August 1958, neither Senghor nor Houphouët-Boigny was ready to contemplate the stark alternative that he put forward: a full break with the *métropole*.

As Frederick Cooper puts it, the French leader's message on his trip to Africa was "an inclusive appeal at one level, an ultimatum on another." All but one colony voted yes, and in overwhelming majorities. De Gaulle hoped that the French Community of Africa would become a model for Algeria, once the rebels were defeated. ("It is for Algeria that I create the Community," he told the French African politician Gabriel d'Arboussier.) The referendum was also an indirect challenge to the FLN, which had just announced the formation of its provisional government. Deprived of the right to set their own foreign policies, the community's member states would in due course vote alongside France, at the United Nations, on the war in Algeria.

Fanon could not have been surprised by Houphouët-Boigny's support for a yes vote; he regarded the leader of Côte d'Ivoire as a French collaborator. But the pro-French position of Senghor, Senegal's head of state, must have stung him, coming from one of the founders of Négritude. Fanon had ultimately rejected Senghor's philosophy in *Black Skin, White Masks*, but he could still recall having "waded in the irrational"—and having discovered himself as a Black man—under the spell of Senghor's verse. Senghor's support for de Gaulle was the clearest possible indictment of Négritude in Fanon's eyes, and he would attack Négritude with increasing vehemence as a "mystification," a mix of race essentialism and political cowardice.

The only African leader to reject de Gaulle's project was the new president of Guinea, the one country whose voters opted for full independence. Ahmed Sékou Touré hadn't studied at the Sorbonne like Senghor, nor did he come from a family of cocoa farmers like Houphouët-Boigny. Just thirty-six years old, he was a former trade union leader, a popular orator, and a man of the people, not an assimilated intellectual. When de Gaulle came to the capital, Conakry, to sell the new arrangements on August 25, Sékou Touré, standing beside the general on the podium, declared that his people would "prefer freedom in poverty to wealth in slavery," to rapturous applause. His intention was not to cut off ties with France so much as to show up his former mentor, Houphouët-Boigny; he didn't even call for a no vote in his speech. But Sékou Touré's display of defiance in the presence of de Gaulle made history and created an irreversible logic of its own. When his turn came to speak, de Gaulle issued a scarcely veiled threat to the effect that France would "of course draw the necessary consequences." Later that evening he had his meal delivered to his room rather than attend an official dinner with "that person," and declined to give Sékou Touré a lift on his plane to Dakar, as he had promised. "Adieu, Guinea," he said at the airport, after shaking the Guinean leader's hand.

When Guinea became independent on October 2, the meaning of de Gaulle's words became clear. All French aid ceased overnight, and all French nationals fled, leaving Guinea without administrators or trained professionals. But before they flew home, they ripped out electrical wires from streetlights, apartment buildings, and offices, destroyed the generators of local hospitals, and removed every piece of equipment they could carry back home. The fury and violence of France's departure made a lasting impression on Fanon. So did Sékou Touré's courage and audacity in standing up to de Gaulle. Two years later, Sékou Touré would set up a brutal one-party dictatorship in Guinea. When Mohammed Harbi traveled to Conakry on behalf of the GPRA in 1961, during a violent purge of supposed traitors, he quickly realized that the plots Touré raved about were pretexts for liquidating rivals, if not paranoid hallucinations, representing little more than the "bloody folly of a tyrannical power." But Fanon's esteem for him never wavered, and he would respectfully cite both Touré and his ruthless interior minister Fodéba Keïta in *The Wretched of the Earth*. Like Abane, Touré was a hard man, an unyielding militant. Fanon once confessed to having a "horror of weaknesses," and Sékou Touré appeared to have none.

In December 1958, two months after the referendum, Fanon flew to Accra, the capital of Ghana, with his FLN colleagues Ahmed Boumendjel (the brother of the assassinated FLN lawyer Ali Boumendjel) and Chawki Mostefaï, an adviser to Krim Belkacem. His passport, issued by the Tunisian consulate of the United Kingdom of Libya, identified him as Dr. Omar Ibrahim Fanon. He had come to Ghana to represent the GPRA and raise support for Algeria's struggle at the All-African People's Congress, a pan-African conference organized by Kwame Nkrumah, who had led the former Gold Coast to independence from Great Britain the year before. Delegates from all the independent states of the continent, as well as anti-colonial leaders such as Patrice Lumumba of the Belgian Congo and Félix-Roland Moumié of French Cameroon, arrived in the former British colony to discuss Africa's decolonization and to salute their host. As the head of the first African state to free itself from colonialism, and an eloquent pan-Africanist, Nkrumah was at the height of his influence, and not only in Africa. As one of the guests at the 1957 independence ceremony—a twenty-eight-year-old pastor from Atlanta named Dr. Martin Luther King Jr.—put it, Ghana's freedom would "give impetus to oppressed peoples all over the world," since "both segregation in America and colonialism in

Africa are based on the same thing—white supremacy and contempt for life."

De Gaulle's effort to exert control over France's African satellites, and to undermine Afro-Algerian solidarity, was very much on Fanon's mind in Accra. So was the betrayal of African leaders like Senghor, who had settled for something less than independence and sided with France against Algeria. Nkrumah was a more militant leader than Senghor, envisioning a union of free and sovereign African states that would pool their economic resources and together achieve the "total liberation of the African continent." He urged that the imperial powers "pack up voluntarily rather than be forced out"; he and most of the participants at the congress made no secret of their preference for a peaceful exit, hoping to build on the success of Gandhi's nonviolent resistance in India.

Fanon delivered his speech in a beige suit, a white shirt, and dark glasses to protect his eyes against the sunlight streaming in through the windows: a model of revolutionary elegance in an era in which militancy and respectability went hand in hand, and African radicals wore suits and ties rather than the guerrilla fatigues and dashikis they would adopt by the end of the 1960s. Dispensing with the cautious, scholarly style (and the rhetorical subterfuge) of his lecture at the 1956 congress sponsored by *Présence africaine* in Paris, when he was forced to conceal his FLN affiliations, Fanon described France's gruesome atrocities in Algeria and made an uncompromising case for armed struggle—the FLN's way—as a uniquely effective route to national liberation. As he spoke, he gripped both sides of the lectern, leaning forward toward the audience and ultimately bringing them to their feet, receiving the event's loudest applause and putting Nkrumah, his host, on the defensive.

Though quite a performance, it was not rehearsed. Fanon would give many such speeches throughout Africa. The cause of African liberation was not a passing, "parallel love"; it was a passion, and an aspiration, that grew out of his commitment to Algeria. Peter Worsley, a British sociologist, remembered that he "appeared almost to break down" during a 1960 speech in Accra. When Worsley asked him afterward what had caused him to tremble, Fanon replied that he had "suddenly felt emotionally overcome at the thought that he had to stand there, before the assembled representa-

tives of African nationalist movements, to try and persuade them that the
Algerian cause was important, at a time when men were dying and being
tortured in his country for a cause whose justice ought to command automatic support from rational and progressive human beings." After all, he
would add, Africa's freedom fighters could count on unswerving Algerian
solidarity. An Algerian, he insisted, "cannot be a true Algerian if he does
not feel at his core the indescribable tragedy that is unfolding in the two
Rhodesias or in Angola."

If that had been true, few would have counted as "true Algerians." In
his identification with Africa, Fanon was in no way a typical Algerian. He
knew this, of course, but pretended not to. Most of his Algerian comrades
saw their national liberation war as a *North* African struggle. In French,
they called it a revolution, but in Arabic they referred to it, more modestly,
as an uprising or revolt. And if they looked beyond the borders of the
Maghreb, they were less likely to identify with the South African anti-
apartheid struggle or the Angolan battle against the Portuguese than with
Vietnam's insurgency against the French, Nasser's revolution in Egypt, or
the struggle to recover Palestine from the Zionists. But Fanon had a rare
gift for portraying Algeria's rebellion as a global model for imperialism's
victims.

Privately, some in the FLN made light of Fanon's rhetoric. In his memoirs, Serge Michel remembers speaking to an Algerian colleague who
criticized Fanon for universalizing the independence struggle beyond reason and overlooking Algerians' attachment to their traditions, especially
their religion. "What does the destruction of the 'survivals from the medieval and feudal era' . . . mean, practically, for most Algerians?" the man
remarked, alluding to one of Fanon's articles in *El Moudjahid*. "You can't
blame him. He makes an effort." Still, he added, "Islam is not the Third
International, nor the Fourth." Another FLN leader in Tunis grumbled
to Michel about the "West Indian who wants to explain Algeria to me . . .
Do you know what he told me? 'The revolution knows me, come and see
me, I'll give you some advice' . . . Do you know that he wants to create a
theoretical journal to give us an ideology? Why not, after all? He has the
right to dream, too. But who would read it?" Certainly not Algerians, he
implied.

Aimé Césaire, the Martinican poet, playwright, and statesman, in 1967. A founder of the Négritude movement, Césaire exerted an enormous influence over the young Fanon. (Photograph by Roger-Viollet via Getty Images)

The writer Suzanne Césaire, née Roussi, the wife of Aimé and cofounder of the Négritude quarterly *Tropiques*, "believed in struggle more than in tears," according to her daughter. (Ville de Fort-de-France)

The Senegalese poet and politician Léopold Sédar Senghor, speaking in Strasbourg as a delegate to the Council of Europe, August 9, 1949. While studying medicine in Lyon in the late 1940s, Fanon was initially entranced by Senghor's mystical version of Négritude. (Photograph by Hulton-Deutsch Collection / Corbis via Getty Images)

ABOVE: Francis Jeanson, Paris, June 1966. The editor of Fanon's first book, *Black Skin, White Masks*, Jeanson was a veteran of the Resistance and a supporter of Algerian independence. When Fanon had to be smuggled out of France in 1957, it was Jeanson's underground network that helped him cross over into Switzerland. (© Marc Garanger / AURIMAGES via AFP)

LEFT: During his residency at the Saint-Alban asylum in the early 1950s, Fanon found a mentor in the Catalan psychiatrist François Tosquelles, a refugee from Franco's Spain whose ambition was to "bring Marx into the asylum." (Photograph by Roman Vigouroux / courtesy of the Archives of the Tosquelles Family)

Fanon became the director of the Blida-Joinville Psychiatric Hospital in Algeria in late 1953. At the clinic, he came to see his Muslim patients as victims of colonial alienation as much as mental illness—and ultimately concluded that psychiatry alone was impotent in the face of colonial oppression. (© Archives Frantz Fanon / IMEC)

Fanon spoke of Algeria's independence fighters as "peasant-warrior-philosophers" and saw them as the vanguard of African resistance to French colonialism. Soldiers he treated were described by their fellow fighters, with affectionate mockery, as having been "Fanonized." (Photograph by Photo12 / Universal Images Group via Getty Images)

Two women soldiers of Algeria's National Liberation Army (ALN), training in the district of Constantine, Algeria, on March 1, 1957. Fanon was impressed by women's roles in Algeria's independence struggle, particularly as fighters, and argued that decolonization would bring about not only national liberation but also women's emancipation from patriarchy and religious authority. (AP Photo)

(From left) Ahmed Ben Bella, Mohamed Boudiaf, Hocine Aït-Ahmed, Mostefa Lacheraf, and Mohamed Khider stand handcuffed outside the French secret service office in Algiers on October 22, 1956. The FLN leaders had been on their way to a conference in Tunis when their plane was intercepted by the French air force. They spent the remainder of the war in French prisons. Ben Bella would become independent Algeria's first president in 1962. (Photograph by Jacques Grevin / AFP via Getty Images)

A Muslim woman and her daughter walk past French soldiers guarding a school in Algiers on October 2, 1956. A few days before, the FLN had carried out a series of bombings in central Algiers, killing several civilians, in retaliation for a French attack on an FLN safe house in the casbah in which more than seventy people had perished. (Photograph by Jacques Grevin / AFP via Getty Images)

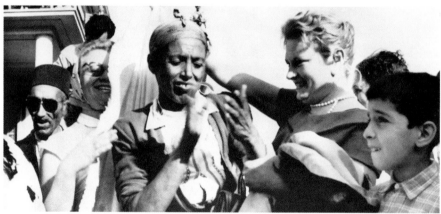

The unveiling ceremonies of May 1958, staged by the French army in an effort to win the hearts and minds of Muslim women, inspired one of Fanon's most influential essays, "Algeria Unveiled." "Every veil that fell," he argued, represented an acceptance of the "rape of the colonizer," submission to colonial rule rather than women's emancipation. (Photograph by AFP via Getty Images)

Fanon at a press conference at the Congress of Writers in Tunis, 1959. As an FLN spokesman in Tunis, Fanon acquired a reputation as a charismatic—and hard-line—exponent of Algeria's armed struggle. (© Archives Frantz Fanon / IMEC)

In Tunis, Fanon founded Africa's first psychiatric day clinic, working with a team that included his secretary and confidante Marie-Jeanne Manuellan (to Fanon's right, in sunglasses); the psychiatrist Charles Geronimi, an FLN sympathizer who had trained with him in Blida (to Fanon's left, also in sunglasses); and Fanon's bodyguard, Youcef Yousfi, a Black Algerian with whom he was often confused (behind Manuellan and to her right). (© Archives Frantz Fanon / IMEC)

Abane Ramdane, seen here in an undated photograph, helped establish the supremacy of the FLN's political wing. In December 1957, Abane was lured to Morocco by his FLN comrades and strangled. The FLN announced that he had died on the battlefield, but Fanon knew better, and blamed himself for his friend's death. (Photograph by AFP via Getty Images)

The historian Mohammed Harbi (seen in this photograph from 1980) met Fanon in Tunis in the late 1950s, when Harbi was a young man working for the FLN's foreign ministry. Harbi recognized Fanon's charisma, but he was also struck by Fanon's "strong need to belong" and disturbed by his almost messianic faith in the revolutionary spontaneity of the peasantry. (Jean-Régis Roustan / Roger-Viollet)

Patrice Lumumba, Léopoldville, Belgian Congo, June 26, 1960, four days before independence was proclaimed and Lumumba became the first prime minister of independent Congo. Fanon befriended Lumumba in December 1958 at a pan-African conference in Accra, and met with him again in Congo weeks before Lumumba was overthrown in a coup backed by the United States and Belgium. After Lumumba's assassination on January 17, 1961, Fanon wrote that his tragic end underscored that the continent could not "advance by regions," but only "in totality," like "a great body that refuses any mutilation." (Photograph by Patrice Habans / Paris Match via Getty Images)

Félix-Roland Moumié, at a pan-African conference in Accra, Ghana, on April 24, 1954. Fanon regarded him as one of Africa's most principled leaders. In November 1960, just before setting out on a dangerous mission in Mali, Fanon learned that Moumié had been killed in Geneva; a French intelligence officer posing as a journalist had poisoned his drink with thallium. (Photograph by Philippe Le Tellier / Paris Match via Getty Images)

Simone de Beauvoir and Jean-Paul Sartre, on Copacabana beach in Rio, September 21, 1960. "Tell him that I think of him each time I sit down at my desk," Fanon said of Sartre, in a letter to his editor, François Maspero. The respect was mutual. Sartre, who spent three days talking to Fanon in Rome in August 1961, would write an incendiary preface to Fanon's 1961 manifesto, The Wretched of the Earth; after Fanon's death, Beauvoir would pay moving tribute to him in her memoir, The Force of Circumstance. (Photograph by AFP via Getty Images)

When Charles de Gaulle visited Algeria in December 1960, Algerians—men, women, children, the elderly—poured into the streets en masse to demand independence, waving the banned flag of the FLN. Fanon was electrified by the events of December, drawing inspiration from the spectacular display of Algerians' support for their liberators. (AP Photo)

On December 12, 1961, a group of ALN soldiers carried Fanon's casket on a long march through the woods, crossing the border from Tunisia into Algeria toward the cemetery of the *chouhada* (war martyrs), in the recently liberated area of Aïn Kerma. According to one of the mourners, Fanon's funeral was "imbued with a great serenity and a strange beauty." (© Section photo—Algérie Presse Service)

After his death, and thanks to the publication of *The Wretched of the Earth* and his own martyrdom in the Algerian independence struggle, Fanon would become an icon of national liberation movements in Africa, the Middle East, and Latin America. (Everett Collection)

Édouard Glissant, 1958, in Essonne, outside Paris, signing copies of his novel *La Lézarde*. A Martinique-born novelist, poet, and philosopher, Glissant first met Fanon in Paris in the mid-1940s, and regarded Fanon's decision to join the Algerian struggle as the only real "event" in the modern history of the French West Indies. But he came to believe that Fanon's radicalism was incompatible with what he called the "ambiguity of the West Indian condition," and that an alternative path to freedom had to be found. (Photograph by AFP via Getty Images)

Stokely Carmichael, at the Roundhouse in London, 1967. Carmichael, Eldridge Cleaver, and other leaders of the Black Power movement embraced Fanon as a French-speaking Malcolm X—and as a uniquely penetrating analyst of the Black condition under white domination. (© John Haynes. All rights reserved 2024 / Bridgeman Images)

Yet the FLN—much like the Spanish Republic in the 1930s and, later, the Palestine Liberation Organization and the African National Congress—welcomed foreign sympathizers like Michel and Fanon precisely because they could speak on its behalf to people abroad. And the leadership in Tunis was especially pleased to have Fanon represent their Africa policy. In a sense, he *was* their Africa policy, a Black man who looked like other Africans and, like them, had experienced the hypocrisy of France's color blindness. He understood—or so they imagined—how the Africans felt about white domination. When Africans asked Fanon if there were many Black people in Algeria, he always said yes, although Black Algerians in the south, like his bodyguard Youcef Yousfi, formed only a small—and oppressed—minority of the country's population. (He reported these exchanges with great amusement to the Manuellans.) After all, as he had written, truth in a colonial war was whatever advanced the victory of the colonized. So long as Fanon represented Algeria in Africa, Algeria was Black.

"We have found in Accra that the great figures of the Algerian Revolution—Ben Bella, Ben M'hidi, Djamila Bouhired—have become a part of the epic of Africa," Fanon reported with satisfaction in *El Moudjahid* after the conference. But as much as he had electrified the audience in Accra with his call for armed struggle, few of Africa's leaders were willing to sign up. Most were pragmatic nationalists like Senghor who had come to power peacefully and had no desire to take up arms: however heroic, Algeria's agony was something to be avoided, not emulated. Still, Fanon made fast friends with two of Africa's most militant young leaders: Patrice Lumumba, soon to be the prime minister of independent Congo, and Félix-Roland Moumié, who had been expelled from Cameroon by the French after helping to launch an armed insurrection two years earlier, and who would follow Lumumba to Léopoldville at independence. Both men embodied, to Fanon, a principled commitment to African self-determination and a repudiation of the tribalism that Western leaders had promoted under colonialism, and now exploited to keep the continent divided, and under their control.

"Reading their writings and deciphering their lives," Sartre wrote of Fanon and Lumumba, "one might take them to be implacable enemies." While Fanon had become an advocate of violent rebellion in a North

African country far from his homeland, Lumumba was a Congolese native son who had built a nationalist movement through peaceful organizing. One man was a worldly and sophisticated intellectual fluent in the latest styles of Parisian thought; the other the son of a farmer, educated by missionaries, who started out as a humble postal clerk in Stanleyville. Yet Fanon and Lumumba took to each other immediately. And though Fanon would reproach Lumumba for his "exaggerated confidence in the people," which blinded him to the traitors in his midst, he also admired this faith in the wisdom of the masses; according to Sartre, he "saw in it a fundamental trait of the African." That Lumumba hoped to take power by means of the ballot, not the bullet, reflected local realities. Like the British and French in their African colonies, the Belgians had no appetite for a colonial war. Algeria, where the French remained determined to maintain power by any means necessary, was the outlier.

There was, however, another leader at the congress in Accra who shared Fanon's belief in the intrinsic value of armed struggle: Holden Roberto, a pastor from northern Angola who had grown up in the Belgian Congo, where he had been trained by American missionaries. A former football star, he went by a number of aliases; in Accra he called himself "Rui Ventura." From his headquarters in Léopoldville, he led an armed movement called the Union of Peoples of Angola (UPA), which aimed to liberate Angola from Portuguese rule. The UPA had its base among the Bakongo, a rural ethnic group who lived on both sides of Angola's northern border with Congo—its original, more accurate name was the Union of Peoples of Northern Angola.

Impressed by Roberto's militancy, Fanon decided that Roberto's UPA was an authentic peasant movement, closer to the people than Angola's Communists, and persuaded his FLN colleagues to allow UPA members to train in ALN camps. But Roberto's political vision was sectarian, and his tactics brutal. Fanon would remain curiously loyal to him, even after the Marxist liberation movement in Angola, the Movimento Popular de Libertação de Angola (MPLA), launched its—ultimately successful—war against the Portuguese army in 1961. Fanon had met one of the MPLA's founders, the poet Mário Coelho Pinto de Andrade, at the Paris congress of 1956, and shared a secular, left-wing culture with the MPLA's militants that was absent among the UPA's rural populists. But Fanon had come to develop an increasing distrust of urban intellectuals and a passionate, almost mystical belief in the peasantry: its wisdom, its refusal of the temptations of Western assimilation, its incorruptibility. Roberto's UPA was also anti-Communist, unlike the pro-Soviet MPLA, and Fanon—in spite of his own intellectual debts to Marxism—had looked askance at communism ever since the Communist Party's betrayal of Algeria in the French Assembly.

There may have been yet another, more intimate reason for Fanon's belief in Roberto: the UPA's leadership was Black, while a high proportion of the MPLA's was mixed-race, comprising Angolans of Portuguese descent, or *mestiços*. Fanon, who had lived his entire life in rejection of blood, was becoming increasingly curious about his own blood—the blood that connected him to the African continent. He had recently learned that his family's origins might be in Luanda, the capital of Angola, and would later flirt with the idea of leaving the FLN and joining Roberto's struggle in the north.

What Fanon did not know was that Roberto's hatred of communism had earned him a place on the CIA's payroll. As an FLN diplomat, Fanon had already attracted the CIA's attention, since the agency wanted to prevent Algeria from falling into the Soviet orbit after independence. It's not clear what the Americans made of his affection for their man in Angola, but the budding friendship could not have gone unnoticed in Langley.

Fanon would have little success in "Algerianizing" the strategies of African liberation struggles.* Instead, the effect of his involvement in the continent's Black liberation movements would be to "Africanize" his own perspective, even his identity. Hardly had he become an Algerian than he began to think of himself as an African. As Harbi reminds us, Fanon had a great desire to belong. Yet he also seems to have had a remarkably elastic sense of what belonging meant, almost as if he could insert himself imaginatively into any group whose struggle he adopted as his own: Algerians,

---

* Only after his death would African independence fighters—notably Amílcar Cabral of Guinea-Bissau and the guerrilla movements in Namibia and Zimbabwe—launch the kind of national liberation wars he advocated.

Africans, the "damned" of the Third World. He was persuaded that their roads to freedom were in fact one, since all were national struggles against imperialism. Together, he insisted, these new nations, forged in violence and armed with the self-confident cultures that emerge uniquely out of collective struggle, would overcome the alienations inflicted by colonialism and generate a new internationalism, or what he would call a "new humanism" at the Second Congress of Black Writers and Artists, scheduled in Rome in the spring of 1959.

Like the first congress in Paris three years earlier, the second was organized by *Présence africaine* and featured some of the Black world's leading intellectuals and politicians: Sékou Touré; Eric Williams, the Trinidadian leader and historian of slavery; the Malagasy poet and politician Jacques Rabemananjara; the Senegalese historian Cheikh Anta Diop; and two of Négritude's founders, Léopold Sédar Senghor and Aimé Césaire. The most notable absence was Richard Wright, a co-organizer of the first congress, who refused to attend: a free discussion, he protested, would be impossible in the city of the Vatican. (Alioune Diop of *Présence africaine* was a convert to Catholicism and a friend of Pope John XXIII, who addressed the event.) The second congress was in some ways more radical than the first, foregrounding the role of culture in the struggle against colonial domination. Rabemananjara set the tone of the event in a rousing speech evoking the "great surge of African unification" stretching from "Tananarive to Port-au-Prince, from Conakry to Harlem, from Bamako to Fort-de-France . . . from Little Rock to Durban."

Fanon, too, had caught the spirit. In his speech, "Mutual Foundations for National Cultures and the Struggles for Liberation," which he would later expand as the chapter "On National Culture" in *The Wretched of the Earth*, he hailed the emergence of a new "literature of combat." Instead of writing with "an eye to the oppressor, whether to charm him, or to denounce him," the colonized writer "gradually assumes the habit of addressing himself to his own people. It is only after this moment that one can speak of a national literature." This shift in address had resulted in new, more urgent literary forms, in the reinvention of older forms, and in the creation of an insurgent national culture. As an example of what he had in mind, he described how storytelling, and the relationship between storytellers and their audiences, had changed in Algeria with the advent of war:

> The epic, with its standardized forms, reemerged. It has become an authentic form of entertainment that has once again taken on a cultural value. Colonialism knew full well what it was doing when it began systematically arresting these storytellers after 1955. The people's encounter with this new song of heroic deeds awakens a new rhythm of respiration, arouses forgotten muscular tensions, and develops the imagination. Every time the storyteller narrates a new episode, the public is treated to a new invocation. The existence of a new type of man is revealed to the public. The present is no longer turned inward but channeled in every direction. The storyteller once again gives free rein to his imagination, innovates, and turns creator . . . Close attention should be paid to the emergence of the imagination and the inventiveness of songs and folk tales in a colonized country. The storyteller responds to the expectations of the people by trial and error, and searches for new models, national models, apparently on his own, but in fact with the support of his audience. Comedy and farce disappear or else lose their appeal. As for drama, it is no longer the domain of the intellectual's tormented conscience. No longer characterized by despair and revolt, it has become the people's daily fare.

In a sense, Fanon was becoming just such a storyteller, although his epic descriptions of decolonization, in *The Wretched of the Earth*, would reach audiences in the colonial world only after his death, in 1961. The speech had all the hallmarks of Fanon's modernizing energy, and of his modernist sensibility. As usual, he was less interested in tradition and memory than innovation and invention as evidence of a "collective awakening." His emphasis on "progress and momentum" reflected his psychiatric training as much as his political outlook. The new storytelling would have to enable the process of disalienation and generate a surge of creative energy across all the arts. He envisaged a radical mutation in the aesthetic traditions of the colonized. "The festival of the imagination produced by struggle," as the Cameroonian philosopher Achille Mbembe wrote later, "is the name that Fanon gives to culture," and it is nowhere better expressed than on this occasion in Rome.

Fanon already foresaw a carnivalesque approach to the plastic arts, in which "jugs, jars, and trays are reshaped, at first only slightly and then quite radically. Colors, once restricted in number, governed by laws of traditional harmony, flood back, reflecting the effects of the revolutionary upsurge . . . Likewise, the taboo of representing the human face, typical of certain clearly defined regions according to sociologists, is suddenly lifted." He warned that "colonialist experts" on so-called native art would be enraged and reinvent themselves as "defenders of indigenous traditions." He had already spotted a dismaying precedent in the resistance of American connoisseurs of New Orleans swing to the innovative musical experiments on the African American scene of the 1940s. Evoking the "reaction of white jazz fans when . . . new styles such as bebop took root" in postwar America, Fanon the modernist was at his most caustic:

> For them jazz could only be the broken, desperate yearning of an old "*nègre*," five whiskeys under his belt, bemoaning his misfortune and the racism of the whites. As soon as he understands himself and apprehends the world differently, as soon as he evinces a glimmer of hope and forces the racist world to retreat, it is obvious he will blow his horn to his heart's content and his husky force will ring out loud and clear. The new jazz styles are not only born out of economic competition. They are one of the definite consequences of the inevitable, though gradual, defeat of the southern universe in the USA. And it is not unrealistic to think that in fifty years or so, the type of jazz lament hiccupped by a poor, miserable "Negro" will be defended by only those whites believing in a frozen image of a certain type of relationship and a certain form of Négritude.

Fanon's argument, which ridiculed the so-called moldy fig critics of bebop, would find a precise echo a few years later in the 1963 book *Blues*

*People,* by the young Black American poet and jazz critic LeRoi Jones.* But the most telling remark in Fanon's invective against the moldy figs is his aside about Négritude, whose nostalgic cultural politics were embodied by Césaire and Senghor, both of whom attended the congress. Under Senghor, as we have seen, Senegal had joined the French Community of Africa. Césaire had broken with his fellow Communists and formed the Martinican Progressive Party, but he continued to argue, on pragmatic grounds, that the island should remain a French department. Fanon's speech in Rome offered another opportunity to take his distance from departmentalization, which he regarded as a pitiful form of "internal autonomy." (It also meant that he could not visit his family back home, since he was now seen as an enemy of France.) That Senghor and Césaire continued to celebrate the Black "shout" of Négritude while making their peace with France was no consolation. Clearly, Fanon could hear in Césaire and Senghor only the "broken, desperate yearning" of the elderly Black man. Clearly, too, he favored the bebop of comprehensive anti-colonial upheaval.

Culture wars, as we think of them now, were meaningless to Fanon. Even a full-on, revolutionary culture war was a lost cause unless it coalesced as a "national" rather than a "racial" project. The recovery of a usable past would not in itself produce a resilient national culture. Only the "organized and conscious struggle taken by a colonized people" could bring this project to fruition. Collective action, struggle, and cultural invention were the three themes of Fanon's speech in Rome. From these an internationalist perspective would follow in the great unfolding of a new political order. Authentic national consciousness, far from encouraging narcissism or xenophobia, would allow Africa's colonized populations to identify the "international dimension" of their own struggles and eventually accede to a community of nations with their African identity intact. "National consciousness," Fanon argued, bore no resemblance to "nationalism." On the contrary, it opened onto an internationalist perspec-

---

* Jones, who later changed his name to Amiri Baraka, contrasted the "willfully harsh, anti-assimilationist sound of bebop" with the Dixieland revival of "young white college students trying to play like ancient colored men" who "revived quite frankly, though perhaps less consciously, the still breathing corpse of minstrelsy and blackface."

tive, a joint awareness that any "independent nation in an Africa where colonialism still lingers is a nation surrounded, vulnerable, and in permanent danger."

By the time he spoke at the Second Congress of Black Writers and Artists, Fanon was deeply engaged in the armed struggle against France, yet the terms in which he defended national consciousness were those of a classically republican French intellectual: if it "reflects the manifest will of the people," he declared in his speech, then it "will necessarily be accompanied by the discovery and the reinforcement of universalizing values." And though he hoped that the liberated nation-states of Africa would eventually form a larger, pan-African union, he gave little consideration to their cultural content (aside from the ferment of collective struggle); nor, strikingly, did he question the geographical boundaries imposed by Europe.

What Senghor and Césaire made of Fanon's speech, we can only imagine. But Joby Fanon, who came to Rome to see his younger brother for the first time in three years, reported an awkward exchange between Fanon and Césaire. "You have chosen the right struggle," Césaire complimented Fanon. "But there is still room for others," the younger man replied, and though he bowed, this was an implicit challenge, if not a rebuke, to his elder, the leader of Martinique, an overseas territory that had failed to decolonize.

Fanon was working hard in Rome to internationalize the Algerian model of armed struggle. In the basement of a café, he met with a group of Angolan revolutionaries, including Pinto de Andrade, and told them that the FLN was ready to train eleven young Angolans in guerrilla warfare at one of its camps in Tunisia: once they were back in the country, they would prepare for the war against the Portuguese. As he explained, the FLN hoped that national liberation wars in southern Africa would scatter the forces of NATO, which was rallying to France's counterinsurgency in Algeria.

Pinto de Andrade and his MPLA comrades were Marxists, unlike Fanon's friend Holden Roberto. But this does not appear to have discouraged Fanon (or the FLN), because they had declared themselves ready to take up arms. The person entrusted with recruiting the eleven Angolan fighters was a young Bissau-Guinean, Amílcar Cabral. A year older than

Fanon, Cabral was the son of middle-class Cape Verdean immigrants. As a student in agronomy in Lisbon, he had devoured Senghor's anthology of Black poetry, which—along with the pervasive anti-Black racism of the *métropole*—had led him to establish a student movement against both the Salazar dictatorship and Portuguese settler colonialism. Like Fanon, he defended an inclusive Marxisant nationalism. He would carry out his mission in Angola and become one of the founders of the African Party for the Independence of Guinea and Cape Verde, which embarked on an armed struggle against the Portuguese.

Shortly before leaving Rome, Fanon sought out the company of a somewhat younger Martinican acquaintance, the writer Édouard Glissant. Glissant had just published his first novel, *La Lézarde*, a dark, turbulent tale about a group of radical young intellectuals in Fort-de-France who murder a corrupt official after concluding that the "power of words" is no surrogate for militant action—the theme of Fanon's youthful writing for the theater. Fanon called him at his hotel in Rome, gave him an address, and told him to meet him there that evening. When Glissant arrived, he discovered it was a brothel. The two men chatted in the salon, then went their separate ways. According to the Algerian novelist Assia Djebar, to whom Glissant recounted the anecdote, Fanon disappeared into the night, but not before turning around to make sure he wasn't being followed, "his expression on the lookout, his gaze inquisitive."

In 1959, Fanon would represent the FLN at events in Delhi, Cairo, and Casablanca. As his prominence grew, so did the dangers that he courted.

On May 22, he traveled to an FLN base near Oujda, a Moroccan town on the Algerian border, to treat soldiers suffering from exhaustion and to meet with Colonel Boumediene, who had emerged as the leader of the army of the frontiers, and as a pivotal figure, along with Abdelhafid Boussouf, in the so-called Oujda clan, which would go on to mold the Algerian state after independence. Fanon's days were spent putting soldiers into "active hibernation" with sedatives, so that they could return to the front; his nights were devoted to reading and writing. Fanon lodged in an ALN hospital equipped by Yugoslavia and East Germany, where he shared a room with the man who would become his assistant, Amar Boukri, a soldier who had retrained as a paramedic.

A few weeks into his stay, Fanon was badly injured in a road accident: he was thrown out of a moving vehicle, and several of his vertebrae were damaged. The Moroccan doctors who arrived on the scene worried that he had suffered a fatal injury to his spine, and—as Fanon would later recall, joking with the Manuellans—seemed as if they were preparing to bury him. Was he a Muslim? they asked the Algerians. Was the scar on his upper left cheek the sign of a religious ritual? Unable to respond, Fanon listened to their conversation in a daze. When Josie heard about the accident in Morocco, she fell into a panic, convinced that he had been the victim of a deliberate attack.

He was not. But in early July, Fanon was the target of an assassination plot in Rome. He arrived in the Italian capital on July 5, bandaged from the neck to the pelvis, for further medical treatment. His passport identified him as the Libyan doctor Ibrahim Omar Fanon. But the assassins of the Main Rouge, the death squad of French intelligence, were tracking his movements. Fanon and his two bodyguards, a Moroccan and a Tunisian, had expected to be received at the airport by Taïeb Boulahrouf, a leader of the FLN's Fédération de France, but were met instead by the carabinieri (the Italian national police). A bomb had exploded beneath the driver's seat of Boulahrouf's car, killing a young boy playing nearby. (Boulahrouf was not in the car at the time.) An armed police officer guarded Fanon's room on the ward, but in a report on the bombing in an Italian newspaper, his presence at the hospital was mentioned. He asked to be moved to a different floor. A gunman entered the hospital soon after and forced his way into Fanon's original room.

On his return to Tunis in August, Fanon participated in a series of discussions on the FLN's political program. It was the only time he exerted any direct influence on the organization's policy, and it led to his appointment to a "specialist" commission on which Omar Oussedik, his friend from Wilaya 4, also sat. Fanon's appointment was a sign of the growing esteem in which he was held by the FLN leadership, and of the interest it was developing in his thoughts about the direction of Algeria's revolution. In a report that bore his imprint, the commission concluded that the peasantry was "still the most revolutionary section of the population." This struck Mohammed Harbi—who had joined the GPRA's Ministry of

Information in Tunis at the request of M'hammed Yazid, and had a series of long discussions with Fanon in the summer of 1959—as an absurd misreading, "in flagrant contradiction with reality." The soldiers of the ALN had benefited from the generosity of some peasants—including being offered sanctuary—in the *bled*; early in the war, they had found it relatively easy to ignite rural uprisings in Philippeville and elsewhere. But in much of the countryside, the ALN had imposed its will, sometimes ruthlessly, on people whose first reflex was a pragmatic wait-and-see policy, negotiating provisional alliances not only with the rebels but also with the French military and the MNA, with the aim of protecting their villages from military incursions and extortion. As Pierre Bourdieu pointed out, moreover, France's "resettlement" campaign had denied the peasantry the possibility of revolutionary mobilization: they had either ended up in camps surrounded by barbed wire or fled to Algiers, Oran, and other cities that became sanctuaries—and ultimately permanent homes—for rural refugees.* According to Bourdieu, who bemoaned (and acutely resented) Fanon's influence on the left, his belief in the revolutionary nature of the peasantry was "pretentious foolishness," both "false and dangerous."

Yet Fanon's line on the peasantry was not unique. Since the 1930s, Algerian nationalists—and some dissident communists, breaking with the party's emphasis on the urban working classes—had advanced similar ideas. As in Vietnam, the war in Algeria was mainly fought over the hearts and minds of rural communities. "The people of Algeria are peasants," the French ethnographer Jean Servier, one of Jacques Soustelle's advisers, observed. "The revolution led by France must be agrarian."

But this sector of the population wasn't looking to become part of a revolution, led by France or by the FLN. In large part they espoused a millenarian vision of an Arab Islamic (or Kabyle Berber) restoration,

---

* In July 1959, Mouloud Feraoun learned from his mother that, under the leadership of a former fervent FLN supporter, their family's village in Kabylia had defected to the French army; ALN fighters had then entered the village, kidnapping old men, slitting people's throats, and demanding money. "The people of the village are feeling tired, unhappy, and battered," Feraoun wrote. "Once inside the barbed wire [of the army's resettlement camps], many of them must have breathed a sigh of relief." Mouloud Feraoun, *Journal 1955–1962: Reflections on the French-Algerian War*, trans. Mary Ellen Wolf and Claude Fouillade (University of Nebraska Press, 2008), 268.

based on codes of patriarchal authority and honor, to which the FLN was forced to adapt. In Albert Camus's novel *Le Premier Homme* (*The First Man*), Saddok, an FLN maquisard, explains to a French friend that, in spite of his own liberal convictions, he's planning to marry a woman he scarcely knows in a traditional Islamic ceremony. "Why subject yourself to a tradition you believe is foolish and cruel?" his friend asks. Saddok—whose name derives from *zadok*, Hebrew for "righteous"—replies: "Because my people are identified with this tradition, they have nothing else, they stopped there, and to part with that tradition is to part with them. That is why I will go into that room tomorrow, and I will strip a stranger of her clothes, and I will rape her to the sound of guns being fired."

Despite the extreme coarseness of the exchange, it captured a real dilemma. The presence of young, urban women in the maquis, hailed by Fanon as evidence of female emancipation under the force of revolution, caused such a disturbance in parts of the *bled* that some ALN commanders—whose own views about gender tended to be equally conservative—imposed strict segregation in their units, with women assigned to stereotypically "feminine" tasks such as nursing and food preparation.* Consensual sexual relations between maquisards were forbidden. In his memoir *Nour le voilé*, Serge Michel reports an incident in which two young lovers in the maquis were brought before an ALN tribunal: the young woman was sent to Tunisia and married off to a wounded soldier; the man was killed. When Michel raised the matter with his colleague Krimou (probably Krim Belkacem), he replied, "What did you expect? That we'd marry them and they'd make lots of little maquisards? . . . The FLN isn't a matrimonial agency, or a brothel . . . What you call love is our worst enemy."

The practice of Islam in rural areas became even more austere and so-

---

* ALN fighters rarely engaged in acts of violence and rape against women, and were severely punished—in some cases executed—when they did. "This was one crucial area in which the ALN won support among rural populations in contrast to the French military in which abuse of women, rape, and sexual humiliation of males was endemic," writes the historian Neil MacMaster in *War in the Mountains: Peasant Society and Counterinsurgency in Algeria, 1918–1958* (Oxford University Press, 2020), 323.

cially conservative during the war, as the Association of Algerian Muslim Ulama—an influential force inside the FLN—made inroads in the countryside, combating the traditions of maraboutism, based on the worship of local saints and holy shrines. Fanon argued in *L'An V de la révolution algérienne* that the decline of maraboutism reflected the FLN's success in channeling popular energies away from superstition toward nationalist goals, but what it really demonstrated was the growing influence of a highly conservative, neo-traditionalist interpretation of Islam that gained a foothold in the nationalist movement at the expense of the more supple and mystical traditions that had beguiled Fanon on his research trips in Kabylia.*

Mohammed Harbi, a libertarian Marxist, suspected that the "adoption of Fanon's theses" about the peasantry was a tactical move by the army of the frontiers and other forces "hostile to liberalism and Marxism, which had an important social base in the cities." Indeed, the term "peasantry" was code for the army of the frontiers, made up largely of soldiers from rural backgrounds. (While Houari Boumediene, the army's leader, may have dismissed Fanon as "a modest man" who "didn't know the first thing about Algeria's peasants," he grasped the usefulness of Fanon's rhetoric.) As Harbi predicted, Fanon's paean to the revolutionary peasantry would lend itself rather easily to a campaign to strengthen the exterior at the expense of the political forces of the GPRA and the interior. When he announced to Fanon and Oussedik that "they were deluded, projecting their political desires and strategic considerations onto a rural world whose sociological nature remained hidden to them," Oussedik laughed, and Fanon pouted, "as if to say there could be little of interest in anything that seemed to him to come from an Orthodox Marxism." It is true that many members of the ALN were from the countryside, where the French were regarded from the outset as invaders—*roumis*, or non-Muslims—who would eventually be forced to leave, but Fanon's ode to the peasant

---

* Although projected as a return to sacred traditions, the Islam of the Ulama was, in fact, a late-nineteenth-century invention—"much younger than the Enlightenment," as the anthropologist Ernest Gellner pointed out.

warriors of the ALN as a group uncontaminated by French culture would help to underwrite a conservative social project he had once dreaded, the nostalgic "return to the self."

That Fanon's writing was being pressed into the service of such an inward-looking version of "national consciousness" was an irony, but perhaps less of an irony than it seems. While he never ceased to support an expansive and pluralistic vision of Algerian identity, his work in Blida had taught him that, in a colonial setting, disalienation could not proceed without a recognition of cultural difference and an acceptance of traditions that, to a Frenchman of his generation and background, would have seemed antiquated, if not exclusionary, such as the *café maure*, where working-class men drank coffee and women were unwelcome. What had happened to the great leap of invention he had praised in *Black Skin, White Masks*? Had he learned to forget that he was a secular man of the left, and encounter colonized Algerian Muslims where they were, rather than where he hoped to lead them (as Memmi had written of European leftists who joined Muslim national liberation struggles)? Or was he simply confident that the independence struggle would trigger a radical revolution inside Algerian society, as he had suggested in *L'An V de la révolution algérienne*, with its portraits of liberated female fighters, sons overthrowing their fathers, and young men and women marrying in the maquis out of love and shared national devotion?

Since Fanon said so little about the content of Algeria's Arab Islamic nationalism, it's hard to know what his real views were. According to the Palestinian American literary critic Edward Said, one of his most celebrated interpreters, Fanon regarded nationalism as an unavoidable rite of passage, "a necessary but far from sufficient condition for liberation, perhaps even a sort of temporary illness that must be gone through." But, as his ethnographic writings about the *bled* suggest, Fanon seems to have found, or imagined, what the Martinican novelist Patrick Chamoiseau has called "atavistic certainties that didn't exist in the blurry mosaic of his native land"; above all, he seems to have discerned a people without white masks. The ALN represented the masses, the "people in arms," and Fanon had little desire to contradict them or to dwell on the predicament of middle-class, French-educated Algerians whose backgrounds were similar to his own, and who wished to achieve both independence as a nation *and* freedom as individuals.


FANON'S IMPATIENCE WITH COLONIZED elites and their sense of being caught in between—and alienated from both—Western culture and their own traditions was on particularly harsh display in an anonymous attack in *El Moudjahid* on Richard Wright's book *White Man, Listen!*, published in August 1959. The author of *Native Son* and *Black Boy* had once been a hero to him; Fanon had considered writing a monograph about his work, a project he described in the fan letter to which Wright never replied. After settling in Paris in 1947, Wright helped found *Présence africaine* with Césaire, Senghor, and Diop, but like most Black writers in Paris, including James Baldwin, he shied away from commenting on the war in Algeria, for fear of being expelled by the state that had offered him a refuge from American racism. Nonetheless, he refused to sign a statement denouncing the Soviet invasion of Hungary unless it condemned the war in Suez as well, and he wrote extensively about decolonization movements in Africa and Asia. Like Fanon, he was fascinated by the new world rising from the ashes of European imperialism.

In his travelogues from Ghana and the Bandung Conference, Wright had left behind the angry didacticism that Fanon had admired in his early fiction in favor of an inquisitive and probing literary journalism that questioned many orthodoxies, including those of the anti-colonial left. While Wright welcomed the fact that Africans and Asians were now able to express their "racial feelings . . . in all their turgid passion," he could not bring himself to embrace Third World nationalism; at Bandung he had been troubled by the growing power of race and faith, the superstitions with which he'd wrestled back in America. "My position is a split one. I'm black. I'm a man of the West . . . I see and understand the West; but I also see and understand the non- or anti-Western point of view. How is this possible? The double vision of mine stems from my being a product of Western civilization and from my racial identity." That "double vision" was not simply a form of torment, as Du Bois had described "double consciousness." It was an intellectual asset, he believed, allowing him to "see both worlds from another and third point of view," and to see the colonized as both "victims of their own religious projections and victims of Western imperialism."

In *White Man, Listen!*, Wright gave a poignant account of the psychological dilemmas experienced by people from backgrounds similar to his and Fanon's: the "westernized and tragic elite of Africa, Asia and the West Indies, the lonely outsiders who exist precariously on the cliff-like margins of many cultures." The "whiteness" of the white world, the spread of white supremacy in countries dominated by imperialism, had left native elites orphaned: they could never be fully Western, but neither could they find a haven in their own traditions.

Wright's argument about the psychic toll of whiteness in the lived experience of the "lonely outsiders" of the colonized world had much in common with Memmi's analysis in *The Colonizer and the Colonized*, and indeed with Fanon's in *Black Skin, White Masks*. But Fanon, by then, was no longer a lonely outsider in the white West: he was an Algerian, an African. And he had lost patience with the private sorrows of colonized elites. Wright's study, he wrote, "suffers from the same shortcomings as Memmi's essay: the Black man, like the Arab . . . is an abstract figure." It's true, he went on,

> that Black writers and poets all endure their own suffering, that the drama of consciousness of a westernized Black man, torn between his white culture and his Négritude, can be very painful; but this drama, which, after all, kills no one, is too particular to be representative: the misfortune of the colonized African masses, exploited, subjugated, is first of all of a vital, material order; the spiritual rifts of the "elite" are a luxury that they are unable to afford . . . Wright misses the point, losing himself in chatter of interest only to "elites" . . . Has history, then, taught Richard Wright nothing?

In fact, it had taught him a great deal: while Wright's sympathies lay with the colonized, he understood—thanks to his own experiences as a Black refugee from the South who had made his way north in the Great Migration—that the road to freedom was mined with obstacles, both economic and psychological. The very nature of imperialism, including the Western education and secular styles of thought and ideology it had exported to the colonies, had created forms of dislocation that political independence would not instantly overcome. In retrospect, Wright's assessment of the postcolonial condition was full of suggestive ambiguities, unsparing in its indictment of the West but also alert to the allure of nativism and other sectarian passions—a problem that Fanon himself would soon be forced to address.

ON JANUARY 4, 1960, only a few days after Fanon celebrated New Year's at the Manuellans' apartment, Camus was driving back to Paris from his house in Provence when his car swerved off the road and crashed into a tree. He was forty-six. His traveling companion, Michel Gallimard—the nephew of his publisher and the driver of the car, a Facel Vega—died five days later. Camus had often described dying in a car crash as the height of the absurd. But by then, he was less identified with the absurd than with the positions he had taken—or failed to take—on France's war in Algeria.

His death carried immense symbolism, as if the hope of reconciliation between Algerian and European Muslims, in an "integrated" Algeria that remained a part of France, had died with him. In reality it had died long before—perhaps as long ago as the original sin of the conquest, as Camus himself came close to acknowledging in *Le Premier Homme*. Camus was repelled by the intellectual rationalizations of the FLN's attacks on civilians, which the writings of Fanon, whom he never met, would come to embody. Camus's name appears only once in Fanon's work (and not even in his own words): in an appendix in *L'An V de la révolution algérienne*, containing Geronimi's testimony of his political awakening as a European supporter of the FLN. But Camus and Fanon had much in common. Both had grown up in port towns, at the edges of the French empire, where they had acquired a love of football, swimming, and physical activity. Both had looked in their youth toward France as a symbol of freedom; both had answered de Gaulle's call to defend it in the war; both wrote about their horror at the misery of Algerian street children; both were fascinated by the question of murder and confession. Camus had enjoyed all the privileges (and blindness) of a European in the colonies, but his origins were far humbler than Fanon's. As a writer and thinker who hadn't attended the *grandes écoles*, and as the Algerian-born son of an illiterate mother, Catherine Sintès, he felt—with some justification—that Left Bank intellectuals looked down on him. (He sniped in his journals at the "petty breed of Parisian writers who cultivate what they believe to be insolence. Servants who at one and the same time ape the great and mock them in the pantry.") Like Fanon, he was both combative and easily wounded. His vanity, like Fanon's, made him doubly susceptible to slights, especially aspersions cast on his virtue, like the character of "the penitent-judge," Jean-Baptiste Clamence, in his 1956 novel, *The Fall*.

But Camus had been raised in Algeria and remained loyal to his community, the Europeans of Algeria, often in an ostentatiously agonized way. None of this was true of Fanon. While Camus used his influence behind closed doors to secure the release of FLN prisoners, he refused to condemn the army's conduct. After the failure of his civilian truce initiative, he swung back and forth between reticence and prickliness; it was not always clear if he was defending France or merely his right to remain silent about a subject that he found too painful to discuss. At Stockholm University on December 12, 1957, two days after Camus received the Nobel Prize, an Algerian student asked him why he spoke out against Stalinist crimes in Eastern Europe but not against French crimes in Algeria. Camus did not appreciate the question, or the torrent of insults that followed. "I have always denounced terrorism," he said. "I must also denounce a terrorism which is exercised blindly, in the streets of Algiers for example, and which one day could strike my mother or my family. I believe in justice, but I shall defend my mother before justice."

For the former *résistant* and opponent of capital punishment, the rooted attachment to tribe and family now took precedence over "abstract" principles. But justice—or rather its absence—had never been an abstraction for Algerian Muslims, and their mothers were at greater risk of indiscriminate violence than his. Two weeks after the exchange in Stockholm, the Berber poet Jean Amrouche, with whom Camus had fallen out over the war, wrote, "I had to break with my mother, because the cause of

justice, that is to say of millions of Algerian mothers, comes before mine."
Camus's "discomfort, in glorious solitude, is very comfortable," he added.

Camus decided to hold his tongue in public. But he began to spend
even more time in Algiers, visiting his aging mother. Some of his Algerian
friends avoided him, but others understood his reasons for not supporting
the rebellion, even if they regretted his position. In his diary after seeing
Camus, Mouloud Feraoun wrote:

> We spent two hours just talking very openly. His position . . . is exactly
> as I thought it would be—incredibly human. He feels tremendous pity
> for those who are suffering. But he also knows that pity or love is impo-
> tent, completely powerless to overcome the evil that kills, that destroys,
> and that would like to wipe everything out and create a new world
> where the timid and the skeptical are banished.

In the last two years of his life, Camus confined his thoughts on Algeria to his journals, where he confessed that his love for his mother country
was so fierce that it had led him to betray the principles he had espoused
throughout his life. "It is myself that for nearly five years I have been criti-
cizing, what I believed, what I lived," he wrote. "This is why those who
shared the same ideas . . . are so angry with me; but no, I'm making war on
myself, and I'll destroy myself or I'll be reborn." In the journals, he turns
decisively against "the moral point of view"—the view he had taken for
decades—concluding that it is "the mother of fanaticism and blindness."
He is clear about the price he has paid for abandoning it, the loss not only
of the moral prestige he had earned in the Resistance but of a coherent
moral outlook: "Now I wander among the debris, I am lawless, torn apart,
alone and willing to be, resigned to my singularity and my infirmities. And
I must reconstruct a truth, having lived my whole life in a kind of lie."

But as he trudged through the debris of his certainties, Camus began
work on his most persuasive work of fiction set in Algeria. Just as psychiatry enabled Fanon to step away from his grandstanding polemical positions
and write with sensitivity and grace about the "mental disorders" produced
by the war, so *Le Premier Homme* allowed Camus to come to terms with

what he recoiled from in his public statements on the war: the honor and dignity of Algeria's maquisards (embodied in the figure of Saddok), and the terminal crisis of French Algeria. *Le Premier Homme* was not "committed" writing; it could not even be read in his lifetime. Steeped in his new sense of his "lawlessness," the novel acknowledges the legitimacy of Algeria's revolt, even as it captures the tragic fate of European Algerians like his mother, who had known no other home, and who would be "repatriated" to France at independence, in one of the greatest exoduses of the twentieth century. In one of the novel's appendixes, Jacques Cormery, the protagonist, cries out to his mother:

> Return the land. Give all the land to the poor, to those who have nothing and who are so poor that they never wanted to have and to possess, to those in the country who are like her, the immense herd of the wretched, mostly Arab and a few French, and who will live and survive here through stubbornness and endurance, with the only pride that is worth anything in the world, that of the poor, give them the land as one gives what is sacred to those who are sacred, and then I, poor once more and forever, cast into the worst of exiles at the end of the earth, I will smile and I will die happily.

Fanon, of course, believed that men like Cormery would never act on their remorse unless their hands were forced, and that neither land nor freedom was the conqueror's to give: only the wretched of the earth could reclaim it for themselves.

PART IV

# THE AFRICAN

# 13

# PHANTOM AFRICA

IN JANUARY 1960, FANON told Michel Martini, his colleague at Charles Nicolle Hospital in Tunis, that he would be leaving the following month for Accra, to take up a new post as the FLN's *ambassadeur itinérant* (roving ambassador) for the GPRA in Black Africa. He announced the news in a world-weary tone, as if he had no choice but to accept all the tasks that "the organization," the FLN, had assigned him. Martini laughed to himself. Everyone in Tunis knew that Fanon had been campaigning for the job for months.

He hardly needed to campaign. The FLN had much to gain by sending a Black man to represent the movement in Accra. He would also be out of the way, exiled even as he was promoted, an outcome that his more resentful colleagues in Tunis surely appreciated.

It was an irresistible posting: Fanon had been galvanized by his attendance at Nkrumah's All-African People's Conference in 1958. Omar Oussedik, his closest comrade in the FLN, became the GPRA's representative in Sékou Touré's Guinea, stationed in Conakry, while Omar's brother Boualem, with whom Fanon was also friendly, was assigned to serve in the same capacity in Bamako. The leftists of the exterior were being promoted to diplomatic positions, and at the same time conveniently exported to West Africa, which the FLN did not consider to be as strategically important as the countries of the Arab world, Europe, or the Soviet bloc. No matter: the liberation of Black African countries occupied an increasingly large place in Fanon's imagination, whatever the FLN's opinions. Martini had the distinct impression that Fanon was happy to be leaving Tunis, even if it meant bidding farewell to the Charles Nicolle Hospital, and to the CNPJ, his proudest achievement as a doctor.

"Fanon *was* the clinic," as Marie-Jeanne Manuellan put it, and after his departure, it began to crumble. By then, Charles Geronimi had left for East Berlin, where Alice Cherki was doing a residency at the Charité, Germany's oldest hospital, while Lucien Lévy returned to private practice. Manuellan stayed on briefly but eventually found work as a high school French teacher. Fanon's replacement in neuropsychiatry at Charles Nicolle was a thirty-eight-year-old doctor from France, Annette Roger, a daring *porteuse de valise* who had been imprisoned for several weeks (while pregnant) for driving an FLN official from Marseille to Paris in her car. Dazzlingly brilliant, flirtatious, and foul-mouthed, she was the talk of radical Tunis; as the Tunisian journalist Guy Sitbon recalls, when Roger was in the room, "everything was sexy."

Life in Accra, however, was not so sexy, especially for Josie. As the GPRA's representative in Black Africa, her husband was as likely to be in Conakry or Addis Ababa as he was to be at home in Accra. In their early years as a couple, Frantz had been a Black man in white Lyon; now, as a white woman in a Black city, raising a métis son on her own while her husband traveled, she was the one who felt out of place. The one time he took her with him to Conakry, the Guineans refused to speak in her presence; she was a white Frenchwoman, not to be trusted. Soon after the Fanons settled in Accra, she wrote to Manuellan, "The Blacks make fun of me because I'm white, and the whites make fun of me because I married a Black man." Before long, Josie and Olivier moved back to Tunis; Frantz visited as often as he could from Accra.

In August, Fanon was on his way to a conference of the World Assembly of Youth (WAY) at the University of Ghana in Accra, when he stopped a woman on campus to ask for directions to the event in his basic English. As it turned out, she was headed in the same direction. Elaine Klein was an American Jewish woman in her early thirties, a fierce advocate of

Algerian independence, and an activist in the World Federalist Movement
and in WAY. She later wrote about what she called her "enlightenment,"
which had come on May Day 1952, in Paris, while she was in the rue du
Faubourg Saint-Antoine, watching the annual workers' parade organized
by the French Communist Party:

> As the parade was breaking up, thousands of men appeared out of
> nowhere, running in formation, ten to twelve abreast . . . They kept
> coming, more and more—young, grim, slightly built and poorly
> dressed. They shouted no slogans, carried no flags, no banners. They
> were Algerian laborers.

The men were supporters of the Algerian nationalist leader Messali
Hadj, protesting their exclusion from the parade. As Klein soon learned,
the Confédération générale du travail, the Communist-backed union, had
blocked their participation because of their support for Algerian independence. A few weeks later, Messali was arrested and placed under house
arrest in France. Klein recalled:

> That May Day 1952 parade was my first contact with Algeria. The events
> I witnessed gave the lie to French egalitarianism: the famous motto *lib-
> erté, égalité, fraternité* was flipped upside down . . . I had fallen in love
> with France even before stepping on board the ship that had carried
> me across the Atlantic . . . But that May Day, I realized that the French
> were not colorblind . . . Something in me associated those gaunt, olive-
> skinned men on the Faubourg Saint-Antoine with the darker wayfarers
> trailing along the dusty roads of the South I had observed in Georgia as
> a student in the late 1940s. I had seen them as desperate and estranged,
> and they had tugged at my heart.

That August day in 1960, recognizing Fanon's accent, Klein answered
him in French. "His first thought was that I was French," Klein recalled
Fanon telling her. "When he realized that I was not, he was relieved." Klein
was struck by his "deep-set, probing eyes" and his "strong, wide jaw."
Fanon was attending the conference as an official observer of the GPRA.

Together with his colleague Mohamed Sahnoun, a leader of the FLN student association, he pushed for a resolution condemning France and supporting Algerian independence. It passed unanimously. In his speech at the conference, Fanon read passages from *L'An V de la révolution algérienne*, describing the psychological effects of colonialism on his Algerian patients, until Sahnoun, growing weary of Fanon's analytic recitation, stole the microphone and brought the audience to its feet with a call to support the national liberation struggle.

Over the course of the conference, Fanon and Klein met frequently. "We were bound by a commitment to African independence and, beyond that, to the anti-imperialist struggle," Klein recalls. Fanon took her to his office in Accra, "no more than a small apartment." She was "struck by how spartan it was, how clinical in appearance." One night, they were out dancing at a club in Accra when Fanon noticed that a photographer was taking their picture. Fanon, who never danced in the presence of his FLN colleagues, asked him to destroy the photo (it was published a few days later in a Ghanaian newspaper). But as keen as he was to keep up appearances, he snuck a Gauloise with Klein, in spite of the FLN's boycott on French cigarettes. "We became partners in guilt," Klein admitted.

Later, Fanon asked her what she desired in a relationship. "To put my head on someone's shoulder," she replied.

"*Non, non, non,*" he said repeatedly. "Stay upright on your own two feet and keep moving forward to goals of your own."

Fanon had not become a sudden convert to women's liberation, but his belief in freedom extended to women as well as men.* And though he was no longer working as a psychiatrist, he could not resist an opportunity to practice disalienation, even when he was flirting.

In late August 1960, while the WAY congress was still in session, Fanon flew to Léopoldville with Omar Oussedik and M'hammed Yazid, the GPRA's information minister, to attend a conference of African leaders, organized by Fanon's friend Patrice Lumumba, who had recently

---

* After independence, he would write in *The Wretched of the Earth*, "women will receive a place identical to men, not in the articles of the Constitution, but in daily life, at the factory, in schools, and in the assemblies."

become prime minister of the Republic of Congo. Lumumba had won enormous prestige for leading the Congolese to independence against a brutal and humiliating colonial regime. But the "greatest Black man who ever walked the African continent," as Malcolm X called him, was in trouble. Weeks into his tenure and less than two months since independence from Belgium, Lumumba was poised on the edge of an abyss as the country descended into violence. Independence had produced a massive sense of entitlement among the former colonial security forces, the so-called Force Publique, who were now in a state of mutiny over pay and conditions, while the former colonial power—stung by the denunciation that Lumumba had delivered impromptu at the handover ceremonies—had deployed troops of its own, ostensibly to protect Belgian citizens: the violence of the Congolese Force Publique showed no sign of abating even when Lumumba "Africanized" its ranks and reconstituted it as the new Congolese army. It was in large part this escalating crisis that the conference in Léopoldville was convened to address. In July, Lumumba had flown to Accra, where he and Kwame Nkrumah had agreed to work rapidly toward a "United States of Africa." The hope was that the deliberations of the delegates might move things forward. Nkrumah had also pledged military support to Lumumba as his fledgling republic began to founder.

Most of the whites still residing in Congo fled the violence of the mutiny and made their way to the mineral-rich province of Katanga, which had become a bastion of neocolonial ressentiment, fortified by Belgian soldiers; others made their way to the N'djili airport outside the capital. But the mining companies dug in and saw an opportunity to shield their assets from a postcolonial leader who believed that Congo's natural resources belonged to its inhabitants. The United States, too, was invested in Katanga's mineral wealth and wished to ring-fence the strategic minerals site at Shinkolobwe, which had supplied the Manhattan Project with uranium ore. The Belgian navy bombarded the strategic port city of Matadi, while Belgian paratroopers seized N'djili. When some of the departing Belgians met Lumumba at the airport, they spat at him.

Katanga seceded from the newly independent country in the second week of July, with support from Belgium and its mining interests as well as French mercenaries sent by the businessman Jacques Foccart, a friend of de Gaulle whose nickname was "Mr. Africa." Before the month was out, Belgian troops had clashed with the new Congolese army, and in August the diamond-rich province of South Kasai made its own bid to secede. Lumumba cast his net wide for support to keep the peace—he had asked the United States for three thousand soldiers as an interventionist force—but when all other avenues were closed and he appealed to the Soviet Union for help, he conspired in the trap that Washington had set for him.

Days before Fanon flew out for the conference, Larry Devlin, the CIA station chief in Léopoldville, warned the Eisenhower administration that if Lumumba stayed in power, the Soviets would acquire a monopoly on the extraction of cobalt and other minerals used in the production of missiles. In an ominous cable, Devlin described Lumumba and his allies as "anti-white" and attacked Lumumba's press attaché, the French radical Serge Michel—Fanon's colleague at *El Moudjahid*, whom the FLN had "loaned" to the Congolese government—as a Communist. Lumumba, he said, should be replaced with a "more moderate and pro-Western government." UN troops were deployed to keep the peace, but they had no mandate to use arms against Katanga—increasingly a militarized redoubt of Western mining interests and American Cold War ambitions—even though they clashed with secessionist forces later. By the time Fanon was able to speak with Lumumba, the tragic fate of his friend had been sealed.

The conference of independent African states opened in Léopoldville on August 25, the same day the CIA decided not to rule out any activity that might contribute to Lumumba's removal or physical liquidation. Lumumba himself was in Stanleyville, his hometown and stronghold, and did not arrive until a few days later. The purpose of the conference was to rally African support for his embattled government, but Léopoldville was the base of President Joseph Kasavubu, a rival of Lumumba's.

The GPRA delegation had arrived in Léopoldville not to defend Lumumba but to promote the FLN's position on self-determination at a forthcoming UN session on Algeria's future, scheduled for December. M'hammed Yazid spent most of his time at the conference approaching African delegates, with, in Michel's words, "an invisible bowl in his hand to collect the maximum promises of African votes." For Fanon and Oussedik, the situation was much more conflicted: they had come to demonstrate their solidarity with a pan-African ally, but they were only now beginning to grasp the full extent of the assault on his authority.

Taking advantage of Lumumba's vulnerability in the capital, the CIA funded rowdy anti-Lumumba demonstrations outside the conference. As he excoriated the Western powers for their interference in the internal affairs of Congo and other African states, he was drowned out by protesters shouting, "Down with Lumumba!" The delegates were shocked: they had expected to see a poised, confident leader like Kwame Nkrumah or Sékou Touré, not an embattled politician fighting for his survival. Serge Michel, who had grown personally close to Lumumba, told Fanon that he despaired of his chances of remaining in power. In fact, the GPRA leadership had already begun to distance itself from Lumumba. The Bourguiba government—without whom neither the GPRA nor the ALN could operate in Tunisia—was not fond of Lumumba, and was keen to maintain good relations with the West, especially the Americans. Lumumba's feud with the UN also gave the GPRA pause, since the organization was crucial to its campaign to achieve a negotiated solution to the war in Algeria. And then there was the fear of angering Lumumba's enemies in Washington at a time when the American government was beginning to exert discreet pressure on France. Lumumba, in short, was becoming a liability for the Algerians, and, as Michel recalled in his memoirs, "even Frantz and Omar preached realism" on their voyage to Congo.

On one of Fanon's first nights in Léopoldville, M'hammed Yazid invited him to dinner at the home of a friend from New York City, Herbert Weiss, a young specialist on African politics. Weiss had fled Austria as a child with his Jewish family in 1938; the family spent nine years in Khartoum, in what was then the Anglo-Egyptian Sudan, before moving to the United States. As a youth activist in the World Federalist Movement, he had championed the cause of African independence alongside his friend Elaine Klein, later Fanon's dancing partner in Accra. Weiss had briefly worked as a research analyst in the State Department but was now in Congo, conducting field research in rural areas for the Massachusetts Institute of Technology. He had developed close relations with Lumumba's inner circle. His girlfriend, the Belgian sociologist Maryse Périn, had just been expelled from Katanga by the leader of the secession, Moïse

Tshombe, and was working as Lumumba's unofficial secretary. The shared sense of being part of world-historical events—Lumumba's revolution and African independence—added to the intensity of their affair, even if what had begun as the long-overdue summer of Congolese freedom had already given way to mutiny and secession, spasms of anti-Belgian violence, white flight, and Cold War intrigue. During the mutiny, they had rented a colonial house with a terrace—abandoned by its Belgian occupants, like all the houses surrounding it—in the suburb of Binza Ma Campagne, somewhat uphill from the capital, and a little cooler. They could see dogs wandering the streets, looking for their owners, who were never to return.

When Yazid told him that Fanon was in town, Weiss was thrilled at the prospect of hosting him, and invited a friend, the Belgian sociologist Benoît Verhaegen, a left-wing scholar of Congo, to join them. Weiss recalls:

> Fanon came with a reputation, and we were admiring of the fact that a man who wasn't an Arab and couldn't speak Arabic had risen to this height in an Arab nationalist movement. The fact that he was Black was another thing that should have counted against him in the eyes of the Algerians, but it didn't. How many examples are there of *that*? I looked up to this man, not because of his titles, but because of what he had accomplished as a writer and as a man, and the absolutely mind-blowing fact that he treated the torturers by day and the tortured at night. Fanon was the ultimate ideal of Western man, since he had completely honed his own identity and fused the two great intellectual movements of the twentieth century, Marxism and Freudianism. He had structured his life not according to blood or soil, but according to values and principles, and then committed himself to become an activist. He had created himself out of that abstract model.

Yazid, who took pride in his cooking, prepared a splendid meal, and the five of them sat down to discuss Congolese politics. Fanon, "an intense listener," mostly asked questions. He seemed especially curious about the work that Weiss and Verhaegen had been doing on pro-independence protest movements in the countryside. The received wisdom among students of African politics at the time was that elites mobilized the peasantry and urged them to support pro-independence parties. But Weiss told him that his research in the lower Congo had suggested the opposite. Congolese elites had mostly been seeking to replace the Belgians in positions of authority and Africanize the administration, while the rural masses wanted to overthrow and replace the system itself, forcing the hand of previously cautious elites. Fanon, whose hopes for radical social change had been shifting from the city to the countryside ever since his time in Blida, listened intently to Weiss's monologue about the peasants of the lower Congo, either drawing inspiration from his conclusions or simply gratified to have his intuitions confirmed by empirical evidence. In *The Wretched of the Earth*, published a year later, he would provide his own starry-eyed, Narodnik gloss on agrarian radicalism:

> The nationalist militant who decides to put his destiny in the hands of the peasant masses, instead of playing hide-and-seek with the police in the urban centers, will never regret it. The peasant cloak wraps him in a mantle of unimagined tenderness and vitality. Veritable exiles in their own country and severed from the urban milieu where they drew up the concepts of nation and political struggle, they take to the maquis . . . Discussions with the peasants now become a ritual for them. They discover that the rural masses have never ceased to pose the problem of their liberation in terms of violence, of taking back the land from the foreigners, in terms of *national struggle* and armed revolt.

Of what country, in this fable of anti-colonial militants learning humbly from their instinctively insurrectionary rural base, was Fanon thinking? It wasn't exactly Algeria's case. But it may have reflected impressions he had formed during his conversations in sub-Saharan Africa, confirming a vision of Africa that took hold of his imagination in his last two years. As a psychiatrist, Fanon had always insisted on the need for patients to *faire face au monde* (confront the world), even if—especially if—it challenged their sense of reality. But in his political analysis, he would often take a detour from discouraging realities and find sanctuary in a kind of utopian poetry, as if, by the force of his words, he could remake the world.

Africa was, in some ways, a phantom for Fanon: a distant memory of his family's history, a premonition of the future he hoped to usher into reality by violent insurrection.

Intrigued by what Weiss and Verhaegen had to say about rural radicalism, he had also taken a keen interest in Weiss's girlfriend. Périn, a radical anti-colonialist with roots on the Catholic left, had been a *porteuse de valise* in Belgium, where she had helped FLN militants to cross the French border and hidden them in her home. She also shared Fanon's revolutionary impatience, his hunger for action. A few days after the dinner with Fanon, Weiss and Périn were at a garden party for the UN secretary general, Dag Hammarskjöld, when Fanon took Weiss aside to ask a question: "Does that woman belong to you?" Weiss, "like a good Western liberal," replied that only Périn could answer that question. When Weiss looked for her later that evening, she had already left with Fanon.

The next morning, Weiss received a call from a friend in Lumumba's office, warning him that if Périn reported to work, she would be arrested immediately, "because she was Belgian and the situation was becoming increasingly tense." Périn's connection to Weiss also stirred suspicion in the minds of Congolese officials, since a member of intelligence had been given his old State Department business card. (Earlier in the week, Yazid had been asked to vouch to the Congolese that Weiss wasn't a spy.) Weiss drove into Léopoldville and approached Fanon in the lobby of his hotel. "This is not what you think," he explained. "I'm not here as a jealous lover. I just need to know where she is."

Fanon looked incredulous, shrugged, and said she'd gone to work. He had bigger things to worry about than the whereabouts of his one-night stand. Lumumba was clearly losing his tenuous grip over Congo, and, before flying home, Fanon and Oussedik were to spend a long, sleepless night trying to persuade him to give up his post as prime minister and reorganize his political party, the MNC.

As it turned out, Périn had indeed gone to work and been arrested on suspicion of espionage. After spending the night in jail, she returned to Binza under armed guard. Weiss was terrified that the soldiers would search the house, since his office was full of documents that officials in Congolese political parties had given him or allowed him to photograph—research that could easily be mistaken for intelligence work. He brandished the letter that Lumumba had written on his behalf, indicating that he enjoyed the prime minister's protection, and the soldiers left. When Lumumba found out what had happened, he told Périn, "Je suis entouré par des fous" (I'm surrounded by madmen).

He was also surrounded by traitors and assassins. On September 5, Lumumba was dismissed from power by President Kasavubu, who accused him of pro-Communist sympathies: Lumumba riposted by dismissing Kasavubu. The argument went to and fro in the Chamber of Deputies and the Senate until September 13, when a joint session agreed that Lumumba should be given emergency powers. The following day Colonel Joseph Mobutu, whom Lumumba had appointed chief of staff of the overhauled army, announced his decision to take charge of Congo; his coup was backed by the CIA.

Far from urging Lumumba to crack down on his opponents during their conversations in Léopoldville, Fanon had advised him to step down, in line with the GPRA's instructions. When Lumumba refused, he and his colleagues in the GPRA appear to have cut their losses. In his memoir, Serge Michel claims that before leaving Congo, Fanon, Yazid, and Oussedik met one more time with Lumumba, who made a moving appeal for aid from the GPRA. They responded enthusiastically, promising that "the enemies of Africa should be on their guard." But outside Lumumba's residence, Fanon took Michel aside and reminded him that he represented the FLN in Congo, not Lumumba: he ought to be more circumspect. Fanon's advice to Michel was to "forget Lumumba" and align himself with Kasavubu. An anti-Lumumba group, Fanon went on, was "working very hard, and it includes some serious people."

Michel asked Fanon why he was so sure. Fanon replied that his friend Holden Roberto, the CIA-backed Angolan leader ("Gilmore" in Michel's memoir), had tipped him off. "He is aware of everything that is going on," Fanon said. Roberto, who also attended the conference, had decided to back Kasavubu: the Congolese president, like Roberto, was an ethnic Bakongo. Shortly after Fanon's briefing, Michel was approached by Roberto. "Fanon told you?" he asked, before launching into a tirade against Lumumba, "a demagogue, a puppet in the hands of international communism, a public

menace," and concluding, "Blood must flow." After the coup, Mobutu put
out an arrest warrant for Michel, who fled back to Tunis. The next time
Michel saw Fanon, they spoke about Africa, but not about the Congo, "so
as not to reopen wounds that hadn't healed." When Fanon met Sartre and
Beauvoir in Rome in August 1961, he would blame himself for failing to
rescue Lumumba.

Fanon was often described by his peers as distrustful, but in some ways
he was too trusting, even gullible, when it came to hard men like Roberto
(as he was toward the rugged peasant of his imagination). A few days after
Périn returned home from jail, she declared to Weiss that she and Fanon
were planning to join Roberto's movement in northern Angola, the UPA.
It was a momentary fantasy of struggle, stoicism, and sacrifice, and probably pillow talk. By then, Fanon was already back in Accra, having failed
to convince Lumumba to resign.

The following spring, the UPA launched an uprising in which more
than a thousand Portuguese were killed in attacks on farms, government
outposts, and markets—a jacquerie reminiscent of the Philippeville insurrection. "This time," Roberto boasted, "the slaves did not cower. They
massacred everything." The Portuguese responded by killing tens of thousands of Angolans and driving hundreds of thousands across the border into Congo. Hardly a month after the massacres, Roberto met with
President Kennedy and was praised in *Time* as a "determined, soft-spoken,
exiled African Angolan." Through the CIA station in Léopoldville, he was
paid a retainer fee as a reliable and "genuine anti-Communist." He would
later divorce his wife and marry Mobutu's sister-in-law, to consolidate his
ties to Congo's pro-American dictator.

Fanon, for his part, had made his pledge to the FLN and was committed to seeing it through to the war's end. Yet Africa had gone to his head,
as much as Algeria had. His next venture, his most daring yet, would be
in Mali.

# 14

# "CREATE THE CONTINENT"

———

AFRICAN UNITY MAY HAVE been Fanon's obsession in 1960, but he was lucid about the obstacles that stood in its way: anti-Black racism—a legacy of slavery—was one; differences in custom were another. He once accompanied a group of delegates from Guinea to a film screening organized by the Tunisian Ministry of Information. At the intermission they saw the kind of French advertisement Fanon had deplored in *Black Skin, White Masks*: a cartoon in which African cannibals danced around a white man tied to a pole, who proceeded to save his skin by handing out ice pops. The delegates said politely that it was too hot inside the theater and walked out. Fanon complained to a Tunisian official in the ministry, only to be told, "You *Africans* are so touchy." On one of his visits to Conakry with the GPRA, the Algerians he'd taken along were mortified by a show that the Guineans had organized on their behalf, featuring women dancing with their breasts exposed. Fanon pretended not to know what the fuss was about.

"Are these decent women?" his colleagues asked.

"They have breasts, and they show them," Fanon responded.

For all his deference to Algerian customs, he remained a West Indian and enjoyed teasing his Algerian colleagues about their prudish misgivings. But in *The Wretched of the Earth*, he would register pointed concerns about these tensions. All too often, he writes, "a citizen of Black Africa hears himself called a '*nègre*' by the children when walking in the streets of a big town in White Africa, or finds that civil servants address him in *le petit nègre.*" He continues:

> Yes, unfortunately it is not unknown for students from Black Africa who attend secondary schools north of the Sahara to be asked by their classmates if there are houses back where they live, if they know what electricity is, or if they practice cannibalism in their families ... At the same time, in certain young states of Black Africa, members of parliament, even governmental ministers, solemnly affirm that the danger isn't a reoccupation of their country by the forces of colonialism, but a possible invasion by "Arab vandals from the north."

In Fanon's view, the only way to overcome the divisions between white and Black, Arab and sub-Saharan, was to make common cause against colonialism. In November 1960, with the FLN's blessing, he embarked on his first and only military mission for the Algerian cause: a reconnaissance trip, aimed at opening a southern front for the ALN, so that weapons and ammunition could be smuggled from Bamako, the Malian capital, north through the Sahara. Algeria's liberation was the ostensible objective, but it is clear from the journal he kept during his trip that he had a wider sense of what was at stake. Colonialism was on the back foot, he argued, but it was still capable of "reviving old particularisms and breaking up the liberating lava ... For us Algerians the situation was clear. But the terrain remained difficult, very difficult ... We had to prove, by concrete demonstrations, that the continent was one."

Days before his expedition, Fanon learned that his friend Félix-Roland Moumié, the anti-colonialist Cameroonian leader, had been murdered in Geneva; a French intelligence agent posing as a journalist had poisoned his drink with thallium. Moumié, one of the "hard" men Fanon most admired, was thirty-five years old; Fanon had last seen him in Accra in mid-September, where they had made plans to meet again in Rome. Aware that he was under constant surveillance, Moumié had avoided flying over French territory, or the airspace of countries in de Gaulle's French Community. "An abstract death striking the most concrete, the most alive, the most impetuous man," Fanon wrote. "A bundle of revolutionary spirit packed into sixty kilos of muscle and bone." When he picked up Moumié's father at the airport in Accra, he was reminded of "those parents in Algeria who listen in a kind of stupor to the story of the death of their children."

Abane and Moumié had been killed; Lumumba, a friend but never one of the GPRA's priorities, had been toppled in a coup; Fanon himself had narrowly dodged an assassination attempt in Rome. It was in this climate of violence and terror—and possibly in a wish to atone—that he conceived of his expedition. In his imagination, the African desert provided a practical answer to the problem of the Morice Line on Algeria's borders with Tunisia and Morocco; it also promised to link the entire continent in a final, apocalyptic offensive against the forces of imperialism. In evocative, dreamlike prose, he envisioned a continental war of liberation on behalf of Algeria, an anti-colonial analogue of his first battle, when he landed in France with the Free French Forces to fight the Germans in 1944:

> Stir up the Saharan population, infiltrate to the Algerian high plateaus. After carrying Algeria to the four corners of Africa, move up with all Africa toward African Algeria, toward the North, toward Algiers, the continental city. What I should like: great lines, great navigation channels through the desert. Subdue the desert, deny it, assemble Africa, create the continent. That Malians, Senegalese, Guineans, Ghanaians should descend from Mali onto our territory. And those of the Ivory Coast, of Nigeria, of Togoland. That they should all climb to the slopes of the desert and pour over the colonialist bastion. To turn the absurd and the impossible inside out and hurl a continent against the last ramparts of colonial power.

Fanon's anti-imperialist rhetoric had the ring of colonial conquest.

He traveled with a modest team: a commando of eight men, led by an ALN major called Chawki,* who "knows the Sahara like the palm of

---

* This was not Chawki Mostefaï, Krim Belkacem's adviser, with whom Fanon traveled to Accra in 1958.

his hand." He was captivated by Chawki, a former maquisard with "implacable eyes." They would share a bed on their journey and talk until the small hours. "Those eyes," he wrote of Chawki, "tell their own story. They say openly that they have witnessed hard things . . . One notes in those eyes a kind of haughtiness, of almost murderous hardness . . . One quickly forms the habit of paying attention to such men . . . One can say anything to them, but they need to feel and to touch the Revolution in the words uttered." Chawki was another beguiling hard man. Among the Algerians Fanon befriended was a young ALN leader, Abdelaziz Bouteflika, a future foreign minister and president, known at the time by his nom de guerre, Abdelkader al-Mali, who—according to widespread rumors—typed some of the first pages of *The Wretched of the Earth*.

The Malian expedition was a risky endeavor, and it "nearly ended in the interrogation chambers of Algeria." Fanon and his men had flown from Accra to Monrovia, where they hoped to catch a plane to Conakry. When they arrived, they were told that the plane was full. They would have to board an Air France flight instead. Fanon wrote that Air France's employees were "abnormally attentive" to his party and offered to have the company pay all their stopover expenses. Their "exemplary solicitude" and the "bar-maid allure of a voluble and excruciatingly boring French lady" raised Fanon's suspicions that the French were planning to intercept their plane, as they had intercepted Ben Bella's in 1956. His hunch proved correct: the plane made a surprise landing in Abidjan, the capital of Côte d'Ivoire, ruled by France's ally Félix Houphouët-Boigny, and was searched by French forces.

Fanon and his companions had wisely decided against the flight and traveled by road. They entered Guinea from Liberia, passing through the Guinean border towns of Diéké and N'Zérékoré, and then headed to Bamako. The Republic of Mali had proclaimed its independence on September 22, 1960, a month after the collapse of its federation with Senegal, an experiment in pan-African governance that lasted only two months. No longer a part of the French Community, Mali quickly declared itself "free of all engagements and political linkages with France." Its president, Modibo Keïta, offered to set up a listening post for the ALN at Kayes, on the Senegal River; supplied Fanon and his men with identification papers issued by the Ministry of the Interior; and gave them a place to stay in Bamako's main barracks. "If one listens with one ear glued to the red earth," Fanon wrote in his journal, "one very distinctly hears the sound of rusty chains, groans of distress, and the bruised flesh is so constantly present in this stifling noonday that one's shoulders droop with the weight of it. The Africa of everyday, oh not the poets' Africa, the one that puts people to sleep, but the one that prevents sleep, for the people is impatient to do, to play, to speak. The people that says: I want to build myself as a people."

On Tuesday, November 22, at five in the morning, they left for Gao, but the Bamako-Timbuktu road was flooded; they were forced to travel by a road leading south of the Niger to Ségou. After refueling, they headed to San, then Mopti, where they ran into a police roadblock. The gendarme asked for their papers, then insisted on seeing their passports. An inquisitive senior officer arrived on the scene. Suspecting that he was working for the French, Fanon decided to call his bluff, daring him to arrest them for failing to show their papers. The officer let them go. They took the road from Mopti to Douentza, through dense tropical forest, doing their best to follow "the tracks of a car that must have passed there six months before." They lost their way more than once, but at two in the morning, they reached their destination, where they fell asleep in their Land Rovers.

At nine the next evening they arrived in Gao, where a friendly local commander showed them a trove of documents left behind by French intelligence officers working along the borders of Morocco and Algeria. In his journal, Fanon rather grandly compared his mission to the capture of Kufra, an oasis in the Libyan desert, in 1941, when Italian troops surrendered to the Free French Forces, led by Colonel Philippe Leclerc de Hauteclocque. "People used to speak admiringly of the odyssey of General Leclerc's march across the Sahara," he wrote. "The one that we are preparing, if the French government does not realize it in time, will make the Leclerc episode look, by comparison, like a Sunday-school picnic."

Before Fanon and his commando left for Aguel'hoc and Tessalit, the last Malian settlements before the border, the commander in Gao issued them with colonial Arab scout uniforms to disguise themselves, along with rifles and a meager supply of ammunition. (Fanon hadn't held a weapon since the Second World War; his only use of guns was to kill a bustard and several deer for food.) In Tessalit, they passed a French military outpost, where a shirtless French soldier gave them a friendly wave, mistaking them for a band of Arab travelers. "His arms would drop off him if he could guess whom these Arab outfits conceal," Fanon thought, laughing to himself. Once they arrived in Boghassa, a wadi in Kidal, northeast of Gao, a group of Malian nomads gave them a "fairly exact idea about the French forces" in the border towns of the Algerian Sahara. These were the people Fanon hoped to recruit as intermediaries once the ALN set up a supply line on the Malian border.

On the way back from Boghassa, Fanon read books about the history of the region that he had acquired in Kidal. "I relive, with the intensity that circumstances and place confer upon them, the old empires of Ghana, of Mali, of Gao, and the impressive odyssey of the Moroccan troops with the famous Djouder"—Judar Pasha, the Spanish Moroccan military leader who overran the Songhai Empire in 1591. Eight years earlier, Fanon had wondered, in *Black Skin, White Masks*, whether he had "anything else to do on this earth but avenge the Blacks of the seventeenth century." Now that he had bound his destiny to Africa's, its history and its future spoke to him with an immediacy he could scarcely have foreseen at the time.

The challenge for Africa, he understood with a new clarity, was to ensure that liberation from formal colonialism would pave the way for genuine independence: economic development, political sovereignty, and the empowerment of Africa's vast rural populations. Africans were not the first to face this problem: one of the great lessons of modern political revolutions, as Hannah Arendt observed, is that while "liberation is indeed a condition of freedom . . . freedom is by no means a necessary result of liberation."

Still, as Fanon had seen to his horror in Congo, the passage from liberation to freedom in Africa was obstructed by forces both internal and external, from ethnic divisions and the predatory appetites of local elites to imperial meddling and the Cold War imperatives of the superpowers. The question of what would happen in Africa after colonialism died its inevitable death weighed heavily on him during his time in Mali. "Not everything is so simple," he admitted in his journal. Anticipating arguments that he would develop in *The Wretched of the Earth*, Fanon argued that the greatest obstacle to African independence was not "colonialism and its derivatives" so much as the "absence of ideology": the lack of a collective political project. The "new middle classes or their renovated princes," he warned, were conducting their political affairs much as they did their businesses, using "perquisites, threats, even despoiling of their victims." The distortions of colonialism had saddled the continent with a corrupt, self-seeking bourgeoisie. "To participate in the ordered movement of a continent," he reflected, "was really the work I had chosen." But it would not be easy to effect the transition from liberation into freedom.

Fanon's quixotic reconnaissance mission came to nothing: the southern Sahara had never been an important combat zone for the FLN, and there was little trust between the Algerians and the desert tribes. The great invasion of Algeria from the south remained what it always was: a radiant hallucination. (In the summer of 1961, Mali's leader, Modibo Keïta, permitted the ALN to set up a southern front, headed by Bouteflika, but it never amounted to much.) The most important legacy of Fanon's adventures in Mali was the journal he left behind, a riveting collage of Afro-pessimism and Afro-optimism, of lucid, sometimes bleak introspection and hypnotic revolutionary incantation. Prose and poetry were, of course, always interwoven in Fanon's work; this was a mark of his debt to Césaire. But the account of his expedition in Mali also reveals a moodiness born of a growing desperation, as his revolutionary dreams for African unity came up against the continent's less-than-revolutionary realities.

The desperation was also physical. While traveling to the Algerian border, Fanon had lost a great deal of weight, and when he came back to Accra in early December, he was utterly run down. He told himself that he was exhausted from the trip, and returned to work. There was plenty to distract him from the possibility that he had a serious medical condition, including encouraging news from Algeria, where de Gaulle had made an official visit, in an echo of his tour around the French Community of Africa in 1958, to rally support for a referendum on self-determination: it would be held the following month. De Gaulle's aim was to secure the transition to an "Algerian Algeria"—in other words, to neocolonial autonomy without national sovereignty: a "third way" that would leave the FLN out in the cold. He was convinced that, having crushed the rebels in both Algiers and the countryside, he could now impose a settlement and pass it off as self-determination, while protecting French interests in Algeria.

But on December 11, 1960, two days into de Gaulle's visit, in all the major cities, Algerians—men, women, children, the elderly—poured into the streets en masse to demand independence, waving the banned flag of the FLN and carrying banners reading "Muslim Algeria!" and "Negotiate with the FLN!" They clashed with police and European ultras, and converged on European neighborhoods. In Belcourt, a poor section of Algiers where Camus's mother lived, more than ten thousand Algerians occupied the streets. Women charged military barricades while soldiers opened fire on them, leaving their white *haïks* splattered with blood. Never had there been such a public demonstration of Algerian unity behind the FLN, or—despite the violence—a more festive one. As the Algerian historian Daho Djerbal has written: "These Algerians confronted Europeans but also sang and danced; in taking back the streets, they repossessed the cities; in freeing up their bodies, they began to make independence a concrete reality. This was an insurrection of human bodies until then bound by the kind of colonial domination described by Frantz Fanon."

More than a hundred demonstrators were killed during the protests. But de Gaulle, who had authorized the use of live ammunition, was so impressed by the scale of the defiance, and the show of support for the rebels, that he cut short his trip and reviewed his narrowing options. He had come a long way. Returned to power in June 1958 in a coup d'état led by military officers aligned with the settlers, he had vowed never to give up Algeria. In his June 4, 1958, speech before a crowd in Algiers, he declared, "Je vous ai compris" (I've understood you), a typically cryptic formulation, interpreted by some as a reassurance to the Europeans of Algeria, by others as a statement that he understood that Europeans and Muslims alike were exhausted by the war. A few days later, in the western port town of Mostaganem, de Gaulle invoked Algérie française, a phrase whose conspicuous absence in his earlier speeches had infuriated the ultras. But over the next two years, even as he tried to crush the rebellion and hold on to Algeria, he developed a grudging admiration in private for the resolve of the FLN—patriotic soldiers who modeled themselves on the French Resistance—and a growing contempt for the settlers, as well as the *harkis*, Algerian Muslims who fought with the army. But it was only the sight of ordinary Algerians demonstrating in the streets that led him to recognize what Fanon called "the reality of a nation," and the sheer futility of remaining in Algeria.

French Algeria's defeat was sealed not by bombs or rifles but by mass civil disobedience. It was an ironic reversal in the FLN's relationship to its constituency. The organization had projected itself as the defender of Algeria's masses, but it was Algeria's masses—both the long-term city dwellers and the rural people who had settled in the cities, fleeing the army's repression—who revived the FLN's fortunes, forcing de Gaulle to abandon his search for an *interlocuteur valable* and his hopeless quest for a third way. If proof was needed of what Abane Ramdane had called the "primacy of the interior," here it was. The GPRA won a major diplomatic victory on December 20 when the UN General Assembly, meeting in New York, affirmed Algeria's right to independence by a handsome majority and upheld the principle of Algerian territorial integrity in the face of de Gaulle's earlier threats of partition. Direct talks with the FLN could no longer be avoided.

For de Gaulle's critics on the left, his shifting stance on Algeria would come as a surprise, to say the least. De Gaulle was known to be an admirer of the late Hubert Lyautey, a colonial administrator and minister of war, who had been notorious for his brutal methods. When de Gaulle first took office, Fanon described him as "the most execrable instrument of the most obstinate, the most bestial colonialist reaction." Yet it was de Gaulle who would end up presiding over France's withdrawal, in the face of violent opposition from settlers and a terrorist campaign led by the Organisation de l'armée secrète. He had not become an anti-colonialist. Rather, he had come to see that, in his words, "Algeria costs us more than it brings us," much as Raymond Aron had argued in *The Algerian Tragedy*. The only alternative to independence, he realized, was the complete integration of Algeria's Muslims into France, which Jacques Soustelle had promoted, and for de Gaulle, this meant the end of France's European, Christian civilization. As he put it to the Gaullist senator Alain Peyrefitte in March 1959, when they met at de Gaulle's residence in the village of Colombey-les-Deux-Églises:

> Have you seen the Muslims with their turbans and their djellabahs? You can see that they are not French. Try and integrate oil and vinegar. Shake the bottle. After a moment they separate again. The Arabs are Arabs, the French are French. Do you think that the French can absorb ten million Muslims who will tomorrow be twenty million and after tomorrow forty? If we carry out integration, if all the Berbers and Arabs of Algeria were regarded as French, how would one stop them coming to settle on the mainland where the standard of living is so much higher? My village would no longer be called Colombey-les-Deux-Églises but Colombey-les-Deux-Mosquées.

As de Gaulle's biographer Julian Jackson has observed, "The irony here was that the logic of Soustelle's progressive republicanism led him to defend any means—including torture—to keep Algeria French while de Gaulle's pragmatic conservatism led him ultimately to accept Algerian independence." De Gaulle's explanation to Peyrefitte was a perfect example of what Fanon had called "cultural racism" at the 1956 congress of Black writers and artists, yet in this instance it underwrote the French leader's decision to withdraw from Algeria. Fanon's outlook made no allowance for ironies of this sort.

Fanon was electrified by the events of December, drawing inspiration from the reemergence of the interior and the spectacular display of Algerians' support for their liberators. "There is no place for an Algeria shorn of the FLN," he wrote in *El Moudjahid*, "because the FLN is nothing less than the regrouping of the Algerian people imbued with the resolute desire to achieve independence." The revolutionary festival in the streets of Algiers and Oran—which de Gaulle had avoided—proved the point.

But Fanon was also in excruciating pain and could no longer dismiss his physical suffering as exhaustion from the trip. When a doctor in Accra found an unusually high level of leukocytes, or white corpuscles, in his blood, Josie implored him to return to Tunis, where further tests revealed that he had a serious—probably fatal—case of leukemia.

At first, Fanon said nothing to friends and plunged into his work. When he came over to the Manuellans' for dinner, Marie-Jeanne noticed that he looked gaunt and "a little greenish." But he spoke animatedly about his recent experiences in Congo and Mali—and about his next intellectual project.

"I am going to need you again," he told her. "To write another book."

The next day she drove to the Fanons' apartment and told him, "I have come for the pages."

"What pages?" he said.

"The pages of your book."

He laughed and, striking his forehead with his index finger, said, "But the book is here!" The subject, he explained, would be the national liberation struggles in Africa; the provisional title, "Alger–Le Cap" (Algiers to Cape Town). Since Manuellan no longer worked at the Charles Nicolle Hospital, he would dictate the book to her at her home in Mutuelleville, whenever he passed through Tunis. He wasn't planning to stay in Accra forever.

On January 17, 1961, Patrice Lumumba was delivered to the Katangan secessionists. He was beaten and tortured by Moïse Tshombe's troops and Belgian officers, before being shot dead. His body was dissolved in a barrel of acid, an operation executed by a pair of Belgians, one of whom kept a tooth as a kind of souvenir; it has only recently been returned to Congo. For African nationalists, Lumumba's assassination was like the passion of the Christ for the church fathers. Fanon would invoke it as an illustration of the limits of nonviolence—and the dangers of sectarian or tribal division. In a powerful essay on Lumumba's death in *Afrique action*, he decried the "coldly planned, coldly executed murder" of his friend. But he also took stock of Lumumba's failures, portraying him as a noble but ultimately naïve man who had placed such "exaggerated confidence in the people" that he could not imagine them being deceived by his enemies. Lumumba had also erred by asking for UN intervention, trusting in its "friendly impartiality." The UN's role, Fanon wrote, was to help manage the "'peaceful struggle' for the division of the world" between the Cold War powers. "Africans must remember this lesson. If we need external help, let us call our friends." Instead of sending troops to the Congolese government in the framework of the UN, the African states ought to have sent them directly, "from one friendly country to another friendly country." He continued:

> The African troops in the Congo have suffered a historic moral defeat. With arms at the ready, they watched without reacting (because they were UN troops) the disintegration of a State and a nation that all Africa had saluted and sung. A shame. Our mistake, the mistake we Africans made, was to have forgotten the lesson that the enemy never withdraws sincerely. He never understands. He capitulates, but he does not become converted.

The other lesson of "Africa's first great crisis" was that there could not be "one Africa that fights colonialism and another that attempts to make arrangements with colonialism." The reality, of course, was not so simple: for the sake of Algerian independence, the GPRA—and Fanon—had been forced to make "arrangements with colonialism" in Congo, at Lumumba's expense. But Lumumba's murder only served to underscore that the continent could not "advance by regions" but only "in totality," like "a great body that refuses any mutilation."

Somatic metaphors, images of amputation and phantom limbs, had proliferated in Fanon's writing, ever since *Black Skin, White Masks*, but now his own physical fragility was inescapable. Returning to his post in Accra was out of the question. Nor could he keep his diagnosis to himself. One evening at the home of the Manuellans, he broke the news while Josie was still on her way from the offices of *Afrique action*.

"You have to help Josie," he said. "But I'm going to look after myself."

Marie-Jeanne asked him how.

"With my cortex!" he declared.

Magical thinking, to be sure, but his cortex had always been his chief weapon.

When Josie arrived at the Manuellans', visibly overwhelmed, she insisted that they eat as soon as possible so that Fanon could go to bed early. He tried to make light of his illness at dinner; at one point he grabbed an apple on the table, examined it, and gave his diagnosis: "This apple looks bad, it must be a leukemic apple."

When Manuellan went over to his apartment to discuss the book a few days later, she found him on the sofa in misery. He had been suffering from retinal hemorrhages; he was listless, his morale low.

The news of Fanon's condition rippled through FLN circles in Tunis "like lightning in a cloudless sky," according to the surgeon Michel Martini. Tunisia didn't have adequate facilities for patients with leukemia, and, as Martini recalled, "everyone was ready to send him to the moon if it was necessary." The moon would have been safer than France, where even a GPRA representative in poor health risked being transferred from a hospital bed to a prison cell, and Fanon ruled out the United States— "the country of lynchers," he called it. So the FLN decided to send him to Moscow. The night before his flight, the Fanons visited the Manuellans. No one mentioned his leukemia at dinner.

"Were we all oblivious?" Manuellan would write more than a half century later. "Fanon emanated such a life force."

# PART V

# THE PROPHET

———

# 15

# ROADS TO FREEDOM

---

IN JANUARY 1961, a referendum on Algerian self-determination was held on both sides of the Mediterranean. Nearly 70 percent of Algeria's residents voted in favor; the yes vote was even higher (75 percent) in metropolitan France, where the war had become increasingly unpopular.* A month later, Fanon returned to Tunis from the Soviet Union, where he had been receiving treatment with busulfan, an innovative chemotherapy drug. He was ten pounds heavier, and his white cell count had greatly improved. According to his doctors in Moscow, he had four to five years to live—by which time, he hoped, medical research would produce a cure. He was grateful for the care he had received, but life in the Soviet Union, not least in the psychiatric hospitals he visited, disturbed him. "You're watched everywhere there," he told Marie-Jeanne Manuellan. "Even the toilets have no doors." The Soviet empire, he soon learned, had its own forms of imperial prejudice: the Russians and Ukrainians, he remarked, "see the Chechnyans and even the Georgians as barbarians." At the People's University of Russia—which had just been renamed Patrice Lumumba University—he

---

* The lower percentage in Algeria reflected not only the strength of settler opposition but also the high rates of abstention among Muslim voters, many of whom were observing the FLN's call to boycott the referendum.

spoke with a number of African students, and they struck him as "very unhappy," according to the surgeon Michel Martini.

Fanon and Martini would soon join forces to save the life of one of the FLN's senior figures, Krim Belkacem, the GPRA foreign minister, whom Fanon had always respected in spite of his hand in Abane's death. In early March, Krim was preparing for the first round of head-to-head negotiations with France, set to begin in May in the French resort town of Évian on the shores of Lake Geneva, when he was laid low by abdominal pain and indigestion. One of Fanon's medical colleagues thought that Krim, the head of the FLN delegation, might be nervous about the talks, and asked Fanon to perform one of his legendary sleeping cures. In an isolated villa outside Tunis without a telephone or a bodyguard, Fanon began to administer sleep-inducing drugs and tranquilizers, but by 2:00 a.m., Krim's pain had gotten worse. At 6:30 am on March 19—the first day of Eid al-Fitr, the holiday marking the end of the holy month of Ramadan—Fanon called Martini from a bistro, told him that Krim's condition was serious, and then dispatched an Algerian colleague to pick him up. When Martini arrived, Krim was barely conscious. As it turned out, he was suffering from acute inflammation of the gallbladder and required immediate hospitalization. "In addition to being a remarkable psychiatrist," Martini recalled, "Fanon was a very good doctor."

Martini had always looked somewhat askance at his West Indian colleague. But from the "moment he knew that he was dying," Fanon seemed to him "another man," "admirably full of lucidity, courage and simplicity." When Fanon asked him what he thought of Algeria's revolution, Martini said that he didn't think it *was* a revolution. The heroic days of the interior, Fanon replied, had been revolutionary, but he didn't press his case, and for once, "he didn't try to prove that I was wrong." He radiated a calm and gallant sense of purpose, pouring all his energy into his writing life, "as if he suspected . . . that death would come to surprise him before he'd finished writing what he had to say."

Martini's impression of a reinvigorated—and transformed—Fanon was shared by Manuellan, to whom he was dictating his new book at an accelerated clip. Although he experienced spells of fatigue, she never saw him take an aspirin or a transfusion, pause for a nap, or even sit down when they worked together. The urgency with which Fanon approached *The Wretched of the Earth*, she thought, reflected his awareness of how little time he had left, and his desire to be the first writer to "denounce the compromises of bourgeois nationalists" in Africa. He had heard that the French agricultural engineer René Dumont was working on a book about the failures of Africa's nationalist elites, and wanted to beat him to it. His body was failing him, but his ambition remained intact.

Fanon had first mentioned the book he was writing in correspondence with his editor François Maspero the previous summer. (He signed his letters with the pseudonym "F. Farès.") His previous book for Maspero, *L'An V de la révolution algérienne*, had exerted a powerful influence on the French left's understanding of the Algerian independence struggle, although it had to be read in secret, since the police had removed it from bookstores. His outline for his new book was more ambitious in thematic scope, and geographically more nomadic. (It appeared in a July 27, 1960, letter to Maspero from Josie, writing from Lausanne, Switzerland, under the name "Nadia Farès.")

"Based on the armed struggle in the Maghreb, the development of consciousness and national struggle in the rest of Africa," he explained, the book had grown out of his travels on the continent and his work as a psychiatrist, but at this point, he warned, it resembled jottings in a journal. "I am moving around a great deal and events go by so quickly," he explained. "Some critics . . . reproach me for my 'jargon,'" he acknowledged, alluding to the book's theoretical underpinnings, but he added, "fear, inferiority complexes, and resentment sometimes give to an event an orientation and a form that 'dialectical' study does not provide for." Fanon's defense of his "jargon" was typically cryptic. What he meant was that Marxist analysis ("dialectical study") could not capture the lived experience of decolonization, especially the fantasies, drives, and desires of the colonized, which only a more psychoanalytic and philosophical vocabulary could bring to light. "If you see Jean-Paul Sartre," Fanon added, "tell him that I was able to get his most recent book and that the ideological elements he develops in it have found an exceptional echo in me."

Published in late April 1961, Sartre's massive tome, *Critique de la raison dialectique* (*Critique of Dialectical Reason*), would become as important to

Fanon's thinking about anti-colonial struggle as *Reflections on the Jewish Question* and the essay "Black Orpheus" had been to his thinking about racism and Négritude. Written in a speed-induced frenzy, Sartre's *Critique* is a convoluted, sometimes forbiddingly difficult work. Its philosophical aim was to reconcile existentialism with the Marxist politics Sartre had embraced, by folding both into a Hegelian philosophy of history. Abandoning the individual-centered framework of *Being and Nothingness*, it focused instead on collectivities, especially "groups-in-fusion," people brought together by a common cause, fighting to alter conditions they have inherited: in Sartre's terminology, the "practico-inert," or "worked matter." In ordinary life, people encounter one another in alienated relations of "seriality," he argued, using the example of strangers standing in line for a bus. But in periods of social and political upheaval, they are reconfigured as self-conscious collectives endowed with agency and the power to change their circumstances. This was exactly the transformation that Fanon had described in *L'An V de la révolution algérienne*, as Algeria's Muslim population achieved national self-consciousness and embarked on an insurgency. In *The Wretched of the Earth*, he would extend this model to the entire colonial world.

Sartre drew his examples mostly from European history, notably the French Revolution and the Paris Commune. But *Critique* also revealed his intensifying interest in problems that preoccupied intellectuals in the Third World: hunger, colonialism, racism, revolutionary violence. The defining condition of political struggle, he argued, was *la rareté* (scarcity), whether historical or natural. "After thousands of years of History," he wrote, "three-quarters of the world's population are undernourished. Thus, in spite of its contingency, scarcity is a very basic human relation, both to Nature and to men." While many of his left-wing peers were bemoaning the numbing effects of abundance on the Western working class, Sartre found a new historical subject, a new agent of revolutionary change: the oppressed masses in the colonial world, for whom scarcity was an ever-present reality. The Black, Arab, or Latin American "other" was not merely the victim of the West, but its potential savior.

In a chapter on colonialism, Sartre argued that the colonizer and the colonized—almost two distinct species, "humans" and "sub-humans"—

were "a couple," neither of whom would exist without the other. Their
identities were fixed by the colonizer as essences: colonialism "defines the
exploited"—the sub-humans—"as eternal because it constitutes itself as
an eternity of exploitation." Racism—a structure, not an ideology or a
doctrine—was the result of this Manichaean division. "*It is not a thought
at all*," Sartre wrote, so much as "the colonial interest lived as a link of
all the colonialists in the colony." Anti-colonial violence was a logical
"counter-violence," a "retaliation against the violence of the Other" and
the "systematic exploitation of man's humanity for the destruction of the
human." The ultimate aim of anti-colonial insurrection was not retaliation but the conquest of scarcity: the reclamation of the land that settlers
had seized, reducing the colonized to misery and famine. In a struggle
of this kind, he declared, "the destruction of the adversary is the only
means."

Sartre's formulations—about the dehumanization of the colonized,
counterviolence, the battle against scarcity and dispossession, and decolonization as the creation of a new world—struck a powerful chord with
Fanon. But the section that resonated with him even more was the discussion of what Sartre called "fraternity-terror": the suspicion, tyranny, and
violence that simmer and sometimes boil over inside groups-in-fusion.
Sartre was thinking about the Terror during the French Revolution and
about the Stalinist purges.

But his interest in the question of treason had a more personal source:
Sartre's close childhood friend, the writer Paul Nizan, had been accused of
treason when he broke with the Communist Party over the Hitler-Stalin
Pact. In early 1960, Maspero asked Sartre if he would write a preface to a
new edition of Nizan's 1931 memoir, *Aden Arabie*, a fiery indictment of
French bourgeois society and the colonial order. When Maspero contacted
Sartre, Nizan had been nearly forgotten—or rather buried, thanks to the
Communist Party's vicious campaign of invective, which continued even
after he was killed at age thirty-five by a stray German bullet during the
Battle of Dunkirk. Sartre observed in his preface, "The Communists do
not believe in hell. They believe in nothingness." Praising Nizan as an
ideal spokesman for the "angry young men" of the lean postwar years, he
wrote, "In his hibernation, he has grown younger by the year. Yesterday

he was our contemporary, today he is theirs." Sartre's preface, written on a monthlong trip to revolutionary Havana, where he and Beauvoir met Fidel Castro and Che Guevara, was a paean to one of the great victims of fraternity-terror.

Yet Sartre's approach was structural, not moralistic. Groups-in-fusion, he argued in *Critique*, were based on a "pledge," a swearing of allegiance that binds the group. "We are brothers insofar as, following the creative act of the pledge, we are *our own sons*, our common creation." But to retain its unity and survive in the face of external threats, the group-in-fusion must instill a fear of violence in its members, "substituting a real fear, produced by the group itself, for the retreating external fear, whose distance is deceptive." The instilled fear, he suggested, was "a coercive action of freedom" against the group's potential dissolution, and "it is called Terror." Those who take the pledge and become brothers in arms are saying, in effect, "'You must kill me if I secede." In Sartre's view, this statement is not merely a negative acceptance of the consequences of disloyalty; it is a positive means by which the group-in-fusion is created.

Fanon had devoted himself to a group-in-fusion, an organization of brothers who imagined themselves as sons of a revolution without a father. (Their common "father," Messali Hadj, had been declared a mortal enemy.) As an FLN spokesman during the Melouza affair, Fanon had taken part in the FLN's war against the MNA; he had seen the Boussouf boys turn against Abane. And by time he began to dictate *The Wretched of the Earth* to Manuellan in Tunis, Lumumba had been murdered, after some of his comrades in Congo—and sympathetic revolutionaries from Tunis, including Fanon himself—had withdrawn their support.

In Sartre's new book, Fanon found a disturbingly familiar reflection on the coercive internal culture of revolutionary movements. Without the constraints imposed on individual members by fraternity-terror, revolutionary groups-in-fusion risked either being crushed by more powerful adversaries or dissolving. For a clandestine movement like the FLN, facing one of the world's most powerful armies, fraternity-terror could be justified as a wartime necessity. But fraternity-terror could also lead to murder, massacres, and further acts of betrayal, subverting the aspirations to freedom that had led to the "pledge" in the first place. And it threatened to establish a new and inhibiting set of constraints on the future, which was certainly Algeria's case: after independence, Algerians would find themselves ruled by a secretive and authoritarian military regime, whose spinal cord was the intelligence apparatus created by Abdelhafid Boussouf. For all of Sartre's belief in revolutionary commitment, *Critique* was a terribly somber book about the prospects for freedom after liberation, suggesting that the freedom that revolutionaries fight for is threatened, if not doomed, by the coercive internal practices that bind them together against external threats (such as the ruling class or imperialism). This was a problem that had begun to obsess Fanon during his time in sub-Saharan Africa, and that he had explored in his travelogue from Mali.

Shortly before Fanon went to Moscow, he received a visit from two of Sartre's colleagues at *Les Temps modernes*, Claude Lanzmann and Marcel Péju, who had come to Tunis for an anti-colonial conference. In 1959, *Les Temps modernes* had published Fanon's essay on the European minority in Algeria, an excerpt from *L'An V de la révolution algérienne*, but this was his first encounter in person with members of Sartre's editorial circle. They spent an afternoon at Fanon's spartan apartment in El Menzah, the suburb of Tunis where he and Josie had moved after his return from Accra. Lanzmann, who would later achieve renown as the director of the Holocaust film *Shoah*, was a left-wing journalist with a history in the Resistance and a temperament even more volatile and impulsive than Fanon's; he was also Beauvoir's lover. As a teenage maquisard in Clermont-Ferrand, he had collected guns at the local railway station under the Gestapo's nose, laid ambushes, and then, after the war, found himself "turned upside down" and "cured" by Sartre's book on antisemitism. His consciousness of being Jewish was as intense as Fanon's consciousness of being Black. According to Beauvoir, he would sometimes wake up from dreams screaming, "You're all Kapos!"

Lanzmann was shocked by Fanon's condition. "Fanon was lying on a sort of pallet, a mattress on the floor," he recalled in his memoirs. "I was immediately struck by his fiery dark eyes, black with fever . . . Fanon spoke with a lyricism I had never before encountered, he was already so suffused with death that it gave his every word the power both of prophecy and of the last words of a dying man." At one point Josie left the room in tears, distressed by the sight of her dying husband. But Fanon said, "Let's talk about something else," and proceeded to pepper Lanzmann with questions about Sartre and his *Critique*, especially the chapter on fraternity-terror; he had been giving lectures on the book to soldiers at ALN training camps. "Everything here is corrupt," he said of Tunis. If Lanzmann wanted to discover the Algerian Revolution, he would have to go to the interior, where the *djounoud* (combatants) were "more true, more pure," and studied philosophy when they weren't fighting the French. Lanzmann was skeptical, but Fanon's "passionate words made it impossible to doubt the existence of these peasant-warrior-philosophers . . . It is impossible to object to a prophet's trance."

Lanzmann visited him once more in Tunis in the spring of 1961. Fanon recited passages from the manuscript of *The Wretched of the Earth* and gave him a copy to take back to Paris; according to Lanzmann, he had "one thought in mind: he wanted Sartre to read it and write the preface." Throughout his career as a writer and militant, Fanon had been thinking of Sartre's ideas on racism, identity, the force of the "gaze," the nature of commitment.

But he was no longer an unknown West Indian student in Lyon; he was a man of stature and influence, a representative of a national liberation struggle, a living example of the committed writing that Sartre had espoused. As Mohammed Harbi discovered when he went to Conakry as a representative of the GPRA in 1961, "all the radical elites" were close readers of Fanon, "the voice of rupture with the European powers that wanted to hand over power while continuing to exploit Africa's riches." Having fought to create a world without masters, Fanon was looking to Sartre not as a *maître à penser* but as an elder comrade and interlocutor with whom he hoped to establish, at last, a direct dialogue and collaboration.

Fanon had traveled a long way in the last decade, but so had Sartre and Beauvoir. Since the late 1940s, Sartre had published uncompromising attacks on colonialism and racism. He had warned that colonial racism would "end up infecting the 'métropole' itself," and denounced the manner in which colonialism dehumanized both colonized and colonizer. But when his protégé Francis Jeanson organized the network of *porteurs des valises* on behalf of the FLN in the mid-1950s, neither Sartre nor Beauvoir was willing to support him. As Beauvoir put it, "We still believed it was possible to work toward independence by legal means." What this meant, at the time, was denouncing the war and calling for peace without explicitly siding with the FLN: the Dreyfusard position advanced by the historian Pierre Vidal-Naquet. In March 1958 in *L'Express*, Sartre published a classic Dreyfusard text on Algeria: an article on *The Question*, Henri Alleg's gruesome account of his torture by the French army in Algiers. Alleg, a Communist intellectual of Jewish origin, was the editor of *Alger républicain* and a supporter of independence; at the time of publication, he was still in prison. "It is in our name that he was victimized," Sartre wrote, "and because of him we regain a little of our pride: we are proud that he is French." Alleg's achievement in refusing to name names while enduring the *gégène* and waterboarding was to "save us"—the French— "from despair and shame because he is the victim himself and because he has conquered torture." Compared to the "little cads" who tortured him, Sartre wrote, "Alleg is the only really tough one, the only one who is really strong."

But Sartre's essay on *The Question* was more than a Dreyfusard celebration of masculine courage under torture. Torture was not simply an "excess" of war; it was part of a system, "imposed by the circumstances and required by racial hatred; in some ways it is the essence of the conflict and expresses its deepest truth." Although he never mentioned the FLN by name, Sartre argued that Algeria's *sous-hommes* (sub-men) had been driven to violent revolt, since they had the "choice of starvation or of reaffirming their manhood against ours . . . It is a bitter and tragic fact that, for the Europeans of Algeria, being a man means first and foremost superiority over Muslims. But what if the Muslim finds in his turn that his manhood depends on equality with the settler? It is then that the European begins to feel his very existence diminished and cheapened."

Sartre's logic led, it seemed, to an inevitable conclusion: only by supporting the rebels among those "sub-men" could the French left help end the "atrocious and bleak cruelty" that Alleg—and many thousands of Algerian Muslims—had experienced. Yet, oddly, he merely called for negotiations leading to peace, a position not far from the "beautiful souls" of the French left whom Fanon had denounced in *El Moudjahid*.

Within a year of Sartre's piece in *L'Express*, however, he and Beauvoir had moved closer to Jeanson's view that supporters of Algerian independence had to undertake active resistance on behalf of the FLN. Alleg's book was confiscated from stores, and other legal forms of protest were falling prey to censorship and repression. Charles de Gaulle, propelled to power by a military coup hatched by colonial ultras in Algiers, had launched the Challe Plan to defeat the resistance in Algeria. And now there were detention camps for Algerians inside France itself, spreading the "gangrene" of repression to the *métropole*.

Beauvoir wrote that she and Sartre were now convinced by Jeanson's reasoning. The French left, she went on, "could only take revolutionary positions in liaison with the FLN." In 1957, Jeanson's network had seemed to Beauvoir "the camp of treason." She wrote, "Something in me . . . held me back from contemplating it." She added that three years later, "[The Algerian War had] invaded my thinking, my sleep, my moods." She became involved in organizing a committee to defend Djamila Boupacha, a maquisarde who had been tortured and raped with a bottle by French soldiers, then put on trial for homicide. Those who wept over "past sorrows—Anne Frank or the Warsaw Ghetto," but failed to condemn France in Algeria, Beauvoir declared, put themselves "on the side of the executioners of those who suffer today."

On April 21, 1961, four pro–Algérie française generals, led by Raoul Salan, the man who had pinned a Croix de Guerre onto Fanon's lapel, launched a coup to prevent de Gaulle's plans for withdrawal. The army remained loyal to de Gaulle, and the putsch crumbled in four days, but Salan became the head of the Organisation de l'armée secrète (OAS), an insurgency of extremist settlers and former army officers, which had been formed three months earlier in Franco's Spain. More than two thousand people, most of them civilians, would be killed by the OAS; the lingering smell of plastic explosives became familiar in the streets of Algiers—and in metropolitan France, where the OAS tried to assassinate de Gaulle and his minister of culture, the writer André Malraux. Sartre's support for the

FLN also made him a target of the OAS. On July 20, his apartment at 42, rue Bonaparte was bombed; he and Beauvoir were absent.*

Sartre, however, does not seem to have given much thought to his own self-preservation. And though he and Beauvoir continued to speak in the name of the Republic and its values, their vision of the world—its vast inequalities and finite resources, the enduring imprint of Western domination, the struggle for recognition and dignity—was reshaped by their travels in the developing world. As Beauvoir put it, using a word that Sartre had made a central category of his *Critique*, "Their scarcity became the truth of the world, and our Western comfort a narrow privilege." They were learning to see the world through Fanon's eyes, even before they met him.

Beauvoir wrote of their month in Cuba in March 1960, "For the first time in our life we were witnesses of a happiness that had been won by violence; our previous experiences, the Algerian War above all, had led us to discover it only under its negative form: the refusal of the oppressor." Sartre noted that Cuba was experiencing the "honeymoon of the Revolution," and pointed out the signs of its impending Stalinization; but he, too, was overjoyed by the seeming absence in Havana of any bureaucracy, "just a direct relationship between ruler and ruled." On August 15 they flew to Brazil, where they spent three months on a tour led by the novelist Jorge Amado. Everywhere Sartre went, he denounced the war in Algeria and defended the FLN, in the face of a French expatriate community that despised him; in the words of his biographer Annie Cohen-Solal, Sartre was "the most honest and the most vehement counter-ambassador of the French Republic." In Copacabana, a representative of the GPRA showed him fake copies of the newspaper Fanon edited, *El Moudjahid*, created by the psychological bureau of French intelligence.

Shortly after their arrival in Brazil, Sartre and Beauvoir learned from Lanzmann that the police had arrested several members of the Jeanson group, although Jeanson himself had evaded capture and gone

---

* On January 7, 1962, the OAS made a second attempt on Sartre's life, bombing the wrong floor but destroying much of the apartment.

underground. On September 6, both signed an open letter on "the right of insubordination in the Algerian War" in the antiwar journal *Vérité-liberté*. The "Manifesto of 121," drafted by a group of intellectuals headed by the philosopher Maurice Blanchot, called on the French government to recognize Algerian independence, denouncing torture and defending the right to conscientious objection. Among its 121 signatories were the novelists Marguerite Duras, Alain Robbe-Grillet, and Nathalie Sarraute; the director Alain Resnais; the composer Pierre Boulez; the actress Simone Signoret; and Fanon's friend from Martinique, the writer Édouard Glissant. Many more asked to add their names, but the publisher, Jérôme Lindon, stopped at 121 because he thought "it sounded nice." The Communist Party, as anxious as ever not to alienate the French working class, opposed the *Manifeste des 121*, insisting that left-wing conscripts should promote revolution inside the army, not desert their posts.

The *Manifeste* was published the day after the Jeanson trial opened at a military court in the rue du Cherche-Midi, the same street where the Dreyfus trial had taken place seventy years earlier. The defense lawyers had hoped Sartre would attend, but he refused to abandon his commitments in Brazil, many of them on behalf of Algeria. By telephone from Bahia, he dictated to Lanzmann and Péju his declaration to the tribunal, which was published in *Le Monde* on September 22.

In his statement, Sartre artfully interwove the themes of Dreyfusard protest and Third Worldist resistance, displaying his unique flair for transcending the divisions between patriotic opponents of torture and the radical supporters of the FLN, thereby making himself a linchpin of left unity. (As he had observed of Richard Wright, Sartre had a gift for speaking to a "split audience.") Algerian independence, he said, "is certain." He continued:

> What isn't certain is the future of democracy in France. For this Algerian war has made our country rot. The progressive reduction of our freedoms, the disappearance of political life, the generalization of torture, the permanent insurrection of military power against civilian power, mark an evolution that one can without exaggeration describe as fascist.

The left would remain "impotent," he argued, unless it joined with "the only force that today really struggles against the common enemy of Algerian freedoms and French freedoms. And that force is the FLN. This was the conclusion that Francis Jeanson had reached, and it is also the one that I have reached." The *porteurs des valises* were not simply aiding an "oppressed people"; they were also "working for themselves, for their freedom and their future. They are working for the establishment in France of a real democracy." If Jeanson had asked him to carry suitcases or to put up Algerian militants, he "would have done so without hesitation." What the French government called "treason" was a higher form of patriotism.

A few weeks later, thousands of right-wing demonstrators flooded the Champs-Élysées, chanting "Shoot Sartre!" When he and Beauvoir returned to France in November, Lanzmann advised them to travel by car from Spain; otherwise they would be heckled, if not attacked, by Algérie française ultras waiting for them at the airport. Far from being chastened by this hostility, Sartre was emboldened by it; at fifty-five, he had never seemed younger. In his writings on Nizan and the Algerian War, in his project to fuse existentialism and radical politics, and in his public defiance of his own government, he had rekindled his youthful rebelliousness and become a symbol of France's New Left: independent of a Stalinist Communist Party, fiercely anti-colonial, inspired by the revolutionary ferment in the Third World. Outside the West, Sartre's moral prestige was unmatched. For intellectuals in countries that had struggled to free themselves from colonial domination, he seemed miraculously uncontaminated by the paternalism—and hypocrisy—of his peers on the European left.

Fanon had been observing Sartre's every move, gratified, no doubt, that the philosopher was coming around to his position, that their roads to freedom were at last intersecting. In *Black Skin, White Masks*, Fanon had wondered where his struggle against racial domination and alienation converged with Sartre's existential socialism. Now he had his answer: in the struggle for national liberation in Algeria.

On April 7, 1961, Fanon wrote to Maspero that *The Wretched of the Earth* was moving forward, and added, in handwriting that had markedly deteriorated, "Ask Sartre to preface me. Tell him that I think of him each time I sit down at my desk . . . Yours in friendship, F. Farès." Sartre would need little convincing. Lanzmann had already told him how "carried away" he was by Fanon, and in May 1961, *Les Temps modernes* published Fanon's essay "De la violence" (On Violence), which would become the first chapter of *The Wretched of the Earth*. According to Beauvoir, "Sartre had realized in Cuba the truth of what Fanon said: in violence, the oppressed achieve their humanity. He agreed with his book: an extreme manifesto of the Third World, uncompromising, incendiary, but also complex and subtle."

When Lanzmann learned that Fanon was heading to Italy for a thermal cure in early August, he invited him to meet with Sartre and Beauvoir in Rome, now the couple's refuge from Paris, where Sartre was under OAS death threats. After a week of treatments for rheumatism in the spa town of Abano Terme, Fanon arrived in Rome on a Friday. At the train station, Sartre and Beauvoir spied him carrying his luggage, with (in Beauvoir's words) "shaky gestures, an agitated face, his eyes on the lookout." In the car, he spoke feverishly, predicting that in the next forty-eight hours the French army would invade Tunisia, and blood would flow. His anxieties were not unreasonable. In late July, a small war between France and Tunisia had broken out in Bizerte, a strategic port on the Mediterranean where, five years after independence, the French government continued to maintain a naval base as part of its operations inside Algeria. After Tunisian forces blockaded the base in the hope of forcing France to finally evacuate, the French army launched a full-scale invasion; three days later, twenty-seven French soldiers and more than six hundred Tunisians lay dead.

At lunch, Fanon and Sartre began their discussion, while Beauvoir and Lanzmann listened in. The conversation lasted until two in the morning, when Beauvoir gently interrupted so that Sartre could get some sleep. "I don't like people who conserve their energy," Fanon sniped. He kept Lanzmann awake until eight. Fanon stayed through Sunday, when he took the train back to Abano Terme. Sartre, who wrote every day, never picked up his pen, so riveted was he by Fanon's company; Lanzmann had never seen him "as charmed, as captivated by a man."

Fanon seems to have spared no detail of his life story, from the injuries he had suffered as a victim of racism in medical school to his work as a psychiatrist in Blida, from his involvement with the FLN in Tunis to his adventures in Congo. During their three days with their guest from Tunis, Sartre and Beauvoir hardly left the apartment. In Beauvoir's memoir *La Force des choses* (translated into English as *The Force of Circumstance*), the Rome meeting suggests a scene from an anti-colonial version of Sartre's play *No Exit*, whose three characters find themselves locked in a room together for eternity. Fanon had never amounted to much as a playwright, but he had become an actor on a much larger stage and retained his sense of theater. In Rome, he gave the performance of a lifetime: the monologue of a young, dying Black revolutionary, delivered in front of an older white man who shares his convictions yet declines to sever his ties with the society he condemns.

It seemed to Beauvoir—as it had to Manuellan—that Fanon was haunted by the awareness of his own death. His political vision was catastrophist, although Algeria's prospects, he admitted, were not entirely bleak. The moderate nationalist Ferhat Abbas, he noted approvingly, had been replaced as president of the GPRA by the more radical Benyoucef Benkhedda, Abane's former lieutenant. Independence was imminent; only its terms remained to be settled by the negotiators in Évian. But he predicted that the days ahead would be terrible, that half a million, even a million, would die before the war was over. Beauvoir sensed that Fanon, "a partisan of violence who was horrified by violence," was at war with himself: "His features changed when he evoked the mutilations inflicted by the Belgians on the Congolese, or the Portuguese on the Angolans," but also "when he spoke of the 'counter-violence' of Blacks and the terrible score settling within the Algerian revolution." Fanon, too, blamed himself for this horror of violence, as if it reflected the shameful weakness of a middle-class intellectual, or perhaps the white mask he was still struggling to expunge. He told Beauvoir that "everything he'd written against intellectuals, he had written against himself."

Like Harbi, Beauvoir was struck by Fanon's "passionate desire to put down roots." She wrote, "He ceaselessly reaffirmed his commitment: the Algerian people were his people . . . About the dissensions, the intrigues, the liquidations, the oppositions that were later to provoke so much turmoil, Fanon knew much more than he could say." Those "dark secrets, and perhaps also personal hesitations, gave his remarks an enigmatic, obscurely prophetic and troubled turn." At times, it seemed to Sartre and Beauvoir, Fanon inflated his contributions and "spoke as if he was the GPRA himself." They were taken aback by his boasting and could not understand why a man of Fanon's stature in the Algerian movement needed to fall back on hyperbole. Yet Fanon made no secret of the sources of his guilt, even if he was unwilling to spell out the nature of his responsibility. "I have on my conscience," he said, "two deaths for which I do not forgive myself: Abane and Lumumba's." If he had forced them to follow his advice, they might still be alive, he believed.

Fanon seemed decidedly more relaxed when he spoke about philosophical issues with Sartre. But, uninterested in small talk, he expressed indifference, even irritation, when Sartre and Beauvoir took him to a trattoria where they hoped he might unwind: the European past, the comforts of bourgeois life, had long ago ceased to matter to him. However much they criticized the actions of their own government, Sartre and Beauvoir remained wedded to a world that he had renounced. "Fanon did not forget that Sartre was French, and reproached him for not sufficiently atoning for it," Beauvoir recalled. He criticized Sartre for remaining in Brazil during the Jeanson trial, instead of returning to France to address the military tribunal in person and face arrest. "We have rights over you," he said. "How can you continue to live normally and to write?" He wondered why Sartre couldn't follow the example set by Fernand Iveton, a *pied-noir* member of the FLN who had gone to the guillotine at the Barberousse Prison in Algiers in 1957.* Beauvoir had the impression that Fanon "lived in another world."

Yet, for all the demands Fanon raised, his purpose was not to indict Sartre but to woo him, since a preface by the world's most famous philosopher would work wonders for his book. Ten days after their first meeting, Fanon passed through Rome again and paid him another visit. He was still smarting from an exchange with a maid at his hotel in Abano Terme. "Is it true what they say about you?" she asked. "That you hate white people?"

---

* "The man's life, my own life, matters little," Iveton reportedly declared before being executed. "What matters is Algeria and its future. And Algeria will be free tomorrow. I am convinced that the friendship between the French and the Algerians will one day be mended."

She might as well have called him a *nègre*. Becoming an Algerian had not insulated him from the indignities of being a Black man in the West, nor had all his accomplishments or his international prestige. One minute he was talking to a distinguished philosopher; the next he was being asked to account for himself by a person cleaning his hotel room. Once again, his hatred of racism had been misconstrued as a hatred of whites, when the fundamental problem, he told Sartre and Beauvoir, was that whites had an almost "physiological horror of Black people."

In Fanon's presence, Beauvoir wrote, life seemed a "tragic adventure, often horrible, but invaluable." Like Sartre, she was overwhelmed by his "power of evocation, the speed and audacity of this thinking." She recalled, "When I held his feverish hand, I felt that I was touching the passion that burned it." Fanon, for his part, was somewhat irritated that he had to share Sartre with Beauvoir and Lanzmann—"I wish I could have had a moment alone with him," he reported to Alice Cherki—but he relished their exchanges in Rome. He told Lanzmann, "I would pay twenty thousand francs a day to speak with Sartre from morning till evening for a fortnight."

# 16

# VOICE OF THE DAMNED

---

FANON FINISHED DICTATING HIS new book, still called "Alger–Le Cap," to Marie-Jeanne Manuellan in July 1961. A month later, he wrote to François Maspero, asking him to "examine carefully the issue of distribution. Among other places, to Africa and to Latin America . . . I think it necessary to publish no fewer than 10,000 copies. Political milieus of the Third World are feverishly awaiting this book." He also revealed his new title: *Les Damnés de la terre* (*The Wretched of the Earth*). It was lifted from a poem by Jacques Roumain, a Haitian Marxist who had died of an illness in 1944, at age thirty-seven—a year older than Fanon was at the time. The title of the poem, "Sales nègres" (Dirty Negroes), powerfully expressed the anger of France's colonized subjects after the sacrifices they had made in the Second World War. Black people, Roumain proclaims, will no longer tolerate being "your *nègres* / your niggers" (a word he renders in English), nor will they take orders to shoot down Arabs in Syria, Tunisia, and Morocco, or "white comrades" who are "despised like us." In an image of a final battle, he envisions a "harvest of vengeance" stretching from "the gold mines in the Congo" to the "cotton plantations of Louisiana" and the "sugar cane fields of the Antilles," in which Black people are joined by equally "filthy" Indochinese, Arabs, Malays, Jews, and proletarians:

*And here we are standing up*
*All the wretched of the earth*
*all the upholders of justice*
*marching to attack your barracks*
*your banks*
*like a forest of funeral torches*
*to be done*
*once*
*and*
*for*
*all*
*with this world*
*of Negroes*
*of niggers*
*of filthy Negroes.*

Fanon may have become an Algerian in Tunis, but he remained an attentive reader of West Indian poetry, and he was obviously moved by the insurrectionary cadences of Roumain's poem.* This was Fanon's voice, too, in *The Wretched of the Earth*, and it bore the imprint of his West Indian experience, both in its depiction of the colonized as the "slaves of modern times" and in its warning that without a social revolution, the former "natives" would never overcome the "supremacy of white values"—any more than the former slaves of the West Indies had after abolition. On his travels in West Africa, Fanon had seen that decolonization could result in what he called a "sterile formalism," with a native elite filling posts deserted by the colonizers, and ruling with as little—and sometimes less—concern for the masses. That sterile formalism had been the fate of France's old colonies, including Martinique. He wrote *The Wretched of the Earth* to sound the alarm about this "nauseating mimicry" of colonial rule under the flag of independence.

---

* Roumain was surely aware of the allusion to the "wretched of the earth" in the 1871 revolutional anthem "L'internationale," a popular chant of the French labor movement—an additional resonance that could not have been lost on Fanon, a Black Jacobin at heart.

Sitting on his bed in El Menzah, Fanon read excerpts of the book to Alice Cherki, Charles Geronimi, and Pierre and Claudine Chaulet. Claudine later said that Fanon's bedside readings reminded her of "a great classical hero who has been wounded in battle." *The Wretched of the Earth* was his last testament, offering further elaborations of his ideas about national consciousness and Négritude; armed struggle and the "revolutionary spontaneity" of the peasantry; and, more broadly, the difficult journey from liberation to genuine freedom. It was addressed to his "brothers" and intended as a manifesto, but it reflected the tempestuous and often contradictory personality that both Beauvoir and Lanzmann had evoked in their descriptions of Fanon. The book brought together piercing analytic insights and militant theatrics, apocalyptic warnings and wildly utopian projections, a passionate faith in violence as a means to achieve freedom, and a lucid awareness of the dangers that violence posed to mental health and the psychiatrist's painstaking task of disalienation. Fanon made no attempt to resolve these tensions in his book, any more than he did in his life. It turned out to be a prophetic work, but not always for the reasons he imagined.

Like other political broadsides—Rousseau's *Social Contract*, Tom Paine's *Common Sense*, Marx and Engels's *Communist Manifesto*—Fanon's book told a story. Its subject was the psychological and political awakening of the colonized as they became a movement (a Sartrian group-in-fusion) under the leadership of revolutionary parties and took up arms in their own defense. Fanon was not the first writer to describe decolonization as a zero-sum struggle between settler and native. Memmi, as we have seen, made a similar argument in *The Colonizer and the Colonized*. But Fanon interpreted this struggle with unequaled force, as an inexorable, epic battle against "atmospheric violence" whose outcome was the destruction of the Western-dominated colonial world, and the culture and values that sustained it. With their "shrinking stomachs," Fanon wrote, the masses of the Third World had mapped "the geography of hunger" and thrown into relief the "scandalous" opulence of the West, "built on the backs of slaves." This was entirely consistent with Sartre's arguments about colonialism and scarcity in the *Critique*. Fanon continued:

Europe is literally the creation of the Third World . . . And when we
hear a European head of state declaring with his hand on his heart that
he must come to the aid of the unfortunate underdeveloped peoples, we
do not tremble with gratitude. On the contrary, we say to ourselves, it
is a just reparation that will be made to us.

Reparations had a recent precedent, he noted: After the Second World
War, the governments of nations occupied by the Nazis demanded financial compensation from Germany, as well as the restitution of "cultural
treasures, pictures, sculptures, and stained glass." The former colonies,
pillaged by European "capitalists [who] have comported themselves like
nothing more than war criminals," had equally strong claims: "The wealth
of the imperialist countries is also our wealth." Shelving the doubts about
the value of retroactive justice that he had expressed in *Black Skin, White
Masks*, Fanon insisted that the West had an obligation to support the development of its former colonies, not merely for their sake but to "rehabilitate
Man and ensure his triumph everywhere." The persistence of inequities
born of slavery and colonialism, not the rivalry between the Communist
and capitalist blocs, was "the fundamental problem of the contemporary
era." The Cold War, he argued, was merely a sideshow at the margins of an
epic struggle that promised to redeem centuries of colonial exploitation.
Where Memmi had described the birth of new nation-states, Fanon saw
the dawn of a new world.

Fanon drew on a great variety of examples in Africa, Asia, Latin
America, and of course Algeria. None were explored in any detail, and
the result in *The Wretched of the Earth* is a broad-brush depiction of a
monolithic Third World. But for all the loss in specificity, the payoff was a
coherent depiction of anti-colonial revolts as an indivisible historical se-
quence, of which the FLN's fighters were the vanguard, and the Black rebels of the West Indies the precursors. *The Wretched of the Earth* is in many
ways a marriage in prose of the two places that had formed Fanon's political imagination: Martinique and Algeria. What Beauvoir had praised in
Rome as Fanon's "power of evocation" had never been on such magisterial
display. *The Wretched of the Earth* was Fanon's most overtly polemical
book; it was also, paradoxically, his most literary.

It begins with a riveting description, rich in anaphora, of the colonial city as a Manichaean confrontation between its separate *villes* (towns). Fanon repeats the word *ville* no fewer than eighteen times, in a passage that captures the economic chasm between settler and native, the drastically segregated spaces they occupy, the erotic undercurrents of power and envy that define their relationship:

> The settler's town is built to last, all stones and steel. It's a brightly lit town with paved roads, where garbage cans are always full of unknown remains, never seen, not even dreamed of. The settler's feet can never be glimpsed, except perhaps in the sea, but then you can never get close enough. Feet protected by solid shoes while the streets of their town are clean, smooth, without holes, without stones. The settler's town is a sated, lazy town, its belly is permanently full of good things. The settler's town is a town of whites, of foreigners.
>
> The town of the colonized, or at least the "native" town, the Negro town, the Medina, the reservation, is a disreputable place inhabited by disreputable men. You are born anywhere, anyhow. You die anywhere, from anything. It's a world with no space, men are piled up one on top of the other, the huts built one on top of the other. The town of the colonized is a hungry town, hungry for bread, meat, shoes, coal, and light. The town of the colonized is a squatting town, a kneeling town, a sprawling town. It's a town of *nègres* and *bicots* [dirty Arabs]. The gaze the colonized casts at the settler's town is a lustful gaze, an envious gaze. Dreams of possession. Every type of possession: sitting at the settler's table, sleeping in his bed, with his wife if possible. The colonized man is an envious man. The settler is aware of this as he catches the furtive glance, and constantly on his guard, bitterly notes: "They want to take our place." And it's true, there isn't a colonized person who does not dream at least once a day of taking the settler's place.

In Fanon's account, settler and native know each other all too well; indeed, the one would not exist without the other: "Just as the racist creates his inferior, so it is the colonizer who creates the 'native.'" In the dichotomized world of settler colonialism, what determines one's place is "first and foremost what species, what race one belongs to. In the colonies the economic infrastructure is also a superstructure. The cause is effect: You are rich because you are white, you are white because you are rich. This is why a Marxist analysis should always be slightly stretched when it comes to addressing the colonial problem." For the colonized, desire is not simply a matter of wanting what they don't have, of what Sartre called "scarcity." It is a matter of wanting what others—the foreigners, the colonizers—have taken from them, starting with their land.

In one of the book's more striking passages, Fanon argues that settler colonialism not only deprives people of their land but also turns them into a dehumanized feature *of* the land. "Algerians, women in '*haïk*,' palm trees and camels," he writes, "form the panorama, the *natural* backdrop of the French presence." The "hostile, restive, fundamentally rebellious nature" of the land that has been occupied is "represented in the colonies by the bush, the mosquitoes, the natives and fever . . . Railways through the bush, the draining of swamps, and a native population that is non-existent politically and economically are in reality one and the same thing." All are subjected to what Theodor Adorno and Max Horkheimer, in their classic 1947 study, *The Dialectic of Enlightenment*, called "instrumental reason," subdued and transformed into objects for the sake of production, efficiency, and profit.

In contrast with the gloomy thinkers of the Frankfurt School, Fanon highlighted the resistances to instrumental, or colonial reason, and located these, above all, in the *bodies* of the colonized. In the colonial imagination, natives hardly exist except as exploitable bodies, yet those very bodies know something that the colonizers strenuously deny: namely, that they are more than bodies; they are human beings, with histories of their own and the same capacity for freedom as their oppressors. What settlers see as their "indolence" is, in fact, "a conscious way of sabotaging the colonial machine; on the biological level it is a remarkable system of self-preservation."

In *Black Skin, White Masks*, Fanon had written that in the racist imagination, the Black man represents "the biological," a proximity to natural impulses that whites prefer to deny. Here he made a similar argument about the "animalization" of natives by the settler community. "The language of the settler, when he speaks of the colonized, is a zoological language," he writes, evoking the "slithery movements of the yellow race, the odors from the native town . . . the hordes, the stink, the swarming, the seething, and the gesticulations." In trying to describe the colonized, the settler is always reaching for "the bestiary." This is not to say that the colonized internalize or "epidermalize" this view of themselves, as Fanon had suggested of West Indians. On the contrary, he argued that the colonized person is under no illusion as to what the settler thinks of him, and "roars with laughter when he hears himself described as an animal. For he knows that he is not an animal. And at the very moment he discovers his humanity, he begins to sharpen his knives to secure its victory."

Once the independence struggle breaks out, "the colonized liberates himself in and through violence." Violence, in this view, is not simply an instrument, a means to an end; it is an epistemological tool. When the colonized attack the colonizer—as they did in Sétif and Philippeville— the savagery of the colonial response lifts the veil of impassive colonial order, revealing the violence that keeps the "natives" in their place. It is in violence that the colonized find the "key . . . to decipher social reality."

Fanon's attraction to violence reflected his background as a former soldier, and as a West Indian who had long believed that Martinique had failed to achieve genuine freedom because abolition had been granted by the French, rather than wrested from them as it had been in Haiti. Moreover, the struggle that he had joined in Algeria was among the most violent wars of national liberation of the twentieth century, matched only by Vietnam's. But Fanon's interest in violence also reflected his psychiatric training, especially his reading of Adler's work on aggression. In his work with his patients in Algeria, he discovered a society where the aggressive instincts of the settler were given free rein, while those of the native were thwarted altogether. The settler was an "exhibitionist" who constantly reminded the native of his power in displays or threats of violence; the native was a jealous, immobilized subaltern whose inability to express rage left him in a permanent state of muscular tension. It was not only the political economy of colonialism that was unjust, but also the libidinal economy.*

* Fanon remarks that one of the signal features of "underdeveloped societies" is that "the libido is above all a concern of the group, of the family"—proof, he adds, that these societies "attach great importance to the unconscious."

If violence was not one of the excesses of settler colonialism but its essence and ultimate guarantee, and if the unraveling of the system could only be a violent process, what could usefully be said about the development of violent impulses in the colonized, from the desires for revenge in their daydreams to the outbreak of organized armed struggle? Clearly it was not unprovoked aggression, but this was not to say that it was inherently good or noble. Fanon had no illusions that the colonized were by nature more virtuous than their oppressors: they were human beings with the same capacity for aggression. "The colonized subject," he notes, "is a persecuted person who constantly dreams of becoming the persecutor."

The dream life of colonial oppression, the collective unconscious of the colonized, is the subject of "On Violence," the opening (and best-known) chapter of *The Wretched of the Earth*:

> The first thing the native learns is to stay in his place and not overstep its limits. This is why the dreams of the native are muscular dreams, dreams of action, aggressive dreams. I dream that I am jumping, that I am swimming, that I am running, that I am climbing. I dream that I'm bursting out laughing, that I'm crossing a river in a single stride, that I'm being pursued by packs of cars that will never catch me. During colonization, the colonized never ceases to liberate himself between the hours of nine in the evening and six in the morning.

The aggressive instincts of the colonized, "sedimented in his muscles," are initially turned inward, in violence and crime against his own people, in wars among "tribes" and other "internecine feuds." The colonized also loses sight of his enemy, the settlers, by finding refuge in religion, "fatalism," or by taking part in "ecstatic dances," a "muscular orgy in the course of which the most acute aggression and the most immediate violence are channeled, transformed, spirited away." Colonialism, Fanon observed, could coexist quite easily with possession ceremonies and religious superstition. And so long as crime and violence were confined to the "Negro town" or the Casbah, they were a police matter, not a threat to the system: if anything, they supplied welcome evidence of the inherent criminality and primitiveness of the "natives."

At a certain point, however, "after years of unreality, after wallow-
ing in the most extraordinary phantasms," the colonized would become
"acutely aware of everything he does not possess"—of the physical scarcity
and mental alienation imposed by colonialism—and take up arms against
"the only forces that challenge him in his being: those of colonialism."
Crime, ecstatic dances, tribal warfare: all these distractions vanish, under
the disalienating force of the struggle. And so, by an "ironic twist of fate,"
it is now the turn of the colonized to say of the colonizer that he "only
understands the language of force."

The initial stages of decolonization, in Fanon's prognosis, would be
fumbling and cruel; the colonized lash out blindly at anyone belonging to
the settler population (as they had in Philippeville). Those who had been
despised as filthy *nègres* or *bougnoules* would naturally understand their
struggle, at first, as a race war, and as a war for all the things their white
masters had denied them: land, education, the right to affirm their languages and cultures. "Anti-racist racism and the will to defend one's skin
that characterizes the response of the colonized to colonial oppression,"
he writes, are "obviously sufficient grounds for joining the struggle." But,
like Négritude, they represent a passing moment, because "one doesn't
endure enormous repression, one doesn't witness the disappearance of
an entire family, so that hatred and racism can triumph." Under a revolutionary leadership, the colonized would realize that not all the settlers
are their enemies, and not all the natives are their allies. Overcoming the
"anti-racist racism" of the colonized would not be easy, he warns: colonial
reprisals would "reintroduce emotional elements into the struggle" and
"give the militant new motives for hatred, new reasons to go in search of
'settlers to slaughter.'" But a visionary leadership would realize that "hatred cannot constitute a program." A national struggle that was originally
grounded in the us-and-them framework of identity and driven by an
understandable desire for score-settling would then evolve into a more
inclusive social revolution, and an assault on all forms of privilege and
ill-gotten gains—including those of the native bourgeoisie.

How this would happen, Fanon did not explain. Nor did he mention
that in Muslim countries colonized by Europeans, Islam—far from being
put into its place or dissolving—had assumed greater significance as an

assertion of anti-colonial identity. But he made it clear that neither the "emancipated slaves" of the native middle classes (code for Algeria's reformist Muslim politicians) nor the "relatively privileged" urban working class (the group anointed by the Communist Party) were qualified to lead. The only revolutionary forces were those most oppressed by colonialism: the peasantry, and the outcasts of the cities, the lumpenproletariat, the unemployed, the criminal. "The pimps, the thugs, the unemployed, . . . all those who, maneuvering between madness and suicide, [would] throw themselves into the struggle for liberation like sturdy workers." Unlike the working classes, they are impervious to the "morality of the dominators. On the contrary, they assume their inability to enter the city except by the force of the grenade or the revolver."

There was a sliver of truth in this fantasy. Some FLN leaders, notably Ali La Pointe, one of the leaders of the Battle of Algiers, had started out as thieves and pimps. (Yacef Saadi, who recruited La Pointe and other members of the underworld to the FLN, believed the "illiterate and the criminal" were "the first victims of colonialism," as he explained in a 1984 BBC documentary.) But people without a stake in society seldom make the most reliable revolutionaries. It was from the same milieu that the *harki* militias—Algerians who fought with the French army—were often recruited. Nonetheless, in his celebration of the damned in the slums of Algiers, Fanon achieved a hallucinatory lyricism worthy of Genet. (Not surprisingly, the Black Panthers would pay close attention to these pages as they organized the African American lumpenproletariat in what they called the internally colonized slums of American cities.)

Fanon's argument for violence was, in part, an official defense of the FLN's historic decision to launch the armed struggle on November 1, 1954, in defiance of Messali Hadj. Yet his observations about violence were often rich and suggestive. As always with Fanon, they were based on a mixture of clinical analysis and literary inspiration. To reinforce his point that violence releases the colonized person from his "inferiority complex and his passive or despairing attitudes," he cited a lengthy passage from Aimé Césaire's play about a slave revolt, *And the Dogs Were Silent*, in which the protagonist, the Rebel, recalls killing his master. As he enters the master's bedroom, he assures him that "it was indeed . . . the good slave, the faith-

ful slave, the slave slave." Then the Rebel says, "Suddenly my eyes were
two cockroaches frightened on a rainy day . . . I struck, the blood spurted:
it is the only baptism that today I remember." Crucially, this sanguinary
encounter produces two deaths: an enslaved man slays his oppressor and
his slave self, emerging a free man.

At the same time, Fanon argues the merits of violence in broader
terms as a force of social cohesion, binding the colonized into a group-
in-fusion, against the divide-and-rule tactics of colonialism: "Violence
in its practice is totalizing, national. As a result, it harbors in its depths
the liquidation of regionalism and tribalism." The armed struggle uni-
fies the colonized population—formerly an undifferentiated mass of "natives," trapped in despair and fatalism—behind a common aim: national
liberation. In an addendum on violence in the international context, he
describes how the armed struggle has transformed the colonized into
"political animals in the most planetary sense of the term." They are no
longer downtrodden people begging for compassion but insurgents, represented by leaders who must be taken into account by the great powers. The "newly independent peoples" now have a "diplomacy in motion,
in fury, which contrasts strangely with the immobile, petrified world of
colonization." (Some leaders from the colonial world, like Fidel Castro, he
notes, appear in military garb at the UN, but this "does not scandalize
the underdeveloped countries," who understand that young revolutionary
nations emerge from "the atmosphere of the battlefield.") The tables have
turned: faced with the dynamism of insurgencies in the Third World, the
West looks stagnant and sleepy.


FANON'S ADVOCACY OF VIOLENCE can, at times, be alarming. In a chilling
passage on the Mau Mau revolt against the British in Kenya (1952–1960),
he writes that "to work means to work toward the death of the settler,"
and suggests that participation in killing becomes a way for "members of
the group who have strayed or been outlawed to come back, to retake their
place and be reintegrated. Violence can thus be understood as the perfect
mediation"—a cohesive activity for the rebels and their supporters among

the masses. But it is hard to read this passage today without thinking of
the Rwandan *génocidaires*, a group-in-fusion whose members also spoke
of killing as work. We are a long way here from the Fanon of 1959, who
wrote that, once their country was decolonized, Algerians would want to
"discover the man behind the colonizer."

The author of *The Wretched of the Earth* was only nine years older than
the author of *Black Skin, White Masks*, but he already sounds like a new
man: assertive, even oracular, in tone, no longer an observer of a people's
struggle but a full-blown participant. He describes the revolutionary process as if it were unilinear—or rather, Algerian. There is, it seems, only one
way to make a proper revolution, and it is the author's—the FLN's—way.
The doubt and self-searching Fanon expressed in "The Lived Experience
of the Black Man" have evaporated. The rhetorical force of *The Wretched of
the Earth* is undeniable. Yet it also has, at times, the air of an official document: a message to the prince, delivered by his most virtuous, incorrigible,
omniscient adviser.

Many of the book's first readers would express horror at Fanon's praise
of violence. "An atrocious book," the novelist François Mauriac, an early
critic of torture in Algeria, declared in *Paris Match*. In his review in the
weekly *L'Express*, Jean Daniel congratulated Fanon on having "realized his
life's dream: to give a revolutionary voice to the Third World," and compared his book to "Lenin's great pages in *State and Revolution*." But in his
journals he expressed a different opinion:

> If *The Wretched of the Earth* becomes the book of reference for the great
> agitators or leaders, all of the Third World will fall into convulsions.
> After having found it necessary to kill the colonialist, they will find it
> essential to kill those among their own who hesitate to kill. Redemp-
> tive murder will be worse than the logical crimes of the Stalinists . . . a
> terrible book, terribly revealing, a terrible harbinger of barbaric justice.
> The disciples of these arguments will be tranquil assassins, justified
> executioners, terrorists with no other cause than to affirm themselves
> by murdering others. If the white man has to die so the Black man can
> live, we've returned to the sacrifice of the scapegoat.

Intellectuals on the anti-colonial left also raised objections to Fanon's belief in violence as an "absolute praxis" of liberation. "When a colonized people abandon *l'arme de la critique* [the weapon of critique] in favor of *la critique des armes* [the critique of weapons]," the philosopher Jean-François Lyotard observed, "they do not simply change strategy. They destroy the very society in which they live, in the sense that the rebellion eliminates the constitutive social relationships of that society." The very class that Fanon anointed as the subject of history, the peasantry, was too fractured to overcome the crisis of rural society. The violent disruption of rural life was less likely to produce a revolutionary society than, in Lyotard's words, "a society in meltdown." The Vietnamese Marxist Nguyen Khac Vien (writing under the pseudonym Nguyen Nghe) argued that Fanon had ignored "a fundamental truth: namely that the armed struggle, while of capital importance, is no more than a moment, a phase in the revolutionary movement that is first and foremost political." In her 1969 book *On Violence*, Hannah Arendt would make a similar point, noting that "no human relationship is more transitory" than the fraternity experienced in war, which "can be actualized only under conditions of immediate danger to life and limb."

The discomfort of critics like Lyotard and Khac Vien was understandable. Fanon's evocation of disintoxication by violence is so vivid that it is sometimes hard to tell whether he is conveying the exhilaration of the colonized or his own. Certainly he identified with the anger of his subjects, in the face of colonial humiliation and France's murderous repression of the Algerian revolt. But if he advocates the logic and necessity of counterviolence by the colonized, he is also explicit in his criticisms of a politics based on revenge: the revolutionary movement's obligation is to direct the violent impulses of the colonized toward pragmatic objectives, not to foment bloodletting or to treat all members of the settler community as legitimate targets.

The seeming exaltation of violence in the opening pages of "On Violence" gives way to a position more nuanced than critics like Daniel—or admirers such as Sartre—understood. And perhaps more qualified than Fanon himself was willing to admit: some of his incendiary rhetoric seems designed to alienate the "beautiful souls" of the French left. As often in his writing, the boundary between diagnosis and prescription is hard to pin down, lending itself to a range of interpretations as to his intentions. "On Violence" can be read either as a psychiatric, phenomenological account of the lived experience of armed struggle or as an impassioned defense of armed struggle as a uniquely authentic path to collective and individual liberation—or, perhaps more accurately, as an unsettled combination of both.

"On Violence" tells a story with only two characters: settler and native. This radical simplification is a deliberate move on Fanon's part. His point is that once an anti-colonial insurrection is launched, every inhabitant in a settler-colonial society is forced to position himself or herself in relationship to the primary contradiction of colonizer and colonized: there is no middle ground. The stark binarism of "On Violence," with its vision of disintoxicated former natives experiencing rebirth as men over the corpses of their colonial tormentors, is, moreover, a source of its disturbing power as *literature*.

Indeed, the chapter is perhaps best read as a Hegelian parable, in which the dialectic of the Lord and the Bondsman is transposed to the struggle of colonizer and colonized. This is very much the Hegel of Alexandre Kojève's Paris lectures of the 1930s, which informed *Black Skin, White Masks*, with the *colonisé* (colonized) and the *colon* (settler)—Fanon almost always refers to them in the singular—as archetypes locked together in fatal contradiction. Mirroring Kojève's reading of *The Phenomenology of the Spirit*, Fanon's colonized achieves freedom and self-consciousness when he engages the settler in a struggle to the death. Fanon's praise of violence as the only way to undo the master-slave dialectic was echoed a century earlier in Frederick Douglass's account of his brawl with the brutal slave breaker Edward Covey. Douglass wrote of his battle with Covey in his 1845 memoir, *The Narrative of the Life of Frederick Douglass*:

> It rekindled the few expiring embers of freedom, and revived within me a sense of my own manhood. It recalled the departed self-confidence, and inspired me again with a determination to be free. The gratifi-

cation afforded by the triumph was a full compensation for whatever else might follow, even death itself . . . I felt as I never felt before. It was a glorious resurrection, from the tomb of slavery to the heaven of freedom.

After the confrontation, Douglass knew that he might be a "slave in *form*" but he was henceforth "a freeman in *fact*." He spoke of a resurrection, rather than a baptism, from the social death of slavery, but his evocations of psychological catharsis by violence were remarkably similar to Fanon's.

There are later echoes of this catharsis—not as a real encounter but as compensatory fantasy—in the writings of Jean Améry, a Vienna-born philosopher, né Hans Maier, who fought in the Belgian Resistance until he was captured by the Gestapo in 1943 and sent to a series of concentration camps, including Auschwitz. "The gaze we directed toward the city of the SS was also that of 'envy' and 'luxury,'" Améry wrote in a 1969 essay on Fanon. "Just like Fanon's colonized, each of us dreamed at least once a day of replacing the oppressor. In the concentration camp as in a 'native' village, envy transformed itself into aggression against other prisoners." The revolutionary violence Fanon espoused, he argued, "creates a negative equality, an equality in suffering. Repressive violence is the negation of equality and man. Revolutionary violence is above all *human*." This humanization of fury may have been what some of Fanon's readers found so disturbing about "On Violence." No less alarming, perhaps, was that it came from the pen of a Black man. As Malcolm X said of America, "The only people who are asked to be non-violent in this country are Black people."

As a work of phenomenology, describing the lived experience of decolonization, "On Violence" vividly captured the collective awakening among the colonized in the early days of an insurgency: the way that hallucinatory, muscular dreams of potency were channeled into violent, organized resistance and given a larger, national shape by a revolutionary movement. Less persuasive was Fanon's professed faith in the enduring—and redemptive—effects of violence. As the Fanon scholar Jean Khalfa reminds us, Fanon saw violence as a kind of shock therapy, like the ECT he used with some of his patients. Once the colonized have been "enlightened by violence," Fanon assures us, they will resist "any pacification," and the entire "business of mystification" by the colonizer "becomes practically impossible." His belief in the healing properties of violence betrayed an unlikely faith in the possibility of a resolution that went against much of what he had learned in his readings of psychoanalytic literature. It was also at odds with his findings as a doctor—the subject of the last chapter in *The Wretched of the Earth*, "Colonial Warfare and Mental Disorders," which seems implicitly to offer a rebuttal to the opening passages of the book.

Drawing upon his work as a psychiatrist in Blida, Tunis, and ALN training camps in Tunisia and Morocco, Fanon gave an unflinching account of the war's psychological injuries. The "human legacy of France in Algeria," he predicted, would be "an entire generation of Algerians, bathed in gratuitous, collective homicide with all the psycho-affective consequences that this entails." For Algerians, the war had often assumed "the air of an authentic genocide," terrorizing even those who kept their distance from the armed struggle. One of Fanon's patients, a thirty-seven-year-old peasant from eastern Algeria, had narrowly survived a massacre in which the army summarily executed a group of twenty-nine male civilians at point-blank range, in retaliation for an FLN ambush. Recovering from two bullet wounds at the day clinic in Tunis, the man began to attack the people around him; in a delirious rage, he imagined that the other patients and the hospital staff were French spies disguised as Arabs, and begged for a machine gun, saying, "They've all got to be killed."

The psychic toll of France's war—hallucinations and muscular rigidity, suicidal and murderous urges, depression, and apathy—is so devastating, Fanon writes, that "the militant sometimes has the grueling impression that he has to drag his people back, up from the pit and out of the cave." The use of the word *grotte* (cave) may be an allusion to the caves of the Aurès Mountains, a hideout for the rebels led by Emir Abdelkader during the French conquest and, a century later, for the "men of 1954," the fighters of the interior. Since the Roman invasion, the caves had been a sanctuary for Berber tribes, but they were also a site of unimaginable suffering at the hands of foreign occupiers: the *enfumades* of the 1840s (in which thousands of Algerians sheltering in place were asphyxiated by troops lighting fires at their entrance) and the napalm bombings of the war of independence.

*La Grotte éclatée* (*The Exploded Cave*), a 1979 novel by Yamina Méchakra set during the war, touches on many of Fanon's intuitions of Algerian trauma. In Méchakra's book, the cave is both a real place and a metaphorical space of refuge, resistance, and irreparable wounds. Like Fanon, Méchakra was a psychiatrist by profession, born a few years before the war of independence in the northern Aurès Mountains. As a young girl, she saw her father tied to the barrel of a tank and tortured to death by the army. The nameless narrator of her devastating novel—a long "poem in prose," in Kateb Yacine's words—is a nurse in the maquis, working in a hospital hidden inside a cave, where she treats wounded Algerians whose anguished confessions are remarkably similar to those of Fanon's patients. After the cave is discovered by the French and her son is blinded in a napalm attack, she winds up at the Manouba Psychiatric Hospital in Tunis, where Fanon briefly worked. Her son, she tells herself, will "see the country with the hands of his memory," and "the land will be reborn." For the survivors of colonial warfare, independence is a tormented birth from which they are always struggling to recover: "We are not heroes, we are the condemned."

The overwhelming impression left by Fanon's case studies in *The Wretched of the Earth* is that the disintoxicating effects of violence are ephemeral at best. Far from illustrating the redemptive force of armed struggle, they address the consequences of extreme colonial violence meted out to Algerians who lived through brutal roundups in villages, escaped from mass executions, withered away in refugee camps, or survived ruthless interrogation. In one rare case—not even Algerian—Fanon recounts the story of a patient whose revolutionary gesture culminated in prolonged anxiety. This patient, he tells us, placed a bomb at a café reputed to be a haunt of colonial extremists, killing ten people. Since independence in the unnamed country where he placed the bomb, the patient had forged friendships with people from the former colonial community who had supported his struggle. Each year, as the anniversary of his action came around, he imagined the same friends, or people like them, torn to shreds by his bombs. In Fanon's account, he was plagued by anxiety, dread, and "thoughts of self-destruction." Colonial soldiers were not the only ones whose sleep was disturbed by their actions during the war; the same was true of the men and women he celebrated as freedom fighters.

Unlike the opening of the chapter on violence, in which we see the armed struggle dragging the colonized masses out of their fatalism and apathy, the concluding chapter suggests that the war dragged many Algerians back into a different sort of cave and abandoned them to their own devices. It's not clear—nor is it likely—that Fanon saw this as a contradiction: the colonized, he believed, had no choice but to fight back; their very existence, over and above their right to self-determination, was at stake. But the sobering litany of case studies injects a striking ambivalence into a work of militant self-certainty. The reader, Fanon warns, "will perhaps find these psychiatric notes in such a book inopportune and singularly out of place. There is nothing we can do about it."

THE SOCIOLOGIST GEORGE STEINMETZ has identified an "overeager messianism around peasants and the Lumpenproletariat" in *The Wretched of the Earth*, but, he adds, the "questionable arguments about violence as 'absolute praxis,' can be sectioned off from this brilliant portrait of a late colony. What is more, they do not necessarily follow from it." In fact, much of the power of the book lies in Fanon's alertness to the difficulties that formerly colonized peoples would face after independence. Some of these were the result of external forces, from the ravages of slavery, colonialism, and imperialism (underdevelopment, poverty, low levels of education, shortages of trained professionals, etc.) to the opposition of the Western powers to nationalization programs (as the overthrow of Mossadegh in Iran and Árbenz in Guatemala, and the Suez crisis had recently illustrated). But Fanon spent more time discussing the internal obstacles that faced formerly colonized nations as they grappled with the challenges of independence.

In *The Wretched of the Earth*, the danger of regression is represented by what he calls the "national bourgeoisie"—the Western-educated, assimilated professional classes for whom he had developed a lasting scorn in Martinique. In the chapter titled "The Misadventures of National

Consciousness," Fanon lashed out at these postcolonial native elites, for whom "nationalization signifies very precisely the transfer into indigenous hands of privileges inherited from the colonial period":

> Lacking in ideas . . . inward-looking, cut off from the people, sapped by its congenital incapacity to evaluate issues on the basis of the nation as a whole, the national bourgeoisie assumes the role of manager for the companies of the West and in effect turns its country into a brothel for Europe.

The national bourgeoisie, he continues, is a "voracious, petty caste, dominated by a small-time racketeer mentality," not so much a "replica of Europe but rather its caricature." According to Fanon, the national bourgeoisie's "congenital weakness" is not merely the result of colonial "mutilation" but of its "laziness and mimicry" and the "deeply cosmopolitan formation of its mind." Infatuated with Western models, and allied to the Western bourgeoisie, it is fundamentally imitative, parasitic, and authoritarian; it "promotes the establishment and reinforcement of the racism that characterized the colonial era." When the national bourgeoisie demands the "Africanization" (Fanon uses the deliberately demeaning term *négrification*) or the "Arabization" of the civil service, its motive is not to pursue "an authentic project of nationalization" but rather to help itself to its share of the public purse in the name of justice. Not surprisingly, he observes, the masses "present the same demand but by restricting the notion of the African [*nègre*] or Arab to members of the nation." Violent demonstrations against non-nationals—people from Benin and Burkina Faso in Côte d'Ivoire, or Malians in Senegal—reflect the same "desperate return to the most odious, the most aggressive chauvinism."

In some of the book's most memorable pages, Fanon predicted that leaders of postcolonial African states—the "moral power under the protection of which the bourgeoisie . . . decides to enrich itself"—would entrench themselves by appealing to "ultranationalism, chauvinism, and racism." It was a startling anticipation of the Mobutus and the Mugabes of the future, the "big men" who would drape themselves in African garb, promote a folkloric form of Black culture, and cynically exploit the rhetoric of anti-colonialism—even, in the bitterest of ironies, invoking Fanon's own words. When the Trinidadian writer V. S. Naipaul visited Mobutu's Zaire—the former Belgian Congo—in 1975, he wrote that the official newspapers, "diluting the language of Fanon and Mao, speak every day of the revolution and the radicalization of the revolution. But this is what the revolution is about: kingship."

Before the leader is crowned, however, Fanon writes, the people "spontaneously trust this patriot," because he embodies their aspirations to freedom, independence, and dignity. But as independence fails to deliver on its promises of land and bread, "the leader will reveal his intimate function: to be the CEO of the company of profiteers impatient to get the most from the situation," and serve as "a screen between the people and the rapacious bourgeoisie." In a passage that prefigures Naipaul's dictator, inspired by Mobutu, in his 1979 novel *A Bend in the River*, Fanon writes of the leader:

> Each time he addresses the people he recalls his life, which was often heroic, the battles he led in the name of the people, the victories that he won in their name, thus conveying to the masses that they must put their trust in him . . . The leader pacifies the people. Years after independence, incapable of offering the people anything of substance, incapable of really opening up the future to the people, of launching the people into the task of nation building and hence their own development, the leader can be heard churning out the history of independence and recalling the sacred union of the liberation struggle. Refusing to break up the national bourgeoisie, the leader asks the people to plunge back into the past and get drunk on the epic that led to independence . . . During the struggle for liberation the leader roused the people and promised them a radical, heroic march forward. Today he repeatedly tries to lull them to sleep and three or four times a year asks them to remember the colonial period to take stock of the immense path they have traveled.

And what is the role of the people in this postcolonial order? The most fortunate rise inside the ranks of the only legal political party, the leader's party, an empty shell whose primary purpose is to oversee the "distribution of the cake of independence." But for everyone else—and even for the apparatchiks—the order from on high is "to follow, and to follow, always and forever," much as they had done under foreign rulers. Meanwhile, the rural masses, in whose name the revolution was made, would continue to live in squalor, while "the army and the police constitute the pillars of the regime," advised by foreign "experts." Eventually, Fanon warns, the regime will devolve into a "tribal dictatorship," in which government officials "are chosen directly from the leader's ethnic group, sometimes even directly from his family . . . These heads of government are the real traitors to Africa because they sell it to the most terrible of her enemies: stupidity."

Fanon was not the only writer to issue this grim warning about the postcolonial order. In his damning 1962 report, *False Start in Africa*, published only a few months after *The Wretched of the Earth*, the French agronomist René Dumont—the grandson of a peasant and an adviser to several African governments after independence—described the continent's new leaders as "a civil service bourgeoisie," "fake revolutionaries" who talked endlessly about the people's revolution while helping themselves to fancy cars, chauffeurs, and well-paid posts in the existing state apparatus. The African farmers he interviewed for his book told him that independence wasn't for them: it was only for the middle classes of the cities, the wealthiest of whom had moved into villas deserted by the settlers while rural people still lived in shacks. Dumont, who admired Fanon's book, considered the peasants of Africa to be the "true proletariat of modern times"; he warned that they were headed toward an even worse form of colonialism, a colonialism of class, albeit with a native elite and flags of their own. The "revolutionary spontaneity" of the peasantry may have been an illusion; the need to include them in the process of decolonization and independence was anything but. If they weren't given a stake, the future for which the colonized had given their lives would be stolen.

In his 1983 book, *The Intimate Enemy: Loss and Recovery of Self Under Colonialism*, the Indian philosopher Ashis Nandy, an astute reader of Fanon, describes colonialism as "the theft of futures." This was also Fanon's understanding. For him, the dictatorship of the national bourgeoisie was endlessly obliged to invoke the past at the expense of the future, whether in its revolutionary commemorations (designed to legitimize the ruling party that led the country to independence) or in nostalgic odes to the splendor of precolonial civilizations: an understandable response to racist denigration that ultimately serves conservative ends.

In the chapter expanding on his 1959 speech in Rome, Fanon once again takes the "racialized" ideologies of Négritude and Arabism to task for ignoring the living culture of ordinary citizens and privileging outmoded traditions they have ceased to practice. "It is not enough to reunite with the people in a past where they no longer exist," he writes. Later he adds, "The African intellectuals who are still fighting in the name of 'Negro-African' culture and who continue to organize conferences dedicated to the unity of that culture should realize that they can do little more than compare coins and sarcophagi." To "imagine that one can create a Black culture is to forget, oddly enough, that the *nègres* are in the process of disappearing, since those who created them are witnessing the demise of economic and cultural supremacy." What matters, in the final analysis, is the "kind of social relations" postcolonial leaders establish, "the conception they have of humanity's future . . . All the rest is literature and mystification."

Curiously, the literary work that Fanon singled out for praise as an example of revolutionary national culture was about the past, albeit the recent past. The prose poem "African Dawn," by the Guinean writer Fodéba Keïta, tells the story of a young soldier from a remote village in the bush who becomes a hero during World War II, only to be gunned down by the colonial forces when he returns home. "This is Sétif in 1945, Fort-de-France, Saigon, Dakar, and Lagos," Fanon writes approvingly. That Fanon was moved by the poem is hardly surprising: he, too, was a Black war hero who had been let down by the country for which he had served. But the author of this long (and rather wooden) piece of agitprop was not an independent intellectual: Fodéba was Sékou Touré's minister of the interior, and he presided over the notorious Camp Boiro, where Touré's alleged enemies were held and in some cases executed. The Guadeloupean novelist Maryse Condé, who was living in Conakry in 1961, was shocked by Fanon's praise of Fodéba, all the more so since the chapter "The Misadventures of National Consciousness" had felt to her like an accurate portrayal of the brutal regime she knew in Guinea. "How could I possibly understand such a contradiction?" she wondered. She decided that as powerful a thinker as Fanon was, "his taste in literature left much to be desired. I felt free to become a true Fanonian." In 1969, Fodéba was himself imprisoned in Camp Boiro, on charges of conspiring against Sékou Touré; he was shot dead without trial.

The contradiction that Condé found so disturbing existed within Fanon himself. For all that he believed in individual as well as collective freedom, he shared the fundamental premise of the native elites he criticized that, after independence, postcolonial states would be ruled by single-party regimes. And he remained, to the end, a soldier, a believer in military discipline who hoped that the army would serve as "a school for civics, a school for politics," helping to "detribalize and unify" the people. His objection to the despotism of the national bourgeoisie was not that they suppressed other parties but that they embodied narrow class interests. Like Rousseau, Fanon had an unshakable belief in the general will, and, like Lenin, an unshakable faith in the revolutionary party's ability to incarnate it, so long as it was "a direct expression of the masses." The role of "the party"—*the* party—is to "awaken the mind, to give birth to the mind. It is, as Césaire said, 'inventing souls.'" In an eerie passage, he adds that "everyone must be compromised in the fight for common salvation. There are no clean hands, there are no innocents, no onlookers. We are all getting our hands dirty in the swamps of our country . . . Every spectator is a coward or a traitor." As a student in Lyon, Fanon had seen Sartre's play *Dirty Hands*, about the execution of a suspected traitor in the Communist Party in a fictional Eastern European country. But in Fanon's account there is none of Sartre's ambivalence or anguish. He knew what it meant to have dirty hands, but if he felt any pangs of conscience, he dismissed them as middle-class squeamishness.

Nonetheless, to read *The Wretched of the Earth* today is to be struck by the prescience of Fanon's warnings about the obstacles to postcolonial freedom: corruption, autocratic rule, xenophobic nationalism, the lingering injury of colonial violence, and the persistence of underdevelopment and hunger—a "bloodless genocide" that consigns "a billion and a half men" to oblivion.

In the closing passages of *Black Skin, White Masks*, Fanon had willed himself into a mood of revolutionary optimism, concluding with a prayer to his body, and a vision of a world liberated from racism, indeed from the very idea of race. Despite its inventory of postcolonial pitfalls, *The Wretched of the Earth* performs a similar pirouette, ending with a rousing exhortation to his readers—"comrades"—to heed his warnings, to press on to the limits of political ambition, and "invent the total man whose triumph Europe has been incapable of realizing." As always, for Fanon, authentic freedom lies in the "leap of invention."

With decolonization, he announces, a new chapter in history has begun. The time has passed for hurling righteous accusations against the West (an "obsolete game") over its colonial crimes. "Europe did what it had to do, and on the whole it did it well . . . We no longer have to fear it, so let's stop envying it . . . No, we do not want to catch up with anyone. What we want is to move forward all the time, night and day, in the company of man, all men." With its hint of Césaire's "rendezvous of victory" in *Notebook of a Return to the Native Land*, Fanon's image of "all men" walking toward freedom celebrates the utopian conquest of alienation. But how would his disalienated man, freed from the "pathological separation of his functions and the crumbling of his unity" that Europe had brought about, come into being? And why would the new "spiritual adventure" that he proposed be any more successful in restoring humanity to a full sense of itself than Europe's had been? He did not say. Like *Black Skin, White Masks*, *The Wretched of the Earth* ends with a beautiful sermon, as vague as it was inspirational. As the French sociologist Philippe Lucas observed, Fanon sounds as if he were imploring his revolutionary comrades to "act *as if* Europe didn't exist, *as if* the world didn't have a history, *as if* it were something to be invented." This was a tall order. The account he gave of colonialism's violence and humiliation—and of the disorders of decolonization—seemed to count greatly against his hopes. For all that he tried to be a hard man, Fanon remained a dreamer.

# 17

# IN THE COUNTRY OF LYNCHERS

ON OCTOBER 3, 1961, François Maspero wrote to Fanon ("F. Farès") with "some very good news. Sartre's preface is ready, beautiful, violent, and useful."

It was certainly violent. In his preface to Paul Nizan's *Aden Arabie*, Sartre had written that Nizan's "words of hate were pure gold, mine were counterfeit." His preface to Fanon's book left a similar impression of a man straining to emulate—but only in the end to parody—the rhetorical fury of a rebel he admired and may have even envied. Dancing around his subject like "an excited small satyr," as the American journalist Harold Isaacs remarked, Sartre wrote:

> Murderous madness is the collective unconscious [for the colonized] . . . To kill a European is to kill two birds with one stone, to eliminate at one and the same time an oppressor and an oppressed, leaving a dead man and a free man: the survivor, for the first time, feels a *national* soil under the soles of his feet . . . We were men at his expense, he becomes a man at ours. Another man; of better quality . . . Violence, like the spear of Achilles, can heal the wounds it has made.

Sartre seemed to have read only the chapter on violence, and not very carefully. For all of Fanon's gusto in evoking the carnage of anti-colonial struggle—the baptismal moment when the envy, muscular tension, and other thwarted emotions and impulses erupt in violence—he set himself the task of explaining how these impulses could be channeled into a disciplined armed struggle, advancing a project inclusive of all those who supported independence, and promoting a political order inhabited by neither natives nor settlers but by citizens equal under the law. Fanon was also aware, in spite of his own belief in violence, that some of the wounds it left behind would never heal. As Hannah Arendt would point out in her 1969 book *On Violence*, he was "much more doubtful about violence than his admirers."

"What verbal masturbation!" Jean Daniel wrote of Sartre's preface in his journals. "What deadly frivolousness!" In her portrait of Fanon, Alice Cherki claims that he took a dim view of the preface, but all she tells us by way of evidence is that he was "extremely silent" about it. Yet it's hard to imagine that Fanon wasn't in some way honored, even flattered, by the homage. In spite of its reckless celebration of bloodletting, the preface is a remarkable moment that registers the impact of radical decolonization as yet another devastating blow—the Bolshevik revolution was the first—to the humanist assumptions of the Western intellectual.

"Not so long ago," Sartre begins, "the earth had two billion inhabitants, i.e., five hundred million people and one billion five hundred million natives. The first had possession of the Word, the others had the use of it." Those who had it on loan, those "gagged" and long-silent "mouths," responded to colonization in different ways. Some tried to mimic the culture of their oppressors ("a golden age" for the latter); others invoked Western "humanism" to throw it back at colonial culture to expose its "inhumanity." But by taking up arms against their rulers, the colonized were no longer repeating the usual loan words about the West's liberal ideals in the vain hope of negotiating their freedom. Instead, they were making themselves heard in a new language—a language of violence articulated "on the rebound" from the violence of colonialism. This, for Sartre, was the last curtain call for Western pretentions to humanist values—values that he himself had celebrated in his 1945 lecture "Existentialism Is a Humanism" and that had been travestied in the colonies. In Fanon's writings he had discovered an echo of Hegel's spirit of history: in the struggle between a

hypocritical humanist colonialism and its authentic discontents, the dialectic had never seemed clearer. "The Third World discovers *itself*," he proclaimed, "and speaks *to itself* through this voice."

Whatever Fanon thought of Sartre's text, it would have been the least
of his worries by the time he read it. His condition had suddenly deteriorated after his return from Rome, and the kind of treatment he ur-
gently needed was not available in North Africa. Since he could not go
to France, his only alternative, the FLN persuaded him, was the United
States; M'hammed Yazid was already in touch with an American diplomat with this in mind. On October 2, Fanon was driven to the El Aouina
airport, nearly silent and moving convulsively. There were no direct flights
between Tunis and the States, and during his stopover in Rome, which he
spent in a hospital, Sartre visited him for a few hours. The next day he flew
to New York.

In *The Wretched of the Earth*, Fanon had described the United States as
"a monster where the defects, the sickness, and the inhumanity of Europe
have reached appalling proportions." That he ended up dying in "the country of lynchers," as he called it, was one of the great incongruities of his
life. Stranger still was the fact that the Central Intelligence Agency helped
to arrange his treatment. Fanon's friend Elaine Klein has expressed horror
at the possibility that he "could have been duped" by the CIA, yet there is
little doubt Fanon's trip was made possible in part by Yazid's American
intermediary, Oliver Iselin, a young staffer at the agency from a family of
Swiss American bankers. While heading the CIA's North Africa desk in
Tangiers, Iselin had developed pro-nationalist sympathies. Once Morocco
became independent in 1956, he turned his attention to Algeria. He made
regular visits to ALN training camps in Morocco, delivering hospital supplies, cigarettes, and lighters made up with an Algerian flag and "Free
Algeria" insignia. By 1960, he had recruited two informants, one of whom
became an influential figure after independence. The Americans wanted
to ensure that Algeria didn't fall under Moscow's influence and were keen
to demonstrate their good intentions to its future rulers.

Fanon's illness provided just such an opportunity. The idea had been
raised as early as December 1960, when the eloquent Yazid, who had first
briefed Kennedy in the run-up to his UN speech on Algeria, alerted Iselin

to the seriousness of Fanon's condition. At the time, Fanon chose to go to a hospital in the Soviet Union, but the benefits of his treatment, initially impressive, were short-lived. In an interview with the American historian Thomas Meaney, Iselin remembered meeting Fanon in his plane at Idlewild Airport, then flying on with him to Virginia. "He was a sick man," Iselin recalled. "When I told him we . . . were landing in Virginia and had to go into the District of Columbia, he thought it was another border: 'Oh my god, another border.'" Fanon was indeed extremely unwell: he later told Klein that "it was a mystery, even to him," how, on arriving in Washington, he had "managed to get from the airport to a hotel."

It was October 10 before Fanon was able to leave his hotel for the National Institutes of Health in Bethesda, Maryland, where Josie and Olivier would join him. The week that had elapsed must have seemed interminable, and he was understandably angry. Both Beauvoir and Lanzmann would claim that he'd been "left to rot" without medical attention; others insinuated that the delay was a CIA plot to hasten his death. More likely there were bureaucratic hurdles in the way of Fanon's admission. What would the Americans have stood to gain by neglecting the care of a leading FLN intellectual, when the point of receiving him in Washington was to make a friendly overture to the future government of Algeria? And while Fanon was hardly a friend of American interests, he was not in all respects an adversary. In *The Wretched of the Earth*, he described America as the heir of the European colonial empires and predicted, correctly, that its early infatuation with anti-colonial movements—an infatuation that Iselin embodied—would be short-lived, as newly independent states embraced socialism or refused to align themselves with either superpower in the Cold War.

Yet the Americans who arranged his trip to the States were surely aware of Fanon's dim view of Soviet-style Communism and the French Communist Party—and, it's safe to assume, of his friendship with the anti-Communist Angolan leader Holden Roberto, who was among his visitors in Bethesda and who went on to become one of Iselin's contacts when he oversaw the agency's operations in Angola. For all his insistence that the Cold War was a distraction from the larger drama of decolonization and the rise of the Third World, Fanon could not avoid becoming

caught in the tentacles of US-Soviet rivalry for the support of newly independent nations.

He had not been duped, much less seduced, by the CIA. He was a dying man who wanted the best medical care he could find, even if it meant
being in a country where so-called miscegenation was still illegal in sixteen states, where families like his own were forced to live in secret. Maryland, less than a half hour's drive from the capital, was one of them. Iselin
claimed to have cooked up a cover story so that Olivier Fanon (whom he
described as "very dark") could attend Howard University's kindergarten
as the son of an Arab diplomat.

It's not clear whether Fanon—aka Farès, also the "Arab diplomat"
Ibrahim Omar Fanon (as his passport identified him)—knew of Iselin's
work behind the scenes. Iselin said he steered clear of politics in their
conversations, aware of Fanon's "distrust of our motives," and focused on
making him "as comfortable as possible." If he had any thoughts about
winning over Fanon's wife, these were quickly dispelled: "If Frantz was to
the left," he told Meaney, "she was further to the left." According to Josie,
Fanon warned his American minder that the US government would soon
face uprisings by Black Americans in the cities and guerrilla movements
in South America. He seldom let down his guard, and in his bleakest,
loneliest moments, he was gripped by terrifying hallucinations, in which
his doctors were trying to whiten his skin—to restore, in effect, the mask
that he had cast off—by running him through a washing machine. At the
innermost core of his psyche, the struggle for liberation went hand in hand
with the defense of his own Blackness, the armor of his skin.

Fanon received visits from Abdelkader Chanderli, the head of the
GPRA's New York delegation, as well as African diplomats and Black
American activists. During his periods of remission, he talked about the
books he hoped to write: a treatise on jealousy, a history of the Algerian
National Liberation Army, and a memoir about his own illness, with the
working title *The Leukemia Patient and His Double*—an allusion to Anto-
nin Artaud's *The Theater and Its Double*. Confined to a hospital bed when
he should have been pursuing his revolutionary duties, he spoke often of
Tunis and his comrades, the men he called *les frères* (brothers), with long-
ing and, perhaps, a sense of uneasiness. Once, when he was alone with

Klein, he sat up and exclaimed: "It's not a bad thing to die for one's country." He meant Algeria, but if there had been a way to die for Martinique, Fanon would have found it.

Fanon's brothers were within an inch of achieving their goals: on March 18, 1962, the French government and the GPRA would sign the Évian Accords, which would end the war and lead to independence in July. But in the fall and winter of 1961, as Fanon lay dying, the violence was intensifying. The OAS was escalating its attacks against Algerian civilians and the French authorities. One of its victims would be the Kabyle writer and teacher Mouloud Feraoun, kidnapped and murdered along with five of his colleagues, three days before the cease-fire. It was the terrorism of the OAS in the closing stages of the war, even more than the FLN's bombings during the Battle of Algiers, that shattered any hope of Muslim-European coexistence in any foreseeable future. After independence, more than a million settlers were "repatriated" to France, a country most of them hardly knew.

Inside France, the FLN and the French police were locked in violent conflicts in the run-up to peace. A week after Fanon's arrival at the hospital in Maryland, the Paris police waded into a demonstration by the FLN, which had taken to the streets protesting a curfew imposed exclusively on the city's Algerian inhabitants. Hundreds were murdered, some drowned in the Seine, others beaten to death in police stations. The architect of the October 17 massacre was the police chief of Paris, Maurice Papon, who had tortured FLN suspects in the Constantinois department of Algeria.

On her visits to the hospital in Bethesda, Klein found Fanon "lucid, rapidly perceiving who among his visitors believed in his recovery and who did not; his discourse changed accordingly." When a Black American minister came to the hospital and offered to advise him if he encountered any racial problems, Fanon replied that he could take care of himself. Klein helped out the family by taking Olivier to New York on a sightseeing trip: the carousel in Central Park, the Empire State Building, the Staten Island ferry. Before they set off, Olivier asked Klein to write her name on the icy window in Fanon's room, then copied it. "He's transferring," his father observed from his deathbed, as if he were describing one of his patients.

Claude Lanzmann flew in from Paris, with news of a French doctor who'd had some success with a pioneering treatment for leukemia. It was already too late. "What shocks me here in this bed, as I grow weaker," Fanon wrote in a letter to his friend Roger Taïeb in Tunis, "is not that I'm dying, but that I'm dying in Washington of leukemia when I could have died in battle with the enemy three months ago. We are nothing on earth if we are not, first and foremost, slaves of a cause, the cause of the people, the cause of justice, the cause of freedom." His last wish was to be buried in Algeria.

On December 3, 1961, an Algerian friend brought Fanon a copy of *The Wretched of the Earth*. Josie read him the admiring review in *L'Express* by Jean Daniel, who had kept his reservations to himself. Fanon's pleasure was clouded by his prognosis: "It won't give me back my bone marrow," he said. Three days later he died of a double bronchial pneumonia, as the police in Paris removed copies of *The Wretched of the Earth* from bookstores. He was thirty-six years old.

Beauvoir scrutinized a photo of Fanon on the cover of *Jeune Afrique*, "younger and calmer than when I had seen him, and very handsome. His death weighed heavily because he had charged his death with all the intensity of his life." In his journals, Jean Daniel compared Fanon to the physicist J. Robert Oppenheimer, the father of the atom bomb, the son of German Jewish immigrants "whose mask had struck me at Princeton"; he recalled his powerful handshake, which always seemed to "carry a message," and his "sharp yet indulgent way of meeting a stare. One always hesitated a few seconds to know if one had been admitted into the demanding universe where he had withdrawn . . . to think about the condition of his people, which, as he saw it, was not yet the human condition."

Fanon's body was flown to Tunis. When Josie and Olivier returned, they moved in for a time with the Manuellans. Marie-Jeanne drove Josie to El Menzah to empty the apartment where she and Frantz had lived. Like their other apartments, Marie-Jeanne recalled, it looked less like a home than a makeshift camp. "These are the letters from Sartre," Josie said, crumpling them and tossing them into the wastebasket. She pointed to a black wallet that Abane Ramdane had left and that Fanon had kept as a memento of his friend and their last encounter. While Marie-Jeanne cleaned the apartment, Josie sobbed. "What will become of us, and what

will become of his Black child?" For the next few years, she would tell
Olivier that his father was traveling. (His daughter in France, Mireille,
learned of his death only when she stumbled on his photograph in *Paris
Match*.) Josie worried that the brothers in the FLN would try to marry her
off again. Still, as desperate as she was, she "never expressed the wish, or
the idea, 'not to return to Algeria.'" The plan was for all of them to make
the move after independence.

As it turned out, Fanon—or rather his remains—got there first.

On December 11, a welcome ceremony was held in the *salle d'honneur*
of the airport of El Aouina in Tunis. Representatives of the GPRA surrounded the casket, draped in an Algerian flag. Later that day, there was a
wake at the headquarters of the Algerian mission. Michel Martini, Fanon's
colleague at the Charles Nicolle Hospital, overcame his "horror of these
ceremonies" and lingered for two hours, chatting with Fanon's FLN comrade Omar Oussedik and reflecting on the "vanity of earthly things." At
nine the next morning, Krim Belkacem, whose life had been saved by
Fanon earlier that year, gave a eulogy—"remarkably written, but poorly
read," according to Martini—in which he praised Fanon's qualities as a
revolutionary as well as his work as a psychiatrist and intellectual. The
independence for which Fanon had fought so hard was only a few weeks
away, he said. "Algeria will not forget you," he promised. That evening,
the ALN leadership hosted a dinner in his memory. Iselin was one of the
guests. When news of his presence at the funeral was reported in the Tunisian press, he left immediately for Morocco.

After Krim's speech, Roger Taïeb and Pierre Chaulet, two of Fanon's
closest friends, accompanied the convoy that took Fanon's body from Tunis to Ghardimaou, a town in the northwest along the Algerian border, in
a cortege of about two dozen vehicles. At 12:30 p.m., the convoy reached
its destination. At this point, a group of ALN soldiers carried his casket on
a long march through the woods, in silence under a brilliant sky, crossing
the border—a moment charged with significance—and heading toward
the cemetery of the *chouhada* (war martyrs), in the recently liberated area
of Aïn Kerma. The coffin was lowered onto a bed of branches cut from
a mastic tree. Another eulogy was delivered, this time in Arabic, by the
ALN commander Ali Mendjeli, who pledged "a free, independent, demo-

cratic and social Algeria, one in which human rights will be respected," as
if in return for Fanon's commitment to these ideals. The only woman in
attendance was Josie Fanon. She stood still, barely able to move, gazing at
the horizon through dark sunglasses.

For all the solemnity of the occasion, as the novelist Assia Djebar remarked in her reflections on his life, Fanon was mourned by leaders of
the exterior who had "adopted him as a master thinker, whereas, if he
had been resurrected ten years later, he would have turned his back on
them." Still, Djebar admitted, these "Bonapartists of an emerging military state . . . had the sense of a staging worthy of a progressive and secular Algeria," the cause to which Fanon had given his life. Buried in the
shade of a cork tree in Aïn Kerma, he was reunited with his beloved interior. Cherki heard later from one of the mourners that the crossing of the
woods and the ceremony had been "imbued with a great serenity and a
strange beauty." Martini reminded himself, "Life continued, and no one
is really indispensable."

The most powerful elegy appeared in *Jeune Afrique*, a week after
Fanon's death. The author was his favorite poet, Aimé Césaire, the distinguished elder who, unlike him, had gone back to Martinique and presided over its departmentalization. Fanon's life had been a "detour"—as
Édouard Glissant thought of it—from the West Indies. Césaire, on the
contrary, embodied the idea of "return": they had taken very different
paths, but Césaire put aside their differences in a moving homage. "If
the word 'commitment' has any meaning," he wrote, "it is to be found in
Frantz Fanon." He continued:

> A violent type, it has been said of him. And it is quite true that Fanon
> established himself as a theoretician of violence, the only weapon, he
> thought, of the colonized against colonialist barbarism. But his vio-
> lence was non-violent, however odd this seems. I mean the violence of
> justice, of purity, of intransigence. It must be understood: his revolt was
> ethical, his approach one of generosity. He didn't simply join a cause.
> He gave himself. Wholly. Without reserve. Without measure. With un-
> qualified passion. A theorist of violence, no doubt, but even more of
> action. Because he hated idle chatter. Because he hated cowardice. No

one was more respectful of ideas, more responsible to his own ideals, more demanding with respect to life, which he did not imagine could be anything other than lived thought . . . Frantz Fanon was a paraclete. It's why his voice is not dead. Beyond the grave, it still calls people to freedom and man to dignity.

In his memoirs, Serge Michel remembered 1961 as the year that had begun with the assassination of Patrice Lumumba and ended with the "militant funeral of Fanon." Eight months later, on July 5, 1962, Algeria declared its independence. Now the most precious—and the last—of France's African possessions, claimed exactly 132 years earlier when a French expeditionary force landed in the coastal town of Sidi Ferruch, was the full-fledged People's Democratic Republic of Algeria. A chapter in history, some of whose most memorable lines had been set down by Fanon, had closed; the next would be written by others. Fanon, who liked to think of himself as a humble servant of the revolution, might have been gratified to know that, in the land of a "million martyrs,"* as post-independence Algeria came to think of itself, he was considered no more important than the thousands of men and women who had given their lives to the cause: he was simply another Algerian. And yet, as the official memory of the struggle evolved, he would be recast as a foreign sympathizer, his global influence and prestige vaguely resented by some of his former comrades. And though the Blida-Joinville Psychiatric Hospital was renamed the Frantz Fanon Psychiatric Hospital, the people closest to him were saddened by how quickly his traces seemed to vanish, as Algerians devoted themselves to rebuilding a country devastated by eight years of war, and as the French did their best to bury the memory of a land they had long considered a part of France.

Marie-Jeanne and Gilbert Manuellan moved to Algiers in 1963. Dur-

---

* The actual number of Algerian deaths—estimated at 200,000 to 250,000 by the French historian Charles Robert-Ageron, and at 430,000 by the Algerian demographer Kamel Kateb—was less than 1 million but still enormous for a country of fewer than 10 million. Approximately 24,000 French soldiers died, as did slightly under 3,000 European civilians. Tens of thousands of Algerians—the exact number will never be known—were killed by other Algerians.

ing the four years they spent in his adoptive land, Marie-Jeanne almost never heard Fanon's name mentioned. She tried to find Josie, who was living with an official in the intelligence services—one of the brothers—but no one could tell her where. Then, one day, buying henna in a perfume shop, Marie-Jeanne heard Josie's voice behind her. They fell into each other's arms, exchanged phone numbers, and promised to see each other soon. As Josie was leaving, she mentioned that her telephone wasn't working: best for Marie-Jeanne not to try, Josie would be in touch, but she never called. When the Manuellans returned to France, in the summer of 1967, none of their left-wing friends in Paris regarded Fanon as "anything other than a madman, when he wasn't described as a bloodthirsty madman. The most enlightened among them had read the preface to *The Wretched of the Earth*, since the author was Sartre, and leafed through the rest." The republication of Fanon's manifesto by François Maspero during the events of May 1968 briefly rekindled interest in his work on the French left, but in the pantheon of radical icons, he stood far behind Mao and Che Guevara. He was a native son who had taken part in a war that most of the French preferred to put behind them. Even French radicals preferred to talk about either Vietnam or the Black Panthers rather than *la guerre sans nom* (the war without a name).

In an essay on Algeria published in 1974, the British anthropologist Ernest Gellner rather smugly observed that "whereas virtually no man in the street knows the name of Fanon, he can be relied upon to know the name of another thinker, Ben Badis—who, however, is totally unknown abroad, other than to specialists." But, unlike the leader of the Association of Algerian Muslim Ulama, Fanon never sought to shape the *content* of Algerian nationalism, something that, in any case, no foreigner could have done. (His apparent lack of interest in the religious and cultural roots of Algerian nationalism was, in part, the expression of a foreigner's humility.) And while he had embraced Algeria's struggle, the revolution he envisioned in *The Wretched of the Earth* did not end at Algeria's borders—or indeed any borders. Throughout his struggles against racism in France, colorism and self-hatred in the West Indies, colonial domination in Algeria and Africa, and confinement in psychiatric wards, Fanon was propelled by the same irrepressible commitment to disalienation and freedom. He stripped bare the pretentions of a French universalism that had existed in name only in the colonies, and imagined a future in which different national cultures—emancipated from foreign colonizers, from their own native elites, from social and psychological forms of suffering—would sit together at Césaire's "rendezvous of victory."

This vision, nourished in equal parts by anger and hope, was never meant for Algeria alone, or even merely for national liberation struggles. It was addressed to the world. And after his death, Fanon's ideas would travel across the globe, where they would acquire an influence, an élan, and, indeed, a universality exceeding those of Sartre himself. Fanon's life as a theoretician, a prophet, and an icon of liberation had only just begun.

# EPILOGUE:
# SPECTERS OF FANON

---

### PIECES OF A MAN

"I don't like Fanon to be chopped into little pieces," Marie-Jeanne Manuellan would often say to me. Those who see only one aspect of his work and personality, she argued, missed the indissoluble whole: psychiatrist and revolutionary, writer and man of action, West Indian and Frenchman, Algerian and African. That Fanon's work was being dissected with exegetical devotion in university seminars both amused and exasperated her. "These were pamphlets!" she protested: texts written in the service of a political movement, not works of philosophical reflection.

Manuellan spoke from personal experience, of course, and in her last years, she shared her memories of Fanon to everyone who visited her at the assisted care facility where she lived in the Fourteenth Arrondissement of Paris. At the entrance to her immaculate room was a framed quote by the Turkish leftist poet Nâzim Hikmet: "Hope is in man," a belief that Fanon had also held and that had continued to inspire Manuellan in her work as an activist on behalf of refugees, immigrants, and

Palestinians under occupation. A white Frenchwoman with tousled gray hair, she was an improbable spokesperson for Fanon's legacy, but to listen to her was to feel closer to the man who wrote *The Wretched of the Earth*. "Marie-Jeanne is the only person who brought my father back to life, for me, the only one who has depicted him as something other than a disembodied icon," Mireille Fanon Mendès-France, Fanon's daughter, told me in Paris in the summer of 2018. "The only thing that I reproach her for is that she's going to die." Marie-Jeanne passed away a year later, at ninety-one.

In writing this book, I spoke to a number of Fanon's people, but I learned more from Manuellan than from anyone else about the whole Fanon. I understood why she preferred the man she knew to the pieces into which his work had been divided, and I have done my best to reassemble them. But the fragments—Fanon's influential afterlives in politics, theory, culture, and psychiatry—are also a vital part of his story.

Today, Fanon is an intellectual celebrity whose writing is enlisted on behalf of a range of often wildly contradictory agendas: Black nationalist and cosmopolitan, pan-African and pan-Arab, secular and Islamist, Marxist and liberal, defenses of identity politics and critiques of identity politics. He has been denounced as a misogynist for suggesting that some white women who fear Black men secretly wish to be raped by them, and praised as a precocious Third World feminist for his writings on Algeria's female fighters. Right-wing intellectuals have attacked him as the founding father of modern terrorism and critical race theory, yet they have also drawn inspiration from his work: the French writer and politician Éric Zemmour, a Jew of Algerian origin and an advocate for the racist "great replacement" conspiracy theory, has cited Fanon's observations about the desire of the colonized to take the place of their colonizers. Fanon is now a canonical intellectual figure who commands respect even from his enemies.

The playwright manqué is also as much a part of radical culture as John Berger, James Baldwin, or Audre Lorde, and, as such, a symbol of left-wing hipsterism: in the recent television series *The White Lotus*, a woke young woman of color reads *The Wretched of the Earth* at a Hawaiian resort where she's plotting against the superrich parents of her white best friend, who've taken her on vacation. The actress Jamie Lynn Spears, Britney's sister, has posted Fanon quotes on her Instagram account. In his project for the 2022 Documenta exhibition in Kassel, Germany, the British Bangladeshi artist Hamja Ahsan erected a sign for "Fanon Fried Chicken: Fast Food for the Wretched of the Earth" above a halal restaurant. (Fanon is not likely to have approved this diet on culinary, health, or indeed environmental grounds.) It's hard to think of another mid-twentieth-century thinker with such enduring star power, with the exception, perhaps, of Hannah Arendt, whose 1969 essay on violence was in part a response to Fanon's vogue among New Left radicals. And Fanon's allure has only grown in an intellectual era preoccupied by white supremacy and privilege, anti-Blackness, settler colonialism, and indigeneity. In the introduction to *Black Skin, White Masks*, Fanon declared, "I do not arrive armed with absolute truths." Yet many of his admirers, after his death, would look to him precisely for such timeless wisdom.

### FANON'S GHOST

No one was more ruffled by the cult that formed around Fanon than Albert Memmi, Fanon's Tunisian-born contemporary and rival explainer of the colonial condition. He envied Fanon's prestige on the left and considered him a somewhat dangerous extremist. And in a fascinating essay published in *Esprit* on the tenth anniversary of his death, "La vie impossible de Frantz Fanon" (The Impossible Life of Frantz Fanon), Memmi sought to settle accounts with him—in effect, to banish his ghost. Fanon's life, he argued, had been a thwarted quest to belong and a deluded flight from his Martinican roots. "Fanon's particular tragedy," Memmi wrote, was that, unlike Aimé Césaire, "he never again returned to Négritude and the West Indies." Instead, Fanon transferred his fierce identification with the country that had spurned him to Algeria's Muslim rebels, who would never accept him as one of their own. Once Muslim Algeria proved too "particularist," it was subsumed by something still larger: the African continent, the Third World, and ultimately the dream of "a totally unprecedented man, in a totally reconstructed world." Fanon's "true problem," Memmi insisted, was not how to be French, or Algerian, but "how to be West Indian."

Memmi's account of Fanon's life, and his struggles to define himself, is suggestive, and I have drawn on it in this book. What I do not accept is the implicit accusation that Fanon abandoned his Black brothers and sisters by making common cause with North African Muslims. The impossibility of Fanon's life was not merely his tragedy; it was also his glory. Alice Cherki wrote in response to Memmi, "The project of being exclusively identified with one's origin was at odds with Fanon's conception of what it meant to be a free subject."

Fanon never disavowed his Martinican roots, or his love of Césaire's writings, from which he drew his images of slave revolt in *The Wretched of the Earth*. And nowhere was Fanon more West Indian than in his writings on Algeria and Africa, in which he transposed the experience of the West Indian plantation onto the entire Third World. (It is no accident that labor exploitation plays a far greater role in his account of French colonialism than the "civilizational" or religious conflict between Christian Europe and North African Islam.) He had not forgotten his people or his past, but he had come to see both as part of a larger story that connected him to other people and other pasts. Algerians may not have been racially Black, but they were victims of the same system that had brought his ancestors on slave ships to the West Indies. He had left Martinique, but it never left him. Only a West Indian could have written *The Wretched of the Earth*.

For Memmi, a North African Jew disillusioned with Arab nationalism (and excommunicated by some of his former comrades over his embrace of Zionism), identity was destiny, and Fanon an outlier, if not a failure, for defying its dictates. But it was precisely Fanon's defiance of identity's claims, his nomadic commitment to other people's causes and to a radical, anti-colonial form of universalism, that enabled him to move readers far beyond Martinique, France, and Algeria, from the Belgian Holocaust survivor Jean Améry and the Catholic mystic Thomas Merton to the young Barack Obama (who discussed Fanon late into the night in his dorm room at Occidental College), and the political prisoner Albert Woodfox, a Black

Panther who spent forty-three years in solitary confinement in Louisiana's notorious Angola Prison for a murder he did not commit.

## PROPHET OF THE THIRD WORLD

There were, of course, more nuanced commentators than Fanon on the Algerian struggle and the subject of decolonization. Several of them—Mouloud Feraoun, Mohammed Harbi, Pierre Bourdieu, Jean-François Lyotard—have made appearances in these pages, providing a counterpoint, and occasionally a corrective, to Fanon's often feverish, if seductive, ardor. But while their contributions to historical knowledge were at times more informed and more subtle, the publication of *The Wretched of the Earth* was a historical *event*. Fanon's book conveyed, as no other book did, the psychic drama—and, often enough, the tragic passion—of anti-colonial revolution. For his readers in the training camps of national liberation organizations in the 1960s and '70s, Fanon was not only a theorist of decolonization but also a trusted comrade, and the sacred aura of his manifesto, the bible of the Third World, was burnished by his premature death. Within a few years of its publication, *The Wretched of the Earth* would be read in Spanish by Latin American guerrillas in a Cuban translation commissioned by Che Guevara; in English, by ANC rebels in South Africa; in Portuguese, by anti-colonial fighters in Angola, Guinea-Bissau, and Mozambique; in Farsi, by Iranian Marxists and Islamic revolutionaries; and, not least, in Arabic, by Palestinian fedayeen in training camps in Jordan, Lebanon, and Syria.

The first Arabic translations of Fanon's last work, which appeared in Beirut bookshops in 1963, helped shape the ideology of the emerging Palestinian resistance to Israel. In his 1981 memoir, *My Home, My Land*, the Palestine Liberation Organization leader Abu Iyad (the nom de guerre of Salah Khalaf) writes that Fanon, one of his favorite authors, taught him that "only a people who doesn't fear the guns and tanks of the enemy is capable of fighting the revolution to the finish." Abu Iyad knew that the PLO could never defeat Israel on the battlefield, but he hoped that the armed struggle "could rally the masses to the people's movement we were trying to create." In 1968, Palestinian fighters defended the Jordanian town of Karameh against a raid by the Israeli army. Their losses were heavy (five times as many as on the Israeli side), but they held their ground and even managed to kill two dozen enemy soldiers. The legend of Karameh—"dignity" in Arabic—was born. Before the battle, Fatah had two thousand fighters; three months later, it had fifteen thousand. In a phrase that might have been lifted from *The Wretched of the Earth*, Yasir Arafat remarked, just after Karameh, that the armed struggle had transformed Palestinians from "downcast refugees" into "aroused fighters." Its target was not so much the Israeli enemy as the wounded Palestinian psyche: violence was collective therapy, a way to create the "new man," to forge a nation, and to announce the existence of the Palestinian people on the world stage.

In sub-Saharan Africa, revolutionaries studied Fanon's work with equally keen attention. They included the influential Bissau-Guinean revolutionary Amílcar Cabral, whom he had met in the late 1950s; Steve Biko, the founder of South Africa's Black Consciousness movement, who was beaten to death in 1977 by agents of the apartheid regime; and a young guerrilla leader named Yoweri Museveni, Uganda's future dictator, whose 1971 dissertation was titled "Fanon's Theory of Violence: Its Verification in Liberated Mozambique." (His opponents in Uganda's democratic opposition would later cite Fanon against Museveni.) Walter Rodney, a Guyanese Marxist historian and pan-African leader, cited Fanon in his critique of the "pitfalls of African national consciousness," an initially "liberatory force" that, he warned, "can turn into blinkers and constitute a barrier for further understanding of the real world." Contrary to Memmi, African revolutionaries saw Fanon not as a Black man estranged from his people but as a fellow soldier in the war against both colonialism and neocolonialist exploitation.

## FANON AND "NATIONAL CULTURE"

Fanon exerted an even more powerful influence on Africa's writers, artists, and filmmakers, the creators of "national culture," who found in his work a guide to the psychology of the oppressed—and, increasingly, to the authoritarian and corrupt governments now ruling in their name. As the Kenyan novelist Ngũgĩ wa Thiong'o has pointed out, African literature in the years just after independence "was really a series of imaginative footnotes to Frantz Fanon." Ngũgĩ himself first read *The Wretched of the Earth* (in an early translation titled *The Damned*) in 1965, shortly after arriving at Leeds University. Kenya had won its freedom from British rule two years earlier, and Ngũgĩ could already "sense a discordance between the promises of the anti-colonial movements and independence." Understanding politics "in terms of Black and White" made sense in settler colonies where "White was power, privilege, wealth; Black was powerlessness, oppression and poverty. But what about the post-colonial African state that follows the white settler state? The terms White and Black became inadequate, if not confusing." When he read the chapter on the pitfalls of national consciousness, he felt that Fanon was describing Kenya: "It was Fanon who really gave us the vocabulary to understand and voice the character of the post-colonial era." What Africa's novelists, from Ngũgĩ and Chinua Achebe to Nadine Gordimer and Abdulrazak Gurnah, understood about Fanon was that his work was far more than a set of catechisms about armed struggle and anti-imperialism, the lexicon of vulgar Fanonism. His psychological insights into the humiliations of colonial rule, the violent (and erotic) fantasies of the colonized, and the arrogance of the national bourgeoisie were not only piercing but also rich in dramatic potential.

In his exploration of the unconscious—and distinctly less noble—impulses unleashed by colonialism, perhaps the most Fanonian of post-colonial novelists was V. S. Naipaul. Naipaul had little use for Fanon's liberationist politics: in his 1975 report from Mobutu's Zaire for *The New York Review of Books*, he sneered at the "diluted version of Fanon" that had become the lingua franca of the official newspapers. Yet Fanon would have had no trouble recognizing the wounded, resentful, envious protagonists of Naipaul's novels—"mimic men" who feel, like his narrator, Salim, in *A Bend in the River*, possessed by "colonial rage," cruelly deprived of their "manhood, or a part of it." As James Wood has observed, "Naipaul's radical pessimism meets Fanon's radical optimism at the point where the cut of colonial guilt, angrily resisted by both men, is converted into the wound of colonial shame."

In Fanon, colonial rage leads, ultimately, to anti-colonial insurrection; in Naipaul, however, it had nowhere to go, because the revolutions Fanon embraced had either come to a halt; turned into grotesque (and murderous) parodies of themselves; or led to tyrannical regimes like Mobutu's, the inspiration for the unnamed country in *A Bend in the River*. Naipaul's masterpiece was published in 1979, a year after Edward Said published his landmark critique of Western representations of the East, *Orientalism*. Both, in very different ways, reflected the end of the anti-colonial era and the birth of the postcolonial. The national liberation struggles in southern Africa would continue for another decade or so; the Palestinian struggle would enter a new phase, focused on popular resistance in the occupied West Bank and the Gaza Strip. But the world was entering a new historical cycle, in which the Fanonian themes of armed struggle, rural spontaneity, and secular nationalism were to lose much of their currency. In 1978, Deng Xiaoping embraced the capitalist market and declared that "to get rich is glorious." A year later, Iran was swept by the Islamic Revolution, infused with Ali Shariati's political spirituality, which Fanon had rejected, however much Shariati sang his praises. That same year, Russian forces invaded Afghanistan, setting in motion a chain of events that would culminate in the collapse of the Soviet bloc and the spread of Sunni Islamist insurgencies against Arab nationalist governments, including that of Algeria. The countries of the Global South—the former Third World—would be dominated increasingly by authoritarian capitalism and nationalism, often with a strong dose of religious piety.

## POSTCOLONIALISM AND ITS DISCONTENTS

Algeria was one of those countries. It is unlikely that Fanon, if he had been cured of his leukemia, would have found a home there for long. In the first few years of independence, a revolutionary spirit of solidarity still lingered. In a defiant message to the French military police still stationed in Algeria,* Ahmed Ben Bella, independent Algeria's first president, promised that the rights of French army deserters who had taken refuge in Algeria would be defended as if they were Algerians. When a group of

---

* The Provost gendarmerie (military police) remained in Algeria until 1964, to assist the new government in maintaining order.

French gendarmes tried to arrest a deserter teaching at a school in a village near Blida, the villagers took up arms to protect him and forced the gendarmes to leave. But the country was turning progressively inward. "We are Arabs, Arabs, Arabs," Ben Bella proclaimed, ignoring the substantial minority of Algerian Berbers, who had made great sacrifices during the war, and whose language, Amazigh, would not be recognized by the state for another two decades. In 1963, the observance of Ramadan became obligatory, and a law was passed restricting Algerian nationality to citizens of Muslim origin. Most of Fanon's friends—the Manuellans, Alice Cherki, André Mandouze—decided it was time to leave.

Claude Lanzmann's infatuation with Algeria ended even more abruptly, when Ben Bella announced his intention to send 100,000 soldiers to help the Palestinians liberate their land from Israel. A committed Zionist, Lanzmann went on to make the epic Holocaust documentary *Shoah* and other films about the Jewish experience, including a paean to the Israeli army, *Tsahal*. Yet, even as he repudiated revolutionary Third Worldism, he remained curiously loyal to its prophet; at one point, he pursued the idea of publishing an anthology of Fanon's writings with Maspero—a project vetoed by Josie Fanon, who disliked him. In both *Tsahal* and *Sobibor*, his documentary about Jewish revolt in the camps, Lanzmann advanced a strikingly Fanonian defense of violence, arguing that Jews had remade themselves as a people only by taking up arms and fighting their oppressors. It is unlikely that Fanon would have approved of Lanzmann's passion for the world's last settler-colonial state. Still, in *Tsahal* and *Sobibor* there was a peculiar tribute to his influence.

The first full-length feature by an African filmmaker, *Black Girl*, released in 1966, illustrated Fanon's ideas about racism and resistance in stark black-and-white cinematography of arresting, poetic force. (The brutally frank French title, *La Noire de . . .*, could more literally be translated as "So-and-so's Black Woman.") Its director was Ousmane Sembène, a *tirailleur sénégalais* in the Second World War who discovered Marxism while working on the docks of Marseille in the late 1940s and became an avid reader of Fanon. In Sembène's film, a young woman from Dakar goes to work for a white family in Antibes, on the Côte d'Azur, with dreams of a better life in the *métropole*, only to find herself subject to racist humiliation and psychological injury. She ends up killing herself, but not before reclaiming the African mask that she has given her host family as a gift. In a haunting finale, the mask becomes a symbol of her spirit, and of African resistance: like the veil in Fanon's essay on Algerian women, the meaning of this traditional object is transformed in struggle, infused with insurrectionary force. In his later films, Sembène satirized Senegal's ruling elites with an often deliciously Fanonian irreverence.

Lanzmann and Sembène were not the only filmmakers to be affected by Fanon's vision of revolt as an affirmation of humanity. The Third Worldist cinema of the 1970s, from Med Hondo's New Wave study of Black and Arab alienation and anger in France, *Soleil Ô*, to the Cinema Nova movement in Brazil, to Ivan Dixon's depiction of the American ghetto as a Fanonian war zone in *The Spook Who Sat by the Door*, was a tribute to his influence. But the greatest Fanonian film ever made, by far, was *The Battle of Algiers* (1966), a vérité-style retelling of the events of 1956–1957 directed by Gillo Pontecorvo, an Italian Jewish radical who revered Fanon. (Serge Michel, Fanon's *El Moudjahid* colleague, worked for Casbah Films, which co-produced it.) Pontecorvo's film featured non-actors who had witnessed, and in some cases participated in, the Battle of Algiers, including the FLN's leader in the Casbah, Yacef Saadi, who played himself and co-produced the film. Several of the sequences—the shots contrasting the rich European quarters and the impoverished Casbah; the scenes of Algerian women removing their veils, dressing up as Europeans, and depositing bombs in French cafés and airports—were directly inspired by Fanon's writings. And the film's hero, Ali La Pointe, a former criminal recruited to the nationalist cause in prison, was a classic Fanonian outcast, seething with rage at colonial humiliation.

Fanon would surely have admired Pontecorvo's insistence on the necessity of violence to defeat the forces of colonialism, and his celebration of the rebels of the interior. Yet the making of the film inadvertently helped seal the final victory of the army of the frontiers. On June 19, 1965, while Pontecorvo was shooting the film, the people of Algiers were led to believe that the tanks stationed in the streets of the capital were part of the mise-en-scène. In fact, Colonel Houari Boumediene was using them to remove Ben Bella from power.

Under Boumediene, Algeria became a leader of the non-aligned movement, and Algiers the mecca of foreign revolutionaries. And in the summer of 1969, Fanon's vision of a revolutionary culture—and of Algerian-African unity against imperialism—received a spellbinding tribute in the capital, when Nina Simone, Miriam Makeba, the free-jazz saxophonist Archie Shepp, the Beat poet Ted Joans, the Black Panthers, and representatives of other national liberation movements arrived for the Pan-African Festival— the Woodstock of the Third World. One of its organizers was Fanon's American friend Elaine Klein, who had settled in Algiers after independence. "We are still Black and we have come back. *Nous sommes revenus*," Joans proclaimed from the stage. "Jazz is an African power! Jazz is an African music!" The festival lasted ten days; nothing of its ambition or scale has ever been repeated. Yet the absences were also telling. The Kabyle Berber singer Taos Amrouche, sister of the poet Jean Amrouche, was not invited to perform, in spite of her support for the FLN during the war. Amrouche's affirmation of her Berber roots, her origins as the daughter of converts to Christianity, and her attachment to the French language were frowned upon by the authorities, who saw the expression of multiculturalism as a threat to Arab-Islamic unity. Fanon had insisted that Algeria would welcome, as a fellow Algerian, anyone who supported Algerian independence, but this idea no longer seemed to apply even to native-born Algerians.

Josie Fanon remained in Algeria, where she worked as a journalist and raised her and Frantz's son, Olivier, who went on to become an Algerian diplomat. According to Elaine Klein, Josie had a long, unsatisfactory liaison with an Algerian who claimed to have been a commander in the liberation forces. But remarriage was out of the question for a woman who styled herself as the widow of a great man. When Klein attended a political conference with her in Havana, she saw Josie being courted by a handsome young Cuban, but Josie did not allow him into her room, where she kept a photograph of her late husband by her bed, "like a bodyguard." She defended his legacy with passion and without compromise. When Jean-Paul Sartre sided with Israel during the 1967 war, she demanded that François Maspero "immediately cease the publication of the preface" to *The Wretched of the Earth* since "his pro-Zionist attitudes were incompatible with Fanon's work."

In 1978, Josie flew to the United States for the first time since Frantz's death, at the invitation of a UN commission on apartheid. During her stay, she spoke at Howard University's African American Center, near the nursery Olivier had attended while his father lay dying. When she was asked about the literature on her husband's life and work, she replied that while much remained to be written about him, she did not expect it to come from "Western intellectuals" who "have not completely understood his works." Only in Africa and the African American community in the States, she said, would "valid works" on her husband's legacy be produced.

## FANON IN BLACK AMERICA

As Josie Fanon understood, African American intellectuals and activists embraced Fanon with a fascination equal to the interest he had taken in Richard Wright and Chester Himes. Their devotion to Fanon's work reflected, in part, the excitement that Algeria's struggle had aroused in progressive Black circles. Angela Davis, who would later praise Fanon as the twentieth century's "most compelling theorist of racism and colonialism," discovered the Algerian question as a student at the Sorbonne in 1962, when she came upon "racist slogans scratched on walls throughout the city threatening death to Algerians" and saw the police ("as vicious as the redneck cops in Birmingham") break up a pro-independence demonstration with high-powered water hoses.

Two years later, Malcolm X celebrated his thirty-ninth birthday in Algiers, where he spoke to FLN veterans who struck him as "true revolutionaries, not afraid of death." In an interview shortly before his death, Malcolm explained that meeting an FLN official who was, "to all appearances," a white man, led him to reexamine his understanding of Black nationalism and to embrace a more internationalist perspective on the struggle against racism. William Gardner Smith had a similar revelation while reporting on the Algerian War from Paris, and, in his 1963 novel *The Stone Face*, described African Americans in American ghettos as "America's Algerians." On a visit to the States a few years later, the young militants he met reminded him of the young leaders of the FLN.

When Grove Press published a translation of *The Wretched of the Earth* in 1965, it struck an immediate chord with the young Black militants of the Student Nonviolent Coordinating Committee (SNCC), who had developed a growing interest in African independence movements. Under the influence of Bob Moses, a reader of Camus, SNCC activists had been powerfully shaped by an ethics of moral action. But the beatings they had suffered, and the intensity of white resistance, had sorely tested this commitment. Black movement workers suffered from especially high levels of fatigue, fear, and anxiety, symptoms that the psychiatrist Robert Coles likened to shell shock and PTSD. By 1965, SNCC had shifted toward an emphasis on Black self-determination, dignity, and psychological empowerment; a year later, Stokely Carmichael, a reader of Fanon, sounded the call of Black Power. Andrew Young, one of Dr. Martin Luther King Jr.'s deputies, lamented Fanon's growing influence and attributed it to "a crisis in faith."

That it may have been: patience with the Gandhian model of resistance was running out. But the growing interest in Fanon also reflected the sense among a younger generation of Black civil rights activists that his work helped illuminate the crisis in America, not least in the cities of the North, which were not legally segregated but which nonetheless resembled the violently divided colonial city in *The Wretched of the Earth*. This conviction was only strengthened by the urban revolts in Watts, Newark, Detroit, and other American cities—and by the brutal response of the police and the National Guard. What were the police if not the agents of a ruthless "internal colonialism," to use a phrase that became commonplace in American sociology in the late 1960s? White radicals, too, were beginning to question whether American society could be transformed, and the Vietnam War ended, by peaceful means.

At a public forum in New York in December 1967, Hannah Arendt pointed out that Fanon's views on violence were more nuanced than Sartre's, but *The Wretched of the Earth* was largely read through the prism of Sartre's fiery preface. The professors Aristide Zolberg and Vera Zolberg wrote in 1967, "The specter who now haunts America is the Fanon of the first chapter of *The Wretched of the Earth*." They added somewhat nervously that "it does not stand up as an allegory of our situation," but during the hot summers of the late 1960s, it was easy to think otherwise, and

Fanon's urgent, apocalyptic tone seemed like common sense to his readers in Black militant circles.

Fanon was adopted by LeRoi Jones (later known as Amiri Baraka) and the Black Arts Movement as a theorist of both cultural and political liberation—a French-speaking Malcolm X. He also attracted the interest of Black doctors such as the Harvard psychiatrist Alvin Poussaint, who found a trove of insights in Fanon's writings on the Black psyche in a white-dominated society. Knowing one's Fanon became a symbol of radical militancy, and sometimes of intellectual superiority: in his 1970 poem "Brother," Gil Scott-Heron complained of "would-be Black revolutionaries" who "read Mao or Fanon" while ignoring the suffering of people in their own communities.

Fanon's most energetic disciples in Black American politics were the Black Panthers, who identified as Marxist-Leninists and styled themselves as an American analogue of the national liberation movements in Africa, Asia, and the Middle East. As the Panthers' chief of staff, David Hilliard, put it, "Fanon—and the Algerian Revolution—has provided our most important theoretical model." In 1969, the Panther leader Eldridge Cleaver and his wife, Kathleen, went into exile in Algiers, where their liaison to the Algerian authorities was Elaine Klein. Cleaver praised *The Wretched of the Earth* as "the Black Bible" and said that "every brother on a rooftop" could quote from it. Fanon's critique of assimilation to white models, his scorn for native elites, his belief that self-defense was of therapeutic value: all these themes spoke to the Panthers. So did Fanon's faith in the masses, his belief that petty criminals and outcasts had more to contribute to the revolution than assimilated urban intellectuals, much less the Black bourgeoisie. Malcolm X had made a similar point in his speech about the difference between rebellious "field Negroes" and docile, white-worshipping "house Negroes," and some of the Panthers—including Cleaver and Huey P. Newton, the party's leader in Oakland—were themselves ex-convicts who had remade themselves as revolutionaries in prison. As Marxists, they strongly identified with Fanon's disdain for cultural nationalism, or what they called "porkchop nationalism" in their often-violent clashes with the Us Organization, an Afrocentric group led by Maulana Karenga, the inventor of Kwanzaa and a bitter foe of the Panthers.

The Panthers also made extensive use of Fanon's writings on medicine. The racist, dehumanizing medical practices that he described in France and Algeria could have taken place in America's slums, where inferior care and contempt from doctors were widespread, and Black people had been subjected to sterilization and other invasive experiments. As the sociologist Alondra Nelson has shown, the Panthers applied Fanon's critique of biomedical power in poor Black communities throughout the States. In response to medical discrimination, the Panthers set up free health clinics in poor urban communities and assigned readings by Fanon to the doctors who partnered with them. In Fanon, Nelson writes, they found "an intellectual template for the Party's critique of medicine" as "an instrument of social control."

## IN SEARCH OF FANON

For one member of the Black Panther Party, Fanon became a lifelong obsession. His story is worth telling, since it captures the spell that Fanon cast on a generation of revolutionary Black intellectuals. James Forman, a leader in SNCC who had become the Black Panthers' minister of foreign affairs, began to research a biography of Fanon in 1968, interviewing Joby Fanon in Paris and taking Aimé Césaire on a tour of Harlem. He was forty years old, an old man by movement standards, and susceptible to stark shifts in mood, oscillating between revolutionary confidence and despair as he pursued his project.

Fanon's memory, he feared, was at risk of being desecrated. A white journalist, Peter Geismar, was at work on a Fanon biography, which Forman considered an example of "white imperialism in writing." (An interest in Black radicalism appeared to run in the family: Geismar's father, the literary critic Maxwell Geismar, had written the introduction to Cleaver's *Soul on Ice*.) And in February 1969, the *Washington Post* columnist Joseph Alsop, an anti-Communist who had used his status as a foreign policy commentator to help gather intelligence for the CIA, revealed the agency's role in bringing Fanon to Washington, DC, for medical treatment. Fanon, Alsop gloated, had died "literally in the arms of the CIA"—a "slander," in Forman's view. The telling of Fanon's story, as Forman saw it, was now a battlefield in a struggle between the Cold War establishment and the insurgent forces of Black Power.

In fact, the battle lines were more complicated than Forman understood. In a strange twist, Alsop, a closeted gay Cold Warrior, and Geismar, a member of the New Left who published in the Marxist *Monthly Review*, had begun working together on a lengthy film treatment about Fanon's life. The script was strongly colored by Alsop's obsessions with race, sexuality, and the blackness of Fanon's body and the size of his penis. The script elicited the curiosity of the producer Melville Tucker at Universal Studios, but in a letter to Alsop, Tucker said that he and his colleagues wanted to know more about Fanon: Did he have a sense of humor? Did he display any personal tendencies toward violence? What were his relations with women like? Did he like to dance? Geismar replied to Alsop that he would answer all their questions except "the most idiotic, which was, Did Fanon like to dance? (Yes, he tap-danced and ate watermelon)." The film was never made, and Geismar died of cancer at age thirty-one in August 1970, just after receiving proofs of his Fanon biography.

By then, Forman was already deep into his own biography. In the fall of 1969, he had made his first trip to Algiers to interview Josie Fanon. His translator—Forman did not speak French—was Richard Wright's daughter, Julia, whom he'd met in Paris. She sent him the transcriptions of his interviews, as well as copies of the tapes, but he never received them, and suspected that French intelligence or the CIA had confiscated them. Whether his research materials were intercepted or simply lost in the post, Forman had begun to develop an unusually intense identification with his subject, and seemed to believe that merely by writing about Fanon, he was engaged in a battle with the American empire as dangerous as Fanon's had been with France.

Forman was intrigued by Fanon's ambition to write a study of jealousy: he, too, had been thinking about his quarrels with other Panther leaders, and the problem of egotism in social movements. During his three-week trip to Martinique in the winter of 1969, he appeared to be reliving Fanon's 1952 return to the island, as he lashed out at the Martinicans' lack of revolutionary spirit, their seeming preference for "pleasure, rum, and banalities." He insisted to the Martinicans he met that he was a fellow "African," but they seemed not to care. When he told Fanon's mother that her son's accomplishments should be used to advance the cause of Black liberation, she responded by showing him one of her proudest mementos: Fanon's citation for his service to the French army in World War II. The French mask, if not the white one, remained firmly in place.

After his return from Martinique, Forman set up a nonprofit foundation, the Frantz Fanon Institute. At a conference of the League of Revolutionary Black Workers in 1971, he proclaimed that the humanity of the oppressed "will be restored as they plunge their bayonets through the hearts of their oppressors" and "fire their rifles at the crouching agents of colonialism." But while Forman continued to work on his Fanon biography, he turned his attention to another book project inspired by his visit to Martinique: "A portrait of a black militant—not so young anymore—who has come to Martinique to learn about the reality of Martinican life to do a book about Frantz Fanon." The title he proposed for this autofiction was "Black Skin, White Masks, 1970." Macmillan rejected the manuscript. Yet Forman remained obsessed by Fanon, writing about him in his journals and asking Sékou Touré for his thoughts on Fanon—and for donations to the institute. There is no indication that Guinea's leader replied, but Forman eventually succeeded in persuading Marion Barry, the mayor of Washington, DC, to declare December 8, 1997, "Frantz Fanon Memorial Day." At the ceremony, Ramtane Lamamra, Algeria's ambassador to the United States, offered an unusual explanation for Fanon's death in the capital: "The anti-colonial tradition of the United States and this country's declared commitment to the inalienable rights to life, liberty, and the pursuit of happiness attracted Fanon to Washington, DC, where he passed at the age of 36, as if a providential destiny wanted him to hold, also, a place in the American historic patrimony."

## THE AMERICANIZATION OF FRANTZ FANON

Fanon, as we know, was in no way pleased by the "providential destiny" that led him to spend his final days in the United States. And the "American historical patrimony" has never exactly embraced him, either. When the scholar Simone Browne wrote to the CIA and the FBI in 2011 to re-

quest any materials pertaining to Fanon's visit under the Freedom of Information Act, the CIA replied that it could "neither confirm nor deny the
existence or nonexistence of records responsive to your request." Nonetheless, Lamamra was onto something: Fanon did have an American, or at
least an Anglo-American, destiny.

With the decline of revolutionary Third Worldism at the end of the
1970s, Fanon had come to be widely seen as a historical figure, of interest
mainly to students of radical left Black liberation movements and African
decolonization. His books seemed at risk of becoming relics, remaindered
alongside copies of Herbert Marcuse's *One-Dimensional Man* and Eldridge
Cleaver's *Soul on Ice*. But in the 1980s and '90s, Fanon achieved recognition as a thinker of global significance, inspiring some of the most exciting work in literary criticism and cultural studies in the Anglo-American
academy. *Black Skin, White Masks*, long overshadowed by *The Wretched
of the Earth*, received its due as a sophisticated phenomenological study
of racism, in the work of theorists of the "Black Atlantic" such as Stuart
Hall, Sylvia Wynter, and Paul Gilroy—and in the 1995 film *Frantz Fanon:
Black Skin, White Mask*, an elegant, if somewhat rarefied, documentary
by the Black British artist Isaac Julien.

Perhaps not surprisingly, the most ardent champion of Fanon's Algerian writings in the American university was a man for whom the anti-
colonial struggle had never ended: the Palestinian American literary critic
Edward Said, who joined the PLO not long after the 1968 Battle of Karameh
and became one of Arafat's advisers. By Said's own account, Fanon freed
him from the relentless pessimism of Michel Foucault's studies of power,
by showing that the oppressed could put forward counternarratives, take
their destiny into their own hands, and contest systems of domination.
He was dazzled by Fanon's depiction of liberation as (in Said's words) "a
*process* and not as a goal contained automatically by the newly independent nations," and by his insistence that anti-colonial revolution must be
social, not merely national, in character. He was equally impressed by the
"anti-identitarian force" of Fanon's understanding of Algerian nationalism, which stressed what Said called "affiliation," conscious allegiance,
over "filiation," belonging by virtue of kinship. Why overthrow French
rule in Algeria, or the Israeli occupation of Palestinian land, if the result

was merely a transfer of wealth and power from a colonial elite to a native one? For Said, as for Fanon, the struggle's ultimate goal was not to reclaim land ownership, or to restore a repressed ancestral identity, but to establish a more just society and to create "new souls."

Said was a Palestinian Arab, and thus more of an insider in his movement than Fanon was in his. But as a Protestant Christian raised in affluence in Cairo and educated in the West, he never entirely fit in among his comrades, some of whom referred to him as "the American Professor." Like Fanon, he was a diplomatic spokesman, not a decision-maker, whose role was to articulate the movement's goals and vision to foreign audiences. Said ultimately resigned from the PLO over the Oslo Accords, which he considered a "Palestinian Versailles." But in his advocacy of the Palestinian struggle, he echoed many of Fanon's themes, insisting upon the secular nationalist character of the Palestinian cause in the face of the increasingly Islamic tenor of Palestinian politics; denouncing the corruption and autocracy of his former comrades who confused flags (and private mansions) with independence; and defending a radically inclusive conception of national culture as an opening to the "Other"—including Israeli Jews who committed themselves to decolonization. Fanon, he wrote admiringly, "wants somehow to bind the European as well as the native together in a new non-adversarial community of awareness and anti-imperialism." This was Said's vision of a future in which indigenous Arabs and Jews who had originally arrived as settlers could live together as citizens of a binational state, liberated from the binary definitions, racial hierarchies, and exclusions imposed by Zionism.

The rediscovery of Fanon in the American academy assumed, at times, a more sectarian (and worshipful) cast, accompanied by fanciful reinterpretation, if not wholesale invention. Henry Louis Gates Jr. dryly observed that "critical Fanonism" often took little interest in the historical Fanon, but was rather "a sort of tableau of narcissism, with Fanon himself as the Other that can only reflect and consolidate the critical self." In one of the more influential readings of "critical Fanonism," Fanon was portrayed as an anguished theorist and a connoisseur of "colonial ambivalence," rather than a revolutionary critic of colonialism. The relationships that meant the most to Fanon—Sartre, Césaire, Tosquelles, Abane—were conveniently elided in favor of his ostensible connections to Lacan, Foucault, Derrida, and other French thinkers whose work had spread through literature departments in the 1970s and '80s. Fanon, who took part in a war against French colonialism, was thus reborn as a French theorist. In yet another ironic twist, many of his postcolonial interpreters have been descendants of the national bourgeoisie Fanon had assailed for their mimicry of the West, their careerism and acquisitiveness. As the South Asian Marxist Aijaz Ahmad suggested, talking back to the West—or to academic rivals— in a Fanonian idiom would become a conventional academic career path.

In the last decade, the most fashionable—and curious—style of Fanonism to emerge in the academic world has been the school of thought known as "Afro-pessimism." For Afropessimists like Frank B. Wilderson III, the authentic Fanon is the Fanon of *Black Skin, White Masks*, before he embraced the Algerian cause and left Blackness behind: a striking echo of Albert Memmi's accusation. Afropessimists cull the bleakest passages of Fanon's writing on the Black condition and the vulnerability of the Black body to advance a defiant yet strangely apolitical project of existential refusal, and a rejection of coalition politics with non-Black allies, including Palestinians, whom Wilderson has portrayed as "junior partners" of white supremacy. For the Afropessimists, the force of white supremacy (or "anti-Blackness") is immutable, and there is no way that Black people can achieve the status of "the human," a category premised, like that of "universality," on their eternal exclusion.

In the most extreme iteration of Afropessimism, Black people remain permanent slaves, regardless of their legal status, victims of "social death": a far cry from Fanon's insistence that he was "not a slave of the slavery that dehumanized my ancestors." Afropessimism's critics have pointed out that its ontology of Blackness is antithetical to Fanon's critique of racialism, his indomitable humanism, and his hope that decolonization would bring about a future beyond race. Fanon was both a ferocious critic of universality and a deeply universalist thinker. Nonetheless, Afropessimism's use of Fanon captures a pervasive mood, a grim sense of rage, grief, and hopelessness in the face of police killings of Black people like Eric Garner, Breonna Taylor, and George Floyd.

Misreading, moreover, is a testament to Fanon's aura—and to the emotional force of his writing. That force has allowed Fanon's writing to travel far and wide, acquiring new meanings while still retaining its power to provoke. Today, a student at an American or British university is nearly as likely to encounter Fanon's work in a course on modern art, the Russian empire, or continental philosophy as she would in a course on North Africa, decolonization, or the Black radical tradition. In one of the more original interpretations of Fanon's work, the radical Swedish ecologist Andreas Malm has argued that Fanon understood that the division of the colonial world into white settlers and nonwhite "natives" was made possible by the "violent diffusion of technologies for dominating nature," and that the conquest of the land and of its people went hand in hand. Citing Fanon's defense of violence as a strategy for liberating the oppressed from "despair and inaction," Malm writes: "Few processes produce as much despair as global heating. Imagine that, someday, the reservoirs of that emotion built up around the world—in the Global South in particular—find their outlets. There has been a time for a Gandhian climate movement; perhaps there might come time for a Fanonian one. The breaking of fences may one day be seen as a very minor misdemeanor indeed."

## RETURN TO THE NATIVE LAND

And what of Fanon's legacy in Martinique and Algeria, his native land and his adoptive one?

Reflecting on Fanon's legacy at a UNESCO meeting in Panama in 1979, Édouard Glissant remarked that it was "difficult for a West Indian to be the brother, the friend, even simply the companion or compatriot of Fanon," because he was "the only one who truly passed into action." Glissant had been one of many who tried to follow Fanon's example. In April 1961, he met with a group of West Indian activists (including Fanon's childhood friend, the radical Martinican lawyer Marcel Manville) to set up the Front Antillo-Guyanais pour l'autonomie, an organization that hoped to break free of France's political and cultural domination, and establish an autonomous federation of the overseas islands. The French government, then contemplating its imminent withdrawal from Algeria, responded to the demand for autonomy by dissolving the organization and placing Glissant under house arrest.

When Glissant came back to Martinique, he found himself in a country where, as James Forman discovered, independence was largely seen as a pipe dream, and Fanon as a traitor who had fought against France and turned his back on his West Indian homeland. Over time, West Indian hostility to Fanon would soften, giving way to pride in a native son's international renown, and in 1982 his life was celebrated at a major conference in Fort-de-France. But while revolutionary advocates of independence for the Antilles continued to cite him as an inspiration, Glissant, Fanon's most significant West Indian intellectual heir, came to believe that Fanon's radicalism was incompatible with what he called the "ambiguity of the West Indian condition," and that an alternative path to freedom had to be found.

Glissant would find his path—and a detour from Fanon's imposing demands—in a lyrical and elusive aesthetics that bypassed the call for anticolonial liberation and national sovereignty, and instead exalted the cross-pollination of cultures at the heart of "Créolité." He called this program of Creolized thought a "poetics of relation" and developed it into a dazzling, if somewhat obscure, body of work, ranging across poetry, philosophy, and the novel. The Creole societies of the West Indies, he argued, were averse to revolutionary doctrines, exclusionary nationalisms, and Fanon's "ideological precision"; their originality lay in their cultural *métissage*, their vibrant mélange of indigenous, African, and French traditions, their openness to what Glissant called the *tout-monde*, the world in its entirety. Still, even as he marked his distance, he continued to pay homage to Fanon for inspiring in himself and other West Indians a "will to self-emancipation." As Glissant put it, the "most beautiful homage" West Indians can pay Fanon is to emulate not his words but rather "the passion that animated him."

One of Glissant's friends, the French Martinican trumpeter Jacques Coursil, did both, in his 2007 jazz oratorio *Clameurs*, set to texts from *Black Skin, White Masks* and Glissant's poem "L'Archipel des grands chaos," evoking the savagery of the white man's arrival in Africa. A linguist and philosopher as well as a musician, Coursil discovered Fanon's work in the late 1960s while traveling through West Africa as part of Léopold Sédar Senghor's entourage. In the track "Black Skin, White Masks 1952," Coursil evokes Fanon's insistence on freedom and self-invention, and his repudiation not just of racism but of the category of race itself. "The 'Negro' is not. No more than the white man," he declares, turning the conclusion of Fanon's first book into poetic verse. "I am a man . . . The Peloponnesian War is as much mine as the invention of the compass . . . I am not a prisoner of history. There is no Black mission; there is no white burden." Coursil told me, "Everyone claims Fanon, but it makes me uncomfortable when they go on to say the exact opposite of what Fanon writes. What Fanon broke with was racialist thought. But try to say this in the United States!"

Another illustrious Martinican protégé of Glissant, the novelist Patrick Chamoiseau, had a similar epiphany reading Fanon. In his youth, Chamoiseau had gone through a passionate phase of exalting his Blackness, as if it were his sole defining characteristic. But when he read Fanon's critique of Négritude in *Black Skin, White Masks*, he realized that he had put on a "Black mask," which offered a certain comfort but "ended up concealing the already open abyss of another complexity"—both his mixed, Creole origins, and his individual voice as a novelist. From Fanon, he learned that "the demands imposed on our drive for humanity are more subtle and complex than a mere decolonization." The "sun of independence," after all, could result in "another form of dependence," festooned with "a national anthem, a flag, frontiers, and nationalist fervor." Yet, like Glissant, Chamoiseau was not persuaded that the kind of liberation struggle Fanon advocated in Algeria and Africa made sense in the French department of Martinique: "Our breath of liberation demands a different view of the world, another imaginary."

The response of figures like Glissant, Coursil, and Chamoiseau has been to underscore the Caribbean contribution to the *tout-monde*, showing the islands to be at the forefront of global thought about borders, identity, and subaltern cultures. What Négritude was for Césaire, Créolité is for them: a local identity of global significance, and one that challenges the homogenizing thrust—and the racism—of the French state. While appearing to turn away from Fanon's dream of an independent federation, they have preserved it, secretly, in what Glissant called "opacity." The question is what sort of politics, if any, this "imaginary" might translate into.

The beguiling, sunlit odes of Glissant and Chamoiseau to Créolité, the "poetics of relation," and West Indian traditions of storytelling cannot conceal the fact that Martinique remains an underdeveloped hinterland of the Republic, valued mainly as a tourist destination and treated with neocolonial disregard. In 2018, it was revealed that for two decades, chlordecone, a pesticide linked to cancer, had been sprayed on banana crops with the French government's permission. Chlordecone is present in the metabolism of nearly all the adult inhabitants of Martinique and Guadeloupe, and much of the land can no longer be used for growing fruits and vegetables. Some Martinicans have described the effects of chlordecone on public health, the environment, and the economy as a modern form of slavery.

In the last few years, anger over the chlordecone scandal, unemployment, and the enduring power of the white *békés* has run high, provoking sometimes violent demonstrations. In 2020, local activists in Martinique, inspired by Black Lives Matter and Rhodes Must Fall, toppled statues of Napoleon's *béké* wife, the Empress Joséphine, and of Victor Schœlcher,* the architect of abolition in the old colonies, the benevolent white man whom the young Fanon was taught to venerate. Fanon might have drawn hope from this explosion of popular rage, as he did from the 1959 anti-government riots in Fort-de-France, which rekindled his faith in the fighting spirit of his native island. But the fury of the French West Indies often expresses itself in ways that would surely have confirmed his despair, notably a boisterous anti-vaccination movement, and a flirtation, among younger radicals, with Kémi Séba, a French Beninese conspiracy theorist who has endeared himself to Iran's former president Mahmoud Ahmadinejad and the Russian ultranationalist Aleksandr Dugin. And in 2022, largely out of frustration with President Emmanuel Macron's neoliberalism, more than 60 percent of voters in Martinique and Guadeloupe

---

* These statues are discussed in chapter 1.

cast their ballots for the far-right leader Marine Le Pen. As Fanon would doubtless have noted, Le Pen's voters in the West Indies could not all have been *békés*.

## STRANGER STILL

In Algeria today, there are few visible signs of Fanon's presence, aside from the Frantz Fanon Hospital in Blida and the streets named after *le docteur Fanon* in Algiers and other cities. The Algerian state did little to cultivate his memory. He was, after all, a foreigner, and a non-Muslim, and since he had died in a hospital he could not be counted among Algeria's martyrs. Fanon's brother Joby was startled by the "climate of secrecy" around Fanon's burial site when he traveled to Algiers to visit his brother's tomb and to see if he could carry out their mother's request to have his remains returned to Martinique. President Boumediene told him that the authorities did not know where he was buried, and that, in any case, the area was riddled with anti-personnel mines. "I was struck by his reticence," Joby writes. "I felt that his professed ignorance of the fate of Frantz's corpse was false, but I did not understand his reasons."*

Writers, painters, and poets embraced Fanon for his defense of cultural modernism, and as a symbol of the Algerian Revolution's internationalist ideals, on which the state had turned its back. But by the early 1970s, Fanon had come under increasing—and not entirely inaccurate—criticism from Algerian intellectuals close to the regime, who pointed out his lack of interest in Islam, Algerian traditions, and the history of Arab nationalism. The great theoretician of decolonization became a casualty of the Algerian state's version of decolonization, which entailed a rejection of foreign models—including Fanon's, which had once proved so useful during the war. Fanon's belief in multiethnic citizenship and his attacks on postcolonial authoritarianism were also out of sync with a regime

---

* Fanon's remains were exhumed and reinterred in the martyrs' cemetery in the commune of Aïn Kerma in July 1965, shortly after Boumediene's coup. A small bust of Fanon was erected two decades later. But Fanon's plot fell into disrepair, and in 2020 the local wali instructed the authorities to renovate it.

founded on Arab Muslim identity and still largely run by the intelligence service set up by Abdelhafid Boussouf during the war.

In October 1988, young Algerians born after independence flooded the streets to protest unemployment, rising prices, and the FLN's authoritarian rule. More than five hundred demonstrators were killed in the ensuing repression. As she watched the protests from her apartment in El Biar, a prosperous neighborhood high in the hills of Algiers, Josie Fanon was reminded of the wretched of the earth evoked by her late husband. Having struggled with depression for years, she grew increasingly despondent. Early in the summer of 1989, she traveled to her husband's gravesite for the first time since he was buried, and then went to Tunis, on a pilgrimage that took in every place where they had lived. On her return, she arranged all her affairs—Frantz's letters, poems she had written, photographs—and had herself admitted to a psychiatric clinic. Six days later, on July 12, she went home to water her plants and say hello to her neighbors. The next morning, at dawn, she jumped from her fourth-floor window. Her friend the novelist Assia Djebar wrote, "In her fall, Josie hurt no one. Only she exploded."

Two years later, the Algerian political system fell into crisis, after the fundamentalist Front islamique du salut (FIS) won the first round of legislative elections in December 1991. The FIS styled itself as the true heir of the wartime FLN. (FIS, in French, sounds like *fils*, "son.") Terrifying the urban middle classes with its slogan, "The Quran is our constitution," the FIS looked certain to win the second round. Always suspicious of the democratic experiment that began after Black October, the army canceled the elections, banned the FIS, and declared a state of emergency.

Within a year, Algeria was at war again, only this time it was not against the foreign occupier. Instead, it was a war among Algerians, pitting radical Islamists against the security forces. Algeria's Islamists claimed to be fighting the agents of France and carrying out an overdue cleansing of all foreign elements in Algeria: a second decolonization, as it were. Fanon's colleagues at *El Moudjahid*, now aging allies of the regime, Redha Malek and Pierre Chaulet, stood squarely on the side of the military hard-liners, or "eradicators." More than 100,000 Algerians would lose their lives in the Black Decade, some of them in Islamist massacres, some in repression by the state. Algeria had barely recovered from the mental disorders of colonial war when it faced another cycle of armed struggle and repression, and suffered from the equally severe psychological stress of civil war.

Once again, Algeria faced the question of violence and the meaning of decolonization. In his essay on colonial war and mental disorders, Fanon had warned that the violence of decolonization could haunt Algeria for generations. But he had also contributed to the exaltation of armed struggle as a political and psychological necessity. Had rhetoric like Fanon's helped to reinforce the resort to violence to settle political problems? Kamel Daoud's celebrated 2013 novel, *Meursault, contre-enquête* (*The Meursault Investigation*), seemed to suggest as much, without ever naming Fanon. Daoud, a journalist from Oran who had reported on the Islamist massacres of the Black Decade, published his novel in response to Albert Camus, who had failed to give a name to the Arab killed by Meursault, the narrator of *The Stranger*. Daoud's narrator is the murdered Arab's brother. He has been haunted ever since by Meursault's erasure of the victim's name (Moussa in the novel). We go on to learn that Daoud's narrator, like Meursault, also has a killing on his conscience: egged on by his mother, he'd murdered a random settler, in retaliation for his brother's death, at the end of the war. He reassures himself that this "was not murder but a restitution," yet he does not quite believe it, and finds himself consumed by remorse: "I killed a man, and, since then, life is no longer sacred in my eyes." Instead of recovering his sense of selfhood, he feels merely a pervasive sense of "strangeness" in a country where the only people who seem to matter are war veterans or martyrs.

That sensation of strangeness may seem to echo Camus, yet it is not the same as the strangeness Meursault feels. It is political and psychological, not metaphysical. What Daoud describes is the feeling, widespread among Algerians, that while they live in Algeria, it does not belong to them, that their self-determination and freedom have been confiscated by others: first the French, then the post-independence state. In her probing study *Colonial Trauma*, the Algerian psychoanalyst Karima Lazali draws on Fanon's psychiatric writings to argue that Algerians have been unable to liberate themselves because they have not yet overcome the "colonized part" of their personality. By this, she does not mean that Muslim Algerians have failed to eradicate the influences of French culture, but rather they remain trapped by a complex of "dispossession" and envy that took root under colonialism, both in their relationships among one another and in their relationship to political power. After being liberated from colonial dispossession, Algerians allowed themselves to become occupied by another force, the postcolonial state—"possessed," she says, as if by a *djinn*. Even today, their psyches are still penetrated by "the spirit of colonialism," which has left them unable to assume responsibility for their actions, or to experience freedom as individual subjects. The appeal of radical Islam, she suggests, resides not in the desire to "decolonize" Algeria from the traces of its colonial heritage but rather in a persistent attachment to dispossession, and a fear of freedom. As she puts it: "The subject fascinated by its dispossession takes refuge in origins and in a narcissism from which it struggles to escape." Lazali's book concludes with a stirring homage to Fanon, and a lament that he is not taught to mental health specialists in Algeria and France. "Fanon's thinking," she writes, "offers an invaluable clinical reflection on freedom on both a personal and collective scale."

The Frantz Fanon Psychiatric Hospital in Blida-Joinville long ago ceased to practice disalienation. But in 2018, the psychiatrist Miloud Yabrir, born in 1984, launched a project to restore Fanon's home on the grounds of the hospital and turn it into a museum. Like many young Algerian intellectuals, Yabrir sought out Fanon's writing not because of his insights into violence or peasant spontaneity but because of his prescient critique of the failures of independence—and his commitment to personal as well as collective emancipation. He was also moved by the extraordinary decision that Fanon, a non-Muslim foreigner, a Black West Indian, made to join the Algerian struggle. Fanon's involvement was, of course, a flattering symbol of the Algerian struggle's importance to the international left, but to Yabrir it was also a reminder of a time when it was possible for a man of Fanon's background to imagine that he, too, might become—and be accepted as—an Algerian. As Yabrir put it to me, Fanon's example raises "the question at the heart of Algerian identity: Can one be an Algerian by choice, and what sort of Algerian would we be if that were possible?"

## EQUAL IN PARIS?

A similar question is being asked by Fanon's readers in France today: Is there an equal place for citizens whose ancestors were colonial subjects, or will they always be seen as *indigènes*, not entirely French, somehow less? The historian Benjamin Stora, who was born in the Algerian city of Constantine in 1950, told me that when he was a young man in the Trotskyist movement, *Black Skin, White Masks* taught him that he could be both French and Algerian Jewish, and that he did not have to repudiate his ethnic roots to be involved in left-wing organizing. But for French citizens from the former colonies—the Antilles, West Africa, and, above all, Muslim North Africa—to insist on one's ancestral origins is to risk being accused of disloyalty to the Republic, especially if they dare to criticize its colonial past, or police brutality, discrimination, and other racist practices in France today. And if they decline to eat pork or drink wine, they might be suspected of rejecting *laïcité* (secularism). Women in hijabs have not been forced to remove their veils on the streets, as in Algiers in 1958, but they are forbidden to wear them in public schools, and those in burkinis have been chased off beaches by the police as if they were a threat to public order.

In recent years, the French government has waged an offensive against what it calls Islamo-leftism in intellectual life—a term as ill-defined and (purposefully) indiscriminate as critical race theory in the hallucinations of the American right. It has also opposed the teaching of the postcolonial theory that Fanon inspired: an incitement, it is claimed, to a dangerous form of identity politics, if not terrorism. The horrifying attacks committed by radical Islamists against the editors of *Charlie Hebdo* and the Bataclan Theater in 2015 are one reason for this moral panic, but they do not explain why the French government is carrying out a purge of ideas it deems subversive—or going to such lengths to make millions of its citizens feel so unwelcome. France appears to be beset by an intense malaise about its identity, one of whose expressions is a fixation on anything that appears to threaten it: immigration (although it has not increased); the dangers of the Black and brown *banlieues*; the refusal of French Muslims to relinquish what makes them "other" in French eyes.

Fanon's writings on racism, identity, the veil, and the hypocrisies of French universalism—and his decision to align himself with the "enemy" in the Algerian War—present a troubling reminder of this insecurity. As a result, the most influential Black French thinker of the postwar era resists the symbolic neutralization of difference that France calls integration. While Aimé Césaire has been honored with a fresco, a plaque, and a commemoration ceremony at the Panthéon, Fanon continues to be regarded with suspicion and fear. In December 2018, Bordeaux's municipal council proposed naming streets after Fanon and Rosa Parks, provoking an outcry from *pieds-noirs* organizations. There is now a rue Rosa Parks in Bordeaux, one of the principal ports of the eighteenth-century transatlantic slave trade. But Alain Juppé, the city's mayor, indefinitely suspended the creation of rue Frantz Fanon. "The naming of the roads of our municipality must be an opportunity to pay tribute to people who embody our shared values," he explained.

Fanon is not without admirers in France. In 2000, Alice Cherki published a passionate biographical portrait of her friend, and he has been the subject of numerous works in French, including a graphic novel about his meeting in Rome with Sartre and Beauvoir. Among his most prominent followers is the filmmaker Claire Denis, a white woman who grew up in French-ruled Cameroon, where her father was a civil servant of anticolonial sympathies. When Denis, who was born in 1946, was a young girl, she witnessed a violent clash between a group of Cameroonians and the police. A young man she knew—the family cook—was shot dead beside her. When she read *Les Damnés de la terre* in her late teens, she experienced "an almost physical feeling" of recognition, "not because I was particularly political, but because I felt things that were very close to me. When you read Fanon, you experience physically the symptoms he's talking about. It's far from the beauty of Césaire, but there's something in it that tears the skin." Fanon's work led her to Algiers in 1969, when she attended the Pan-African Festival, and strongly influenced the exploration of race in her films, many of them set in Black milieus in Africa and the Parisian suburbs. But when she decided to include a reference to Fanon in a classroom scene in her 2008 film, *35 Shots of Rum*, a professor she consulted dismissed Fanon as "totally passé." When we met in Paris in 2018, she told me that she went ahead anyway. "And it's what everyone ended up talking about," she said. "But there's still a resistance to him in France. People prefer Césaire because he makes them less uncomfortable. Another reason for the resistance is the trauma of Algeria. But sometimes I wonder, why are we talking about Hannah Arendt? Why aren't we talking about Fanon?"

In fact, Fanon *has* emerged, over the last few decades, as a hero of French writers, artists, and activists of Black and Arab origin, many of whom cite his aphorisms in the manner that Black intellectuals in the States quote James Baldwin or Malcolm X. The French rapper known as Rocé (né José Kaminsky)—the son of the late Adolfo Kaminsky, who forged passports for the FLN during the war, and a Black Algerian mother—told me that when he first read Fanon's description of the colonial city in *The Wretched of the Earth*, he was instantly reminded of the *banlieues*, whose residents live in drab public housing units on the outskirts of Paris, where they are frequently hassled by the police. The Parti des indigènes de la République (Party of the Natives of the Republic), a small but influential group of radical intellectuals and activists, mostly of North African origin, has invoked Fanon as their spiritual father. Like the Afropessimists in the States, it could be argued, the party's leaders turn their condition as "native" victims of neocolonial racism into an essentialist, unchanging ontology. Yet this rhetorical extremity, too, owes much to Fanon, who had a taste for provocation and relished what he called the "charge" of words.

## CLINICAL FANONISM

Fanon's writings have also exerted a growing influence in the institution that gave birth to his mature thought: the rebel's clinic, where politically engaged doctors treat the symptoms of mental illness and distress as forms of social suffering. Among the first psychoanalysts to seize upon the importance of Fanon's work was Félix Guattari, who, in *Anti-Oedipus*, a 1972 manifesto coauthored with the philosopher Gilles Deleuze, credited Fanon with helping to overthrow Freudian psychiatry's emphasis on the "family romance" (parent-child relations in the nuclear family) at the expense of the political roots of trauma. Around the same time, Francis Jeanson, Fanon's editor and the leader of the *porteurs des valises*, retrained as a radical psychiatrist in the early 1970s, as if he were retracing Fanon's steps.

Over the next few decades, what we might call clinical Fanonism began to emerge, largely developed by psychiatrists, therapists, and public health experts working in the Global South. The most faithful practitioners of clinical Fanonism today are psychiatrists in Israel-Palestine, where the occupation has severely affected the mental health of Palestinian citizens and colonial warfare has produced an abundance of mental disorders among both Palestinians and Israelis. Fanon himself never addressed the question of Palestine.* But, as the Palestinian psychiatrist Samah Jabr puts it, "his prophetic insights remain a source of inspiration to Palestinians," since he understood that colonial "subjugation is not only political, economic or military" but also "profoundly and inherently psychological," and that the "struggle for justice and the struggle for mental health" are inseparable. In their applications of Fanon, Jabr and her Israeli colleague the psychiatrist Ruchama Marton, the founder of Israeli Physicians for Human Rights, have also mounted a sharp critique of Israeli psychiatry, exposing its complicity with the Israeli army and its racist assumptions about the Arab mind. In a paper reminiscent of Fanon's essays on French psychiatry in Algeria, Marton has argued that Israeli psychiatrists asked to provide evaluations of mentally ill Palestinians in Israeli military courts have systematically "diagnosed them as impostors and manipulators," denying them their "right to madness." Unable to see that they are "un-

---

* Fanon refers to Israel only twice in his work: in his travel diary from Mali, in which he evokes "Israel reclaiming the desert" in a brief list of Western powers seeking to influence the direction of the colonial world; and in the passage on reparations for colonialism in *The Wretched of the Earth*, in which he discusses Germany's payment to the Jewish state of "enormous sums that are supposed to serve as compensation for the crimes of Nazism." In neither case does he mention the Palestinians.

critically accepting the government's worldview," they imagine themselves as apolitical, objective scientists, and attack anyone who questions their diagnoses as "acting out of 'political motives' which counter the 'purity' of the psychiatric profession." As in Algeria, she points out, psychiatric "objectivity" in Israel-Palestine is all but designed to support the occupation authorities.

Clinical Fanonism has also found inventive—if less obviously militant—applications in the West. In Italy, where Fanon's work has enjoyed unusual prestige, it has inspired a clinic named in his honor, the Centro Frantz Fanon in Turin, whose patients are mostly migrants and refugees, often victims of trafficking or torture. The center's approach to therapy can be traced back to the left-wing psychiatrist Franco Basaglia, who was born in 1924 into a wealthy Venetian family. Steeped in existentialism and phenomenology, Basaglia made a name for himself in 1961, the year of Fanon's death, by unlocking the wards of the notorious Gorizia asylum, on Italy's border with communist Yugoslavia, where he had been appointed director. In refusing the "absurd, disgraceful logic of the asylum," Basaglia drew upon the example of Fanon's work in Blida. But while "Fanon was able to choose revolution," he noted, he and his colleagues could not:

> We, for objective reasons, are prevented from doing so. In our reality, we still need to continue to experience the contradictions of the system that overdetermines us, by managing an institution that we deny, by performing a therapeutic act that we refuse, by preventing the institution . . . from continuing to be *only* functional to the system.

Basaglia was aware of the "absurdity of this wager," but he was determined to "keep the values alive, while nonrights, inequality, and the quotidian death of man are turned into legislative principles."

The psychiatrist Roberto Beneduce and his colleagues have made a similar wager at the center in Turin, which was founded in the mid-1990s in response to the growing population of African and Arab immigrants and asylum seekers. Its clinical approach is informed by an awareness of, in Beneduce's words, "the relationships of force between colonized nations and colonizing nations," as well as ethno-psychiatry's roots in colonial power. At the entrance is a photograph of Fanon—a warning to the staff, according to Beneduce, that "representations and stereotypes become masks, imagos that can fix and trap us, and others; that representations efface people, objects, practices, and experiences."

The psychiatrists at the Centro Frantz Fanon have gone still further than Fanon in combining the cultural rituals and healing practices of their patients with traditional Western medicine, with the purpose of creating a nonhierarchical space of exchange. As the anthropologist Cristiana Giordano has observed in a study of the center's work, the accounts that patients give of their pain tend to be "more complex than what psychiatric diagnosis ('psychotic episode') or state's category ('victim') could contain and explain." While the center's patients are not colonial subjects, most have suffered from racism, marginalization, and the fear of being seized and expelled by the police (in operations sometimes called "negro hunting" or "ethnic cleansing"). In their efforts to achieve recognition and a sanctuary, they often embellish their histories or tell stories designed to win sympathy and secure asylum.

The French doctors described by Fanon in "The 'North African Syndrome'" might have attributed such tales to a penchant for mendacity or a congenital inability to distinguish between truth and lies. But for Beneduce, who has also worked as a medical anthropologist in Africa, these fables are "revealing lies," reflecting the political setting of their composition. "We could paraphrase Fanon and claim that today's objectivity, that of identification measures, fingerprints, and bone measurements used to calculate 'real' age, always backfires against migrants," he writes, in much the same way that colonial objectivity always worked against natives. The lies his patients tell him are often "their only possible reply to the hypocrisies that regulate migration, or the laws on human rights."

Like Basaglia, Beneduce and his colleagues are radical reformers rather than revolutionaries. But like Fanon and Jabr, they respond to the needs of their patients with a sensitivity to identity and difference, an awareness of the political dimensions of mental disorders, and an unswerving belief in the indivisibility of humanity. To insist on the political and cultural specificity of a person's suffering, they understand, is not an obstacle to the universal but rather its secret, indispensable ally.

## TOWARD A "NEW MAN"

The rhetoric of universalism has fallen on hard times. The persistence of racism in Western societies—and the recrudescence of explicit white supremacy, which might have shocked even Fanon, who believed that overt appeals to racism were giving way to a more subtle and insidious cultural racism—is one reason. Talk of a common humanity can seem quaint, if not fraudulent—a rhetorical ploy by right-wing activists who claim the mantle of color blindness and invoke universal standards as a cudgel in their opposition to racial justice. A Nigerian friend of mine wrote me from Munich:

> To live in Europe today is to wake up every day to the drum beat of naked racial hostility, with politicians and their supporters lumping us poor Black souls together as the wretched and dregs of the earth, vermin for which there is no legal protection or even empathy. Everywhere you turn, you are a negative, a constant subject of dehumanization and depersonalization. I am sick of the claim of a common humanity. There is no such thing as a common humanity.

My friend, the late curator and critic Okwui Enwezor, was an admirer of Fanon, but he considered it naïve, and even offensive, to invoke the idea of a shared humanity when it had been betrayed—and then abandoned—by much of the West.

Yet neither walls nor racism have put an end to what V. S. Naipaul called the "great movement of peoples." Today, people from the former colonial world are more likely to seek to enter the West than to struggle against it. They have made the societies of the West far more diverse, and their children have dual identities. While the diversity of Western societies has hardly brought about equality, it has demonstrated that people from different backgrounds can work on common projects and can preside over what Fanon, in a language that has aged, called the future of "man." Yet the citizenship of people from the poor world—and even their very presence, their right to cross borders and exist as equals—has met with fierce resistance from the West that, in the colonial era, claimed to want to civilize them.

While opening its doors to (white) refugees from Ukraine, Europe—Germany being a notable exception—has shut them to darker-skinned refugees from Africa and the Middle East. Economic crisis and climate change have led to a kind of hoarding: of resources, vaccines, and living space. The question of scarcity, which Sartre identified as at the root of political struggle, has returned with a vengeance. Buoyed by white grievance, an international far-right movement has acquired growing influence and entered the political mainstream. Volatile and angry, it invokes the language of righteous victimhood—of a just struggle against being "colonized" by the former colonized, or what the anti-Muslim French writer Renaud Camus, much admired by Éric Zemmour, calls the great replacement.

In Eastern and Central European countries, disenchantment with liberal democracy (and neoliberalism) has provoked a popular rebellion against their leaders' "mimicry" of the West—as Ivan Krastev and Stephen Holmes have argued, citing Fanon's observations in *The Wretched of the Earth*—and fed the forces of xenophobia and authoritarian populism.

The United States, meanwhile, has come to look more and more like the monstrous successor of European imperialism Fanon evoked in *The Wretched of the Earth*. Influential figures in the Republican Party have engaged in their own kind of mimicry, embracing the great replacement theory and sidling up to Viktor Orbán and Vladimir Putin. To listen to a speech by Trump or Zemmour or Orbán is to wonder whether colonialism and imperialism were not, in the end, more damaging to their exponents in the West than to those they once ruled, as the Indian philosopher Ashis Nandy, one of Fanon's most original heirs, has suggested.

Would Fanon have been surprised? Probably not. He shared Enwezor's bleak view of Europe and never forgot his experience of being called a *nègre* by a child in France. Yet he insisted that if the world was to have a future, it lay in the struggle for a common humanity. Since the leaders of the West had failed at the task, and forced the rest of humanity to pay a steep and bloody price "for every one of its spiritual victories," it was time for others to try to achieve it. This was his project for the Third World, to "endeavor to create a new man": "If we want humanity to take one step forward, if we want to take it to another level than the one where Europe has placed it, then we must innovate, we must be pioneers."

Today Fanon's project for the postcolonial world lies in ruins. Narendra Modi's anti-Muslim crusade in India has transformed the world's largest democracy into an increasingly ugly sectarian regime. China has presided over the world's most extraordinary growth rates and raised hundreds of millions out of poverty. But liberty of expression is nonexistent, and the Tibetan and Uighur minorities have been subject to extreme levels of repression. In the Democratic Republic of the Congo and other parts of Africa, China has been prospecting for minerals like the Western imperial powers of the past, albeit without a civilizing mission. The corrupt network of French officials, entrepreneurs, and African autocrats known as Françafrique has been eclipsed by Chinafrique—and by the Wagner Group, a Russian-backed private security firm whose often brutal mercenaries have expanded their presence in the Central African Republic and Mali, and are welcomed by many Africans as a stabilizing force. The monarchies and dictatorships of the Arab world withstood the challenge of the Arab revolts, and in a number of countries, including Algeria, became even harsher in their suppression of democratic aspirations. Patriarchy—abetted by the forces of Islamic traditionalism—has left women in a deplorable state, unable to enjoy the increasingly paltry fruits of independence. The treatment of sub-Saharan migrants in South Africa and Black asylum seekers in the Maghreb is no better, and some ways worse, than that of African migrants in the cities of the West. National consciousness in Africa has proved strong enough to lend itself to pogroms, but not strong enough to prevent murderous resource wars or internal ethnic conflicts.

The geography and architecture of modern power would be mostly unrecognizable to Fanon. As he predicted, de jure occupations have all but vanished, with the exceptions of Palestine and Moroccan control of the Western Sahara. Today, the West's power is secured as much by the indirect coercions of the market and surveillance technology as by bases and

military interventions. After its catastrophic invasions and occupations of
Iraq and Afghanistan, the United States has much less of an appetite than
Russia for ground wars.

Our world is not Fanon's, yet his critique of power and international
relations retains much of its force. The racial divisions and economic inequalities that he protested were not so much liquidated as reconfigured.
Today's political order is no less divided between North and South, no less
shaped by exploitation, violence, and selective compassion, as the war in
Ukraine has illustrated. Would Fanon's sympathies have been with Ukrainians under Russian assault, or would he have seen the war as a sideshow, a
family quarrel in white Europe? A prominent historian of Eastern Europe
has described Ukraine's resistance as a Fanonian anti-colonial struggle.
But Fanon could not have failed to notice that the West's outpouring of
sympathy for Ukraine's refugees was never extended to others from the
equally brutal wars in Yemen and Syria. Some bodies, some lives still matter more than others.

The boundaries that separate the West from the rest, and from its
internal others, have been redrawn since Fanon's death, but they have not
disappeared: if anything, they have multiplied. In the United States, the
killings of unarmed Black people by the police have furnished a grim new
genre of reality television. An American president welcomed the support
of white supremacists, imposed a ban on citizens from seven Muslim-
majority countries, and promised to build a wall between the United
States and Mexico, all to keep out the "bad hombres." The era of alternative
facts and hypernationalism has been a breeding ground for the racialized
fears that Fanon so brilliantly diagnosed. The gated enclaves, surveillance
cameras, and prisons of the liberal West have created cities nearly as compartmentalized as Fanon's Algiers.

To his American admirers, Fanon's present-day relevance is so obvious
that it hardly needs stating. In his ingenious 2008 novel, *Fanon*, John Edgar Wideman remembers being asked by his imprisoned brother, Robert,
why he was writing a book about Fanon. "*Why Fanon*," he says to himself,
feeling disappointed that a Black man who's spent decades behind bars
could be puzzled by interest in "a visionary philosopher who argued that
humankind must liberate itself from the shackles of race to become truly

EPILOGUE: SPECTERS OF FANON                          389

human." He continues, "The answer's obvious, isn't it . . . C'mon, bro, I said to myself. Mize well ask, *Why me. Why you. Why those goddamn fucking stone-cold-ass walls.*" He finally replies, "Fanon because no way out of this goddamned mess . . . and Fanon found it."

Fanon, however, lived in a time of great hopes, the era of anti-colonial revolutions and the civil rights movement in the United States. We live in an era in which the neoliberal economic model and democratic governance have fallen into crisis, but in which alternative horizons have also receded from view. Today's radical movements and insurgencies are religious, identitarian, or both, and many of them are on the hard right. Both radical Islamists and radical nationalists are more likely to express nostalgia for an imagined community than a desire to build a new society. The idea of creating a new man is foreign to them.

The idea of decolonization, on the other hand, is anything but foreign to young people on the left, except that the concept is now applied not to the settler colonies Fanon fought against but rather to museums, universities, concert programs, even restaurant menus. Would Fanon have seen the symbolic gestures of today's "decolonial" movements as working toward a measure of retroactive, ritual justice, or as a leap into an imagined past? Although he eventually argued in favor of reparations for colonial exploitation and the repatriation of stolen artifacts, he remained skeptical of the Négritude movement's emphasis on the reclamation of cultural heritage, and of the "return to the self" promoted by the more pious members of the FLN.*

As the Cameroonian philosopher Achille Mbembe has written, Fanon envisioned "a world finally freed from the burden of race, a world that everyone has the right to inherit." He was not alone. In Fanon's era, the discovery that race was a construction, not a biological reality, fueled a sense of optimism about our ability to overcome racial conflict. "The race problem was *made*," the Black sociologist E. Franklin Frazier wrote in 1955, and therefore "men can *unmake* it."

Today this confidence strikes most of us as utopian—all the more so when a Black American teenager can be shot for knocking on the wrong

---

* By the standards of today's advocates of "indigeneity," Fanon was a resolute modernist.

door. "We know, we declare vehemently that race is construction," the critic Margo Jefferson writes. "We also know that race is a construction site we're not going to be leaving anytime soon." In *Black Skin, White Masks*, Fanon asked whether we can dismantle that construction site if we continue to reinforce it with a race-based politics. He had no patience for color blindness. But he believed that racial consciousness would have to evolve into *national* consciousness, and finally into more international and inclusive forms of attachment, the matrix of a new humanity.

But the national liberation movements ran their course, while Black cultures of art-making and political dissent have continued to thrive in the States and other parts of the African diaspora. Black Lives Matter, though born in America, has focused attention on matters of policing, incarceration, and public health throughout the world, and it has attracted a remarkably diverse group of supporters. It is possible, of course, that Fanon would have seen the politics and culture of diaspora Blackness as a mirage, like Négritude. Some critics of contemporary anti-racism, both liberal and Marxist, have claimed Fanon as an inspiration. Thomas Chatterton Williams, a Black critic of identitarianism, has invoked Fanon's commitment to creating a "new man" in his argument on behalf of a post-racial liberal politics. Writers in Marxist journals like *Jacobin*, meanwhile, have stressed that, at the end of his short life, Fanon was seeking to liberate not Black people but rather "the wretched of the earth," only some of whom were Black. (Indeed, Fanon's remarks about the Black and African middle classes were often withering.) Moreover, they have pointed out, the concepts of Blackness and white privilege threaten to essentialize the idea of race, to erase the realities of social class, and to discourage (and even preemptively discount) the possibility of alliances between oppressed people from different racial groups.

There is some merit to these claims. Although Fanon might have raised his eyebrows at Williams's call for "unlearning race," he, too, abhorred the kind of racial essentialism that, in recent years, has become the lexicon of American liberalism. He wanted to create a world in which the poor and the oppressed of what was then called the Third World, liberated from colonial domination, could take pride in their political and intellectual achievements, not in belonging to a specific race—much less in "Black excellence," a phrase that would surely have reminded Fanon of the rhetoric of Négritude.

But in its most vital forms, today's progressive Black politics is not nostalgic; it is focused on institutional change and open to coalition-building, both with sympathetic whites and with other oppressed groups, including Palestinians. And for the more radical currents in Black Lives Matter and the prison abolition movement, the term "Blackness" refers to a shared culture and condition, as much as a particular skin color. It is the supple and inclusive sign under which a diverse array of concerns, including matters of social class and the rights of women and queer people, come together, in intersectional fashion. In these circles, Fanon is increasingly a point of reference, as a revolutionary theorist who understood that decolonization is an intellectual and not merely a political process. To be sure, few of his admirers in these movements would share his belief in armed struggle as a means of overcoming oppression and recovering selfhood. Then again, Fanon, an admirer of the civil rights movement and the bus boycotts in the South, did not consider armed rebellion to be an auspicious strategy for ending segregation in the United States. Black Americans, he insisted, would have to pursue different strategies for emancipation than colonized Africans, because their conditions were not the same.

It is true, as Williams has argued, that today's anti-racists lack Fanon's faith in the possibility of transcending race. But it's also worth stressing that Fanon did not think that race could be overcome (or "unlearned") by liberal color blindness, or by the class struggle advocated by Marxists. One of his criticisms of the French Communist Party was precisely that it saw European workers in Algeria as a reservoir of support for socialism, while failing to register the significance of Muslim nationalism. Fanon believed that with their voting rights, and superior access to education and housing, Algeria's European proletariat was structurally aligned with the colonial project. His distrust of the white French—including members of the French left—was legendary. It is by no means clear that he would have rejected the emphasis on Black and brown leadership and self-organization among later activists of color: on the contrary, he may have seen these as crucial preparation for mass struggle, and a necessary prelude to alliance-building. His version of anti-racism was anti-essentialist and universalist, but to reach the shores of the universal, where the color of one's skin would be as politically meaningful as the color of one's hair, one first had to pass through the murky—and sometimes perilous—waters of racial consciousness. To pretend otherwise was to deny the lived experience of racism.

In the minds of the young anti-racist activists of the early twenty-first century, the shores of nonracialism have all but receded. Blackness and other forms of identity, not national consciousness, seem, at times, to be not only their raft but their destination itself. Fanon's declaration that the Black man does not exist "any more than the White man" is perhaps even more of a provocation today than it was in 1952—not just to anti-Black racists but also to opponents of white supremacy. The contemporary left's intense preoccupation with race might well have struck him as "the illness that takes itself for the cure," as the Viennese essayist Karl Kraus wrote of psychoanalysis. But Fanon was only thirty-six when he died, and still evolving, and it is hard to imagine him not being moved by the image of millions of young people, of all complexions, taking to the streets to oppose racism and police brutality: if there was one thing he admired, it was active, bodily resistance to oppression.

Although the watchwords of today's anti-racist movements are Black liberation, prison abolition, decolonization, and indigeneity, not the creation of a new humanity, their urgent, existential style of activism, and their emphasis on dignity and self-determination, would surely have struck a chord with him. For all his discomfort with Senghor's mystical version of Négritude, for all his belief in a future beyond both colonialism and race, I also suspect that Fanon would have seen, in the contemporary embrace of Blackness, and in the inventive expansion of its meanings, not a retreat into racialism or an abandonment of the universal but rather a liberatory national culture, although one without territorial borders. And in the BLM slogan "I can't breathe," the last words of Eric Garner and George Floyd, he might have heard echoes of his own observation that the oppressed revolt simply because they can no longer breathe.

# A NOTE ON SOURCES

————

I WAS A TEENAGER when I first saw a picture of Frantz Fanon, on the back of my father's hardcover copy of *Black Skin, White Masks*, the original 1967 Grove edition. He appeared in a tweed jacket, a freshly pressed white shirt, and a striped tie, with a five-o'clock shadow and an intense, somewhat hooded expression. He seemed to be issuing a challenge or perhaps a warning that if his words weren't heeded, there would be hell to pay. *Who is this man?* I remember thinking. I was no less intrigued by *where* I found *Black Skin, White Masks* and *The Wretched of the Earth*, the latter of which is often described as the bible of decolonization. In the small library of radical literature that my father kept in our basement, Fanon's books were sandwiched, appropriately, between *The Autobiography of Malcolm X* and Isaac Deutscher's *The Non-Jewish Jew*: the former a classic memoir of Black nationalism, the latter an essay on socialist internationalism.

It would be an exaggeration, but only a slight one, to say that it was Fanon who sparked my interest in the history of French-occupied Algeria. In 2000, I reviewed David Macey's magisterial biography of Fanon for *The New York Times*. Two years later, I arrived in Algiers, forty years after independence, to report on the end of the "Black Decade," or civil war, for *The New York Review of Books*. I returned for another extensive reporting trip in 2015, observing the achievements, but also the ruins, of the independence struggle to which Fanon dedicated the last years of his life. I met young Algerian intellectuals who were fascinated by Fanon and wistful for the era he embodied, which they themselves had never seen. I had hoped to return to retrace Fanon's steps in Blida, but the Algerian government, facing a wave of weekly protests known as the Hirak (movement), rejected my request for a visa on two separate occasions. Still, my memories of Algeria and its people, and my conversations with Algerian friends, have strongly shaped this book.

In tracing the movements and encounters of Fanon's peripatetic life, I have drawn extensively upon Macey's account as well as Alice Cherki's moving biographical portrait, and the memoirs of Mohammed Harbi, Marie-Jeanne Manuellan, Elaine Klein Mokhtefi, Jean Daniel, Michel Martini, and Serge Michel. My interviews with Cherki, Harbi, Manuellan, Mokhtefi, and Daniel—and with Guy Sitbon and Herbert Weiss—helped me arrive at a more intimate picture of Fanon as an individual. (Daniel and Manuellan both passed away during the writing of this book.) All these people have immeasurably enriched my sense of Fanon: the partygoer and the ascetic, the rebel and the dutiful psychiatrist, the ambitious striver and the selfless militant, the urbane intellectual who romanticized the peasantry, the opponent of France who believed fervently in its revolutionary Jacobin traditions, the nomad who never stopped looking for a home.

The major source remains Fanon's own writings, the repository of his torments and hopes, his insights and innovations, his prophecies and hallucinations. While I sometimes quote from the English translations of his work—Richard Philcox's are the most recent—I cite the French originals and have often adjusted the translations to better approximate the meaning of his words in French. Fanon dictated his writing, but he was exacting, and pointed, when it came to the words he used, especially when they were philosophical and psychiatric terms, or racial designations for colonized and oppressed peoples. The subtleties and nuances of Fanon's writing—and its powerful debt to the idioms of Négritude, psychoanalysis, existentialism, and phenomenology—are often lost in translation, and wherever possible I have sought to restore them.

Fanon was not an autobiographical writer; he disdained memoir as a bourgeois pastime and usually hid behind his professional identities: the mask of the doctor or the mask of the spokesman, depending on the occasion. Yet each of his books—*Black Skin, White Masks*; *A Dying Colonialism*; *The Wretched of the Earth*; and the posthumously collected articles in *Toward the African Revolution*—contains an abundance of asides, often partially concealed, about his "lived experience," and the thinking it inspired. In 2015, the scholars Jean Khalfa and Robert J. C. Young performed an invaluable service by assembling Fanon's unpublished writings in a breathtaking volume, *Écrits sur l'aliénation et la liberté* (titled *Alienation and Freedom* in the 2018 English translation), which includes his two surviving student plays, as well as the psychiatric papers he wrote or co-wrote while in Algeria and Tunisia. Most of these papers can also be found at the Fanon archives of the Institut Mémoires de l'édition contemporaine (IMEC), at the Ardenne Abbey near Caen, in Normandy, where I read Fanon's extraordinary journal from his expedition in Mali, located in the same file as the *vrai faux* passport issued by the Libyan government.

A certain amount of conjecture is, however, a requirement in interpreting Fanon's writings, and I would be the first to admit that this book is, in part, a work of imagination. Fanon grew up on an island where freedom had been nearly synonymous with secrecy and flight from captivity since the days of *marronage*: his inner life will always elude us. My reading of his work seeks to be symptomatic: attuned to gaps, silences, tensions, and contradictions; the barely visible trace, in Fanon's forceful prose, of the distance between the world he inherited and the world that he and many others hoped to create after the collapse of Europe's empires. As the Tunisian Jewish writer Albert Memmi remarked, Fanon, as a West Indian atheist in a Muslim-led national liberation movement, led an "impossible life." But his impossible life, and the work it inspired, was the stranger's gift to the world.

# NOTES

## Prologue

3 *"This part of the Sahara is not monotonous"*: Frantz Fanon, "Cette Afrique à venir," in *Pour la révolution africaine: Écrits politiques* (1964; repr. La Découverte, 2006), 197–211.

6 *classic history of the Haitian Revolution*: C. L. R. James, *The Black Jacobins: Toussaint L'Ouverture and the San Domingo Revolution* (Random House, 1963, second edition).

6 *"is not a wanderer"*: Georg Simmel, "The Stranger," trans. Ramona Mosse, *The Baffler* 30 (March 2016): 176–79. (This is a reprint of the original 1908 essay.)

7 *"in the shadow of infancy"*: See Ralph Ellison, "Richard Wright's Blues," in *The Collected Essays of Ralph Ellison* (Modern Library, 1994), 135.

8 *"History," in the words of the Marxist*: Fredric Jameson, *The Political Unconscious: Narrative as a Socially Symbolic Act* (Cornell University Press, 1981), 102.

8 *"a zone of nonbeing"*: Frantz Fanon, *Peau noire, masques blancs* (Seuil, 1952), 6.

9 *"the Third World discovers itself"*: Sartre, preface to Frantz Fanon, *Les Damnés de la terre*, (1961; repr. La Découverte, 2002), 20.

9 *"the heart and soul of a movement"*: Orlando Patterson, "Frantz Fanon: My Hope and Hero," *New World Journal* (Guyana Independence Issue, 1966), 95.

10 *"an affirmation of dignity"*: Jean Améry, "L'Homme enfanté par l'esprit de la violence," *Les Temps modernes* 1–2, nos. 635–36 (2006): 175–89.

11 *"O my body"*: The quotes in this and the following paragraph are from Fanon, *Peau noire, masques blancs*.

11 *"a yes that vibrates to cosmic harmonies"*: Fanon, *Peau noire, masques blancs*, 6.

12 *"The Negro is not"*: Fanon, *Peau noire, masques blancs*, 187.

12 *"'A man without a mask'"*: R. D. Laing, *The Divided Self: An Existential Study in Sanity and Madness* (Tavistock, 1960), 95.

## 1. A Small Place

17 *"small place"*: Jamaica Kincaid, *A Small Place* (Farrar, Straus and Giroux, 1988), 81.

18 *"stinking pearl"*: Joby Fanon, *Frantz Fanon, My Brother: Doctor, Playwright, Revolutionary*, trans. Daniel Nethery (Lexington Books, 2014), 10–12.

18 *"looked at life"*: Derek Walcott, *Dream on Monkey Mountain and Other Plays* (Farrar, Straus and Giroux, 1970), 9.

19 *"The appetite for knowledge"*: Édouard Glissant, *La Lézarde* (Seuil, 1958), 18. "Lézarde" means "crack" or "crevice," but the novel appeared in English under the title *The Ripening*.

20 *"never had that imperceptible but very real core"*: Alice Cherki, *Frantz Fanon: A Portrait*, trans. Nadia Benabid (Cornell University Press, 2006), 7.

21 *"more for the thrill"*: Joby Fanon, *Frantz Fanon, My Brother*, 12.

21 *The son of a wealthy porcelain manufacturer*: Robin Blackburn, *The Overthrow of Colonial Slavery, 1776–1848* (Verso, 1988), 492–506.

22 *novelist Victor Hugo offered a telling description*: Victor Hugo, *Choses vues*, tome I, *Oeuvres complètes*.

22 *"While Schoelcher's humanitarianism and good intentions"*: Blackburn, *The Overthrow of Colonial Slavery*, 506.

22 *"world of statues"*: Frantz Fanon, *Les Damnés de la terre* (La Découverte, 2002), 53.

23 *"lined by worm-eaten tamarind trees"*: Frantz Fanon, *Peau noire, masques blancs* (Seuil, 1952), 19.

23 *"In the Antilles"*: Fanon, *Peau noire, masques blancs*, 175.

24 *"the cadavers of nègres"*: Fanon, *Les Damnés de la terre*, 94.

25 *"We made practically everything in order to survive"*: Joby Fanon, *Frantz Fanon, My Brother*, 18.

25 *Casimir Fanon fell under suspicion*: Joby Fanon, *Frantz Fanon, My Brother*, 18. The Barbadian writer George Lamming, who worked on but never completed a novel about Fanon, argued that the key event in his formation, and the origin of his "wounds," was the Vichy government's "fascist possession of Martinique." See David Scott, "The Sovereignty of the Imagination: An Interview with George Lamming," in *Small Axe* 6, no. 2 (September 2002): 72–200.

25 *"the darkest of my children"*: Fanon, *Peau noire, masques blancs*, 132.

26 *" a land that was learning the new violence of the world"*: Glissant, *La Lézarde*, 20.

26 *"close symbolic connection"*: See Julius S. Scott, *The Common Wind: Afro-American Currents in the Age of the Haitian Revolution* (Verso, 2018), 38.

26 *"nègres of the lowest category"*: David Macey, *Frantz Fanon: A Life* (Granta, 2000), 171.

27 *" frenzied women of color"*: Fanon, *Peau noire, masques blancs*, 39.

27 *"less carried away by patriotic declarations"*: The quotes in this paragraph are from Joby Fanon, *Frantz Fanon, My Brother*, 22.

28 *"Fire burns and war kills"*: Joby Fanon, *Frantz Fanon, My Brother*, 23.

28 nègres: During Fanon's childhood, the French word *nègre* often carried highly negative connotations and could, in some cases, be translated as "nigger." In a 1927 essay, "The Word 'Nègre,'" the Senegalese Marxist Lamine Senghor described it as "the dirty word . . . by which some of our race brothers no longer wish to be called." For Senghor, the purpose of the word *nègre* was to divide Black people into three groups: *hommes de couleur* (people of color), often of mixed race, who did not see themselves as Black; *noirs*, middle-class Blacks who considered themselves superior to *nègres*; and finally the *nègres*, society's "leftovers." But, as we shall see, the word *nègre*, sometimes capitalized, was recuperated in the 1930s by the Négritude movement, much as "queer" would be by the modern gay rights movement. As a result, the word's meaning would increasingly depend on usage, inflection, and context: sometimes it is simply an antiquated term for someone with African ancestry, like "Negro"; sometimes it is a racist epithet; and sometimes it is an affirmation of racial pride and Black consciousness. Fanon used the word in all three senses, although mostly the first two. For this reason, I have decided to leave *nègre* untranslated throughout this book, only occasionally rendering it as "Negro."

28 tirailleurs sénégalais: The Senegalese riflemen originated as an army of slaves who had been purchased in 1857 by the French army at the behest of Louis Faidherbe, the governor of Senegal. Recruited en masse in World War I, they were praised for their valor and courage,

and for having a supposed greater resistance to pain, a trope common to racist discourse about Black people. They were often the first to be sent to the front lines, because, as Georges Clemenceau, France's head of government in World War I, explained, enough "French blood" had already been spilled.

28 *"We knew about them"*: Fanon, *Peau noire, masques blancs*, 132.

29 *selling a bolt of cloth*: Macey, *Frantz Fanon*, 88.

29 *still trying to change his brother's mind*: Joby Fanon, *Frantz Fanon, My Brother*, 24.

29 *"a logic of stubbornness and morbid perseverance"*: Joby Fanon, *Frantz Fanon, My Brother*, 25.

29 *"ultimate resort of a people"*: Édouard Glissant, *Le Discours antillais* (Gallimard, 1997), 48.

30 *"Hitler, we're going to knock you off"*: Macey, *Frantz Fanon*, 92.

## 2. Wartime Lies

31 *"I doubt everything"*: Frantz Fanon to his family, April 12, 1945, in Joby Fanon, *Frantz Fanon, My Brother: Doctor, Playwright, Revolutionary*, trans. Daniel Nethery (Lexington Books, 2014), 34.

32 *European settlers from Algeria*: The *Français d'Algérie*—the French-speaking European colonists of Algeria—came to be known as *pieds-noirs*, "black feet," toward the end of the Algerian War. I will refer to them mostly as "European Algerians" or as "settlers," because the term *pied-noir*, whose origin remains a mystery, was not widely used until the late 1950s.

33 *"rage and hatred"*: Such scenes were not hard to come by in Algeria; Camus wrote of similar episodes in "Misery in Kabylia," his 1939 report for the Communist newspaper *Alger républicain*.

33 *"We were astonished to see for ourselves"*: Frantz Fanon, *Peau noire, masques blancs* (Seuil, 1952), 83.

33 *"beginning of my real education"*: Harold Cruse, *Rebellion or Revolution?* (University of Minnesota Press, 2009), 168–92.

34 *"an intelligent pupil but of difficult character"*: Quoted in Joby Fanon, *Frantz Fanon, My Brother*, 28.

35 *When one of them asked*: Fanon, *Peau noire, masques blancs*, 20.

35 *"rice, chicken, red lentils, mangoes"*: Joby Fanon, *Frantz Fanon, My Brother*, 32.

36 *"wounded to the core of his being"*: Joby Fanon, *Frantz Fanon, My Brother*, 38.

36 *"We had fought the war"*: Marcel Manville, *Les Antilles sans fard* (Harmattan, 1992), 48.

37 *"You have at times been very inferior"*: Frantz Fanon to his family, April 12, 1945, in Joby Fanon, *Frantz Fanon, My Brother*, 34–35.

37 *"He tells us that he was mistaken"*: Quoted in Joby Fanon, *Frantz Fanon, My Brother*, 36.

37 *"When you hear someone insulting the Jews"*: Fanon, *Peau noire, masques blancs*, 98.

38 *volcanic, explosive, capricious, and violent*: Romuald Fonkoua, *Aimé Césaire* (Perrin, 2013), 29–30.

39 *"Do not say that I do not love France"*: Léopold Sédar Senghor, "Poème liminaire," *Hosties noires* (1948) in *Œuvre poétique* (Seuil, 1990), 55–56.

40 *"rub your nose"*: Léon-Gontran Damas, "Pour sûr," quoted in Lilyan Kesteloot, *Black Writers in French: A Literary History of Negritude*, trans. Ellen Conroy Kennedy (Howard University Press, 1991), 136.

40 *"masks of living chalk"*: Kesteloot, *Black Writers in French*, 141.

40 *"stubborn refusal to alienate ourselves"*: Romuald Fonkoua, *Aimé Césaire* (Perrin, 2010), 48.

40 *pays natal*: In using the phrase *pays natal* in the title of his poem, Césaire meant to evoke his birthplace, not to play on his "native" origins as a colonized Black man; "country of origin" might be a more faithful translation than "native land."

40 *"It's Martinique!"*: See Fonkoua, *Aimé Césaire*, 51.

41 *"My Négritude is neither a tower"*: Aimé Césaire, *Journal of a Homecoming/Cahier d'un retour au pays natal*, trans. N. Gregson Davis (Duke University Press, 2017), 124. I have taken the liberty of adapting some of Davis's translations in this bilingual edition.

41 *"The Negro is not deprived of reason"*: See the texts assembled in Léopold Sédar Senghor, *Liberté 1, Négritude et humanisme* (Seuil, 1964).

42 *"before Césaire"*: Frantz Fanon, "Antillais et Africains," in *Pour la révolution africaine: Écrits politiques* (1964; repr. La Découverte, 2006), 35.

42 *"read Chekhov with her morning coffee"*: Ina Césaire, "Suzanne Césaire, My Mother," in *The Great Camouflage: Writings of Dissent (1941–1945) / Suzanne Césaire*, ed. Daniel Maximin, trans. Keith L. Walker (Wesleyan University Press, 2009), 65.

42 *"The circle of shadow is tightening"*: Aimé Césaire, "Presentation," *Tropiques*, no. 1 (April 1941).

43 *"obscurity in which, paradoxically"*: Fonkoua, *Aimé Césaire*, 72. Fonkoua speculates that the *Tropiques* may have been protected from censorship by Georges Pelorson, the publisher of Césaire's epic poem, who had become the Vichy regime's head of youth propaganda services in the Occupied Zone.

43 *"the racism of Toussaint Louverture"*: Quoted in Daniel Maximin, "Editor's Introduction," in *The Great Camouflage*, xxix.

43 *"after the emancipation of people of color"*: Suzanne Césaire, "Malaise of a Civilization," in *The Great Camouflage*, 28–33.

43 *"a state of pseudo-civilization that one can describe as abnormal"*: Suzanne Césaire, "Malaise of a Civilization," in *The Great Camouflage*, 32.

44 *"Millions of Black hands"*: Suzanne Césaire, "1943: Surrealism and Us," in *The Great Camouflage*, 38.

44 *His stay in the capital*: Joby Fanon remembered that when they visited the Bibliothèque Sainte-Geneviève, Frantz showed little interest in reading the original text of the infamous 1685 Code Noir. Comprising sixty articles regulating the treatment of slaves in the colonies, the "Black Code" authorized torture, amputation, and decapitation in cases of revolt, and encouraged "all our officers to chase from our islands Jews who have established residence there." Fanon was drawn, rather, to the section devoted to Descartes's *Discourse on the Method of Rightly Conducting One's Reason and of Seeking Truth in the Sciences*. See Joby Fanon, *Frantz Fanon, My Brother*, 74.

44 *"There are too many* nègres *in Paris"*: Joby Fanon, *Frantz Fanon, My Brother*, 44.

## 3. Black Man, White City

46 *"We know full well"*: Frantz Fanon, *Peau noire, masques blancs* (Seuil, 1952), 73.

46 *"Did you hear that, Whitey?"*: Joby Fanon, *Frantz Fanon, My Brother: Doctor, Playwright, Revolutionary*, trans. Daniel Nethery (Lexington Books, 2014), 45. Fanon earned a reputation for prickly and sometimes aggressive behavior, but Nicole Guillet, one of his closest friends at the medical school, believed that Fanon's displays of anger were a defense against feelings of insecurity, when they weren't a response to explicit incidents of racism.

47 *"We really worked like—"*: This incident is reported by Simone de Beauvoir in the second volume of her memoirs, *La Force des choses* (Gallimard, 1963).

47 *"no difference between us"*: Fanon, *Peau noire, masques blancs*, 179.

47 *Fanon was fascinated by Bigger Thomas*: Fanon, *Peau noire, masques blancs*, 113.

48 *But one freezing day in winter*: See the chapter "L'Expérience vécue du Noir," in Frantz Fanon, *Peau noire, masques blancs*, 88–114.

48 *"Neger! Neger!"*: James Baldwin, "Stranger in the Village," in *Collected Essays*, ed. Toni Morrison (Library of America, 1998), 119.

48 *"fixed, in the same way you'd fix a preparation with a dye"*: Fanon, *Peau noire, masques blancs*, 88.

49 *"At last I was liberated from my rumination"*: Fanon, *Peau noire, masques blancs*, 92.

49 *"It is the innocence which constitutes the crime"*: James Baldwin, *The Fire Next Time* (Vintage, 1963), 14.

51 *"that larval, stocky, obsolete life"*: Joby Fanon, *Frantz Fanon, My Brother*, 111.

51 *"piled everywhere, even on the floor"*: Joby Fanon, *Frantz Fanon, My Brother*, 54.

51 *The third play*, The Conspiracy, *has vanished*: The play likely took its title, *La Conspiration*, from Paul Nizan's eponymous novel about a cell of student revolutionaries in Paris, published in 1938.

52 *"love takes off the masks"*: Baldwin, *The Fire Next Time*, 95.

52 *Fanon proposed marriage*: I base this account on my conversation with Fanon's daughter, Mireille Fanon Mendès-France. David Macey, in *Frantz Fanon: A Life* (Granta, 2000), claims that Fanon left Weyer when she became pregnant.

52 *"his position as an absent father"*: Joby Fanon, *Frantz Fanon, My Brother*, 55.

52 *"way of speaking under her breath"*: Elaine Mokhtefi, *Algiers, Third World Capital: Freedom Fighters, Revolutionaries, Black Panthers* (Verso, 2018), 46.

53 *"ways that would not have been possible"*: Macey, *Frantz Fanon*, 134.

53 *"psychiatric desert"*: Quoted in Macey, *Frantz Fanon*, 134.

53 *recently published a paper*: See Paul Balvet, "La Valeur humaine de la folie," *Esprit* (September 1947): 289–305.

54 *"The strange impression that death is not far away"*: Frantz Fanon, *Pour la révolution africaine: Écrits politiques* (1964; repr. La Découverte, 2006), 15.

55 *"Stay in your place"*: In *The Practice of Diaspora: Literature, Translation, and the Rise of Black Internationalism* (Harvard University Press, 2003), 52, Brent Hayes Edwards writes: "*Petit nègre* is one of the strangest legacies of World War I: it was a simplified, deformed version of French that the military codified and deliberately *taught* to African soldiers as they came to fight in Europe, as a means both to infantilize them and to control their modes of interaction with their mainly white French commanding officers."

55 *"indulge in any form of paternalism"*: Fanon, *Peau noire, masques blancs*, 26.

56 *"Who are they"*: Frantz Fanon, "Le 'Syndrome nord-africain,'" *Esprit* (February 1952). The article was published as part of a special section on the North African proletariat in France, and reprinted in Fanon, *Pour la révolution africaine*, 11–25.

57 *"the reductive discourse of the doctor"*: Michel Foucault, *The Birth of the Clinic: An Archaeology of Medical Perception*, trans. Alan Sheridan-Smith (Routledge, 2003), xi.

59 *"logician of madness"*: Frantz Fanon, *Écrits sur l'aliénation et la liberté*, ed. Jean Khalfa and Robert J. C. Young (La Découverte, 2015), 220.

## 4. Toward a Black Existentialism

60 *"A genuine rebellion of the intellectuals"*: Hannah Arendt, "What Is This New Philosophy They Call 'Existentialism'?," *The Nation*, February 23, 1946.

62 *became aware of Richard Wright*: Wright's 1945 memoir, *Black Boy*, was serialized across six issues of *Les Temps modernes* in 1946 and 1947.

62 *"We are in the world through our bodies"*: Maurice Merleau-Ponty, *The Phenomenology of Perception*, trans. Donald A. Landes (Routledge, 2012), 213.

62 *"phenomenal body"*: Merleau-Ponty, *The Phenomenology of Perception*, 456.

62 *"A war-wounded man"*: Merleau-Ponty, *The Phenomenology of Perception*, 83–88.

62 *"The phenomenological world is not pure being"*: Merleau-Ponty, *The Phenomenology of Perception*, xxxiv. Donald Landes translates *engrenage* as "gearing together," but "meshing" seems more apt to me.

62 *"whose philosophy soared above the earth"*: Jean-Paul Sartre, *Portraits*, trans. Chris Turner (Seagull Books, 2009), 269–70.

63 *a "flesh memory" of this violence*: The literary theorist Hortense Spillers uses this term in Arthur Jafa's 2013 documentary film, *Dreams Are Colder Than Death*. Describing the pain that a relative continued to feel in his amputated limb, she suggests that the physical oppression of slavery and Jim Crow imprinted itself on the collective unconscious (and "phenomenal"

bodies) of African Americans. The Algerian psychoanalyst Karima Lazali makes a similar argument in her 2018 study, *Le Trauma colonial: Une enquête sur les effets psychiques et politiques contemporains de l'oppression colonial en Algérie* (La Découverte, 2018). The violent conquest of Algeria, she writes, and the accompanying murder of Algerian civilians and erasure of the country's Arab and Muslim identity, inflicted "a pain comparable to that of a mutilated person: the latter experienced the pain of a 'phantom limb' to the point of ignoring the fact that the limb has disappeared." The independence struggle, she suggests, was "a means to erase the disappearance, to make it disappear."

63   *"I refuse this amputation"*: Frantz Fanon, *Peau noire, masques blancs* (Seuil, 1952), 114.

63   *"bodily schema"*: Merleau-Ponty himself derived this term from the French neurologist Jean Lhermitte.

63   *he found that he could not accept*: My argument about Fanon's recasting of Merleau-Ponty owes much to the philosopher Gayle Salamon's perceptive essay, "The Place Where Life Hides Away: Merleau-Ponty, Fanon, and the Location of Bodily Being," in *Differences* 17, no. 2 (September 2006): 96–112.

63   *Their "bodily schema"*: Fanon, *Peau noire, masques blancs*, 89–90.

64   *"white mythologies"*: Derrida was referring to Western reason rather than imperialism or racial domination; it was left to postcolonial theorists to make explicit what was only implicit in the term. "Metaphysics," he wrote, is "the white mythology which reassembles and reflects the culture of the West: the white man takes his own mythology, Indo-European mythology, his own *logos*, that is the *mythos* of his idiom, for the universal form of that he must still wish to call Reason."

64   *Sartre published a short book*: See Jean-Paul Sartre, *Anti-Semite and Jew*, trans. George J. Becker (Schocken, 1948), esp. 13, 22, 48, 53–54, 76–77, 78–79, 83, 117–19, 134–36, 146, 153–54.

65   *created the Jew*: Sartre, *Anti-Semite and Jew*, 69: "It is the anti-Semite who *makes* the Jew."

65   *"Some day they must learn the truth"*: Sartre, *Anti-Semite and Jew*, 75.

65   *"It is a peculiar sensation"*: W. E. B. Du Bois, *W. E. B. Du Bois: Writings* (Library of America, 1986), 364–65.

66   *"the most beautiful we've ever read"*: Fanon, *Peau noire, masques blancs*, 146.

66   *"I am a slave"*: Fanon, *Peau noire, masques blancs*, 128–35.

66   *"would never think of castrating the Jew"*: Fanon, *Peau noire, masques blancs*, 132–34.

66   *"the anti-Semite is inevitably a Negrophobe"*: Fanon, *Peau noire, masques blancs*, 98.

66   *"concrete liberalism"*: Sartre, *Anti-Semite and Jew*, 146.

67   *"When you removed the gag"*: Jean-Paul Sartre, "Black Orpheus," in *"What Is Literature?" and Other Essays* (Harvard University Press, 1988), 291.

67   *Black poets had no choice*: Sartre was channeling Hegel's idea that freedom lies in the recognition of necessity and in the acceptance of responsibilities that history has imposed.

69   *Fanon was incensed*: Sartre has come under harsh criticism for his conclusions in "Black Orpheus." In the words of the Fanon scholar David Marriott: "White theory . . . like a practiced magician or con artist, no sooner sees black experience than it instinctively begins correcting its posture, language and speech." But the nature of Sartre's relationship to Fanon, as we will see, was less one of appropriation or tutelage than of exchange, reciprocal influence, and political solidarity.

69   *"I sensed my shoulders"*: Fanon, *Peau noire, masques blancs*, 112.

70   *"the* nègre *suffers in his body differently"*: Fanon, *Peau noire, masques blancs*, 112.

70   *"You'll change, my child"*: Fanon, *Peau noire, masques blancs*, 109.

70   *"reveals itself to be false"*: Fanon, *Peau noire, masques blancs*, 107–11.

72   *"Isn't the superiority of the* nègre *real?"*: Fanon, *Peau noire, masques blancs*, 129.

74   *"The white man's unadmitted"*: James Baldwin, "Down at the Cross," in *Collected Essays*, ed. Toni Morrison (Library of America, 1998), 341.

74   *"The analysis of reality is a delicate task"*: Fanon, *Peau noire, masques blancs*, 136.

75 *"wonder if [colonial administrators]"*: Fanon, *Peau noire, masques blancs,* 175.

75 *"Let us have the courage to say"*: Fanon, *Peau noire, masques blancs,* 75.

75 "in its time, *and this time"*: Fanon, *Peau noire, masques blancs,* 86.

76 *the implicitly subversive suggestion*: See Livio Boni and Sophie Mendelsohn's discussion of Mannoni in *La Vie psychique du racism* (La Découverte, 2021).

77 *"Constantly preoccupied with self-assertion"*: Fanon, *Peau noire, masques blancs,* 170–72.

77 *"97 percent"*: Fanon, *Peau noire, masques blancs,* 123–24.

77 *"I am afraid the Caribbean"*: Stuart Hall, "The After-Life of Frantz Fanon: Why Fanon? Why Now? Why *Black Skin, White Masks?*," in *The Fact of Blackness: Frantz Fanon and Visual Representation,* ed. Alan Read (Bay Press, 1996), 30.

78 *"I'm convinced that the next great arena"*: Quoted in Gabriel N. Mendes, *Under the Strain of Color: Harlem's Lafargue Clinic and the Promise of an Antiracist Psychiatry* (Cornell University Press, 2015), 22.

78 *"the frequency of mental illness"*: Richard Wright, *Black Boy* (Harper Perennial Modern Classics, 2007), 284.

79 *"Bigger Thomas is afraid"*: Fanon, *Peau noire, masques blancs,* 113.

79 *the first outpatient mental health clinic*: My account of the Lafargue Clinic has been shaped by the following works: Mendes, *Under the Strain of Color*; Jay Garcia, *Psychology Comes to Harlem: Rethinking Race Questions in Twentieth-Century America* (Johns Hopkins University Press, 2012); and Eli Zaretsky, *Political Freud: A History* (Columbia University Press, 2015).

79 *"Negroes don't need psychiatry"*: Mendes, *Under the Strain of Color,* 86.

80 *"Negro Americans are in desperate search for an identity"*: Ralph Ellison, *The Collected Essays of Ralph Ellison* (Modern Library, 1995), 322–23.

80 *"I am invisible"*: Ralph Ellison, *Invisible Man* (Penguin, 1952), 7.

80 *replacing his "corporeal schema"*: Fanon, *Peau noire, masques blancs,* 89–90.

81 *"insulting name"*: Ellison, *Invisible Man,* 16.

81 *"great black mirage"*: The phrase "great black mirage" first appears in Frantz Fanon, "Antillais et Africains," in *Pour la révolution africaine: Écrits politiques* (1964; repr. La Découverte, 2006), 31–36. Fanon argues that "after the great white error," the West Indian "is now living in the great black mirage." What, he asks, "could be more grotesque than an educated man, a college graduate . . . claiming that his skin is beautiful and that the 'great black hole' is the source of truth?"

## 5. Refusal of the Mask

82 *The seventy-five-page thesis*: Frantz Fanon, "Altérations mentales, modifications caractérielles, troubles psychiques et deficit intellectuel dans l'hérédo-dégénération spinocérébelleuse. À propos d'un cas de maladie de Friedreich avec délire de possession," in *Écrits sur l'aliénation et la liberté,* ed. Jean Khalfa and Robert J. C. Young (La Découverte, 2015), 168–232.

82 *"a whole, an indissoluble unity"*: Fanon, "Altérations mentales," 168–232.

83 *managed to impress Sartre*: Jeanson's first book, *Le Problème moral et la pensée de Sartre* (Myrte, 1947), was a study of Jean-Paul Sartre's work.

83 *Algeria appeared to be*: Francis Jeanson, "Cette Algérie conquise et pacifiée," *Esprit* (April 1950): 841–61.

84 *one of Jeanson's readers*: A lengthy citation from Jeanson's dispatch in *Esprit* appears in Frantz Fanon, *Peau noire, masques blancs* (Seuil, 1952).

84 *"a Black man plunged in a white world"*: Francis Jeanson, preface to the first edition of Fanon, *Peau noire, masques blancs.*

85 *"pariah writer who had to reinvent"*: See Francis Jeanson, afterword to the 1965 edition of Fanon, *Peau noire, masques blancs.* Genet and Fanon never met, but Genet included a strikingly Fanonian prefatory note in his 1958 play *Les Nègres,* suggesting that "white masks be

distributed to the Black spectators as they enter the theater. And if the Blacks refuse the masks, then let a dummy be used."

85  *"irrationally, almost sensually"*: Quoted in Robert J. C. Young, introduction to Frantz Fanon, *Écrits sur l'aliénation et la liberté*, 49.

86  *"What's all this about Black people"*: Fanon, *Peau noire, masques blancs*, 164.

87  *"all great works of literature found a genre or dissolve one"*: Walter Benjamin, *Illuminations*, trans. Harry Zohn (Schocken, 1968), 201.

87  *"will not recognize themselves"*: Fanon, *Peau noire, masques blancs*, 9.

88  *"the end of the world"*: Fanon, *Peau noire, masques blancs*, 175.

88  *"racism was dead"*: Michel Leiris, *Race and Culture* (UNESCO, 1951), 7.

89  *"ethnocentrism" and "false evolutionism"*: See Claude Lévi-Strauss, *Race et histoire* (UNESCO, 1952), especially chapters 2, 3, and 10.

89  *"The world is white no longer"*: James Baldwin, *Collected Essays* (Library of America, 1998), 129.

89  *"one is not born"*: Simone de Beauvoir, *Le Deuxième sexe 1* (Gallimard, 1949), 285–86.

89  *"erased any trace"*: See Matthieu Renault, "Le Genre de la race: Fanon, lecteur de Beauvoir," *Actuel Marx* 1, no. 55 (2014): 36–48. The only mention of Beauvoir in Fanon's work appears in *Peau noire, masques blancs*, in which he mentions that Beauvoir was once harassed in New York City by an old white American woman who objected to Beauvoir walking alongside a Black man—her friend the novelist Richard Wright. See Fanon, *Peau noire, masques blancs*, 148.

90  *a hero for Fanon*: See Frantz Fanon, "Antillais et Africains," in *Pour la révolution africaine: Écrits politiques* (1964; repr. La Découverte, 2006), 30–33.

90  *"works to decivilize the colonizer"*: Aimé Césaire, *Discourse on Colonialism*, trans. Joan Pinkham (Monthly Review Press, 2000), 35.

90  The *"Christian bourgeois of the twentieth century"*: Césaire, *Discourse on Colonialism*, 36.

91  an *"authentic disalienation"*: Fanon, *Peau noire, masques blancs*, 9.

92  *"racecraft"*: See Karen E. Fields and Barbara J. Fields, *Racecraft: The Soul of Inequality in American Life* (Verso, 2014).

92  *"Yes, I have to watch my diction"*: Fanon, *Peau noire, masques blancs*, 16.

92  *"extremely toxic foreign bodies"*: Fanon, *Peau noire, masques blancs*, 28.

93  *"Every time we see an Arab"*: Fanon, *Peau noire, masques blancs*, 73.

93  *In the early days of colonial conquest*: William B. Cohen, *The French Encounter with Africans: White Responses to Blacks, 1530–1880* (Indiana University Press, 1980). See especially chapter 3, "The Philosophes and Africa."

93  *Thus the* mission civilisatrice, *or "civilizing mission"*: Among the philosophes, Rousseau stood out for his condemnation of the "civilizing mission." He wrote, "If I were the chief of one of the peoples of Black Africa, I would set up on the frontier gallows on which I would hang without mercy the first European who dared enter and the first citizen who tried to leave" (quoted in Cohen, *The French Encounter with Africans*, 179). Yet Rousseau never demanded that France retreat from its expeditions on the West African coast, where it had been active since the late seventeenth century, or from its possessions in the West Indies.

94  *"a screen onto which they projected"*: Cohen, *The French Encounter with Africans*, 33.

94  *"immoral impulses, the unmentionable desires"*: Fanon, *Peau noire, masques blancs*, 153.

94  *"For the majority of whites"*: Fanon, *Peau noire, masques blancs*, 143. In the original French, "whites" is capitalized.

94  *"You think like a European"*: Fanon, *Peau noire, masques blancs*, 52–66.

95  *the Marxist Martinican poet René Ménil*: See René Ménil, "The Situation of Poetry in the Caribbean," in *The Refusal of the Shadow: Surrealism and the Caribbean*, edited by Michael Richardson, trans. Michael Richardson and Krzysztof Fijalkowski (Verso, 1996), 127–33. Fanon appears to have located Ménil's observation not in *Tropiques* but rather in an essay by the ethnographer Michel Leiris.

96  *"ready to revolt"*: Cohen, *The French Encounter with Africans*, 57.

96  *"the Black Man was acted upon"*: Fanon, *Peau noire, masques blancs*, 175–80.

97  *"Woman . . . gives Life"*: Simone de Beauvoir, *The Second Sex*, translated and edited by H. M. Parshley (Vintage Books, September 1989), 64.

97  *"from time to time"*: Fanon, *Peau noire, masques blancs*, 179.

98  *"the Wolf, the Devil"*: Fanon, *Peau noire, masques blancs*, 119.

98  *"The Black man who enters France"*: Fanon, *Peau noire, masques blancs*, 18.

99  *"On the other side of the white world"*: Fanon, *Peau noire, masques blancs*, 98.

99  *"We will speak of black genius"*: Fanon, *Peau noire, masques blancs*, 151.

100 *"Every time a man has brought victory"*: Fanon, *Peau noire, masques blancs*, 183–84.

101 *"wish for a guilt complex"*: Fanon, *Peau noire, masques blancs*, 185–87. I have translated *pères* (fathers) in the phrase "l'Esclavage qui déhumanisa mes pères" as "ancestors."

102 *"good colonial conscience"*: For Chastaing's review, see *Esprit* (October 1952): 556–59; for Balandier's, see *L'Année sociologique* 4 (1951): 169–71.

102 *"Mr. Fanon is sick from being black"*: Quoted in Francis Jeanson's preface to the 1965 edition of *Peau noire, masques blancs*.

103 *"without ever taking into account"*: Quoted in David Macey, *Frantz Fanon: A Life* (Granta, 2000), 13.

103 *"The piece shocked and revolted us"*: Maryse Condé's account of her first encounter with Fanon's work, excerpted from her memoir *What Is Africa to Me? Fragments of a True-to-Life Autobiography*, can be read online at https://www.frieze.com/article/maryse-condes-first-encounter-frantz-fanons-black-skin-white-masks.

## 6. The Practice of Disalienation

104 *"the cynicism and rapaciousness"*: Joby Fanon, *Frantz Fanon, My Brother: Doctor, Playwright, Revolutionary*, trans. Daniel Nethery (Lexington Books, 2014), 69–70.

105 *"out of the question"*: Frantz Fanon, *Écrits sur l'aliénation et la liberté*, ed. Jean Khalfa and Robert J. C. Young (La Découverte, 2015), 233.

105 *"Many West Indians, after a fairly long stay"*: Frantz Fanon, *Peau noire, masques blancs* (Seuil, 1952), 15.

106 *a laboratory of radical psychiatry*: My account of Saint-Alban draws from Camille Robcis, *Disalienation: Politics, Philosophy, and Radical Psychiatry in Postwar France* (University of Chicago Press, 2021); Julian Bourg, *From Revolution to Ethics: May 1968 and Contemporary French Thought*, 2nd ed. (McGill-Queen's University Press, 2017); and Didier Daeninckx, *Caché dans la maison des fous* (Bruno Doucey, 2015).

108 *"in the mud"*: François Tosquelles, "Une Politique de la folie," *Chimères: Revue des schizo-analyses* 13 (1991): 66–81.

108 *"must be a foreigner"*: Tosquelles, "Une Politique de la folie," 67.

108 *"they are thus obliged to translate"*: Tosquelles, "Une Politique de la folie," 67.

110 *"When poetry was called to the Resistance"*: Robcis, *Disalienation*, 35.

110 *"Fanon came from Lyon"*: François Tosquelles, "Frantz Fanon à Saint Alban," *Sud/Nord* 1, no. 22 (2007): 9–14.

111 *"the radical difference between the color"*: François Tosquelles, "Frantz Fanon et la psycho-thérapie institutionnelle," *Sud/Nord* 1, no. 14 (2001): 167–74.

112 *the creativity that can arise from the quotidian*: Fanon, *Écrits sur l'aliénation et la liberté*, 234–37.

112 *a series of papers*: Fanon, *Écrits sur l'aliénation et la liberté*, 237–49.

113 *"If you want to go deeper"*: Frantz Fanon, *Alienation and Freedom*, edited and compiled by Jean Khalfa and Robert J. C. Young, trans. Steven Corcoran (Bloomsbury, 2018), 279.

113 *"My name must be unknown to you"*: Frantz Fanon to Richard Wright, January 6, 1953, Richard Wright papers, Beinecke Rare Book and Manuscript Library, Yale University.

## 7. A World Cut in Two

117 *"I still have a big debt"*: Joby Fanon, *Frantz Fanon, My Brother: Doctor, Playwright, Revolutionary*, trans. Daniel Nethery (Lexington Books, 2014), 73.

118 *"kingdom [built] on top of corpses"*: The controversy around Maran's novel is examined in Brent Hayes Edwards's study *The Practice of Diaspora: Literature, Translation, and the Rise of Black Internationalism* (Harvard University Press, 2003).

119 *"colonialism imposes itself"*: Frantz Fanon, *L'An V de la révolution algérienne* (1959; repr. La Découverte, 2011), 35.

120 *"foreigners with whom history"*: Mohammed Harbi, *Une Vie debout: Mémoires politiques* (La Découverte, 2001), 33.

120 *"The colonist always remains a foreigner"*: Frantz Fanon, *Les Damnés de la terre* (La Découverte, 2002), 43.

120 *"We have rendered Muslim society much more miserable"*: Quoted in Alistair Horne, *A Savage War of Peace: Algeria 1954–1962* (1978; repr. New York Review Books, 2006), 29.

121 *"returning from the expedition"*: Quoted in Karima Lazali, *Le Trauma colonial: Une enquête sur les effets psychiques et politiques contemporains de l'oppression colonial en Algérie* (La Découverte, 2018), 51.

121 *"The colonist is an exhibitionist"*: Fanon, *Les Damnés de la terre*, 55.

121 *confiscating all the fertile land*: As the historian Muriam Haleh Davis has argued, the French justified these confiscations on the grounds that the land belonged not to its original owners but to those who knew how to develop it ("la mettre en valeur") with superior techniques of exploitation. See Muriam Haleh Davis, *Markets of Civilization: Islam and Racial Capitalism in Algeria* (Duke University Press, 2022), 25–26.

122 *Only a few thousand became citizens*: The law granting former colonial subjects French citizenship was known as the "Lamine Guèye law," after the socialist politician Amadou Lamine-Guèye, who (along with his fellow deputy Léopold Sédar Senghor) represented Senegal in the National Assembly. See Laure Blévis, "La Citoyenneté française au miroir de la colonisation: Étude des demandes de naturalisation des 'sujets français' en Algérie coloniale," *Genèses* 53 (2004): 25–47.

122 *"was not the Warsaw Ghetto"*: Harbi, *Une Vie debout*, 67.

122 *exemplified by slurs such as* bougnoule, bicot: Because the etymological origins of these slurs are difficult to retrace, it is nearly impossible to provide univocal English translations: "bicot" is usually construed as an aphaeresis of "arbicot" (Arab); "bougnoule" is said to come from the Wolof "ñuul" (black).

122 *"second breaking of the umbilical cord"*: Quoted in Malika Rahal, *Ali Boumendjel: Une affaire française, une histoire algérienne* (La Découverte, 2022), 82.

124 *"I have given you peace"*: Horne, *A Savage War of Peace*, 28.

124 *"We heard very little"*: The reactions of Kateb Yacine, Ferhat Abbas, and Simone de Beauvoir to the Sétif massacre are quoted in Horne, *A Savage War of Peace*, 27–28. Kateb Yacine's classic novel, *Nedjma* (Seuil, 1956), was permeated by the trauma of his ordeal. He finished it in the early 1950s, but said, "[French publishers] kept telling me: 'But since you have such beautiful sheep in Algeria, why don't you write about them?'"

125 *"Arab boys as beautiful as bronze statues"*: Quoted in Horne, *A Savage War of Peace*, 46.

125 *"compartmentalized" world of colonialism*: Fanon, *Les Damnés de la terre*, 41.

125 *"we are here by the force of bayonets"*: Fanon, *Les Damnés de la terre*, 81. The colonial world offered a perfect illustration of Walter Benjamin's famous observation that "there is no document of civilization which is not at the same time a document of barbarism."

126 *"a primitive being"*: Antoine Porot and Jean Sutter, "Le 'Primitivisme' des indigènes nord-africains. Ses incidences en pathologie mentale," *Sud medical et chirurgical*, April 15, 1939.

126 *"on the psychophysiological level"*: Frantz Fanon, *Écrits sur l'aliénation et la liberté*, ed. Jean Khalfa and Robert J. C. Young (La Découverte, 2015), 344.

127 *"An unhappy patient comes to a doctor"*: John Berger, with the photographer Jean Mohr, *A Fortunate Man: The Story of a Country Doctor* (1967; repr. Vintage, 1997), 75.

128 *"Eating is not inferior to thinking"*: See Fanon's article in the March 17, 1955, issue of the staff newsletter *Notre journal*, in Fanon, *Écrits sur l'aliénation et la liberté*, 279.

128 *"a pretentious idiotic Martinican with a complex"*: Alice Cherki, *Frantz Fanon: A Portrait*, trans. Nadia Benabid (Cornell University Press, 2006), 74.

128 *"Not even the civil servant"*: Fanon, *L'An V de la révolution algérienne*, 122.

129 *"Here, you have the impression"*: Fanon, *Écrits sur l'aliénation et la liberté*, 295.

129 *"On a ship"*: Fanon, *Écrits sur l'aliénation et la liberté*, 263.

130 *"Writing is certainly the most beautiful discovery"*: Fanon, *Écrits sur l'aliénation et la liberté*, 263.

130 *"performs a dazzling feat"*: Fanon, *Écrits sur l'aliénation et la liberté*, 282–83.

130 *"adopt an attitude of punishment"*: Fanon, *Écrits sur l'aliénation et la liberté*, 262.

130 *"If care is not taken"*: Fanon, *Écrits sur l'aliénation et la liberté*, 291.

130 *"Future generations will wonder"*: Fanon, *Écrits sur l'aliénation et la liberté*, 266–67.

131 *relish the failure*: Fanon would have had the same experience in any colonized country. In her novel *The Grass Is Singing* (M. Joseph, 1950), set in British-ruled Southern Rhodesia, Doris Lessing writes: "When old settlers say 'One had to understand the country,' what they mean is, 'You have to get used to our ideas about the native.' They are saying, in effect, 'Learn our ideas, or otherwise get out: we don't want you.' Most of these young men were brought up with vague ideas about equality. They were shocked, for the first week or so, by the way the natives were treated. They were revolted a hundred times a day by the casual way they were spoken of, as if they were so many cattle; or by a blow, or a look. They had been prepared to treat them as human beings. But they could not stand out against the society they were joining. It did not take them long to change."

132 *"you can only understand with your guts"*: Cherki, *Frantz Fanon: A Portrait*, 71.

132 *In a joint paper*: Frantz Fanon and Jacques Azoulay, "La Socialthérapie dans un service d'hommes musulmans: Difficultés méthodologiques," in *Écrits sur l'aliénation et la liberté*, 297–314.

133 *"Why . . . make things abnormal"*: Fanon, *Écrits sur l'aliénation et la liberté*, 270–71.

133 *the French psychiatrist Albert Gambs*: For Gambs's letter and Fanon's response, see Fanon, *Écrits sur l'aliénation et la liberté*, 270–71.

134 *another intern*: Fanon also advised two younger Muslim colleagues, Dr. Ziza and Dr. Slimane Asselah, in their research on Algerian medicine.

134 *"the stranger is also the other"*: Fanon, *Écrits sur l'aliénation et la liberté*, 314–24.

134 *Fanon and his fellow psychiatrists visited communities*: The psychiatric papers discussed in this chapter are in the Fanon archives of the Institut Mémoires de l'édition contemporaine (hereafter IMEC), at the Ardenne Abbey in Normandy, France; they can also be read in Fanon, *Écrits sur l'aliénation et la liberté*.

135 *Algerian attitudes about mental illness*: See Fanon, "Attitude du musulman maghrébin devant la folie," in *Écrits sur l'aliénation et la liberté*, 356–60.

135 *including Germaine Tillion*: Tillion, who was imprisoned at Ravensbrück for her activities in the Resistance, would advise the French government during the Algerian Revolution, and become its liaison to FLN leaders in Algiers.

136 *"a closed society"*: Fanon, "Introduction aux troubles de la sexualité chez le Nord-Africain," in *Écrits sur l'aliénation et la liberté*, 325–32.

136 *"combats magical sorcery by a sort of counter-magic"*: Fanon, *Écrits sur l'aliénation et la liberté*, 330.

138 *"The accused Muslim's refusal"*: Fanon, *Écrits sur l'aliénation et la liberté*, 348.

139 *"L'Algérie montait à la tête"*: Quoted in Horne, *A Savage War of Peace*, 49.

## 8. The Algerian Explosion

140 *"the story that would change his destiny"*: Talk by Jean Aymé, given on September 28, 1999, in Martinique, in the Fanon archives at IMEC.

141 *Algerian war of independence*: Algerians refer to the war either as the "guerre de libération" (liberation war), or as the Algerian Revolution; French historians refer to it as the "guerre d'Algérie," the Algerian war. I use "Algerian war" when referring to the battle itself, "Algerian war of independence" when describing the Algerian struggle for liberation from French rule, and "Algerian Revolution" when evoking the political project of revolutionaries such as Fanon and his comrades.

141 *poorly armed fighters*: The rebels had only a few hundred firearms on All Saints' Day. Hence they often resorted to slitting the throats of French soldiers. The so-called Kabyle smile would become an effective psychological weapon, terrifying French soldiers who discovered their comrades with their throats slit (and often their genitals stuffed in their mouths), but the FLN was initially making a virtue of necessity.

141 *"a group of responsible young people"*: The FLN's original communiqué is reprinted in Martin Evans and John Phillips, *Algeria: Anger of the Dispossessed* (Yale University Press, 2007), 56–58.

142 *Algerians fighting alongside the French*: The *harkis*, who fought in mobile auxiliary units (*harka* means "mobile" in Arabic), were seldom ideological partisans of Algérie française. Most either had been forcibly conscripted into the French army or had sided with the French to protect their villages from FLN harassment or extortion. Whatever their motivations, tens of thousands would be executed as collaborators in the purges after independence; some were wrapped in French flags and burned alive before cheering crowds.

143 *they were patriots*: The FLN—and Fanon—would cast Algeria's elected officials as *béni-oui-oui* (yes men). But as the historian Malika Rahal argues, the Muslim deputies in the second college "refused to be made inferior in relationships that were marked by Orientalism and paternalist control" and worked to promote genuine reforms, often in the face of racist insults from European legislators. See Malika Rahal, *Ali Boumendjel: Une affaire française, une histoire algérienne* (La Découverte, 2022), 25.

143 *"We have been waiting 116 years"*: Quoted in Rahal, *Ali Boumendjel*, 25.

144 *left-wing European Catholics*: Fanon was always more at home among secular-minded people, but he was never a secularist—and one reason may be that he often found religious progressives to be more reliable allies of the struggles he supported.

144 *"a Church of the Whites"*: Frantz Fanon, *Les Damnés de la terre* (La Découverte, 2002), 45.

145 *"landed on another planet"*: See André Mandouze, *Mémoires d'outre-siècle: D'Une résistance à l'autre* (Editions de CERF, 1998).

145 *a lacerating critique of French rule*: André Mandouze, "Impossibilités algériennes ou le mythe des trois départements," *Esprit*, July 1947, 10–30.

145 *"Algerian conscience"*: André Mandouze, "Manifeste," in *Un chrétien dans son siècle: De Résistance en résistances*, ed. Olivier Aurenche and Martine Sevegrand (Karthala, 2007), 109–10. For more on Mandouze and Catholic anti-colonialism in Algeria, see Darcie Fontaine, *Decolonizing Christianity: Religion and the End of Empire in France and Algeria* (Cambridge University Press, 2016).

146 *"in the classical Greek sense"*: André Mandouze, speech at a 1982 celebration of Fanon's life held in Martinique, in the Fanon archives at IMEC.

147 *the institution of a future state*: By the end of the war in 1962, more than half of Algeria's medical professionals would end up working for the health services established by the FLN and the ALN. When the American ambassador William Porter visited one of the FLN's clinics in Algiers just before independence, he described it as "impeccable," even "cheerful." Quoted in Malika Rahal, *Algérie 1962: Une histoire populaire* (La Découverte, 2022), 182.

148 *"I'll say this despite how it might come off"*: Quoted in Adam Shatz, "An Interview with Alice Cherki," *Historical Reflections/Réflexions historiques* 28, no. 2 (2002): 293–300.

148 *"the sparkle in his eyes"*: Alice Cherki, *Frantz Fanon: A Portrait*, trans. Nadia Benabid (Cornell University Press, 2006), 3.

149 *"one of the few people"*: Quoted in Joby Fanon, *Frantz Fanon, My Brother: Doctor, Playwright, Revolutionary*, trans. Daniel Nethery (Lexington Books, 2014), 78–79.

149 *he wanted to be sure his son was born in France*: Joby Fanon, *Frantz Fanon, My Brother*, 80.

150 *launched a new uprising*: For an account of the events in Philippeville, see Alistair Horne, *A Savage War of Peace: Algeria 1954–1962* (1978; repr. New York Review Books, 2006), 118–22.

151 *"When you see hundreds of people"*: Quoted in Peter Batty's five-part documentary film, *The Algerian War: 1954–1962*, produced for the BBC in 1984.

151 *"physical suppression of the foreigner"*: Mohammed Harbi, *1954, la guerre commence en Algérie* (Éditions Complexe, 1998), 148–49. In Philippeville, Harbi observes, "impulsiveness ruled"—an "impulsiveness with deep roots" among the rural masses, for whom Islamic traditionalism had provided a shield against colonial oppression.

152 *"had never sounded hollower"*: Quoted in Horne, *A Savage War of Peace*, 125.

152 *"The Arab personality will be recognized"*: Quoted in Conor Cruise O'Brien, "Camus, Algeria, and 'The Fall,'" *New York Review of Books*, October 9, 1969.

152 *"a sweet sister speech"*: Annexe I in Fanon, *L'An V de la révolution algérienne* (La Découverte, 2011), 161.

153 *he had long believed*: Abbas's nationalist critics would never cease to remind him of the doubts that he had expressed, in 1936, about the existence of an Algerian nation: "Had I discovered the Algerian nation, I would be a nationalist . . . However, I will not die for the Algerian nation, because I know it does not exist . . . One cannot build on the wind." Quoted in Horne, *A Savage War of Peace*, 40.

153 *"The methods that I have upheld"*: Horne, *A Savage War of Peace*, 141.

153 *"Each day, El Mouhoub"*: Quoted in Karima Lazali, *Le Trauma colonial: Une enquête sur les effets psychiques et politiques contemporains de l'oppression colonial en Algérie* (La Découverte, 2018), 138.

154 *"We have not intertwined"*: Quoted in Jean Daniel, *La Blessure* (Grasset, 1992), 126.

154 *"Why is it that all of a sudden"*: Mouloud Feraoun, *Journal 1955–1962: Reflections on the French-Algerian War*, trans. Mary Ellen Wolf and Claude Fouillade (University of Nebraska Press, 2000), 42–43.

154 *"as welcome as any official decree"*: Feraoun, *Journal 1955–1962*, 45.

155 *"the point of no return"*: Fanon, *Les Damnés de la terre*, 86.

155 *"just under the skin"*: Fanon, *Les Damnés de la terre*, 70.

155 *"For the colonized"*: Fanon, *Les Damnés de la terre*, 89–90.

156 *"Racism, hatred, resentment"*: Fanon, *Les Damnés de la terre*, 133–40.

157 *"Gestapo tactics"*: Claude Bourdet, "Votre Gestapo d'Algérie," *L'Observateur*, January 13, 1955.

157 *two Algerian adolescent boys*: Fanon, *Les Damnés de la terre*, 259–61.

158 *"just which stage the interrogation has reached"*: Fanon, *Les Damnés de la terre*, 253–55.

158 *"mental disorders of colonial warfare"*: Fanon, "Guerre coloniale et troubles mentaux," in *Les Damnés de la terre*, 238–97.

159 *"the most hallucinatory war"*: Fanon, *L'An V de la révolution algérienne*, 5.

159 *Shaken by the traumas he observed*: It was not until 1992, three decades after the cease-fire, that the French state offered compensation to soldiers suffering from psychological issues related to the war.

159 *"Every passing hour is an indication"*: David Macey, *Frantz Fanon: A Life* (Granta, 2000), 272.

160 *her husband was plotting an attack*: This incident is recounted in André Mandouze's autobiography, *Mémoires d'outre-siècle: D'une résistance à l'autre* (Vivian Hamy, 1998), as well as in an unpublished paper by Fanon's colleague Charles Geronimi, "Fanon à Blida."

161   *He had joined the party*: Romuald Fonkoua, *Aimé Césaire* (Perrin, 2010), 227.

162   *"The apparition of racism"*: The quotes in this and the following four paragraphs are from Frantz Fanon, "Racisme et culture," in *Pour la révolution africaine: Écrits politiques* (1964; repr. La Découverte, 2006), 37–52.

164   *"behaved differently than those who dominated Africans"*: Fanon, *Les Damnés de la terre*, 205.

165   *executed under Krim's orders*: Mohammed Harbi, *Une Vie debout: Mémoires politiques* (La Découverte, 2001), 262.

168   *"One corpse in a jacket"*: Horne, *A Savage War of Peace*, 132.

169   *"There are more and more"*: Feraoun, *Journal 1955–1962*, 138.

169   *"girl who places a bomb in the Milk Bar"*: Horne, *A Savage War of Peace*, 186.

170   *"Carrying revolvers, grenades"*: Fanon, *L'An V de la révolution algérienne*, 40.

170   *"When you told me"*: See Frantz Fanon, "Lettre à un français," in *Pour la révolution africaine*, 55–58.

172   *"For nearly three years"*: Frantz Fanon, "Lettre au minister résident," in *Écrits sur l'aliénation et la liberté*, ed. Jean Khalfa and Robert J. C. Young (La Découverte, 2015), 367–68.

## 9. Vertigo in Tunis

177   *"since they and I continued to be"*: Gabriel García Márquez, "From Paris, with Love," in *The Scandal of the Century and Other Writings*, ed. Cristóbal Pera, trans. Anne McLean (Knopf, 2019), 279–80.

179   *the permanent moral corrosion of the Republic*: Until his death in 2006, Vidal-Naquet led the campaign for recognition by the Republic of France's responsibility for the murder and disappearance of the Communist mathematician Maurice Audin, who was arrested in June 1957 and never seen again. In 2018, President Emmanuel Macron admitted that Audin had been tortured and executed by the army.

179   *a liberal philosopher of conservative temperament*: According to Alice Cherki, Fanon described Aron, whom he met in Tunis, as "an intelligent and erudite man who doesn't want to know anything about alienation, not even his own."

180   *"technical knowledge, ingenuity"*: Sarah Kaminsky, *Adolfo Kaminsky, Une vie de faussaire* (Calmann-Lévy, 2009), 250. According to Kaminsky, it was in large part thanks to the *porteurs des valises*, and especially to Francis Jeanson's pleading, that the FLN's Fédération de France confined its attacks inside France to military, police, and industrial targets.

181   *"So, my brothers, how could we fail"*: Frantz Fanon, *Les Damnés de la terre* (1961; repr. La Découverte, 2002), 302–303.

182   *La Santé prison in Paris*: Hocine Aït-Ahmed, one of the prisoners at La Santé, would remark years later that the hijacking had inadvertently saved the FLN from a "terrible crisis," since the Cairo-based Ben Bella had been at odds with the leadership inside Algeria.

183   *"We resembled each other physically"*: Yousfi's remembrance of Fanon is in the Fanon archives at IMEC.

185   *"The Taïebs were older than we were"*: Marie-Jeanne Manuellan, correspondence with the author, 2018.

186   *"Even the most liberal"*: Fanon, *Les Damnés de la terre*, 75.

186   *"His formulations were original"*: Guy Sitbon, conversation with the author, Paris, summer 2019. Fanon and Sitbon briefly shared a mistress, a young North African Jewish doctor. "One day," Sitbon recalls, "we were making love when Fanon arrived at her apartment. She closed the door and walked out. I waited for a half an hour, hiding in the bedroom."

187   *a documentary he had been making*: René Vautier's 1958 film, *Algérie en flammes*, a twenty-minute documentary shot in the Aurès Mountains, was the first to depict the national liberation war from the FLN's perspective. It provoked such outrage, even before its release, that Vautier was forced to go underground for two years. The film was not screened in France until 1968, during the student uprising.

188 *"pompously idiotic style of a certain regional weekly"*: Mouloud Feraoun, *Journal 1955–1962: Reflections on the French-Algerian War*, trans. Mary Ellen Wolf and Claude Fouillade (University of Nebraska Press, 2000), 169.

188 *"The Frenchman in Algeria"*: See Frantz Fanon, "Les Intellectuels et les démocrates français devant la révolution algérienne," in *Pour la révolution africaine: Écrits politiques* (1964; repr. La Découverte, 2006), 83–98.

189 *"Injustice, injury, humiliation and insecurity"*: Quoted in Adam Shatz, "On Albert Memmi," *London Review of Books* 42, no. 16 (August 13, 2020), https://www.lrb.co.uk/the-paper/v42/n16/adam-shatz/on-albert-memmi.

189 *"the couple is not an isolated cell"*: Albert Memmi, *The Colonizer and the Colonized*, trans. Howard Greenfield (1957; repr. Souvenir, 2016), 3.

189 *"participates in and benefits from those privileges"*: Memmi, *The Colonizer and the Colonized*, 64.

190 *his account of leftists*: Memmi, *The Colonizer and the Colonized*, 77–88.

190 *"temporarily forget that he is a leftist"*: Memmi, *The Colonizer and the Colonized*, 81.

190 *"it was possible to be born poor"*: Albert Memmi, *La statue de sel* (Gallimard, 1966), 137.

190 *"I wanted to reject with all my indignation"*: Memmi, *La Statue de sel*, 301.

191 *"As a Tunisian Jew of French culture"*: Albert Memmi, *Tunisie, An I*, ed. Guy Dugas (CNRS, 2017), 148.

191 *"Fanon had a very strong need to belong"*: Mohammed Harbi, conversation with the author, Paris, 2017.

192 *"diplomatic revolution"*: See Matthew Connelly, *A Diplomatic Revolution: Algeria's Fight for Independence and the Origins of the Post-Cold War Era* (Oxford University Press, 2003).

192 *"the myth of French empire"*: John F. Kennedy, "Remarks of John F. Kennedy in the Senate, Washington, D.C., July 2, 1957," https://www.jfklibrary.org/archives/other-resources/john-f-kennedy-speeches/united-states-senate-imperialism-19570702.

193 *"The colonizer and the colonized are old acquaintances"*: Fanon, *Les Damnés de la terre*, 40.

193 *"For the people, only fellow nationals"*: Fanon, *Les Damnés de la terre*, 52.

194 *One of Fanon's acquaintances*: Mohammed Ben Smaïl became known as *le journaliste fellagha* because of his pro-FLN sympathies. I am grateful to his grandson, the historian Youssef Ben Ismail, for pointing me to Ben Smaïl's reporting on Melouza.

195 *"Gentlemen of the FLN"*: Feraoun, *Journal 1955–1962*, 223.

195 *"The French ministers Lacoste and Soustelle"*: Fanon, *L'An V de la révolution algérienne* (1959; repr. La Découverte, 2011), 6.

196 *more than two million villagers*: The existence of the resettlement camps was first revealed in 1959 in a scathing report, soon leaked to the press, by the socialist politician Michel Rocard, then a twenty-eight-year-old inspector of finances in French Algeria.

196 *In their letters home*: See Raphaëlle Branche, *Papa, qu'as-tu fait en Algérie? Enquête sur un silence familial* (La Découverte, 2020), and my essay on Branche's book: Adam Shatz, "Dynamo Current, Feet, Fists, Salt," *London Review of Books* 43, no. 4 (February 18, 2021).

196 *threaten its unity*: Reflecting on the Melouza massacre in his memoirs, Mohammed Harbi writes, in *Une Vie debout: Mémoires politiques* (La Découverte, 2001), of having "found myself in an organization . . . where authoritarianism inculcated in everyone the idea that evil could be converted into good if it were done in the name of the revolution." Yet, like Fanon, Harbi remained in the FLN throughout the war.

196 *Born Lucien Douchet in 1922*: For an account of Serge Michel's life, see Émile Carme, "Serge Michel—amour, anarchie, Algérie," *Ballast*, February 8, 2015, https://www.revue-ballast.fr/serge-michel/.

197 *"Don't trust anyone"*: Serge Michel, *Nour le voilé: De la casbah au Congo, du Congo au desert: La Révolution* (Seuil, 1982), 121.

198 *"Oriental despots in the making"*: Alice Cherki, *Frantz Fanon: A Portrait*, trans. Nadia Benabid (Cornell University Press, 2006), 101–102. (I have slightly adjusted the translation.)

200 *who never spoke of what they had done*: The psychoanalyst Karima Lazali has attributed the FLN's rejection of charismatic leadership to colonialism's aggression against indigenous paternal authority. Because their fathers had been humiliated (and in some cases killed) by the French state, the men who formed the FLN constituted themselves as a band of brothers and saw anyone who claimed the mantle of authority as an illegitimate father who had to be eliminated so that they could hold on to power themselves and "the place of the father" would remain empty.

## 10. Disalienating Psychiatry

202 *"lively and brilliant eyes"*: The quotes in this and the following two paragraphs are from Michel Martini, *Chroniques des années algériennes 1946–1962* (Editions Bouchène, 2002), 368–75.

202 *"run down and less well ventilated"*: Joby Fanon, *Frantz Fanon, My Brother: Doctor, Playwright, Revolutionary*, trans. Daniel Nethery (Lexington Books, 2014), 95–96.

204 *"We do not believe in the curative value"*: The quotes in this and the next paragraph are from Frantz Fanon, "L'Hospitalisation de jour en psychiatrie, valeur et limites," in *Écrits sur l'aliénation et la liberté*, ed. Jean Khalfa and Robert J. C. Young (La Découverte, 2015), 397–416.

204 *"classical hospitalization"*: Fanon's critique bore a notable resemblance to Erving Goffman's 1961 study *Asylums: Essays on the Social Situation of Mental Patients and Other Inmates* (Anchor, 1961), as well as Michel Foucault's *Naissance de la Clinique: Une archéologie du regard medical* (Presses universitaires de France, 1963).

205 *he gave the impression of a mind on fire*: See Lilia Ben Salem's notes in Fanon, *Écrits sur l'aliénation et la liberté*, 430–46.

205 *"the aggressiveness of the Black man"*: Fanon, *Écrits sur l'aliénation et la liberté*, 441.

206 *"whose energy has not yet been claimed"*: Fanon, *Écrits sur l'aliénation et la liberté*, 445.

206 *small but passionate literature of denunciation*: See Gwen Bergner, "Who Is That Masked Woman? Or, the Role of Gender in Fanon's *Black Skin, White Masks*," *PMLA* 110, no. 1 (January 1995): 75–88.

207 *a markedly less normative direction*: See Alice Cherki, *Frantz Fanon: A Portrait*, trans. Nadia Benabid (Cornell University Press, 2006), 121.

207 *"His personality fascinated us"*: Quoted in Fanon, *Écrits sur l'aliénation et la liberté*, 435.

207 *"We were enormously impressed"*: See "'When I Was a Student of Fanon': An Interview with Frej Stambouli," in *Review of African Political Economy*, June 2, 2021, https://roape.net/2021/06/02/when-i-was-a-student-of-fanon-an-interview-with-frej-stambouli/.

207 *One ALN soldier*: This story was told to me by Dridi's daughter, the journalist Daikha Dridi.

208 *"Few Algerians would have dared"*: From Youcef Yousfi's remembrance of Fanon in the Fanon papers at IMEC.

209 *whom he revered as "warrior-philosophers"*: Claude Lanzmann, *The Patagonian Hare: A Memoir*, trans. Frank Wynne (Atlantic Books, 2009), 341.

211 *"Colonial War and Mental Disorders"*: The quotes in this and the next few paragraphs are from Frantz Fanon, "Guerre coloniale et troubles mentaux," in *Les Damnés de la terre*, 239–97. Fanon's analysis of trauma resulting from the Algerian War was also prescient. At the time, French doctors dismissed accounts of psychological distress among veterans of the Algerian War by claiming that a damaged patient was "talkative, boastful and happy with himself and his uncontrollable stories." Not until 1992 would veterans be entitled to compensation for war-induced trauma. According to an article in *Le Monde* published in 2000, as many as 350,000 veterans suffered from PTSD. See Raphaëlle Branche, *Papa, qu'as-tu fait en Algérie? Enquête sur un silence familial* (La Découverte, 2020).

## 11. Fanon's "Tape Recorder"

214 *vilified him as a misogynist*: The feminist writer Susan Brownmiller denounced Fanon as a rape-obsessed "man who hated women," as if she had confused him with the Black Panther Party

leader Eldridge Cleaver, who boasted of raping white women as a form of political resistance. See Brownmiller, *Against Our Will: Men, Women, and Rape* (Simon & Schuster, 1975), 250.

214 *"He was a terrorist"*: Marie-Jeanne Manuellan, conversations with author, 2017–2019.

215 *"We had lost Communism"*: All of the quotes from here to page 217 are from Marie-Jeanne Manuellan, *Sous la dictée de Fanon* (L'Amourier, 2017).

217 *"As soon as I'm finished"*: Manuellan, *Sous la dictée de Fanon*, 126.

217 *While treating a young Algerian woman*: Manuellan, *Sous la dictée de Fanon*, 93.

218 *"If I understand correctly"*: Manuellan, *Sous la dictée de Fanon*, 96.

219 *"Fanon worked like the first Viennese psychoanalysts"*: Manuellan, *Sous la dictée de Fanon*, 123.

219 *an incident that troubled her*: Manuellan, *Sous la dictée de Fanon*, 132–33.

220 *a short documentary about the CNPJ*: I watched the only surviving copy of this documentary at IMEC.

220 *the detail that "pricks me"*: Roland Barthes, *Camera Lucida: Reflections on Photography*, trans. Richard Howard (Farrar, Straus and Giroux, 1981), 27.

220 *"If it's too much for you"*: Manuellan, *Sous la dictée de Fanon*, 67.

221 *She felt humiliated*: Manuellan, *Sous la dictée de Fanon*, 76.

221 *"I'm going to need you"*: Manuellan, *Sous la dictée de Fanon*, 111.

221 *"the ceremony of the book"*: Manuellan, *Sous la dictée de Fanon*, 114–15.

223 *as the historian Neil MacMaster has shown*: Neil MacMaster, *Burning the Veil: The Algerian War and the "Emancipation" of Algerian Women, 1954–62* (Manchester University Press, 2010).

223 *"converting the woman"*: Frantz Fanon, *L'An V de la révolution algérienne* (1959; repr. La Découverte, 2011), 21.

223 *"In the face of the Algerian intellectual"*: Fanon, *L'An V de la révolution algérienne*, 23.

224 *"test-women, with their bare faces"*: Fanon, *L'An V de la révolution algérienne*, 24.

224 *"Every veil that fell"*: Fanon, *L'An V de la révolution algérienne*, 25–28.

224 *visible to the male European gaze*: The steely resolve of Algerian women not to be seen by French soldiers was memorably documented by Marc Garanger, a young conscript who took identity card photos in resettlement camps in 1960. Forced to remove their veils for Garanger, they stared back in defiance at (in his words) "the first witness to their silent and smoldering protest."

225 *"a new life to this dead element"*: Fanon, *L'An V de la révolution algérienne*, 29.

225 *"It is the white man"*: Fanon, *L'An V de la révolution algérienne*, 29.

226 *"withdrawal into oneself"*: Frantz Fanon, "Lettre à Ali Shariati," in *Écrits sur l'aliénation et la liberté*, ed. Jean Khalfa and Robert J. C. Young (La Découverte, 2015), 543–44.

226 *"birth of a new woman"*: Fanon, *L'An V de la révolution algérienne*, 94.

226 *"Each time she ventures"*: Fanon, *L'An V de la révolution algérienne*, 34–35.

227 *"The absence of the veil"*: Fanon, *L'An V de la révolution algérienne*, 41.

227 *"there is no character to imitate"*: Fanon, *L'An V de la révolution algérienne*, 32.

228 *"the only means of entering"*: Fanon, *L'An V de la révolution algérienne*, 67–68, 73.

228 *"integral part of colonization"*: Fanon, *L'An V de la révolution algérienne*, 123.

229 *"all the things that seemed to be part"*: Fanon, *L'An V de la révolution algérienne*, 132.

229 *"knocked over and challenged"*: Fanon, *L'An V de la révolution algérienne*, 93.

229 *"The united militant couple"*: Fanon, *L'An V de la révolution algérienne*, 98.

230 *"[It] contained for me an exact analysis"*: Safia Bazi's recollections are in the Fanon papers at IMEC.

230 *persisted in the strongly patriarchal idea*: See MacMaster, *Burning the Veil*.

230 *"Perhaps a new world"*: Mouloud Feraoun, *Journal 1955–1962: Reflections on the French-Algerian War*, trans. Mary Ellen Wolf and Claude Fouillade (University of Nebraska Press, 2000), 242.

230 *"save brown women from brown men"*: See Gayatri Chakravorty Spivak's essay "Can the Subaltern Speak?" in *Marxism and the Interpretation of Culture*, eds. Cary Nelson and Lawrence Grossberg (Macmillan, 1988).

231  *"eyes and ears of the Revolution"*: Fanon, *L'An V de la révolution algérienne*, 145.

232  *"multiracial reality of the Algerian Nation"*: Fanon, *L'An V de la révolution algérienne*, 146.

232  *the "earthquake" of his childhood*: Jacques Derrida would later speak of his "African" roots and pay homage to Fanon in a 1981 lecture on "geopsychoanalysis." But during the war he opposed independence and deplored the violence of the FLN, in much the same manner as Camus. "Any attempt to justify or condemn either group is not just obscene, just a way of quietening one's conscience, but also abstract, 'empty,'" he wrote to a friend who, while serving in the army, had witnessed the torture of an Arab teenager. See Edward Baring, "Liberalism and the Algerian War: The Case of Jacques Derrida," *Critical Inquiry* 36, no. 2 (Winter 2010): 239–61.

232  *the solidarity of their Muslim neighbors*: The abrogation of the Crémieux Decree in 1940 also led Muslim leaders like Ferhat Abbas to the conclusion that Algeria's "natives" should create their own country, instead of advocating integration: after all, if Jewish citizenship could be revoked by the French at a stroke, so could Muslim citizenship.

233  *"open to all"*: Fanon, *L'An V de la révolution algérienne*, 14.

233  *"two decisive sinister legacies"*: "'When I Was a Student of Fanon': An Interview with Frej Stambouli," in *Review of African Political Economy*, June 2, 2021, https://roape.net/2021/06 /02/when-i-was-a-student-of-fanon-an-interview-with-frej-stambouli/.

234  *"Your book has represented"*: Letter from François Maspero to Fanon, September 24, 1960, repr. in Fanon, *Écrits sur l'aliénation et la liberté*, 559.

234  *He later admitted his error*: Albert Memmi, *Les Hypothèses infinies: Journal 1936–1962*, ed. Guy Dugas (CNRS, 2021), 1,228. In a November 23, 1959, entry, Memmi writes that he was initially "a little irritated" that Fanon had borrowed "a certain number" of his arguments in *The Colonizer and the Colonized* without crediting him. Then, passing by the offices of Seuil, he saw a copy of *Black Skin, White Masks* and realized that it had been published five years before his own book. Ashamed of his irritation, he wondered if he had unconsciously lifted some of Fanon's ideas.

234  *"Who told you I was going to have a preface"*: Manuellan, *Sous la dictée de Fanon*, 119.

234  *brought them closer*: Manuellan, *Sous la dictée de Fanon*, 140–44.

236  *"The* nègres *invented nothing"*: Manuellan, *Sous la dictée de Fanon*, 39.

237  *"This Manuellan is sapping my morale!"*: Manuellan, *Sous la dictée de Fanon*, 148.

237  *Alain Resnais's new film*: Manuellan, *Sous la dictée de Fanon*, 153–57.

237  *"dangerous paranoids"*: Manuellan, *Sous la dictée de Fanon*, 155.

238  *Josie seems to have taken a lover*: Claude Lanzmann makes this claim in his memoir *The Patagonian Hare: A Memoir*, trans. Frank Wynne (Atlantic Books, 2012).

238  *"We were all as serious as he was"*: Manuellan, *Sous la dictée de Fanon*, 155–56.

238  *Abdelhafid Boussouf's spies*: Mohammed Harbi, in *Une Vie debout: Mémoires politiques* (La Découverte, 2001), reports being followed by Boussouf's intelligence services when he worked for the GPRA in Tunis.

## 12. Black Algeria

240  *"Each generation must discover its mission"*: Frantz Fanon, *Les Damnés de la terre* (1961; repr. La Découverte, 2002), 197.

240  *"an African victory"*: Frantz Fanon, *Écrits sur l'aliénation et la liberté*, ed. Jean Khalfa and Robert J. C. Young (La Découverte, 2015), 527.

241  *"gift for suggestive obscurity"*: Julian Jackson, *A Certain Idea of France: The Life of Charles de Gaulle* (Penguin, 2018), 490.

241  *"recognized and overcome"*: Frederick Cooper, *Citizenship Between Empire and Nation: Remaking France and French Africa, 1945–1960* (Princeton University Press, 2014), 36. I am greatly indebted to Cooper's subtle and revelatory account of the debate over decolonization and citizenship in French West Africa.

241  *"vertical solidarity"*: Cooper, *Citizenship Between Empire and Nation*, 203.

242  *"interdependence with France"*: Cooper, *Citizenship Between Empire and Nation*, 285.

242  *"an inclusive appeal at one level"*: Cooper, *Citizenship Between Empire and Nation*, 308.

243  *"prefer freedom in poverty"*: See Cooper's intricate reconstruction of Sékou Touré's speech during de Gaulle's visit in *Citizenship Between Empire and Nation*, 314–17.

244  *"bloody folly of a tyrannical power"*: Mohammed Harbi, *Une Vie debout: Mémoires politiques* (La Découverte, 2001), 341–42.

244  *"give impetus to oppressed peoples"*: Quoted in Susan Williams, *White Malice: The CIA and the Covert Neocolonisation of Africa* (Hurst, 2021), 13.

245  *"appeared almost to break down"*: Peter Worsley, "Frantz Fanon: Evolution of a Revolutionary," *Monthly Review* 21, no. 1, May 1969.

246  *"What does the destruction"*: Serge Michel, *Nour le voilé: De la casbah au Congo, du Congo au desert: La Révolution* (Seuil, 1982), 139–41, 150–52.

247  *Fanon reported with satisfaction*: Fanon, "Accra l'Algérie à Accra," *El Moudjahid*, December 24, 1958, repr. in Frantz Fanon, *Pour la révolution africaine: Écrits politiques* (1964; repr. La Découverte, 2006), 168–70.

247  *Félix-Roland Moumié*: Moumié was a leader of the Union of the Populations of Cameroon (UPC); in 1959, the UPC would be rebaptized the Armée de libération nationale du Kamerun (ALNK).

247  *"Reading their writings and deciphering their lives"*: Jean-Paul Sartre, "The Political Thought of Patrice Lumumba," in *Colonialism and Neocolonialism*, trans. Azzedine Haddour, Steve Brewer, and Terry McWilliams (1964; repr. Routledge, 2006).

248  *"exaggerated confidence in the people"*: Fanon, *Pour la révolution africaine*, 214.

248  *a pastor from northern Angola*: For an account of Holden Roberto's background, see Williams, *White Malice*, 49.

249  *He had recently learned*: Herbert Weiss, conversation with the author, 2019.

251  *"The epic, with its standardized forms, reemerged"*: Fanon, *Les Damnés de la terre*, 229.

251  *"it has become the people's daily fare"*: There are echoes here of Walter Benjamin's classic essay on the storyteller, in which he describes the vanished tradition of storytelling as an "artisan form of communication" promoting "instruction" and "epic remembrance," and connecting listeners to past generations. But Fanon is not speaking in an elegiac mode here, and his argument about the transformation of storytelling in revolution is more reminiscent of "The Author as Producer," a text Benjamin delivered as a speech in Paris in 1934. A revolutionary writer's "mission," Benjamin argued, "is not to report, but to struggle; he does not play the role of spectator, but actively intervenes." Like Benjamin, Fanon argued that artists were duty bound to participate directly in the struggle, and to create their work in a dialectical exchange with their audiences.

251  *he was less interested in tradition and memory*: Fanon has been criticized for his modernist bias, notably by the decolonial scholar Françoise Vergès, who has argued that Fanon belittles "memories" as "shackles to progress and momentum" and offers little more than "militarised virility." But if Fanon had been so dismissive of memory as a foundation of national culture, he might well have avoided the example of the storyteller. See Vergès, "Chains of Madness, Chains of Colonialism: Fanon and Freedom," in *The Fact of Blackness: Frantz Fanon and Visual Representation*, ed. Alan Read (Bay Press, 1996), 46–75.

252  *"The festival of the imagination"*: Achille Mbembe, *Necropolitics*, trans. Steve Corcoran (Duke University Press, 2019), 141.

252  *"jugs, jars, and trays are reshaped"*: Fanon, *Les Damnés de la terre*, 231.

254  *"You have chosen the right struggle"*: Quoted in Joby Fanon, *Frantz Fanon, My Brother: Doctor, Playwright, Revolutionary*, trans. Daniel Nethery (Lexington Books, 2014), 90.

254  *The person entrusted with recruiting*: António Tomás, *Amílcar Cabral: The Life of a Reluctant Nationalist* (Oxford University Press, 2021), 109.

255  *Shortly before leaving Rome*: According to the scholar Wilbert J. Roget, Glissant and his friend Albert Béville, a writer who published under the pen name Paul Niger, had a separate meeting in Rome with Fanon and Césaire at which they discussed the creation of a West

Indian political organization that would campaign for the autonomy of the French Caribbean, but this seems unlikely, given the differences between Fanon and Césaire over Martinique's political status. See Roget, "Édouard Glissant and Antillanité" (PhD diss., University of Pittsburgh, 1975).

255  *"his expression on the lookout"*: Assia Djebar, *Le Blanc de l'Algérie* (Albin Michel, 1995), 113.

257  *"in flagrant contradiction with reality"*: Harbi, *Une Vie debout*, 29.

257  *"false and dangerous"*: See the discussion of Bourdieu's views on Fanon in Michael Buroway, *Symbolic Violence: Conversations with Bourdieu* (Duke University Press, 2019), 76–93.

258  *"Why subject yourself to a tradition"*: Albert Camus, *The First Man* (Penguin Classics, 1996), 250.

258  *"What did you expect?"*: Michel, *Nour le voilé*, 131–33.

259  *"adoption of Fanon's theses"*: This and the other quotes in this paragraph are from Harbi, *Une Vie debout*, 297–98.

260  *"a necessary but far from sufficient condition"*: Edward Said, *Reflections on Exile and Other Essays* (Harvard University Press, 2000), 449.

260  *"atavistic certainties that didn't exist"*: Patrick Chamoiseau, *Écrire en pays dominé* (Gallimard, 1997), 249.

261  *an inquisitive and probing literary journalism*: See my essay on this topic: Adam Shatz, "Outcasts and Desperadoes: Richard Wright's Double Vision," *London Review of Books* 43, no. 19 (October 7, 2021).

262  *"suffers from the same shortcomings"*: See Frantz Fanon, "Écoute homme blanc! de Richard Wright," in *Écrits sur l'aliénation et la liberté*, 524–27.

264  *"I have always denounced terrorism"*: "Albert Camus face à la question algérienne, par Christiane Chaulet Achour," *Histoire coloniale et postcoloniale*, August 28, 2013, https://histoirecoloniale.net/Albert-Camus-face-a-la-question.html.

264  *"I had to break with my mother"*: Jean Amrouche, letter to J. Falcou-Rivoire, repr. *Expressions Maghrébines* 9, no. 1 (Summer 2010): 165–69.

265  *"We spent two hours just talking"*: Mouloud Feraoun, *Journal 1955–1962: Reflections on the French-Algerian War*, trans. Mary Ellen Wolf and Claude Fouillade (University of Nebraska Press, 2000), 244.

265  *"It is myself"*: Albert Camus, *Carnets III: Mars 1951–Décembre 1959* (Gallimard, 1989), 301.

266  *it could not even be read in his lifetime*: Camus died before *Le Premier homme* was finished to his satisfaction, and it wasn't published until 1994. Catherine Camus, his daughter, transcribed the handwritten manuscript, which was discovered in the mud at the site of his car crash.

266  *"Return the land"*: Albert Camus, *The First Man*, 255.

## 13. Phantom Africa

269  *Fanon had been campaigning for the job*: Fanon also told Martini that after independence he planned to make Geronimi the head of the center for psychiatry in Oran, as if he had the power to distribute posts—surely a case of "Fanonian delirium," Martini thought, wondering if Fanon might appoint him rector of Oran's university.

270  *"everything was sexy"*: Guy Sitbon, conversation with the author, Paris, 2019.

270  *she wrote to Manuellan*: Marie-Jeanne Manuellan, *Sous la dictée de Fanon* (L'Amourier, 2017), 161.

271  *"As the parade was breaking up"*: Elaine Mokhtefi, *Algiers, Third World Capital: Freedom Fighters, Revolutionaries, Black Panthers* (Verso, 2018), 6.

271  *"His first thought was that I was French"*: Mokhtefi, *Algiers, Third World Capital*, 39.

273  *"greatest Black man who ever walked the African continent"*: Malcolm X made this statement about Patrice Lumumba on June 28, 1964, at a rally of the Organization of Afro-American Unity, at the Audubon Ballroom.

275  *personally close to Lumumba*: The feelings were mutual. When a journalist asked Lumumba about his white press attaché, he replied, "That guy? He has a black heart. He's an African."

275 *"even Frantz and Omar preached realism"*: Serge Michel, *Nour le voilé: De la casbah au Congo, du Congo au desert: La Révolution* (Seuil, 1982), 213–14. Like many memoirs in France, *Nour le voilé* was published as a *roman* (novel), in large part because of its style and voice. Michel, like Norman Mailer, writes about himself in the third person and refers to his character as "Troisième-College" (Third College), an allusion to the double electoral college that divided native Algerians and Europeans in France's National Assembly, and an indication of his position as an outside observer. Nonetheless, *Nour le voilé* is a work of nonfiction.

275 *Herbert Weiss, a young specialist*: My account of Herbert Weiss's encounters with Fanon is based on extensive conversations with Weiss, by phone and over email, from 2019 to 2022.

277 *his research in the lower Congo*: Weiss published his findings in the monograph *Political Protest in Congo: The Parti Solidaire Africain During the Independence Struggle* (Princeton University Press, 1967).

277 *"The nationalist militant who decides"*: Frantz Fanon, *Les Damnés de la terre* (1961; repr. La Découverte, 2002), 123.

278 *Dag Hammarskjöld*: On September 18, 1961, Hammarskjöld was killed in an airplane crash while en route to negotiate a cease-fire between UN troops and Moïse Tshombe's secessionist forces in Katanga. The causes of the crash have never been solved.

279 *"the enemies of Africa"*: The quotes in this and the next paragraph are from Michel, *Nour le voilé*, 239.

280 *"determined, soft-spoken, exiled African Angolan"*: Susan Williams, *White Malice: The CIA and the Covert Neocolonisation of Africa* (Hurst, 2021), 457.

## 14. "Create the Continent"

281 *differences in custom were another*: According to Mohammed Harbi, who later represented the GPRA in Guinea, a further obstacle to Afro-Arab unity at the time was the question of Israel-Palestine. Many of the African leaders he met "tended to think that the fate of Jews was identical to that of Black people," while for Arabs the recovery of Arab Palestine was "primordial."

281 *"Are these decent women?"*: Simone de Beauvoir, *La Force des choses* (Gallimard, 1963), 2:423.

281 *"a citizen of Black Africa"*: Frantz Fanon, *Les Damnés de la terre* (1961; repr. La Découverte, 2002), 157.

282 *"reviving old particularisms"*: Frantz Fanon, *Pour la révolution africaine: Écrits politiques* (1964; repr. La Découverte, 2006), 197.

282 *"An abstract death"*: Fanon, *Pour la révolution africaine*, 200.

283 *"Stir up the Saharan population"*: The quotes in this and the following two paragraphs are from the travel diary "Cette Afrique à venir," in Fanon, *Pour la révolution africaine*, 197–21.

284 *an experiment in pan-African governance*: The Mali Federation, which linked the French colonies of Senegal and French Sudan (Mali) under the auspices of the French Community, was founded on June 20, 1960, but tensions immediately erupted between the Sudanese, who advocated a more centralized government with a strong executive, and the Senegalese, who feared that Sudan, with nearly twice the population, would dominate the state. Léopold Sédar Senghor also promoted a closer relationship with France, which led Modibo Keïta to accuse him of trying to "colonize" Senegal and "return Mali to France."

285 *"If one listens with one ear"*: Fanon, *Pour la révolution africaine*, 199.

285 *"People used to speak admiringly"*: Fanon, *Pour la révolution africaine*, 205.

286 *"I relive"*: Fanon, *Pour la révolution africaine*, 206.

286 *"anything else to do on this earth"*: Fanon, *Peau noire, masques blancs* (Seuil, 1952), 185.

286 *"liberation is indeed a condition of freedom"*: Hannah Arendt, "The Freedom to Be Free," *New England Review* 38, no. 2 (2017): 60.

286 *"Not everything is so simple"*: Fanon, *Pour la révolution africaine*, 206.

289 *If proof was needed*: A similar reversal in the power dynamics of interior and exterior would take place in the Palestinian national movement in the late 1980s, when the exiled leadership of the PLO—headquartered in Tunis, like the FLN—was rescued by the First Intifada, as

Palestinians in the West Bank and the Gaza Strip launched a popular revolt, characterized by strikes, stone-throwing at Israeli soldiers, and other acts of civil disobedience.

289 *"the most execrable instrument"*: Frantz Fanon, *Écrits sur l'aliénation et la liberté*, ed. Jean Khalfa and Robert J. C. Young (La Découverte, 2015), 506.

290 *"The irony here"*: Julian Jackson, *A Certain Idea of France: The Life of Charles de Gaulle* (Allen Lane, 2018), 511.

290 *"There is no place for an Algeria shorn"*: Fanon, *Écrits sur l'aliénation et la liberté*, 540.

291 *"coldly planned, coldly executed murder"*: The quotes in this and the following paragraph are from Frantz Fanon, "La Mort de Lumumba: Pouvions-nous faire autrement?," in *Pour la révolution africaine*, 212–18.

292 *"You have to help Josie"*: Marie-Jeanne Manuellan, *Sous la dictée de Fanon* (L'Amourier, 2017), 164.

293 *"like lightning in a cloudless sky"*: See Michel Martini, *Chroniques des années algériennes 1946–1962* (Editions Bouchène, 2002), 319–20, 367–77.

293 *"Were we all oblivious?"*: Manuellan, *Sous la dictée de Fanon*, 165.

## 15. Roads to Freedom

297 *"You're watched everywhere"*: Quoted in Marie-Jeanne Manuellan, *Sous la dictée de Fanon* (L'Amourier, 2017), 166.

297 *"see the Chechnyans"*: Quoted in Alice Cherki, *Frantz Fanon: A Portrait*, trans. Nadia Benabid (Cornell University Press, 2006), 156.

298 *Fanon and Martini would soon join forces*: Michel Martini, *Chroniques des années algériennes 1946–1962* (Editions Bouchène, 2002), 319–21.

298 *"moment he knew that he was dying"*: The quotes in this paragraph are from Martini, *Chroniques des années algériennes 1946–1962*, 373–74.

299 *"denounce the compromises of bourgeois nationalists"*: Manuellan, *Sous la dictée de Fanon*, 166.

299 *working on a book*: René Dumont's unsparing anatomy of the early days of independence, *L'Afrique noire est mal partie* (translated into English as *False Start in Africa*) appeared in 1962, a year after *The Wretched of the Earth*, and cited Fanon's book admiringly.

299 *"Based on the armed struggle"*: The quotes in this paragraph are from Frantz Fanon to François Maspero, July 20, 1960, in *Écrits sur l'aliénation et la liberté*, ed. Jean Khalfa and Robert J. C. Young (La Découverte, 2015), 557.

300 *extend this model to the entire colonial world*: Edward Said hypothesized that Fanon's account of anti-colonial revolt was inspired by the Hungarian Marxist philosopher Georg Lukács's 1923 work, *History and Class Consciousness*. But Lukács's book—a virtuoso description of how the working class overcomes the paralysis of "reification" in a society of class domination and commodification and achieves a revolutionary self-consciousness—was translated into French only in 1960, and it's unlikely that Fanon read it. Said's account may have been inspired by flawed English translations that render *chosification* (thingification), a term Fanon borrowed from Césaire's account of colonial dehumanization, as "reification."

300 *"After thousands of years of History"*: Jean-Paul Sartre, *Critique of Dialectical Reason*, new ed., trans. Alan Sheridan-Smith, ed. Jonathan Rée (Verso, 2004). See especially the section on scarcity, 1:122–52.

301 *"The Communists do not believe in hell"*: Jean-Paul Sartre, *Portraits*, trans. Chris Turner (Seagull Books, 2009), 180. I have translated "le néant" as "nothingness" rather than "oblivion."

302 *"We are brothers"*: See Jean-Paul Sartre, "Fraternity and Fear," in *Critique of Dialectical Reason*, 1:428–44.

303 *As a teenage maquisard in Clermont-Ferrand*: For an account of Claude Lanzmann's life, see my review of his memoirs: Adam Shatz, "Nothing He Hasn't Done, Nowhere He Hasn't Been," *London Review of Books* 34, no. 7 (April 5, 2012).

303 *"Fanon was lying on a sort of pallet"*: The quotes in this and the following paragraph are from Claude Lanzmann, *The Patagonian Hare: A Memoir*, trans. Frank Wynne (Atlantic Books, 2012), 328–52.

305 *"We still believed it was possible"*: Simone de Beauvoir, *La Force des choses* (Gallimard, 1963), 2:127–28.

305 *Henri Alleg's gruesome account*: Jérôme Lindon, Alleg's editor at Éditions de Minuit, had published classic books by Resistance writers during the Nazi occupation.

305 *"It is in our name that he was victimized"*: The quotes in this and the following two paragraphs are from Jean-Paul Sartre, "Une victoire," *L'Express* 350 (March 6, 1958).

306 *"could only take revolutionary positions"*: Beauvoir, *La Force des choses*, 2:120.

307 *"Their scarcity became the truth"*: Beauvoir, *La Force des choses*, 2:96.

307 *"For the first time in our life"*: Beauvoir, *La Force des choses*, 2:286.

307 *a representative of the GPRA*: According to Benyoucef Benkhedda, who replaced Ferhat Abbas as the GPRA's president in August 1961, Sartre rendered enormous service to the Algerian cause during his time in Brazil: when Benkhedda went there in the fall of 1961, the authorities wanted to turn him back, but left-wing students came out en masse to welcome him—and they immediately talked about Sartre. He left the airport in triumph.

308 *"What isn't certain"*: Beauvoir, *La Force des choses*, 2:359.

309 *"Ask Sartre to preface me"*: Frantz Fanon to François Maspero, April 7, 1961, in *Écrits sur l'aliénation et la liberté*, 560.

310 *"Sartre had realized in Cuba"*: Beauvoir, *La Force des choses*, 2:420.

310 *"shaky gestures, an agitated face"*: Beauvoir, *La Force des choses*, 2:421.

310 *a full-scale invasion*: After the fighting, Fanon had gone to Bizerte on behalf of the FLN to visit one of the wounded: the journalist Jean Daniel was recovering from French machine-gun fire, which nearly killed him. Daniel, who admired Fanon's courage and charisma even though he disagreed with his praise of armed struggle, appreciated the visit. Fanon seems to have been merely discharging one of his official responsibilities.

311 *the performance of a lifetime*: The meeting in Rome inspired a graphic novel by the writer Frédéric Ciriez and the illustrator Romain Lamy, *Frantz Fanon*, published in 2020 by Éditions de la Découverte, the successor of Maspero.

311 *"a partisan of violence"*: Beauvoir, *La Force des choses*, 2:420–27.

313 *"I wish I could have had a moment alone"*: Cherki, *Frantz Fanon, a Portrait*, 162.

313 *"I would pay twenty thousand francs"*: Quoted in Beauvoir, *La Force des choses*, 2:421.

## 16. Voice of the Damned

314 *"examine carefully the issue of distribution"*: Frantz Fanon, *Écrits sur l'aliénation et la liberté*, ed. Jean Khalfa and Robert J. C. Young (La Découverte, 2015), 562.

315 "And here we are standing up": Jacques Roumain, "Sales nègres," June 14, 2017, https://afropoesie.com/2017/06/14/sales-negres/.

315 *"slaves of modern times"*: The quotes in this paragraph are from Frantz Fanon, *Les Damnés de la terre* (1961; repr. La Découverte, 2002), 72.

316 *"shrinking stomachs"*: Fanon, *Les Damnés de la terre*, 94.

317 *"Europe is literally the creation"*: Fanon, *Les Damnés de la terre*, 99.

317 *"The wealth of the imperialist countries"*: Fanon, *Les Damnés de la terre*, 98–99.

318 *Fanon repeats the word* ville: In Richard Philcox's translation, *ville* (town) is rendered as "sector."

318 *"The settler's town is built to last"*: Fanon, *Les Damnés de la terre*, 42.

319 *"what species, what race"*: Fanon, *Les Damnés de la terre*, 43.

319 *"The language of the settler"*: Fanon, *Les Damnés de la terre*, 45.

320 *"roars with laughter"*: Fanon, *Les Damnés de la terre*, 46.

321 *"The first thing the native learns"*: Fanon, *Les Damnés de la terre*, 53.

321 *"sedimented in his muscles"*: Fanon, *Les Damnés de la terre*, 53.

322 *"after years of unreality"*: Fanon, *Les Damnés de la terre*, 58.

322  *"only understands the language of force"*: Fanon, *Les Damnés de la terre*, 81.

322  *"obviously sufficient grounds for joining the struggle"*: Fanon, *Les Damnés de la terre*, 133.

323  *"emancipated slaves"*: Fanon, *Les Damnés de la terre*, 66.

323  *"The pimps, the thugs, the unemployed"*: Fanon, *Les Damnés de la terre*, 126.

323  *"his passive or despairing attitudes"*: Fanon, *Les Damnés de la terre*, 90.

323  *"it was indeed . . . the good slave"*: Fanon, *Les Damnés de la terre*, 85.

324  *"Violence in its practice"*: Fanon, *Les Damnés de la terre*, 90.

324  *"diplomacy in motion"*: Fanon, *Les Damnés de la terre*, 76.

324  *"to work means to work toward"*: Fanon, *Les Damnés de la terre*, 85.

325  *"discover the man behind the colonizer"*: Frantz Fanon, *L'An V de la révolution algérienne* (1959; repr. La Découverte, 2011), 14.

325  *"If The Wretched of the Earth becomes the book of reference"*: Jean Daniel, *La Blessure* (Grasset, 1992), 81.

326  *"When a colonized people"*: Jean-François Lyotard, best known for his later writings on postmodernism, taught in Constantine in the early 1950s and published a series of trenchant essays on the Algerian war of independence for the collective Socialism or Barbarism.

326  *"a society in meltdown"*: See Jane Hiddleston, "Lyotard's Algeria: Experiments in Theory," *Paragraph* 22, no. 1 (March 2010): 52–69; and Jean-François Lyotard, *La Guerre des Algériens: Écrits 1956–1963* (Galilée, 1989).

326  *"a fundamental truth"*: Nguyen Nghe, "Frantz Fanon et les problèmes de l'indépendance," *La Pensée* 107 (February 1963): 23–36.

326  *"no human relationship is more transitory"*: Hannah Arendt, *On Violence* (Harvest/HBJ, 1969), 69.

327  *"It rekindled the few expiring embers"*: Frederick Douglass, *Narrative of the Life of Frederick Douglass* (Penguin Classics, 2014), chapter 10.

328  *remarkably similar to Fanon's*: I owe this insight to Margaret Kohn, "Frederick Douglass's Master-Slave Dialectic," *Journal of Politics* 67, no. 2 (May 2005): 497–514. As Kohn points out in her perceptive essay, Douglass does not appear to have read Hegel, but his argument that "the slave prefers death to the inhumanity of slavery" was a Kojèvian rewriting of Hegel avant la lettre.

328  *"The gaze we directed toward"*: Jean Améry, "L'Homme enfanté par l'esprit de la violence," *Les Temps modernes* 1–2, nos. 635–36 (2006): 175–89.

328  *as a kind of shock therapy*: Jean Khalfa, "Fanon, psychiatrie révolutionnaire," in Fanon, *Écrits sur l'aliénation et la liberté*, 137–67.

329  *"human legacy of France in Algeria"*: Fanon, *Les Damnés de la terre*, 241.

330  *"poem in prose"*: In his preface to Méchakra's novel, Kateb Yacine declared that "a woman who writes is worth her weight in gunpowder."

330  *"see the country with the hands of his memory"*: Yamina Méchakra, *La Grotte éclatée* (ENAG Editions, 2000), 27, 102.

331  *"thoughts of self-destruction"*: Fanon, *Les Damnés de la terre*, 242.

331  *"will perhaps find these psychiatric notes"*: Fanon, *Les Damnés de la terre*, 239.

331  *"overeager messianism around peasants"*: George Steinmetz, "An Oblique Encounter with Sociology: Frantz Fanon's *Les Damnés de la terre*," *Soziopolis*, June 12, 2021, https://www.soziopolis.de/an-oblique-encounter-with-sociology.html.

333  *"diluting the language of Fanon and Mao"*: V. S. Naipaul, "A New King for the Congo," *New York Review of Books*, June 26, 1975.

334  *"tribal dictatorship"*: Fanon, *Les Damnés de la terre*, 174.

334  *"the theft of futures"*: Ashis Nandy, *The Intimate Enemy: Loss and Recovery of Self Under Colonialism* (Oxford University Press, 1983), 119.

335  *"It is not enough to reunite"*: Fanon, *Les Damnés de la terre*, 215.

335  *"The African intellectuals who are still fighting"*: Fanon, *Les Damnés de la terre*, 222.

335  *"How could I possibly understand"*: Maryse Condé, "How to Become a Fanonian," in *What Is Africa to Me? Fragments of a True-to-Life Autobiography*, trans. Richard Philcox (Seagull Books, 2021).

336  *"everyone must be compromised"*: Fanon, *Les Damnés de la terre*, 187–89.

336  *"bloodless genocide"*: Fanon, *Les Damnés de la terre*, 304.

337  *"invent the total man"*: Fanon, *Les Damnés de la terre*, 302.

337  *"Europe did what it had to do"*: Fanon, *Les Damnés de la terre*, 303–304.

337  *"act* as if *Europe didn't exist"*: Philippe Lucas, *Sociologie de Frantz Fanon, contribution à une anthropologie de la libération* (SNED, 1971), 21.

## 17. In the Country of Lynchers

338  *"some very good news"*: Frantz Fanon, *Écrits sur l'aliénation et la liberté*, ed. Jean Khalfa and Robert J. C. Young (La Découverte, 2015), 561.

338  *"an excited small satyr"*: Harold R. Isaacs, "Portrait of a Revolutionary," *Commentary*, July 1965.

338  *"Murderous madness is the collective unconscious"*: Jean-Paul Sartre, preface to Frantz Fanon, *Les Damnés de la terre* (1961; repr. La Découverte, 2002), 26–29.

339  *"much more doubtful about violence than his admirers"*: Hannah Arendt, *On Violence* (Harvest/HBJ, 1969), 14.

339  *"What verbal masturbation!"*: Jean Daniel, *La Blessure* (Grasset, 1992), 80–81.

339  *"Not so long ago"*: Sartre, preface to Fanon, *Les Damnés de la terre*, 17.

340  *"The Third World discovers itself"*: Sartre, preface to Fanon, *Les Damnés de la terre*, 20.

340  *"a monster where the defects"*: Fanon, *Les Damnés de la terre*, 302.

341  *"He was a sick man"*: Quoted in Thomas Meaney, "Frantz Fanon and the CIA Man," *American Historical Review* 124, no. 3 (June 2019): 983–95.

341  *"it was a mystery, even to him"*: Elaine Mokhtefi, *Algiers, Third World Capital: Freedom Fighters, Revolutionaries, Black Panthers* (Verso, 2018), 43.

343  *The architect of the October 17 massacre*: More than three decades later, Maurice Papon was convicted in a French court of complicity with the Nazis, for his role in organizing the deportation of more than sixteen hundred Jews under Vichy.

343  *"lucid, rapidly perceiving"*: Mokhtefi, *Algiers, Third World Capital*, 44.

344  *"younger and calmer"*: Simone de Beauvoir, *La Force des choses* (Gallimard, 1963), 2:440–41.

344  *"whose mask had struck me"*: Daniel, *La Blessure*, 79.

344  *"These are the letters from Sartre"*: Marie-Jeanne Manuellan, *Sous la dictée de Fanon* (L'Amourier, 2017), 171.

345  *"horror of these ceremonies"*: Michel Martini, *Chroniques des années algériennes 1946–1962* (Editions Bouchène, 2002), 367.

346  *"adopted him as a master thinker"*: Assia Djebar, *Le Blanc de l'Algérie* (Albin Michel, 1995).

346  *"a great serenity and a strange beauty"*: Alice Cherki, *Frantz Fanon: A Portrait*, trans. Nadia Benabid (Cornell University Press, 2006), 168.

346  *"Life continued"*: Martini, *Chroniques des années algériennes 1946–1962*, 367.

346  *Fanon's life had been a "detour"*: Édouard Glissant, *Le Discours antillais* (Gallimard, 1997), 55–57.

346  *"If the word 'commitment' has any meaning"*: Aimé Césaire, "La Révolte de Frantz Fanon, par Aimé Césaire," *Jeune Afrique*, https://www.jeuneafrique.com/178228/politique/la-r-volte-de-frantz-fanon-par-aim-c-saire/.

348  *"anything other than a madman"*: Manuellan, *Sous la dictée de Fanon*, 172–73.

348  *rekindled interest in his work on the French left*: The most impressive study to emerge from Fanon's rediscovery in France was *Sociologie de Frantz Fanon, contribution à une anthropologie de liberation*, published in 1971 by the sociologist Philippe Lucas, a student of the Romanian Jewish Marxist philosopher Lucien Goldmann. Underscoring the tragic dimensions

of Fanon's search for a liberation politics beyond Négritude, Lucas was struck by the parallels between his account of decolonization and Georg Lukács's Hegelian Marxist interpretation of class struggle—a subject that Edward Said would pick up two decades later.

348    *"whereas virtually no man in the street"*: Ernest Gellner, "The Unknown Apollo of Biskra: The Social Basis of Algerian Puritanism," *Government and Opposition* 9, no. 3 (July 1974): 277–310.

## Epilogue: Specters of Fanon

352    *"Marie-Jeanne is the only person"*: Mireille Fanon Mendès-France, who bears a striking re-semblance to her father, grew up at the experimental psychiatric clinic known as La Borde, a successor to Saint-Alban, where her mother, Michèle Weyer, who had married a psychiatrist, worked as an administrator. Although Fanon's books were in the house, her mother never spoke of him. "It was a complete blackout," Mireille told me. Not until she was in her teens, after Fanon's death, did she read his work, and even then, it was a difficult inheritance. "I didn't understand what I read," she said. "It took me years to understand it." While her half brother, Olivier, was raised in Algiers in the shadow of a great man, Mireille came of age in a country where many people still regarded her father as an enemy. For years as an adult, she used only the last name of her second husband, Bernard Mendès-France, the son of Pierre Mendès-France, who presided over the Republic's withdrawals from Indochina, Morocco, and Tunisia—but not from Algeria. In more recent years, however, she has embraced her father's legacy with pride and vigor, establishing a foundation in his name.

353    *a response to Fanon's vogue among New Left radicals*: See Hannah Arendt, *On Violence* (Harvest/HBJ, 1969).

353    *an intellectual era*: See, for example, the application of Fanon's ideas to the condition of First Peoples in Glen Sean Coulthard, *Red Skin, White Masks: Rejecting the Colonial Politics of Recognition* (University of Minnesota Press, 2014).

353    *"I do not arrive armed"*: Frantz Fanon, *Peau noire, masques blancs* (Seuil, 1952), 5. I have translated Fanon's phrase *vérités décisives* as "absolute truths."

353    *"Fanon's particular tragedy"*: Albert Memmi, "La Vie impossible de Frantz Fanon," *Esprit* (September 1971): 248–73.

354    *"The project of being exclusively identified"*: Alice Cherki, *Frantz Fanon: A Portrait*, trans. Nadia Benabid (Cornell University Press, 2006), 193.

355    *"only a people who doesn't fear"*: Abu Iyad, with Éric Rouleau, *My Home, My Land: A Narrative of the Palestinian Struggle* (Times Books, 1981), 34–35.

356    *the influential Bissau-Guinean revolutionary Amílcar Cabral*: Like Fanon, Cabral defended an inclusive, class-based nationalism as a way of overcoming internal divisions of ethnicity and tribe that might be exploited by the colonial authorities—in his case, the often-bitter distrust between native Bissau-Guineans and the wealthier Cape Verdean minority, who had arrived there as colonial administrators for the Portuguese and were still widely seen as colonizers. In 1973, Cabral, the son of parents from Cape Verde, became a victim of "fraternity terror," murdered by militants in his own party. According to his biographer António Tomás, his killers were partly motivated by ethnic resentment. See António Tomás, *Amílcar Cabral: Life of a Reluctant Nationalist* (Oxford University Press, 2021).

356    *"pitfalls of African national consciousness"*: Walter Rodney, *Decolonial Marxism: Essays from the Pan-African Revolution*, ed. Asha Rodney, Patricia Rodney, Ben Mabie, and Jesse Benjamin (Verso, 2022), 86–87. Rodney made this point in a speech on Angola in the United States, where he defended the Marxist MPLA, led by Angolans of Portuguese descent, including *mestiços*, against Jonas Savimbi's Black-led UNITA, and warned his mostly African American audience not to be misled by Savimbi's appeals to Black consciousness: "To declare for blackness is one of the easier things to do . . . If we want to understand Angola and the complex of relationships between social strata and race, and so forth, we must then understand Angola. We cannot sit in Washington or in Detroit and imagine that what we are seeing around the block is Angolan society." Rodney was assassinated in a car bombing in 1980.

357 *"was really a series of imaginative footnotes"*: Ngũgĩ wa Thiong'o's remarks on Fanon are drawn from his book *Moving the Center: The Struggle for Cultural Freedoms* (James Currey, 1993), and from a 2018 email exchange with the author.

357 *"colonial rage"*: V. S. Naipaul, *A Bend in the River* (Vintage, 1979), 171.

357 *"Naipaul's radical pessimism"*: James Wood, "Wounder and Wounded," *The New Yorker*, December 1, 2008.

358 *a group of French gendarmes*: Malika Rahal, *Algérie 1962: Une Histoire populaire* (La Découverte, 2022), 251.

361 *Fanon's vision of a revolutionary culture*: See my essay on the legacy of the 1969 Pan-African Festival: Adam Shatz, "Rapping with Fanon," in *The New York Review of Books*, January 22, 2019, https://www.nybooks.com/online/2019/01/22/rapping-with-fanon/.

361 *she saw Josie being courted*: Elaine Klein Mokhtefi, conversation with the author, New York City, 2019.

362 *the twentieth century's "most compelling theorist"*: Angela Davis: An Autobiography (Haymarket Books, 2022), 104–105.

362 *"true revolutionaries, not afraid of death"*: Malcolm X, as told to Alex Haley, *The Autobiography of Malcolm X* (Grove Press, 1965), 366.

362 *"America's Algerians"*: William Gardner Smith, *The Stone Face* (1963; repr. New York Review Books, 2021), 204.

363 *"internal colonialism"*: The concept was developed by the sociologist Robert Blauner in a 1969 paper, "Internal Colonialism and Ghetto Revolt," in the journal *Social Problems*. In his 1969 essay "Looking for the Meat and Potatoes—Thoughts on Black Power," Norman Mailer quoted Fanon extensively, and declared that there was "no force in Africa, Asia, or Latin America which we need think of as being any more essentially colonial in stance than the American Negro." See Norman Mailer, *Mind of an Outlaw: Selected Essays* (Penguin, 2013), 252.

363 *"The specter who now haunts America"*: Aristide Zolberg and Vera Zolberg, "The Americanization of Frantz Fanon," *Public Interest* (Fall 1967): 51.

364 *his readers in Black militant circles*: A group of young members of the Kerner Commission, established by the Johnson administration to investigate the 1968 urban revolts, wrote a paper comparing rioters to Algerians fighting French colonialism, and were dismissed from the commission.

364 *the interest of Black doctors*: *Black Skin, White Masks* was often read as a companion volume to the 1968 work *Black Rage*, by the Black psychiatrists William H. Grier and Price M. Cobbs.

364 *their liaison to the Algerian authorities*: Elaine Klein, who moved to Algiers after independence, worked for the Ministry of Information and married a war veteran, the former ALN signals operator Mokhtar Mokhtefi. In 1973, she was expelled by the authorities when she refused to inform on her friend Zohra Sellami, the wife of the deposed president, Ahmed Ben Bella.

364 *Malcolm X had made a similar point*: Malcolm X, "Message to the Grassroots" (1963), https://www.blackpast.org/african-american-history/speeches-african-american-history/1963-malcolm-x-message-grassroots/.

365 *"an intellectual template for the Party's critique"*: Alondra Nelson, *Body and Soul: The Black Panther Party and the Fight Against Medical Discrimination* (University of Minnesota Press, 2011), 67–87.

365 *"white imperialism in writing"*: All Forman quotes are from the James Forman Papers at the Library of Congress, Washington, DC.

367 *"The anti-colonial tradition of the United States"*: James Forman Papers at the Library of Congress.

368 *the CIA replied that it could "neither confirm nor deny"*: Simone Browne, *Dark Matters: On the Surveillance of Blackness* (Duke University Press, 2015), 9.

368 *"a process and not as a goal"*: The quotes in this paragraph and the next are from Edward Said, *Culture and Imperialism* (Knopf, 1993), 267–74.

369  *"a sort of tableau of narcissism"*: Henry Louis Gates Jr., "Critical Fanonism," *Critical Inquiry* 17, no. 3 (Spring 1991): 457–70.

369  *"colonial ambivalence"*: See Homi K. Bhabha, *The Location of Culture* (Routledge, 1994).

370  *talking back to the West*: See Aijaz Ahmad, *In Theory: Nations, Classes, Literatures* (Verso, 1992).

370  *"junior partners" of white supremacy*: In *Afropessimism* (Liveright, 2020), Frank B. Wilderson III writes about a Palestinian friend who told him that the "shame and humiliation" of being searched "runs even deeper if the soldier is an Ethiopian Jewish soldier." Wilderson concludes, "In the collective unconscious, Palestinian insurgents have more in common with the Israeli state and civil society than they do with Black people."

370  *its ontology of Blackness is antithetical*: Imprecise translations of Fanon have contributed to such misperceptions of Fanon's views on race. In 1996, the Institute of Contemporary Art in London published an anthology of writings on "Fanon and visual representation" titled *The Fact of Blackness*, a mistranslation of "the lived experience of the Black man."

371  *"violent diffusion of technologies"*: Andreas Malm and the Zetkin Collective, *White Skin, Black Fuel: On the Danger of Fossil Fascism* (Verso, 2021), 390.

371  *"Few processes produce as much despair"*: Andreas Malm, *How to Blow Up a Pipeline* (Verso, 2021), 161.

371  *"difficult for a West Indian"*: Édouard Glissant, *Le Discours antillais* (Gallimard, 1997), 56. For a fascinating account of Glissant's political and intellectual trajectory, see Andrew M. Daily, "'It is too soon . . . or too late': Frantz Fanon's Legacy in the French Caribbean," *Karib—Nordic Journal for Caribbean Studies* 2, no. 1 (2015): 3, http://doi.org/10.16993 /karib.28.

373  *"ended up concealing the already open abyss"*: Patrick Chamoiseau, *Écrire dans un pays dominé* (Gallimard, 1997), 249–55.

374  *what Glissant called "opacity"*: The "right to opacity," Édouard Glissant argued, supplies the oppressed with a protective shield against the intrusive gaze of outsiders.

374  *a modern form of slavery*: Tim Whewell, "The Caribbean Islands Poisoned by a Carcinogenic Pesticide," BBC News, Martinique, November 20, 2020, https://www.bbc.com/news/stories -54992051.

375  *Le Pen's voters in the West Indies*: When Marine Le Pen's father, Jean-Marie Le Pen, flew to Martinique in 1987, demonstrators assembled at the airport to prevent his plane from landing, forcing it to land in Guadeloupe.

375  *"climate of secrecy"*: Joby Fanon, *Frantz Fanon, My Brother: Doctor, Playwright, Revolutionary*, trans. Daniel Nethery (Lexington Books, 2014), 104–105.

375  *riddled with anti-personnel mines*: The French army left behind as many as ten million anti-personnel mines, mostly in the frontier regions.

375  *criticism from Algerian intellectuals*: Around the same time, Fanon came under criticism from his former colleague in the FLN Mohammed Harbi, now an exiled dissident in Paris. Harbi, an adviser to President Ben Bella, had been imprisoned in 1965 for refusing to endorse the Boumediene coup. In 1973, he fled house arrest to Switzerland, before settling in France, where he published a series of historical works dismantling the myths of the FLN, including Fanon's ideas about rural revolution.

376  *"In her fall, Josie hurt no one"*: Assia Djebar, *Le Blanc de l'Algérie* (Albin Michel, 1995), 184–86. Djebar had befriended Frantz and Josie Fanon in Tunis, where she went to study after publishing her first novel, *La Soif* (titled *The Mischief* in the English translation).

377  *"I killed a man"*: Kamel Daoud, *The Meursault Investigation* (Other Press, 2015), 75, 91, 97.

377  *first the French, then the post-independence state*: Some would go still further back. The writer Nabile Farès, in his 1971 autofiction, *A Passenger from the West*, dreamed of a pagan revolution that would rescue Algeria from "the many conquests" it has known, including the Islamic conquest. "The Islamization of Algeria," he wrote, "is not a divine phenomenon, but, like any phenomenon, a historic one."

378  *"an invaluable clinical reflection"*: Karima Lazali, *Colonial Trauma: A Study of the Psychic and Political Consequences of Colonial Repression in Algeria* (Polity, 2021), 194–218.

380  *"The naming of the roads"*: Claire Mayer, "Il n'y aura finalement pas de rue Frantz-Fanon à Bordeaux," *Le Monde*, February 15, 2019.

380  *"an almost physical feeling"*: Claire Denis, conversation with the author, Paris, summer 2018.

381  *The French rapper known as Rocé*: In 2019, Rocé released an anthology of twenty-four musical tracks of anti-colonial popular music, recorded between 1969 and 1988, with the explicitly Fanonian title, *Par les damné.e.s de la terre.*

381  *has invoked Fanon as their spiritual father*: See Houria Bouteldja, *Whites, Jews, and Us: Toward a Politics of Revolutionary Love* (Semiotext(e), 2017).

381  *Among the first psychoanalysts*: Gilles Deleuze and Félix Guattari, *Anti-Oedipus: Capitalism and Schizophrenia* (University of Minnesota Press, 1983), 117–18.

382  *as if he were retracing Fanon's steps*: In the 1970s, Jeanson obtained a degree in "specialized psychiatric studies" at the University of Lyon and began to work in hospitals and asylums in the Aquitaine region, cultivating an approach to psychiatry that would pay implicit—perhaps unconscious—tribute to Fanon's. Psychiatry led Fanon to his politics of liberation; the politics of liberation led Jeanson back to psychiatry. Oddly, Jeanson never mentions Fanon in his 1979 book, *Éloge de la psychiatrie* (In praise of psychiatry). His feelings about Fanon were a complex mixture of admiration and hurt. And after the horrors of the Algerian Revolution, he may have wished to separate himself from a figure associated with violence in the minds of the French. In a remarkable appearance as himself in Jean-Luc Godard's 1967 film *La Chinoise*, Jeanson attempts to dissuade a young Maoist woman from carrying out acts of terrorism. She is taken aback, because of his work with the FLN, but he insists that her actions "will lead to nothing if they're not supported by a class or a large enough group of people," as in Algeria. "You can participate in a revolution, but you can't invent it."

382  *"his prophetic insights"*: Samah Jabr, "Fanon, the Struggle for Justice and Mental Health," August 24, 2021, posted to YouTube by Firoze Manji, https://www.youtube.com/watch?v=h_6TMJnqb3A&t=1128s, 9:59.

382  *"diagnosed them as impostors and manipulators"*: Ruchama Marton, "The Right to Madness: Les Luttes contre la psychiatrie institutionelle en Israël," Université Paris Diderot, Centre de sociologie des pratiques et des représentations politiques, http://www.csprp.univ-paris-diderot.fr/IMG/pdf/marton.pdf.

383  *"absurd, disgraceful logic of the asylum"*: Quoted in Mike Jay, "'I'm Not Signing,'" *London Review of Books* 38, no. 17 (September 8, 2016).

384  *"more complex than what psychiatric diagnosis"*: Cristiana Giordano, *Migrants in Translation: Caring and the Logics of Difference in Contemporary Italy* (University of California Press, 2014), chap. 2. Thanks to Giordano for discussing the center's work with me.

384  *"revealing lies"*: Roberto Beneduce, "The Moral Economy of Lying: Subjectcraft, Narrative Capital, and Uncertainty in the Politics of Asylum," *Medical Anthropology* 34, no. 6 (2015): 557, 562.

385  *"To live in Europe today"*: Okwui Enwezor, email correspondence with author, 2018.

386  *a just struggle against being "colonized"*: Éric Zemmour is not the only far-right reader of Fanon. One MAGA-adjacent conservative invoked "Fanon's concept of the colonized intellectual" in a Twitter attack on the Never Trump conservative columnist David French: "He's a go-between who translates the colonized for the colonizer, in the colonizer's language and for the political, social, and cultural purposes of the colonizer."

386  *"mimicry" of the West*: See Ivan Krastev and Stephen Holmes, *The Light That Failed: Why the West Is Losing the Fight for Democracy* (Pegasus, 2020).

386  *as the Indian philosopher Ashis Nandy*: Ashis Nandy, *The Intimate Enemy: Loss and Recovery of Self Under Colonialism* (Oxford University Press, 1983), 11. According to Nandy, colonialism "handicaps the colonizer much more than it handicaps the colonized."

387  *"for every one of its spiritual victories"*: Fanon, *Les Damnés de la terre*, 302.

387 *the Wagner Group*: See Roger Cohen, "Putin Wants Fealty, and He's Found It in Africa," *New York Times*, December 24, 2022.

388 *A prominent historian of Eastern Europe*: Timothy Snyder, "The War in Ukraine Is a Colonial War," *The New Yorker*, April 28, 2022, https://www.newyorker.com/news/essay/the-war-in-ukraine-is-a-colonial-war. For a forceful rebuttal of Snyder's argument, and of the decolonization paradigm as applied to Ukraine, see Volodymyr Ishchenko, "Ukrainian Voices," *New Left Review* 138 (November/December 2022), https://newleftreview.org/issues/ii138/articles/volodymyr-ishchenko-ukrainian-voices.

388 "Why Fanon": John Edgar Wideman, *Fanon* (Houghton Mifflin, 2008), 94–95. In the final pages, Wideman's wheelchair-bound mother "rolls herself by Fanon's room" at the hospital in Bethesda where he spent his last days. Marie-Jeanne Manuellan told me that it was only after reading Wideman's novel, and this invented scene, that she was able, at last, to imagine Fanon on his deathbed. When I mentioned her reaction to Wideman, he replied, "I didn't even have to imagine it. It *happened*."

389 "*a world finally freed from the burden of race*": Achille Mbembe, *Critique of Black Reason* (Duke University Press, 2017), 161, 167.

389 "*The race problem was made*": Quoted in Eric Foner, "What Is There to Celebrate?," *London Review of Books* 44, no. 20 (October 20, 2022).

390 "*We know, we declare vehemently*": Margo Jefferson, *Constructing a Nervous System: A Memoir* (Penguin, 2022), 64.

390 *Fanon's commitment to creating a "new man"*: See Thomas Chatterton Williams, *Self-Portrait in Black and White: Unlearning Race* (W. W. Norton, 2019), as well as Williams's remarks on Fanon in "Il faut défendre le droit d'offenser, de dire les choses qui ne sont pas à l'unisson du nouveau consensus," an interview with *Charlie Hebdo*, February 17, 2021.

391 *armed struggle as a means of overcoming oppression*: The George Floyd uprising inspired a few Fanonian celebrations of violence, notably Tobi Haslett, "Magic Actions: Looking Back on the George Floyd Rebellion," *n + 1* 40 (Summer 2021), https://www.nplusonemag.com/issue-40/politics/magic-actions-2/. But on the whole, Fanon's contemporary Black admirers in the United States (and not only the Afropessimists among them) tend to emphasize his psychological insights about the impact of racism, rather than his defense of violence.

# ACKNOWLEDGMENTS

———

DURING THE SIX YEARS that I spent researching and writing *The Rebel's Clinic*, I had a loyal and determined ally in the Wiley Agency's Sarah Chalfant, who tirelessly championed the project from its inception. The idea for the book was originally suggested by my friend Pankaj Mishra, a writer of immense talent and intelligence from whom I have never ceased to learn.

Miles Davis famously instructed his sidemen to "play what you know, and then play above that." Alex Star, my editor at Farrar, Straus and Giroux and a synonym for intellectual integrity in book publishing, has a rare, almost magical gift for inspiring his authors to write above what they know. Working with Alex, who edited my writing for *Lingua Franca* in the late 1990s, was the realization of an old dream. His editorial suggestions and ideas have made this a vastly better book.

*The Rebel's Clinic* grew out of an essay I published in the *London Review of Books* in 2017. I would like to thank Mary-Kay Wilmers for commissioning that article, and Alice Spawls and Jean McNicol for giving me a generous sabbatical that allowed me to complete the book. Thanks also to Jackson Lears at *Raritan*, Isabelle Saint-Saens at *Vacarme*, and Matt Seaton at *The New York Review of Books*, all of whom published portions of the manuscript-in-progress.

Thanks to Alice Kaplan, who hosted my talk "The Americanization of Frantz Fanon" at Yale, and to Nasser Rabat at MIT, Sean Jacobs at the New School, and Tom Keenan at Bard College, for inviting me to lecture on Fanon's life and legacy.

When I began my research on the book, whatever doubts I may have entertained as to the contemporary urgency of Fanon's writing were dispelled by the experience of teaching his work to a group of incarcerated men at the Eastern Correctional Facility in Ulster County, New York. Thanks to Max Kenner for inviting me to be a part of the Bard Prison Initiative, and to my students at Eastern for their inspiring engagement with Fanon's work and their insights into the lived experience of racism and confinement.

A substantial portion of this book was written during the pandemic, on a fellowship from the Leon Levy Center at the CUNY Graduate Center. Thanks to Shelby White, Kai Bird, and Thad Ziolkowski at the center, and to the wonderful fellows, who, in their readings of early chapters, combined criticism and support in just the right measure. Julián González de León Heiblum and Sarah Weber, my research assistants, were remarkably resourceful, and kept me supplied with books, articles, and enthusiasm for the project. My fellow biographers at the center were a model of intellectual camaraderie, combining critique and supportiveness in just the right measure. Thanks also to Misha Glenny, Ivan Krastev, Ayşe Çağlar, and the staff of the Institute for Human Sciences in Vienna, where I was able to finish my manuscript in a setting of tranquility and Old World charm that could not have been more conducive to reflection.

Insofar as I have succeeded in restoring an iconic figure to the condition that the white world had denied him, that of a man, it is in large part thanks to Alice Cherki, Mohammed Harbi, Elaine Klein Mokhtefi, Guy Sitbon, and Herbert Weiss, all of whom shared their memories and impressions of Fanon. My understanding of Fanon and his work has also been enriched by conversations with Fazia Aitel, Sid Ahmed Semiane, Claire Denis, Daikha and Fatima Dridi, Brent Hayes Edwards, Paul Gilroy, Sofiane Hadjadj, Selma Hellal, Youssef Ben Ismail, Jean Khalfa, Pierre-Étienne Manuellan, Mireille Fanon Mendès-France, Malika Rahal, Benjamin Stora, Ngũgĩ wa Thiong'o, Enzo Traverso, John Edgar Wideman, Miloud Yabrir, and Eli Zaretsky.

I am grateful to Jeanne Sauvage, who fact-checked the completed work with exemplary precision, and to Caroline Abu-Sada, Roane Carey, Arun Kapil, Jessica Loudis, Brian Morton, Gregory Pierrot, Marc Saint-Upéry, and Joan Scott, who read earlier versions of the manuscript. Their astute comments helped me to avoid factual errors and stylistic infelicities, while also encouraging me in my efforts. Thanks also to Yves Chevrefils Desbiolles and Hélène Favard, who graciously steered me through the Fanon archives at IMEC-Abbaye d'Ardenne.

Jeremy Harding, my colleague at the *London Review of Books* and a writer of enviable gifts, was my indispensable interlocutor throughout the process of writing this book. With his background of reporting in North and sub-Saharan Africa, his knowledge of French intellectual and political history, his passion for the drama of decolonization, and his unusual sensitivity to the political and ethical demands of this subject, Jeremy was an ideal reader for *The Rebel's Clinic* and improved it in ways large and small. To say that I am grateful to him would be an understatement; this is a different book because of his extraordinary and selfless input.

Thanks to the friends whose warmth and laughter have sustained me through the writing of this book: Sasha Abramsky, Alžběta Ambrožová, Ratik Asokan, Leonard Benardo, Carl Bromley, Tammy Kim, James Lasdun, Jordan Mintzer, Eyal Press, Nermeen Shaikh, Clifford Thompson, Kelvin Williams, and Richard Woodson. A special thanks to my personal marabout, Lisa Grey, who helped exorcise the djinn that possessed me when I began this project.

Last but not least, thanks to my loving family: Leslie and Stephen Shatz, my parents; Sarah Shatz, my sister; Ella Shatz, my daughter; and my partner, Sayeeda Moreno, whose distrust of Fanon's machismo never got in the way of her support for this book.

# INDEX

Feraoun, Mouloud, 154–55, 169, 188, 195, 230, 257*n*, 265, 343, 355
Ferenczi, Sándor, 107, 148, 210
Ferradj, Abdelkader, 168
Fields, Barbara, 91–92
*Figaro, Le*, 102
*First Man, The* (Camus), 258, 263, 265–66
First World War, 24, 28, 208
FIS (Front islamique du salut), 376
FLN (Front de libération nationale), 5, 124, 140–44, 146–48, 150–55, 157, 165–73, 177–200, 202, 207, 208, 229, 232–33, 238, 270, 274, 279, 288–89, 306, 312, 317, 323, 325, 343, 345, 360–62, 376, 381, 389, 410*n*, 412*n*, 414*n*; Abane's murder and, 199–200; Algerian politicians and, 153; Algerian self-determination referendum and, 297*n*; ALN forces of, *see* ALN; Angolan fighters and, 254; bombing of, 168–69; Camus and, 152, 153, 263, 264; diplomatic revolution of, 192–93; Fédération de France, 178, 179, 182, 186, 192, 225, 256; foreign sympathizers and, 247; founders of, 142–43; fraternity-terror and, 302; French vote on special powers against, 160–61, 187; Froger assassinated by, 171; GPRA (provisional government) of, *see* GPRA; hijacking of leaders of, 182, 192; interior versus exterior and, 166–68, 173, 197–98, 289; Jeanson's support for, 179–81, 239, 304–306; Jewish members of, 231, 232; Melouza massacre and, 194–96; MNA and, 142, 178, 194, 302; peasants and, 257–60; Philippeville uprising of, 150, 151, 155, 156, 197, 280, 320; *porteurs des valises* and, 179–80,

239, 270, 278, 304–305, 309, 382; public support for, 288; radio broadcast of, 228, 231; Red Hand and, 182–83; relationship to constituency, 289; rural Algerians and, 152; Sartre and, 304–309; self-description and purpose of, 141–42; Soummam Conference of, 165–68, 198, 232, 233; in Tunis, 5, 166, 167, 173, 177–200, 247; UPA and, 248; urban terrorism campaign of, 168–69; Wilayas of, 147, 148, 150, 155, 165, 168, 174, 178, 184, 192, 194, 197, 199, 230, 233, 256; women in, 169, 170, 226–27, 229–30, 258
FLN, Fanon's work for, 124, 140–44, 157, 171, 173, 203, 205, 221, 231, 235–36, 245, 280, 302, 341, 419*n*; as ambassador, 7, 269–72, 274; *L'An V de la révolution algérienne* and, 234; in Blida, 5, 147–49, 171, 216; with exterior leadership, 209; leukemia treatment and, 293, 340; on military mission, 3–5, 240, 282–87, 291; Mollet plot and, 159–60; request to join the maquis, 239, 240; on specialist commission, 256; as spokesman, 7, 183–84, 186, 193–97, 201, 212, 239, 249, 255; in Tunis, 5, 177, 182–84, 191, 219, 239
Floyd, George, 370, 392
Foccart, Jacques, 273–74
*Folie et déraison* (Foucault), 130
Fonkoua, Romuald, 43
*Force of Circumstance, The* (Beauvoir), 311
Forman, James, 365–67, 372
Fort-de-France, 17–20, 24, 25, 28, 29, 37, 38, 104, 240, 372, 374
*Fortunate Man, A* (Berger), 127
Foucault, Michel, 57, 130, 368, 370

France, 6, 113, 188, 379–80; Allied
liberation of, 33, 36; citizens' status
in, 86, 241, 379; crackdowns on
Algerians in, 177; fall of Fourth
Republic in, 178; Fanon in, after
expulsion from Algeria, 172, 177,
180–82; Fanon's postwar return
to, 33, 44; Fanon's relationship
to, 6, 29, 45, 86, 181, 191; German
occupation and Vichy government
of, 24–27, 29, 31, 42, 43, 61, 65,
83, 105, 106, 110, 125, 232; Main
Rouge in, 182–83, 256; medical
establishment in, 55–58, 71–72,
215, 384; Muslims in, 379–80;
National Assembly of, 21, 37, 90,
96, 143, 160–61, 241, 242, 249;
racism in, 55–58, 86–87, 92–93, 98,
111, 113; Resistance in, 5n, 36, 40n,
58, 61, 100, 105, 110, 144, 145, 264,
265, 289, 303; in Suez War, 178;
Tunisia's war with, 310; Vietnam
and, 100, 143, 173, 246
France, Anatole, 121
Franco, Francisco, 83, 107, 306
*Frantz Fanon: Black Skin, White
Mask*, 368
fraternity terror, 200, 301–304, 422n
Frazier, E. Franklin, 389
Free French Forces, 27–30, 31–37, 83,
143, 181, 187, 283, 285
French colonies, 17, 20–22, 95, 117,
163, 315, 354, 370, 379; in Africa,
20, 21n, 40, 92, 241, 248; citizenship
in, 122; departmentalization of,
38; racism in, 92–93; World War II
soldiers from, 36
French Communist Party, 61, 90, 102,
123, 129, 145, 161, 187, 214, 249,
271, 301, 308, 309, 341, 391
French Community of Africa,
241–43, 253, 282, 284, 287
*French Encounter with Africans, The*
(Cohen), 93–94

French Revolution, 6, 26, 29, 300, 301
Freud, Sigmund, 76, 77, 80, 85, 88,
105, 107, 108, 129, 148, 159, 210,
217–19, 276, 382
Friedreich's ataxia, 59, 82–83
Frobenius, Leo, 39, 41
Froger, Amédée, 171

Gallimard, Michel, 263
Gambs, Albert, 133–34
Gandhi, Mahatma, 245, 363, 371
García Márquez, Gabriel, 177–78
Garner, Eric, 370, 392
Garvey, Marcus, 81
Gates, Henry Louis, Jr., 369
Geismar, Peter, 365
Gellner, Ernest, 259n, 348
"Gender of Race, The" (Renault),
89–90
Genet, Jean, 85, 180, 323
Germany, Nazi, *see* Nazi Germany
Geronimi, Charles, 128, 132, 148, 152,
171, 181n, 184, 195, 202, 204, 216,
263, 270, 316
Ghana, 244, 261, 286
Gide, André, 125
Gilroy, Paul, 81, 368
Giordano, Cristiana, 384
Glissant, Édouard, 19, 26, 29, 44, 114,
161, 255, 308, 346, 371–74
Gobineau, Arthur de, 126
Gordimer, Nadine, 357
GPRA (Gouvernement provisoire de
la république algérienne), 193, 219,
234, 240, 242, 244, 256–57, 259,
269, 281, 283, 289, 292, 293, 298,
304, 307, 311, 312, 342, 343, 345;
Fanon as ambassador for, 269–72,
274, 281; Lumumba and, 274, 275,
279, 283
Gramsci, Antonio, 13
Great Britain, 178, 244, 248, 324
*Grotte éclatée, La* (Méchakra), 330

**A Note About the Author**

Adam Shatz is the US editor of the *London Review of Books* and a contributor to *The New York Times Magazine*, *The New York Review of Books*, *The New Yorker*, and other publications. He is the author of *Writers and Missionaries: Essays on the Radical Imagination* and the host of the podcast *Myself with Others*. He lives in Brooklyn, New York.